WRITER
ANTONY JOHNSTON

ARTIST
EDUARDO BARRETO

THE LONG HAUL

★

Letterer: Marshall
Cover Illustrator: Eduar
Book Designer: Antony J
Deputy: Randal C. Ja
Sheriff: James Lucas Jones

oni
PRESS

PUBLISHED BY ONI PRESS, INC.

1305 SE Martin Luther King Jr. Blvd, Suite A
Portland, OR 97214 USA

Publisher: Joe Nozemack
Editor-In-Chief: James Lucas Jones
Managing Editor: Randal C. Jarrell
Editorial Intern: Daniel Ray

Oni Press: www.onipress.com
Antony Johnston: www.mostlyblack.com

To Carina.
—Eduardo

First Edition February 2005
ISBN 1-932664-05-X

1 3 5 7 9 10 8 6 4 2
Printed in Canada

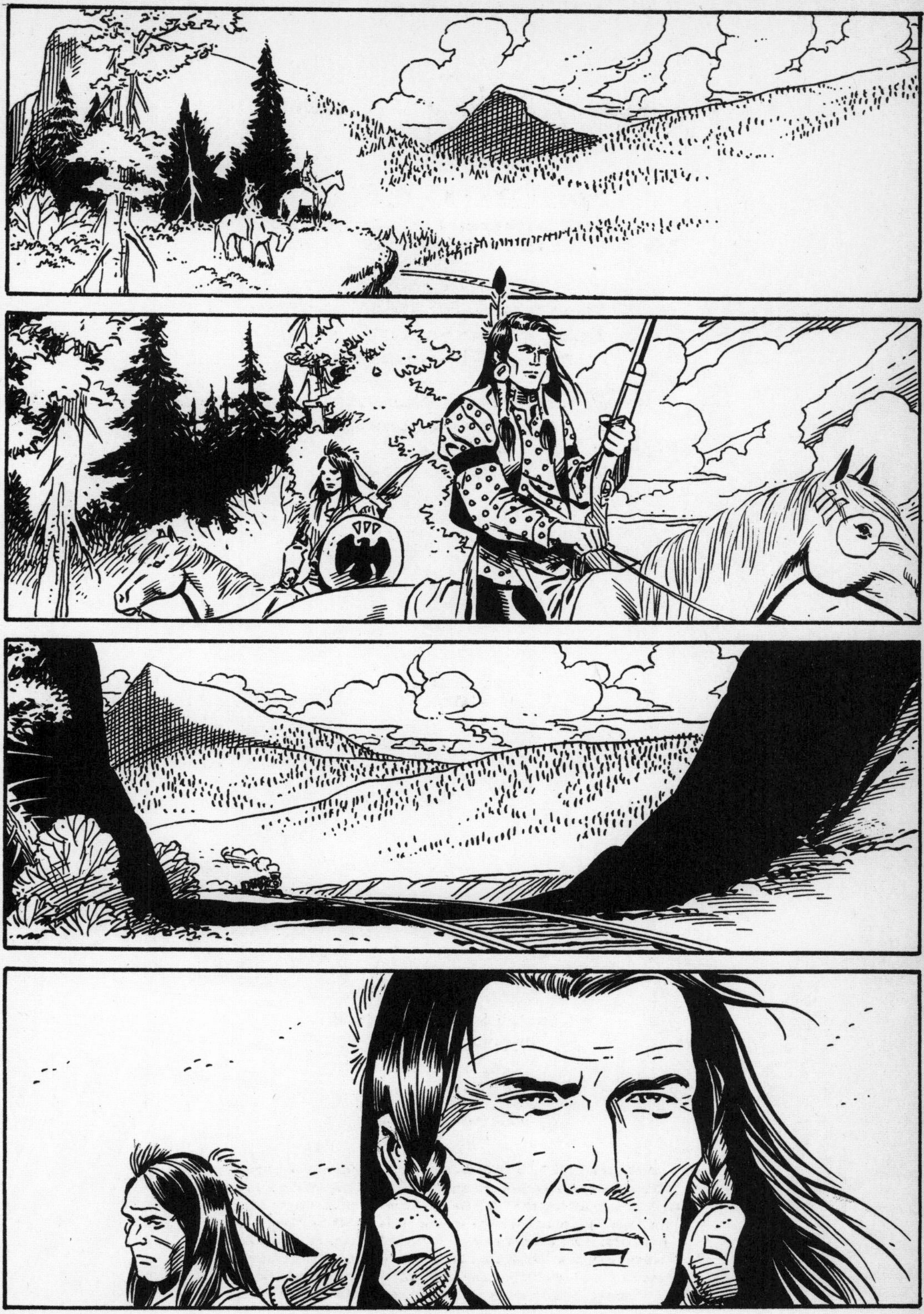

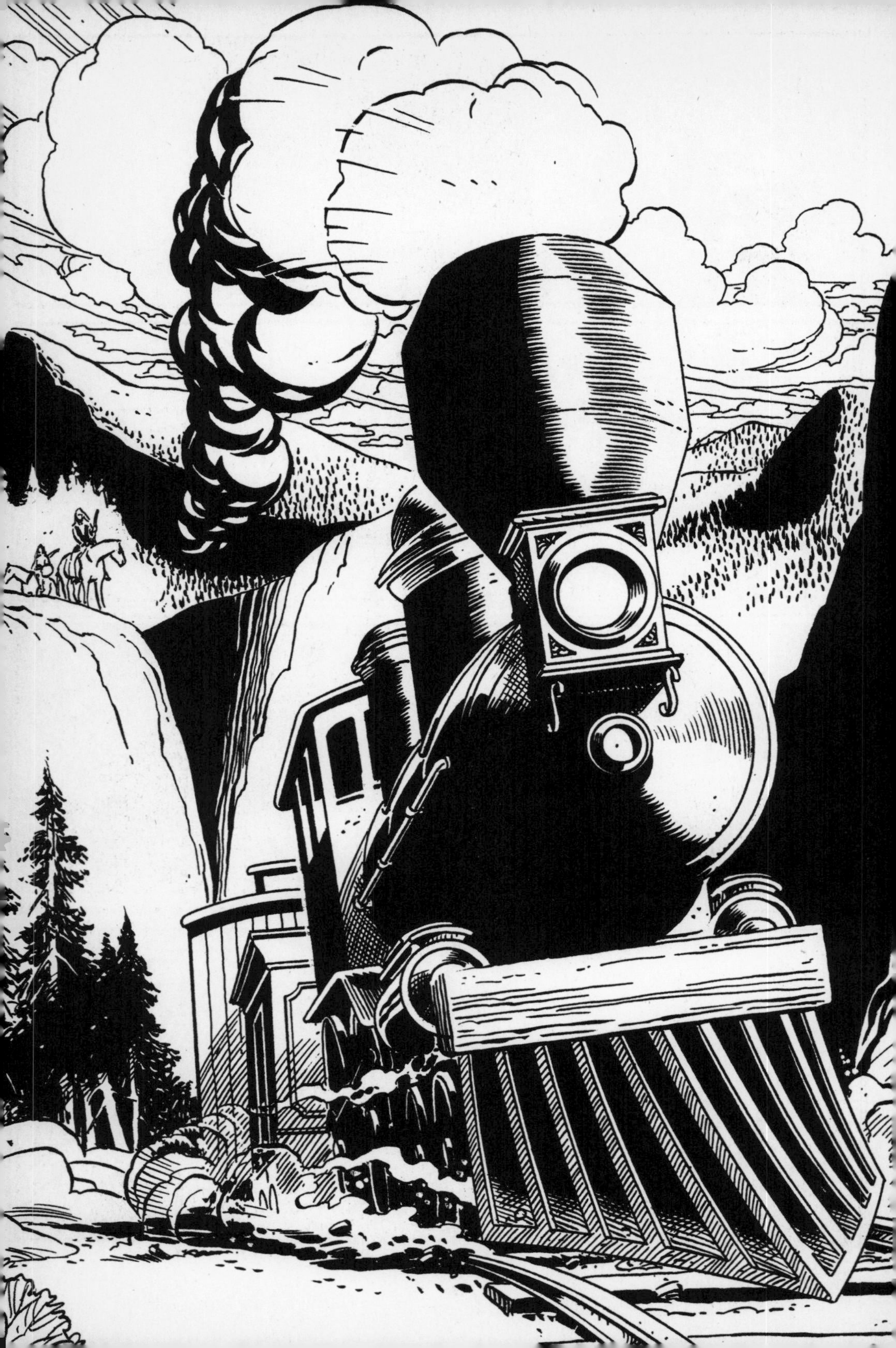

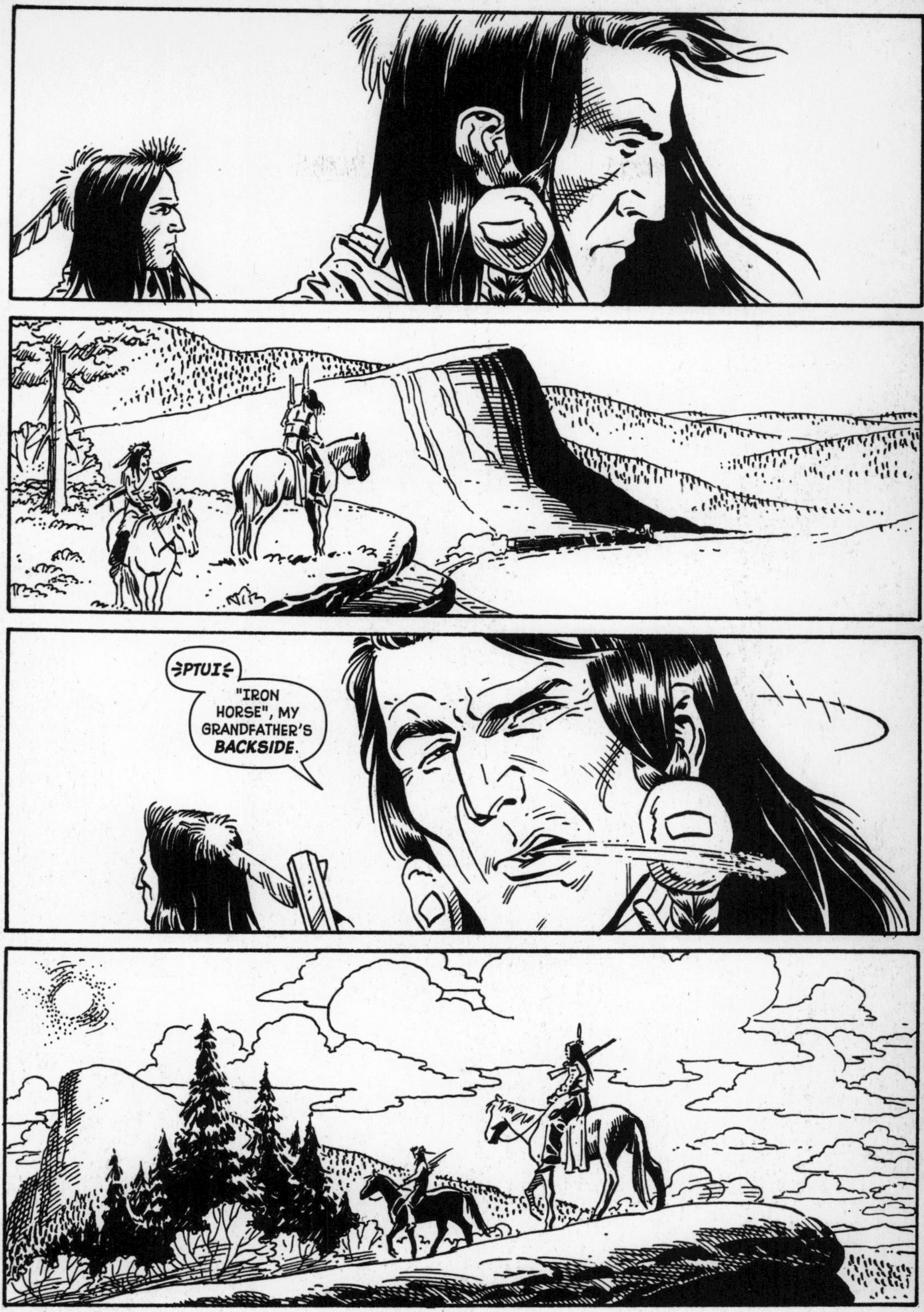
PTUI
"IRON HORSE", MY GRANDFATHER'S BACKSIDE.

ONE

★

"THE MAN WITH THE PLAN"

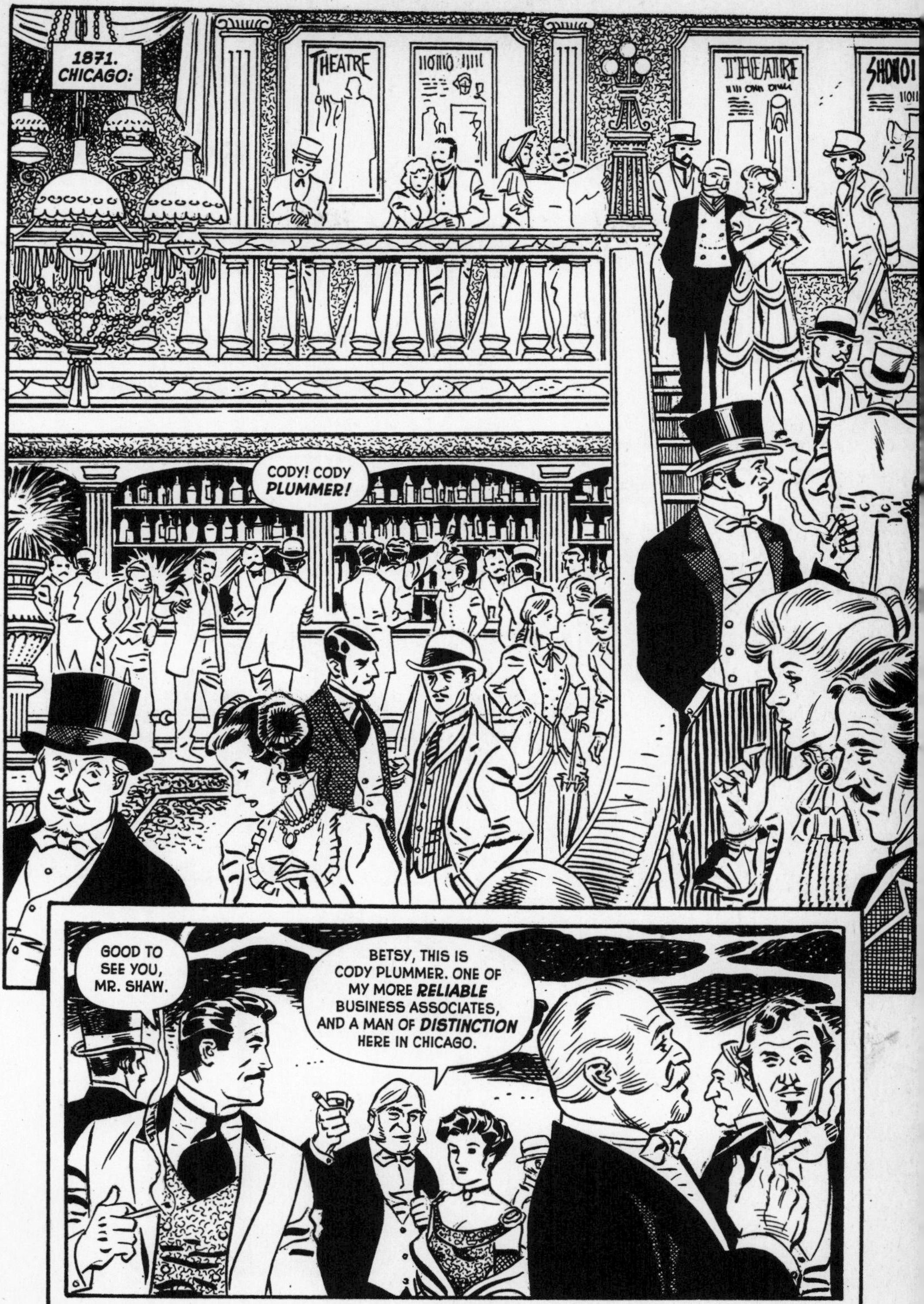
1871. CHICAGO:
THEATRE
THEATRE
CODY! CODY *PLUMMER!*
GOOD TO SEE YOU, MR. SHAW.
BETSY, THIS IS CODY PLUMMER. ONE OF MY MORE *RELIABLE* BUSINESS ASSOCIATES, AND A MAN OF *DISTINCTION* HERE IN CHICAGO.

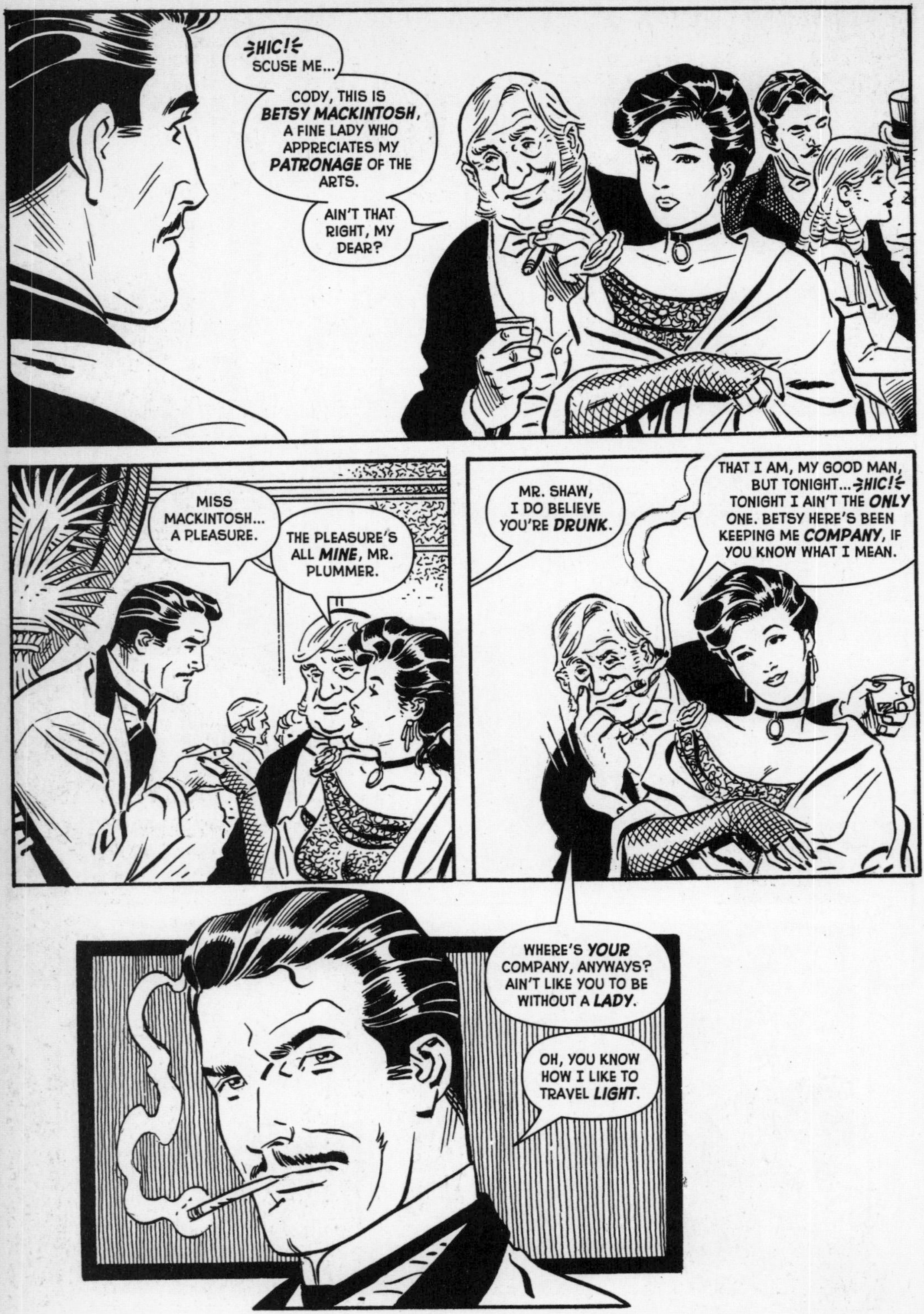
HIC! SCUSE ME...
CODY, THIS IS BETSY MACKINTOSH, A FINE LADY WHO APPRECIATES MY PATRONAGE OF THE ARTS.
AIN'T THAT RIGHT, MY DEAR?
MISS MACKINTOSH... A PLEASURE.
THE PLEASURE'S ALL MINE, MR. PLUMMER.
MR. SHAW, I DO BELIEVE YOU'RE DRUNK.
THAT I AM, MY GOOD MAN, BUT TONIGHT... HIC! TONIGHT I AIN'T THE ONLY ONE. BETSY HERE'S BEEN KEEPING ME COMPANY, IF YOU KNOW WHAT I MEAN.
WHERE'S YOUR COMPANY, ANYWAYS? AIN'T LIKE YOU TO BE WITHOUT A LADY.
OH, YOU KNOW HOW I LIKE TO TRAVEL LIGHT.

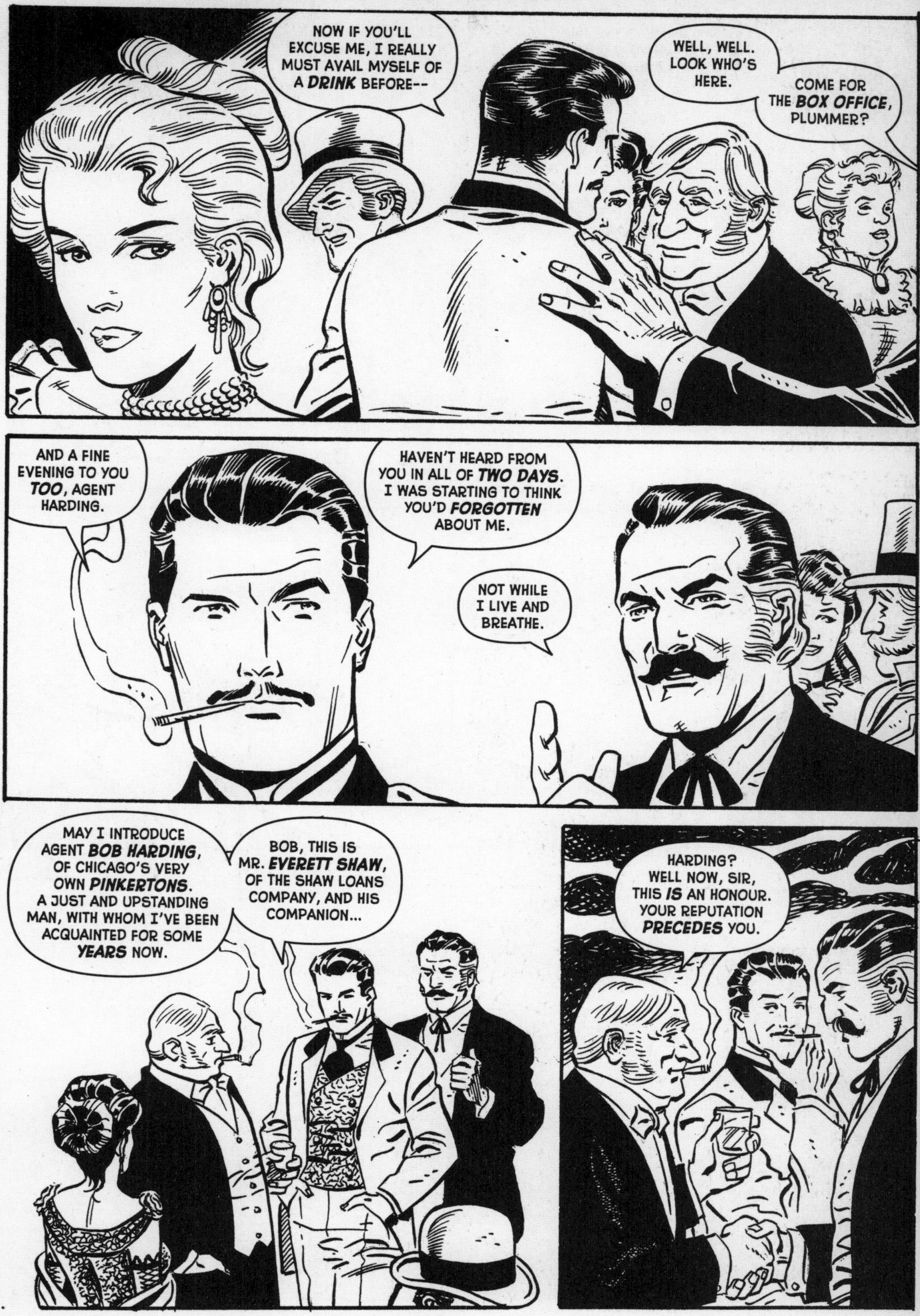
NOW IF YOU'LL EXCUSE ME, I REALLY MUST AVAIL MYSELF OF A DRINK BEFORE--
WELL, WELL. LOOK WHO'S HERE.
COME FOR THE BOX OFFICE, PLUMMER?
AND A FINE EVENING TO YOU TOO, AGENT HARDING.
HAVEN'T HEARD FROM YOU IN ALL OF TWO DAYS. I WAS STARTING TO THINK YOU'D FORGOTTEN ABOUT ME.
NOT WHILE I LIVE AND BREATHE.
MAY I INTRODUCE AGENT BOB HARDING, OF CHICAGO'S VERY OWN PINKERTONS. A JUST AND UPSTANDING MAN, WITH WHOM I'VE BEEN ACQUAINTED FOR SOME YEARS NOW.
BOB, THIS IS MR. EVERETT SHAW, OF THE SHAW LOANS COMPANY, AND HIS COMPANION...
HARDING? WELL NOW, SIR, THIS IS AN HONOUR. YOUR REPUTATION PRECEDES YOU.

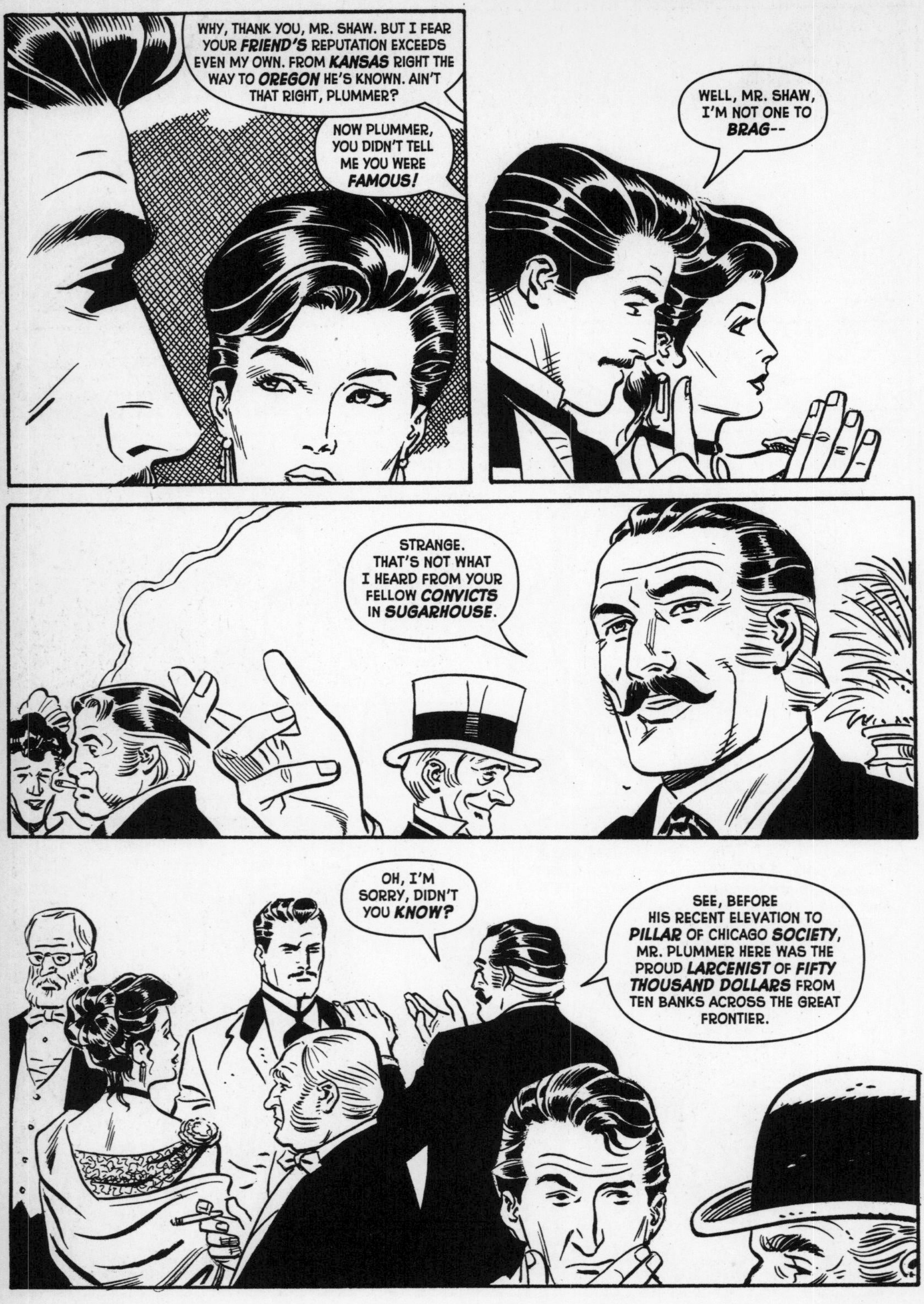
WHY, THANK YOU, MR. SHAW. BUT I FEAR YOUR FRIEND'S REPUTATION EXCEEDS EVEN MY OWN. FROM KANSAS RIGHT THE WAY TO OREGON HE'S KNOWN. AIN'T THAT RIGHT, PLUMMER?
NOW PLUMMER, YOU DIDN'T TELL ME YOU WERE FAMOUS!
WELL, MR. SHAW, I'M NOT ONE TO BRAG--
STRANGE. THAT'S NOT WHAT I HEARD FROM YOUR FELLOW CONVICTS IN SUGARHOUSE.
OH, I'M SORRY, DIDN'T YOU KNOW?
SEE, BEFORE HIS RECENT ELEVATION TO PILLAR OF CHICAGO SOCIETY, MR. PLUMMER HERE WAS THE PROUD LARCENIST OF FIFTY THOUSAND DOLLARS FROM TEN BANKS ACROSS THE GREAT FRONTIER.

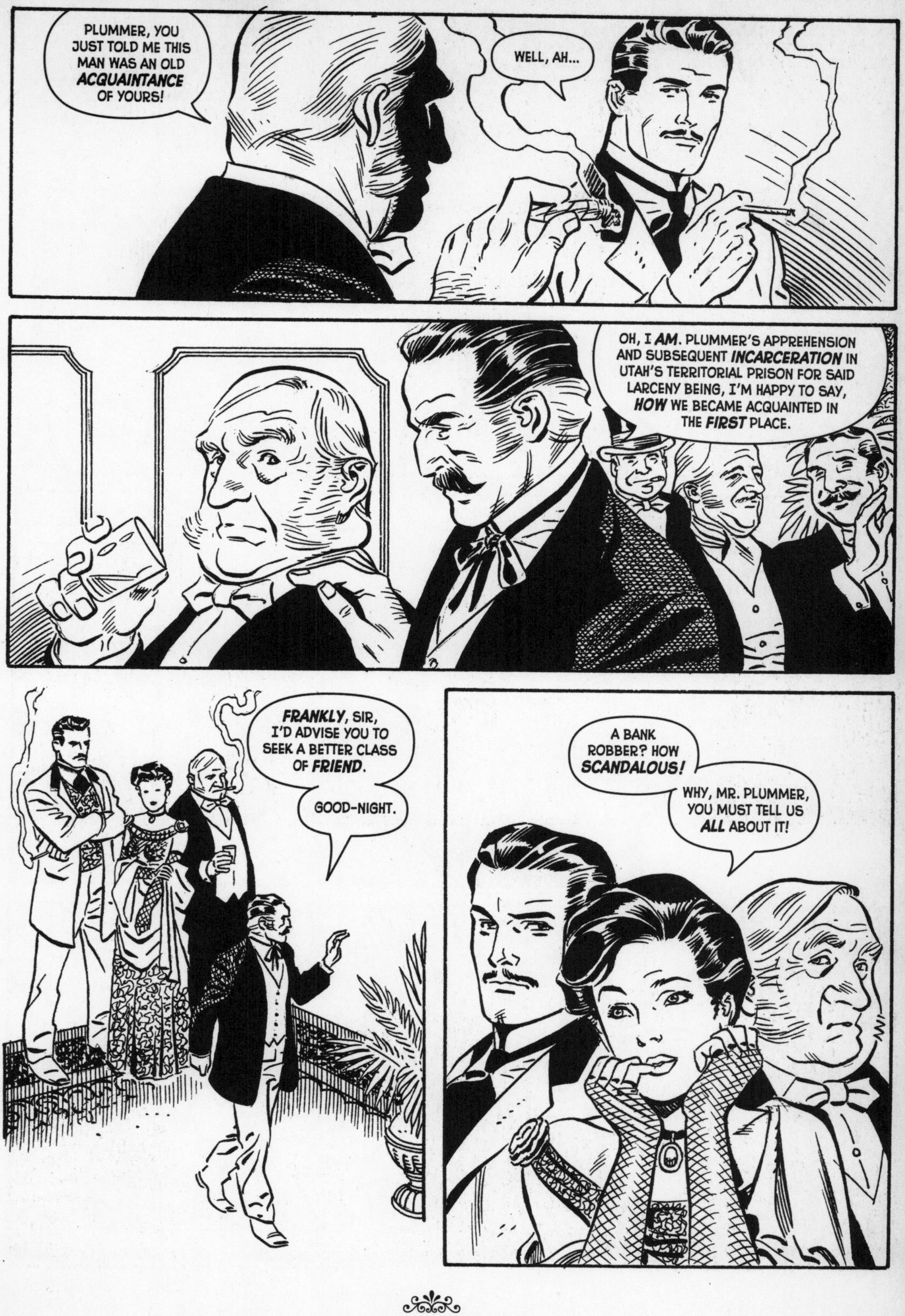
PLUMMER, YOU JUST TOLD ME THIS MAN WAS AN OLD ACQUAINTANCE OF YOURS!
WELL, AH...
OH, I AM. PLUMMER'S APPREHENSION AND SUBSEQUENT INCARCERATION IN UTAH'S TERRITORIAL PRISON FOR SAID LARCENY BEING, I'M HAPPY TO SAY, HOW WE BECAME ACQUAINTED IN THE FIRST PLACE.
FRANKLY, SIR, I'D ADVISE YOU TO SEEK A BETTER CLASS OF FRIEND.
GOOD-NIGHT.
A BANK ROBBER? HOW SCANDALOUS!
WHY, MR. PLUMMER, YOU MUST TELL US ALL ABOUT IT!

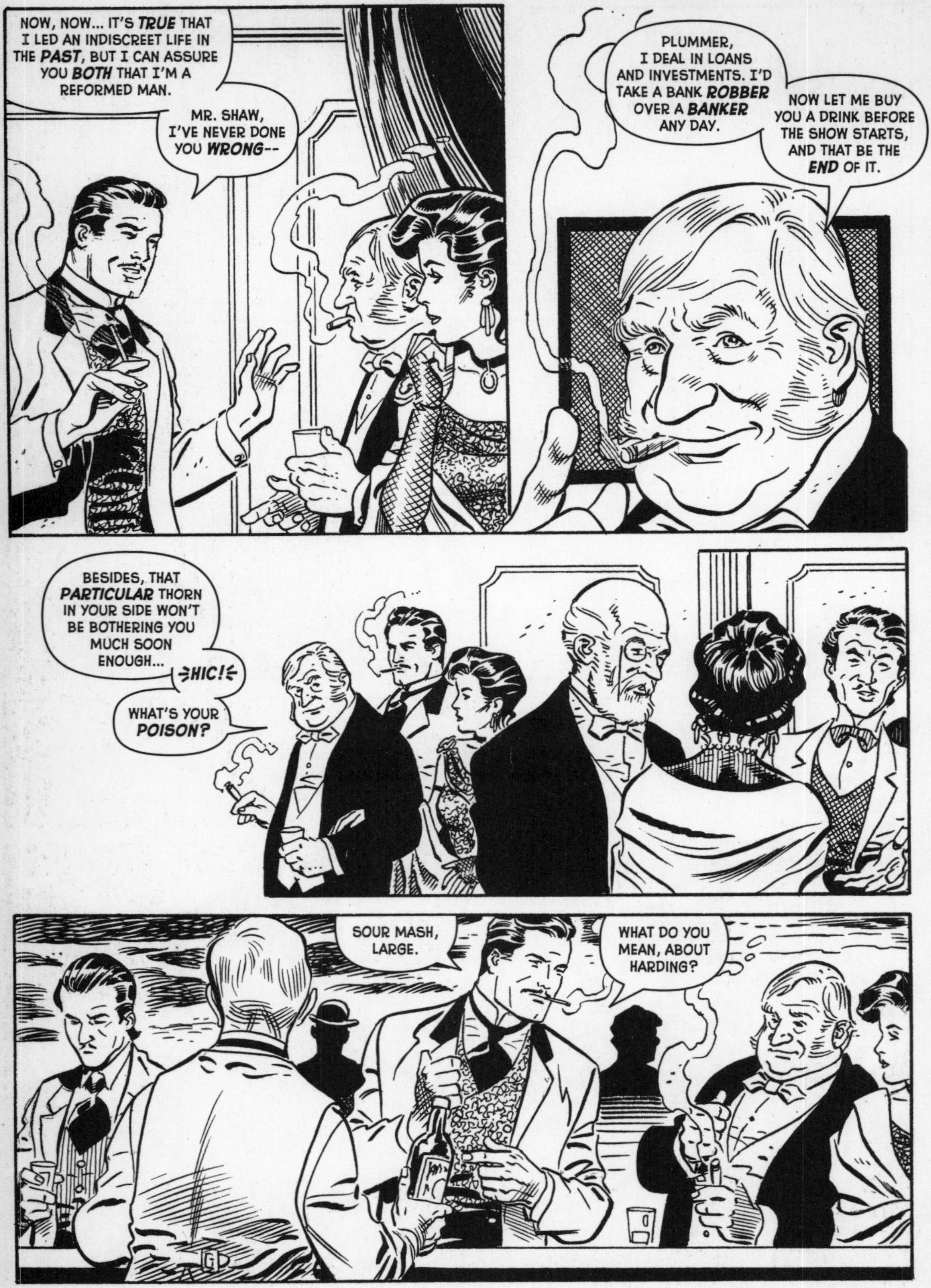
NOW, NOW... IT'S TRUE THAT I LED AN INDISCREET LIFE IN THE PAST, BUT I CAN ASSURE YOU BOTH THAT I'M A REFORMED MAN.
MR. SHAW, I'VE NEVER DONE YOU WRONG--
PLUMMER, I DEAL IN LOANS AND INVESTMENTS. I'D TAKE A BANK ROBBER OVER A BANKER ANY DAY.
NOW LET ME BUY YOU A DRINK BEFORE THE SHOW STARTS, AND THAT BE THE END OF IT.
BESIDES, THAT PARTICULAR THORN IN YOUR SIDE WON'T BE BOTHERING YOU MUCH SOON ENOUGH...
HIC!
WHAT'S YOUR POISON?
SOUR MASH, LARGE.
WHAT DO YOU MEAN, ABOUT HARDING?

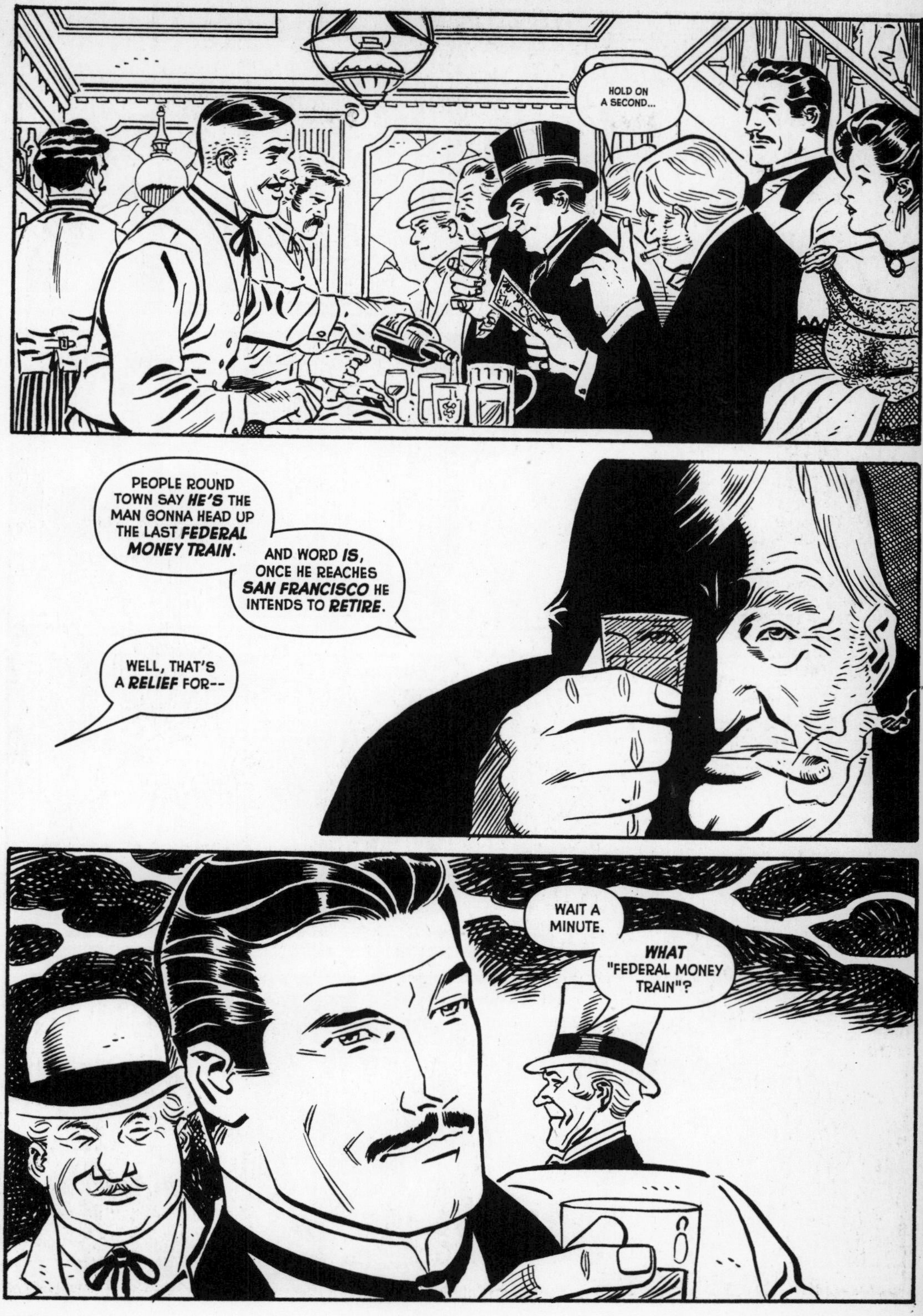

HOLD ON A SECOND...
PEOPLE ROUND TOWN SAY HE'S THE MAN GONNA HEAD UP THE LAST FEDERAL MONEY TRAIN.
AND WORD IS, ONCE HE REACHES SAN FRANCISCO HE INTENDS TO RETIRE.
WELL, THAT'S A RELIEF FOR--
WAIT A MINUTE.
WHAT "FEDERAL MONEY TRAIN"?

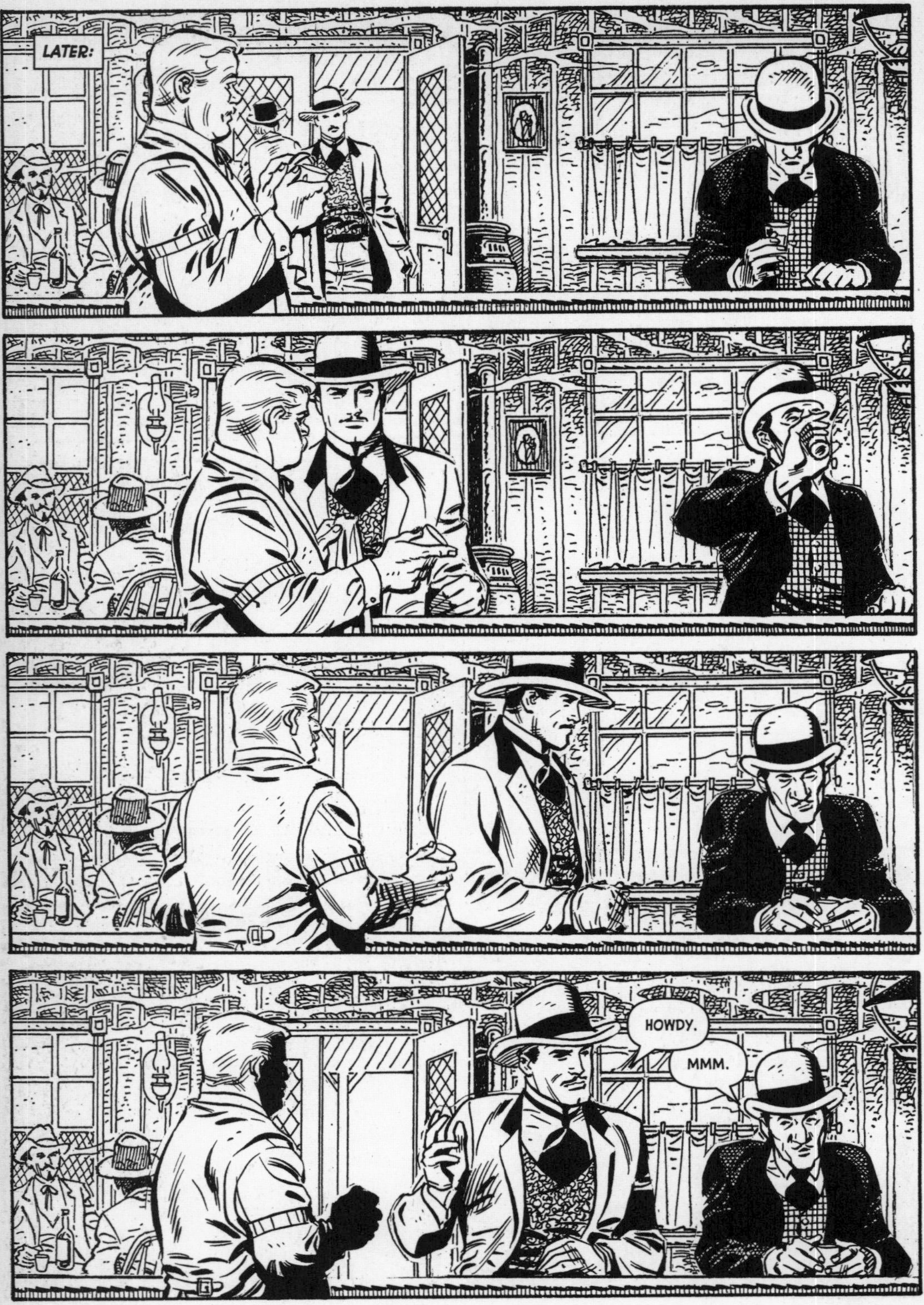
LATER:
HOWDY.
MMM.

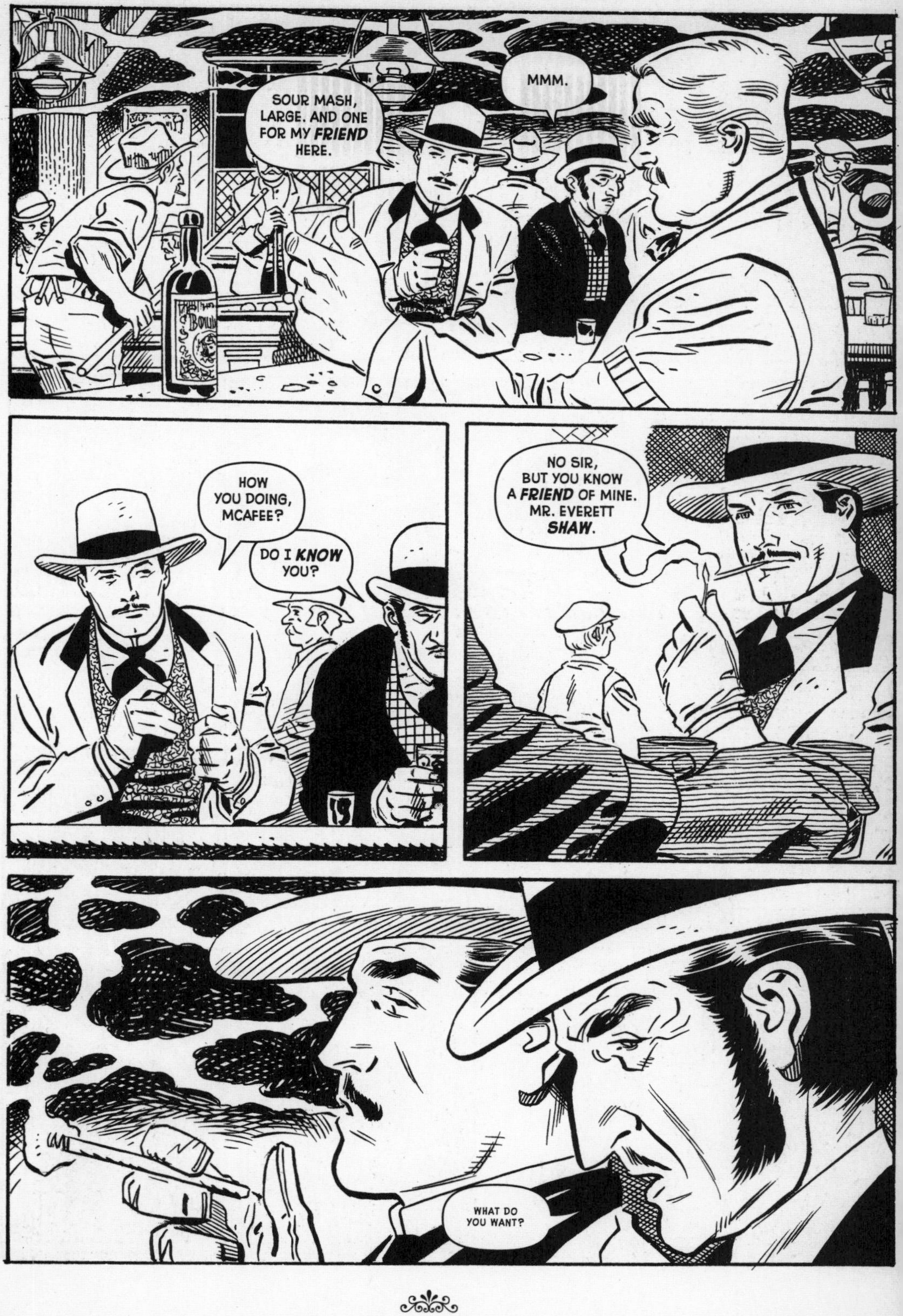
SOUR MASH, LARGE. AND ONE FOR MY FRIEND HERE.
MMM.
HOW YOU DOING, MCAFEE?
DO I KNOW YOU?
NO SIR, BUT YOU KNOW A FRIEND OF MINE. MR. EVERETT SHAW.
WHAT DO YOU WANT?

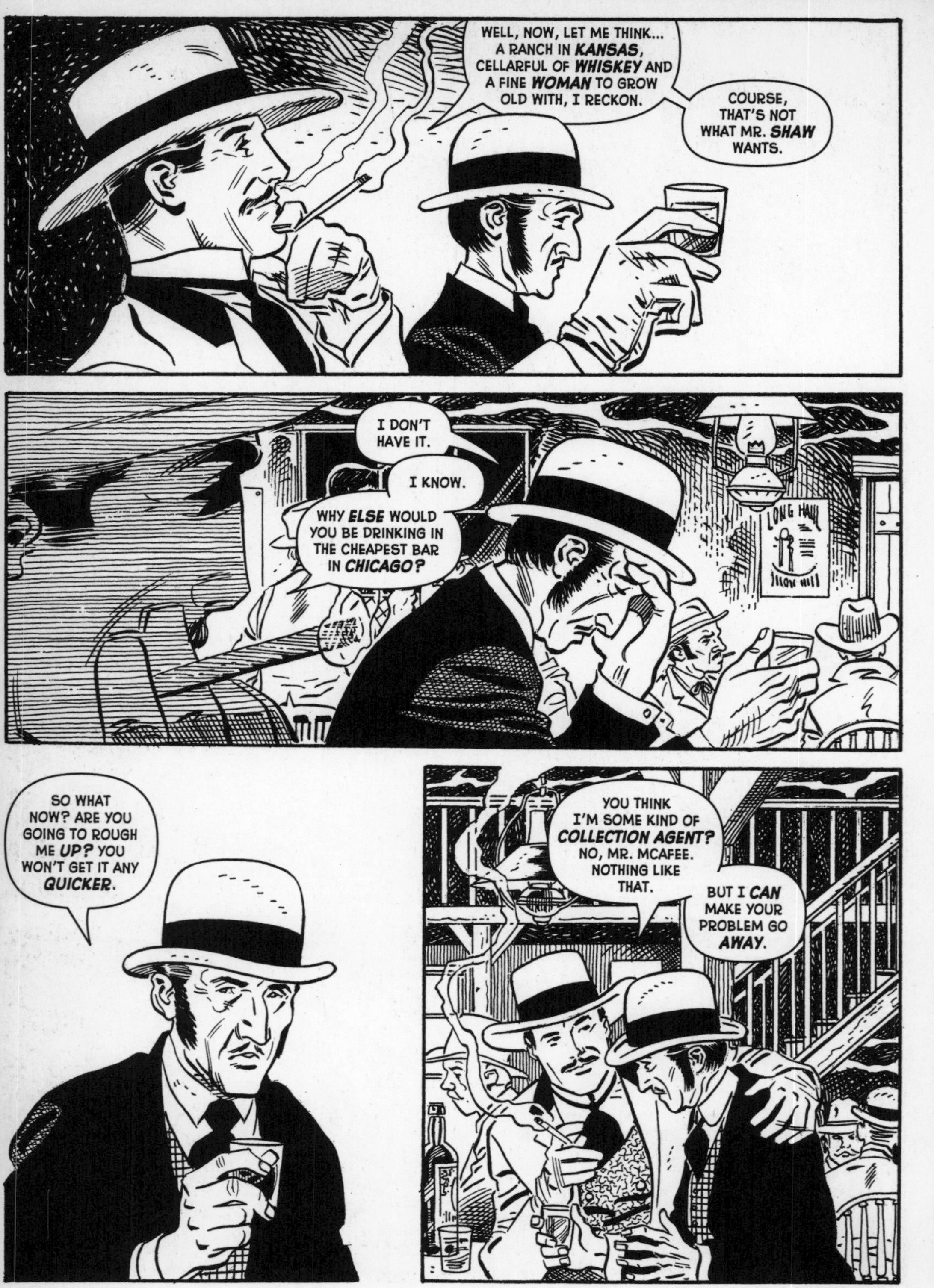
WELL, NOW, LET ME THINK... A RANCH IN KANSAS, CELLARFUL OF WHISKEY AND A FINE WOMAN TO GROW OLD WITH, I RECKON.
COURSE, THAT'S NOT WHAT MR. SHAW WANTS.
I DON'T HAVE IT.
I KNOW.
WHY ELSE WOULD YOU BE DRINKING IN THE CHEAPEST BAR IN CHICAGO?
LONG HALL
SO WHAT NOW? ARE YOU GOING TO ROUGH ME UP? YOU WON'T GET IT ANY QUICKER.
YOU THINK I'M SOME KIND OF COLLECTION AGENT? NO, MR. MCAFEE. NOTHING LIKE THAT.
BUT I CAN MAKE YOUR PROBLEM GO AWAY.

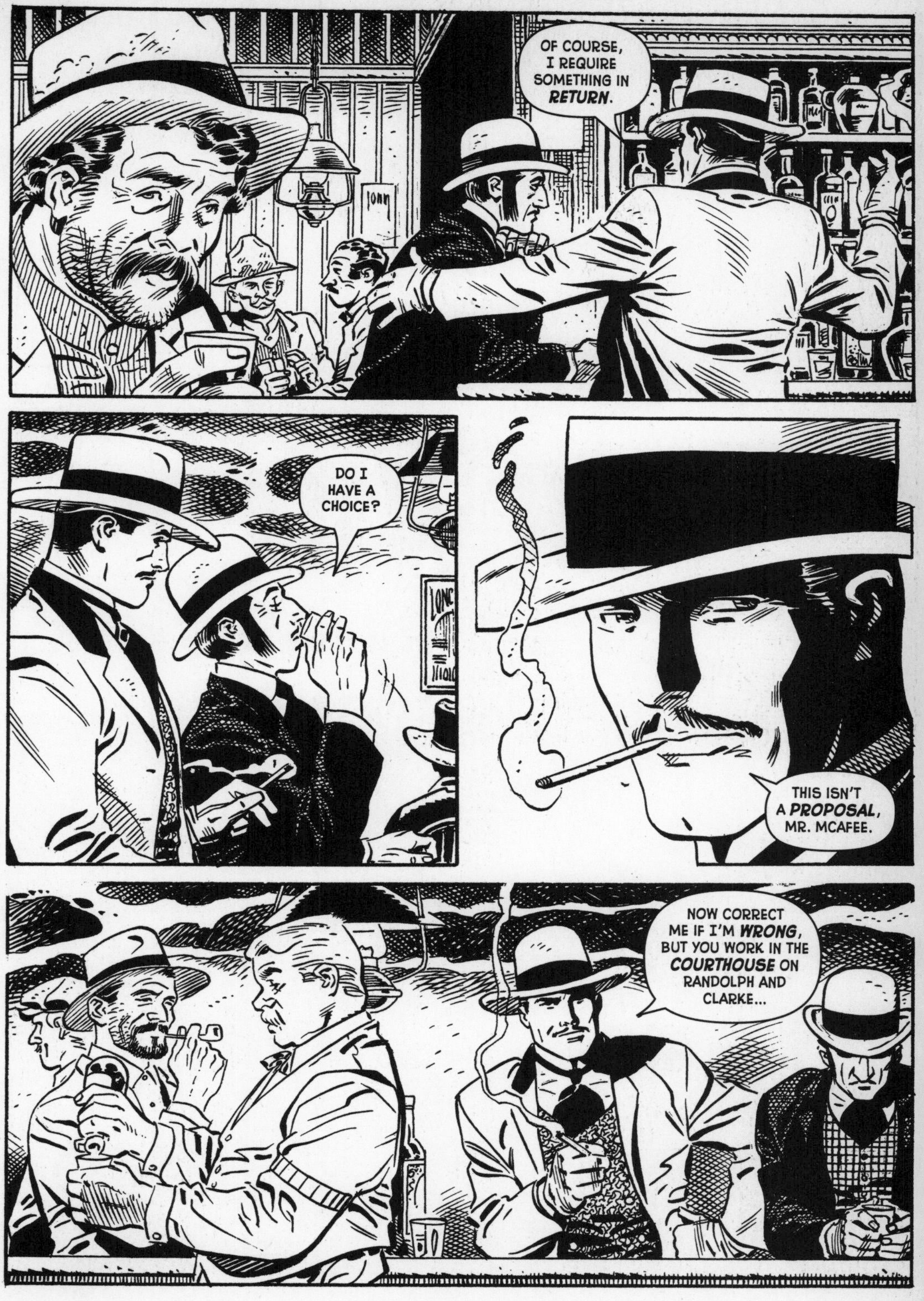
OF COURSE, I REQUIRE SOMETHING IN RETURN.
DO I HAVE A CHOICE?
THIS ISN'T A PROPOSAL, MR. MCAFEE.
NOW CORRECT ME IF I'M WRONG, BUT YOU WORK IN THE COURTHOUSE ON RANDOLPH AND CLARKE...

TWO

---★---

"THE WOMAN"

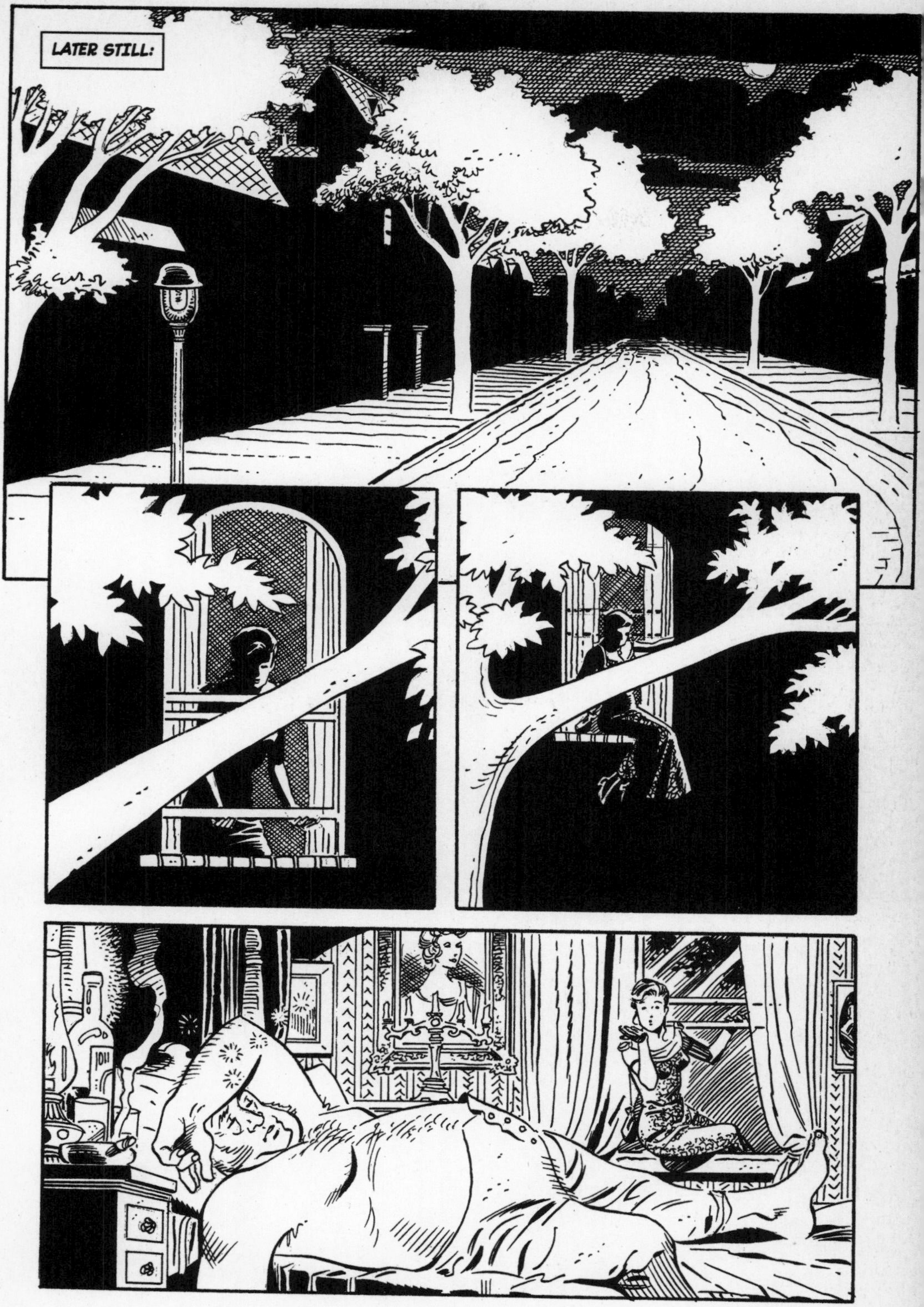
LATER STILL:

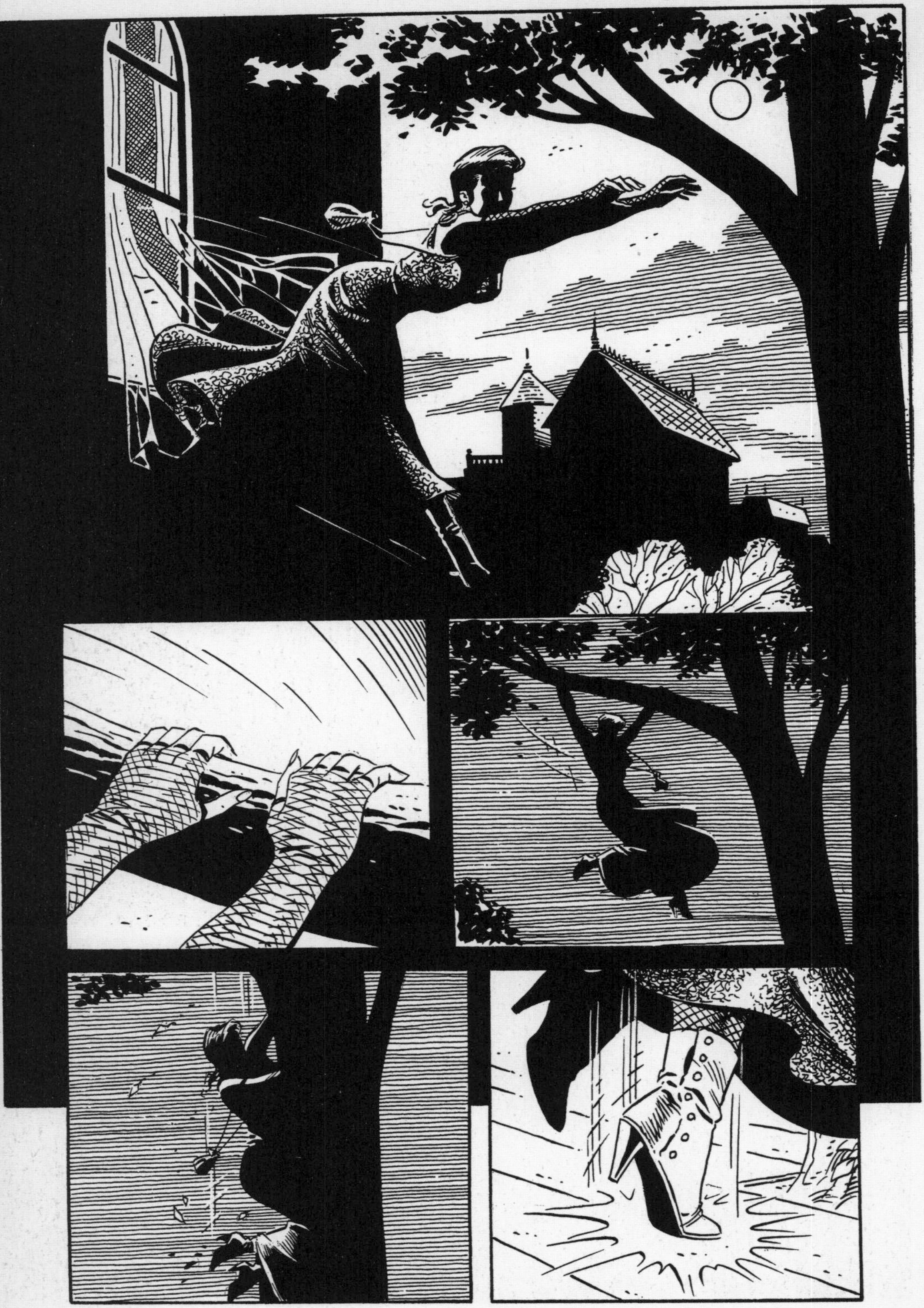

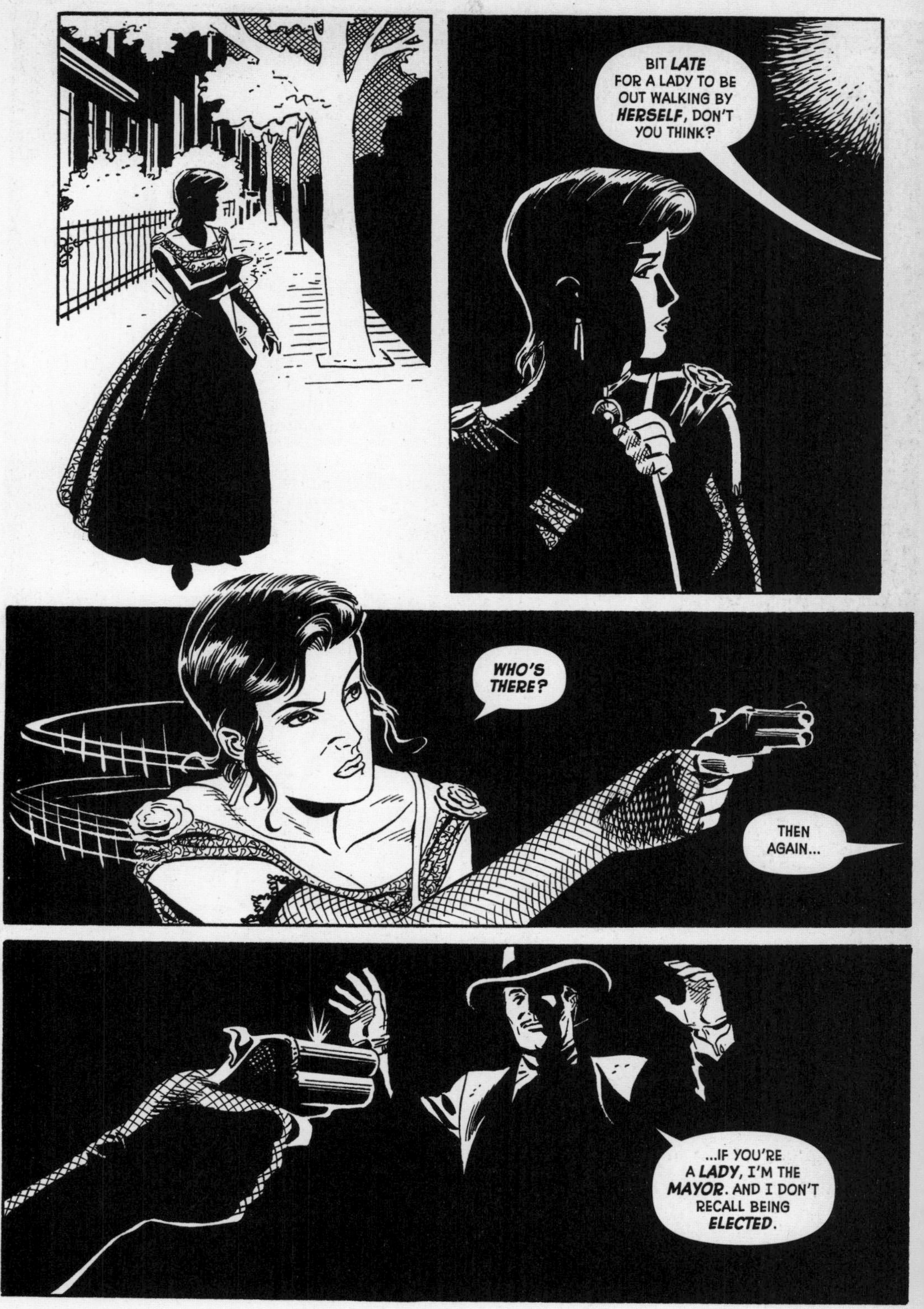

BIT LATE FOR A LADY TO BE OUT WALKING BY HERSELF, DON'T YOU THINK?
WHO'S THERE?
THEN AGAIN...
...IF YOU'RE A LADY, I'M THE MAYOR. AND I DON'T RECALL BEING ELECTED.

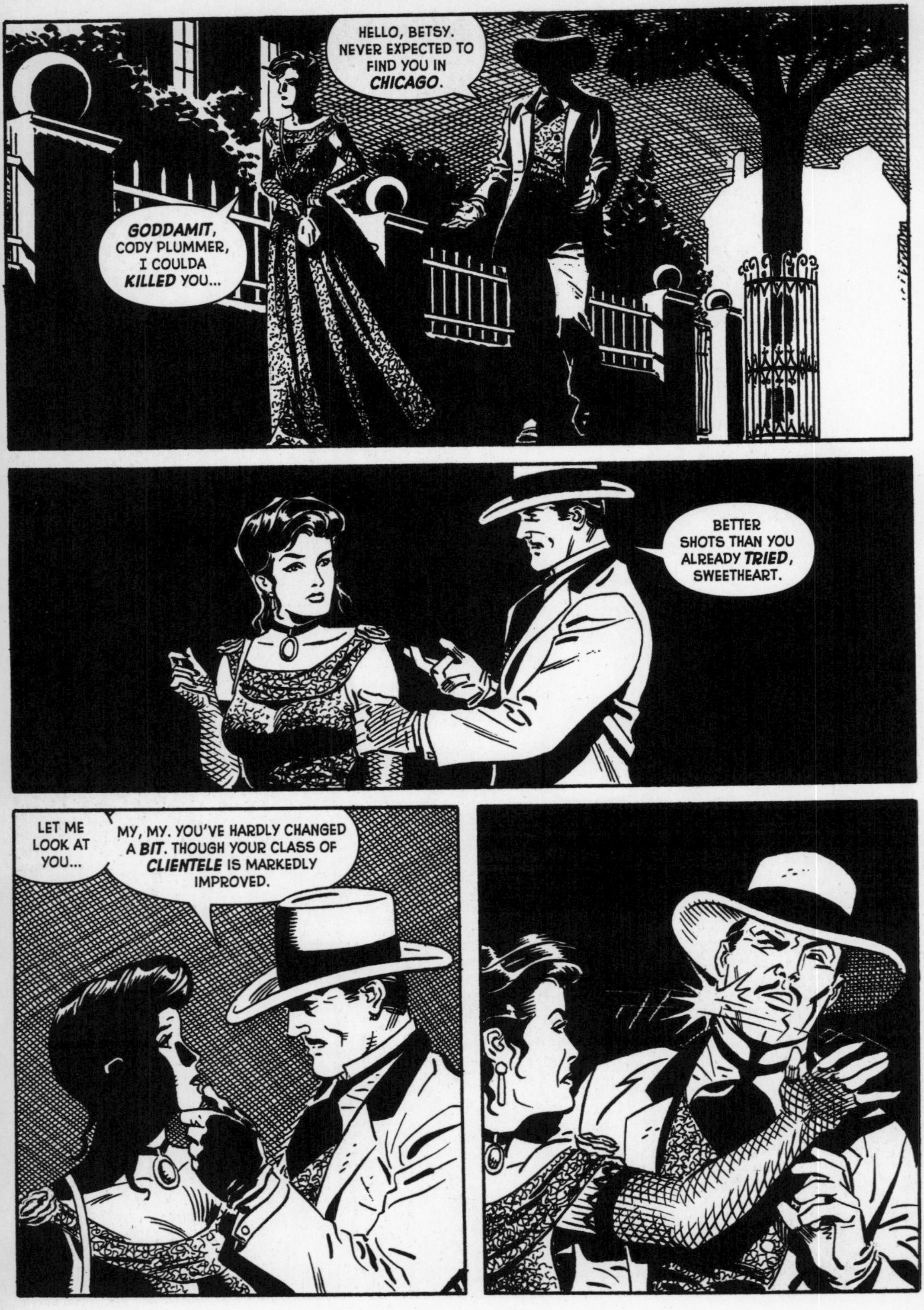
HELLO, BETSY. NEVER EXPECTED TO FIND YOU IN CHICAGO.
GODDAMIT, CODY PLUMMER, I COULDA KILLED YOU...
BETTER SHOTS THAN YOU ALREADY TRIED, SWEETHEART.
LET ME LOOK AT YOU...
MY, MY. YOU'VE HARDLY CHANGED A BIT. THOUGH YOUR CLASS OF CLIENTELE IS MARKEDLY IMPROVED.

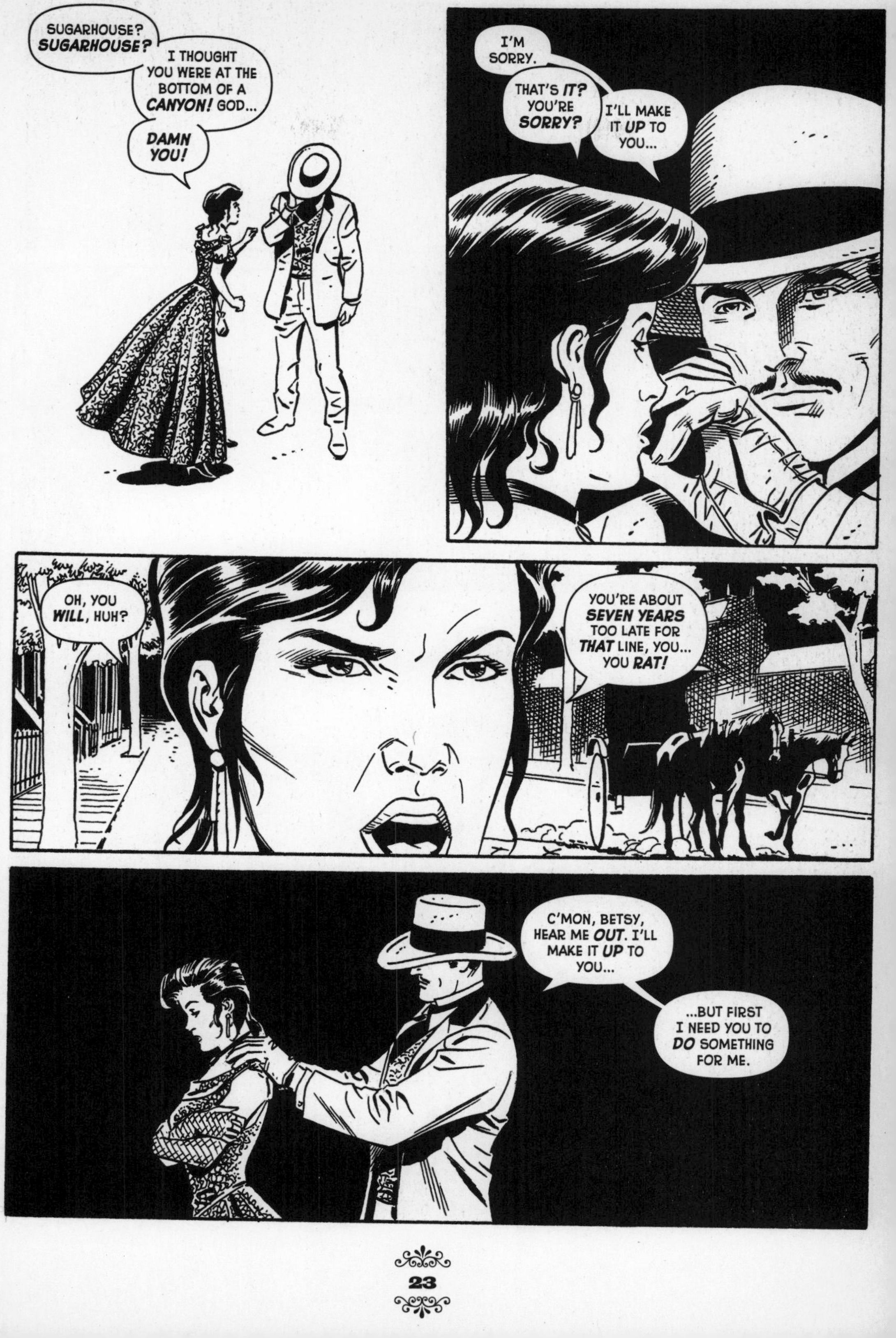
SUGARHOUSE? SUGARHOUSE?
I THOUGHT YOU WERE AT THE BOTTOM OF A CANYON! GOD...
DAMN YOU!
I'M SORRY.
THAT'S IT? YOU'RE SORRY?
I'LL MAKE IT UP TO YOU...
OH, YOU WILL, HUH?
YOU'RE ABOUT SEVEN YEARS TOO LATE FOR THAT LINE, YOU... YOU RAT!
C'MON, BETSY, HEAR ME OUT. I'LL MAKE IT UP TO YOU...
...BUT FIRST I NEED YOU TO DO SOMETHING FOR ME.

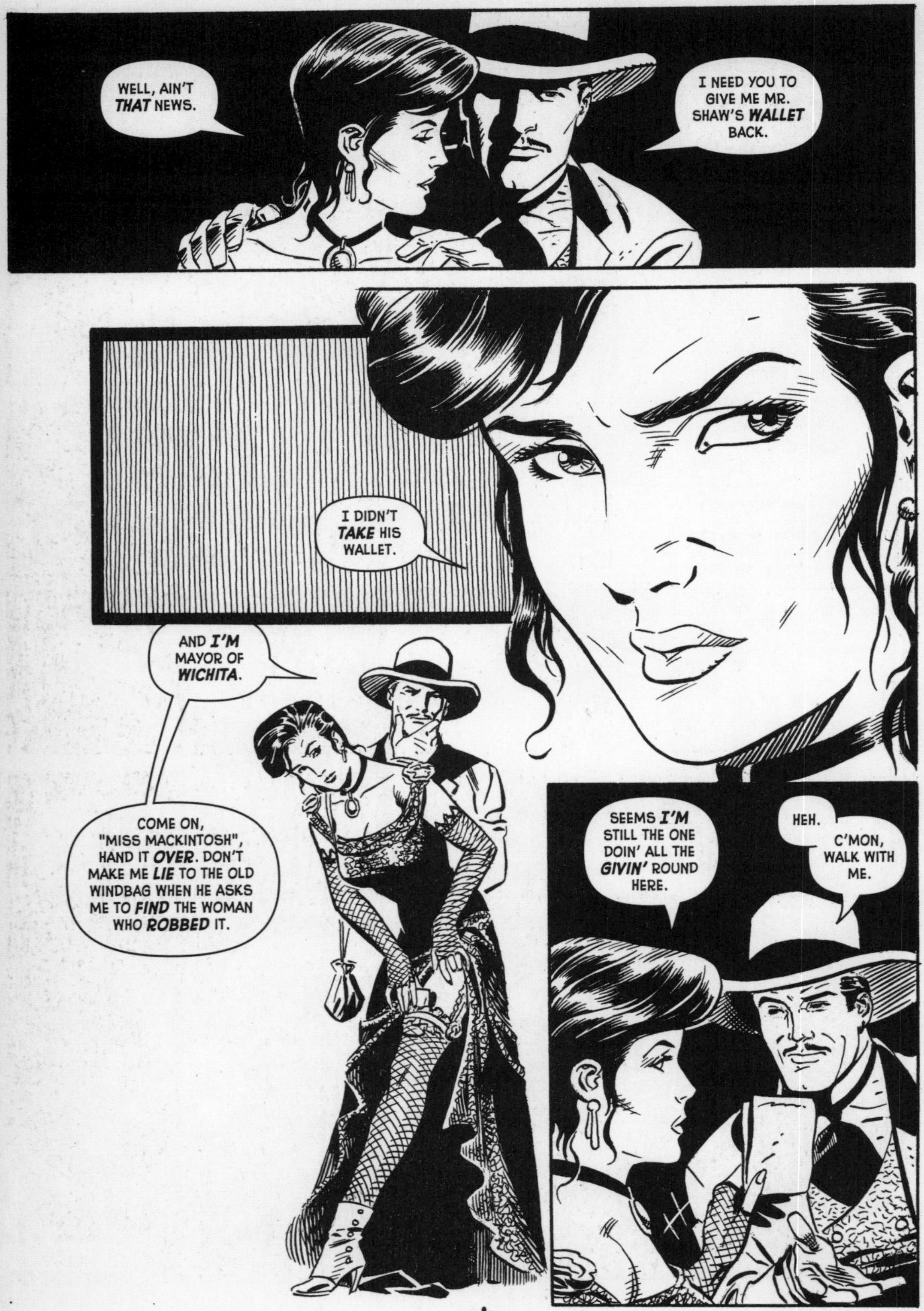
WELL, AIN'T THAT NEWS.
I NEED YOU TO GIVE ME MR. SHAW'S WALLET BACK.
I DIDN'T TAKE HIS WALLET.
AND I'M MAYOR OF WICHITA.
COME ON, "MISS MACKINTOSH", HAND IT OVER. DON'T MAKE ME LIE TO THE OLD WINDBAG WHEN HE ASKS ME TO FIND THE WOMAN WHO ROBBED IT.
SEEMS I'M STILL THE ONE DOIN' ALL THE GIVIN' ROUND HERE.
HEH.
C'MON, WALK WITH ME.

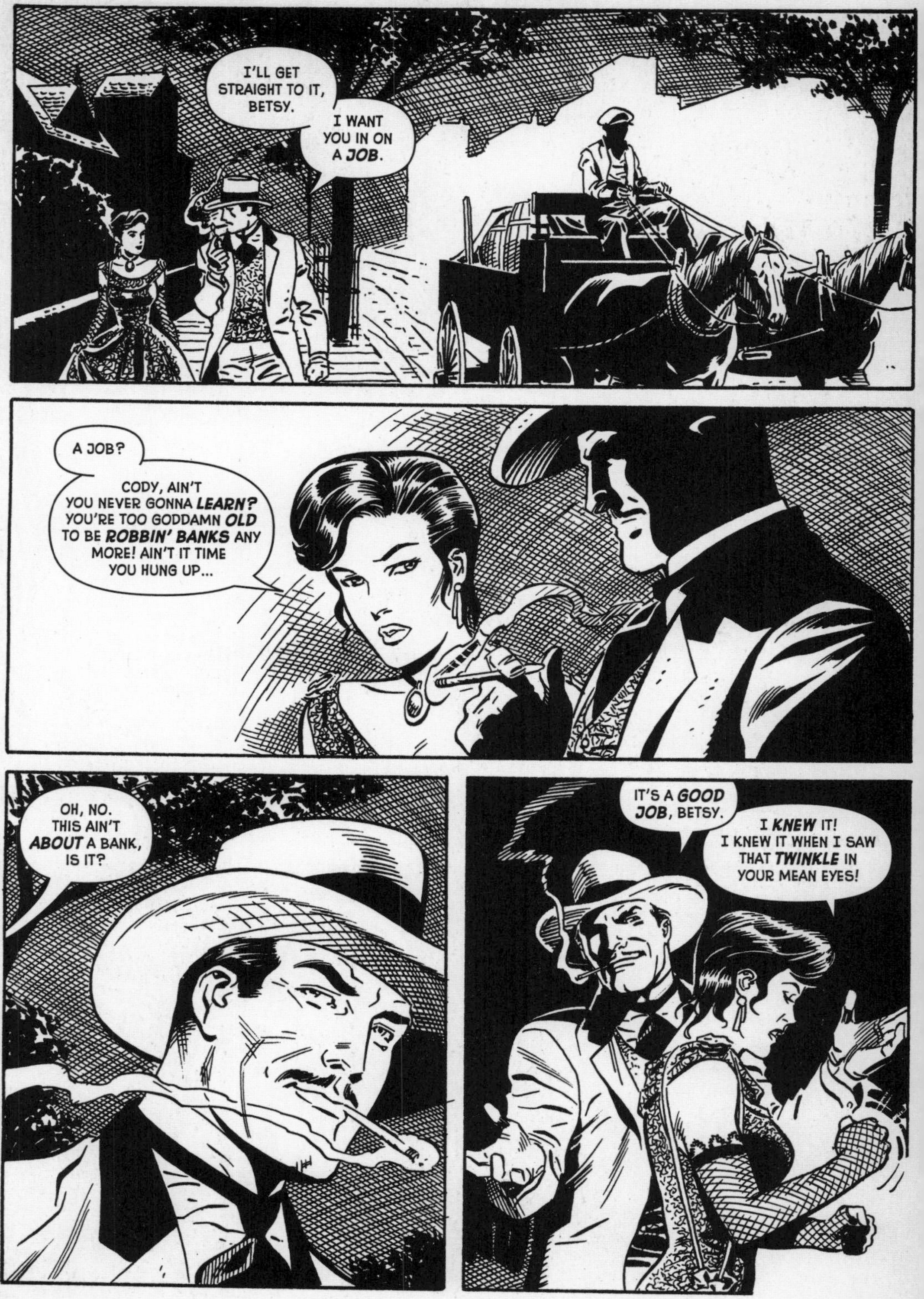
I'LL GET STRAIGHT TO IT, BETSY.
I WANT YOU IN ON A JOB.
A JOB?
CODY, AIN'T YOU NEVER GONNA LEARN? YOU'RE TOO GODDAMN OLD TO BE ROBBIN' BANKS ANY MORE! AIN'T IT TIME YOU HUNG UP...
OH, NO. THIS AIN'T ABOUT A BANK, IS IT?
IT'S A GOOD JOB, BETSY.
I KNEW IT! I KNEW IT WHEN I SAW THAT TWINKLE IN YOUR MEAN EYES!

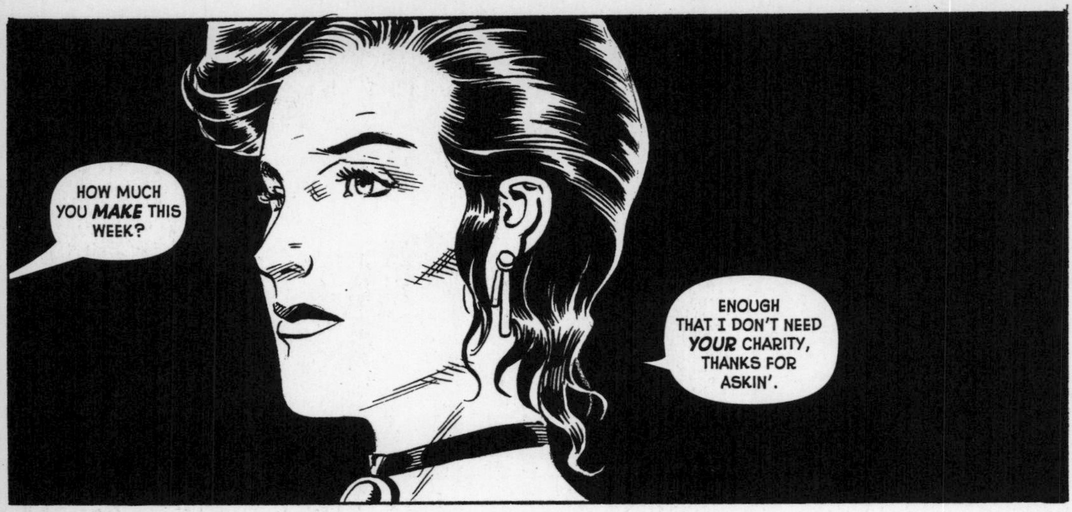
HOW MUCH YOU MAKE THIS WEEK?
ENOUGH THAT I DON'T NEED YOUR CHARITY, THANKS FOR ASKIN'.

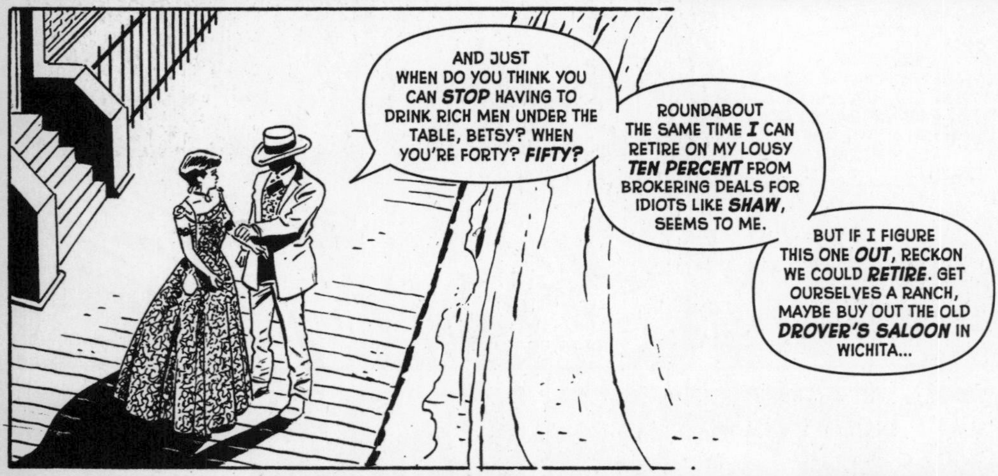
AND JUST WHEN DO YOU THINK YOU CAN STOP HAVING TO DRINK RICH MEN UNDER THE TABLE, BETSY? WHEN YOU'RE FORTY? FIFTY?
ROUNDABOUT THE SAME TIME I CAN RETIRE ON MY LOUSY TEN PERCENT FROM BROKERING DEALS FOR IDIOTS LIKE SHAW, SEEMS TO ME.
BUT IF I FIGURE THIS ONE OUT, RECKON WE COULD RETIRE. GET OURSELVES A RANCH, MAYBE BUY OUT THE OLD DROVER'S SALOON IN WICHITA...

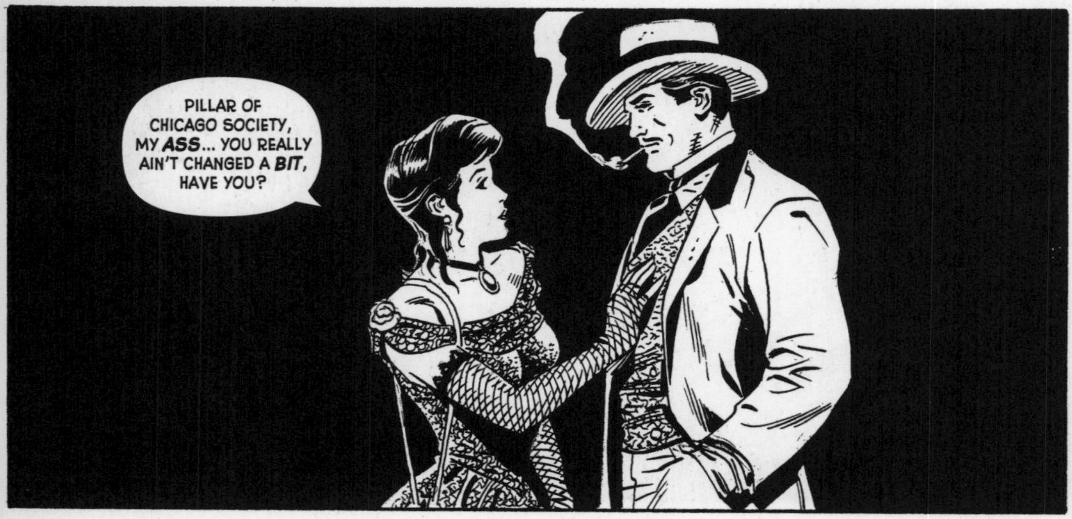
PILLAR OF CHICAGO SOCIETY, MY ASS... YOU REALLY AIN'T CHANGED A BIT, HAVE YOU?

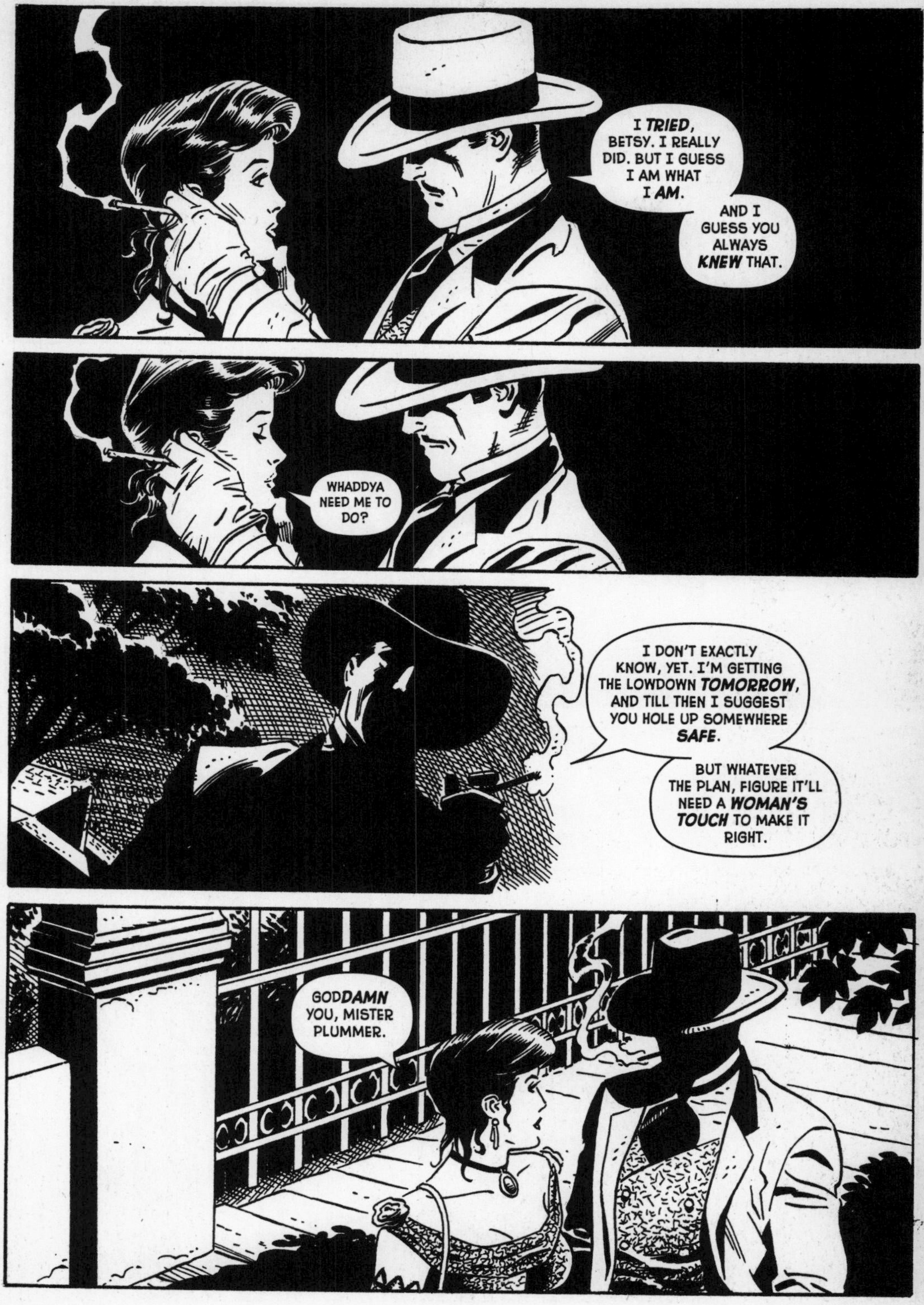
I TRIED, BETSY. I REALLY DID. BUT I GUESS I AM WHAT I AM.
AND I GUESS YOU ALWAYS KNEW THAT.
WHADDYA NEED ME TO DO?
I DON'T EXACTLY KNOW, YET. I'M GETTING THE LOWDOWN TOMORROW, AND TILL THEN I SUGGEST YOU HOLE UP SOMEWHERE SAFE.
BUT WHATEVER THE PLAN, FIGURE IT'LL NEED A WOMAN'S TOUCH TO MAKE IT RIGHT.
GODDAMN YOU, MISTER PLUMMER.

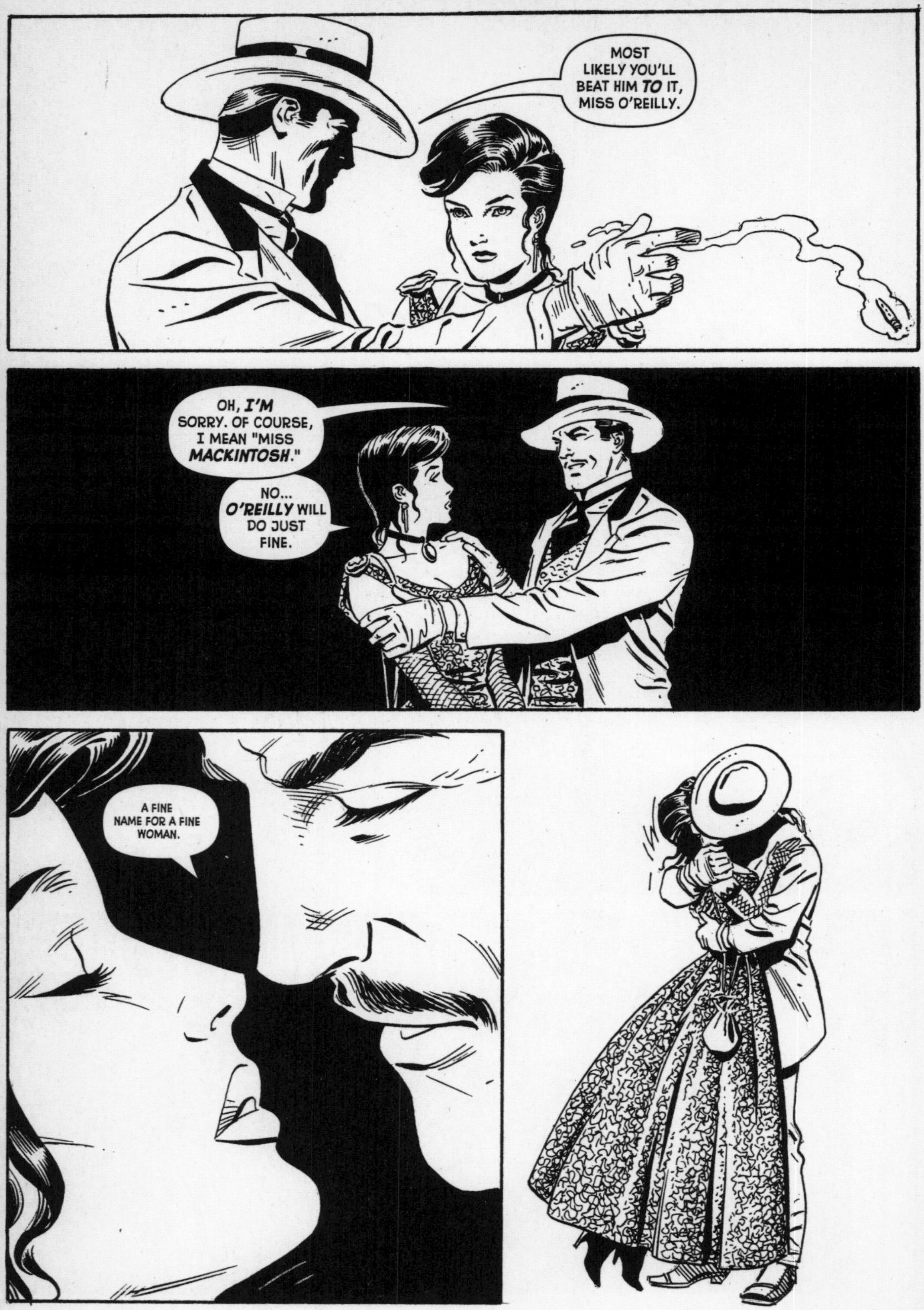
MOST LIKELY YOU'LL BEAT HIM TO IT, MISS O'REILLY.
OH, I'M SORRY. OF COURSE, I MEAN "MISS MACKINTOSH."
NO... O'REILLY WILL DO JUST FINE.
A FINE NAME FOR A FINE WOMAN.

THREE

★

"THE MONEY MAN"

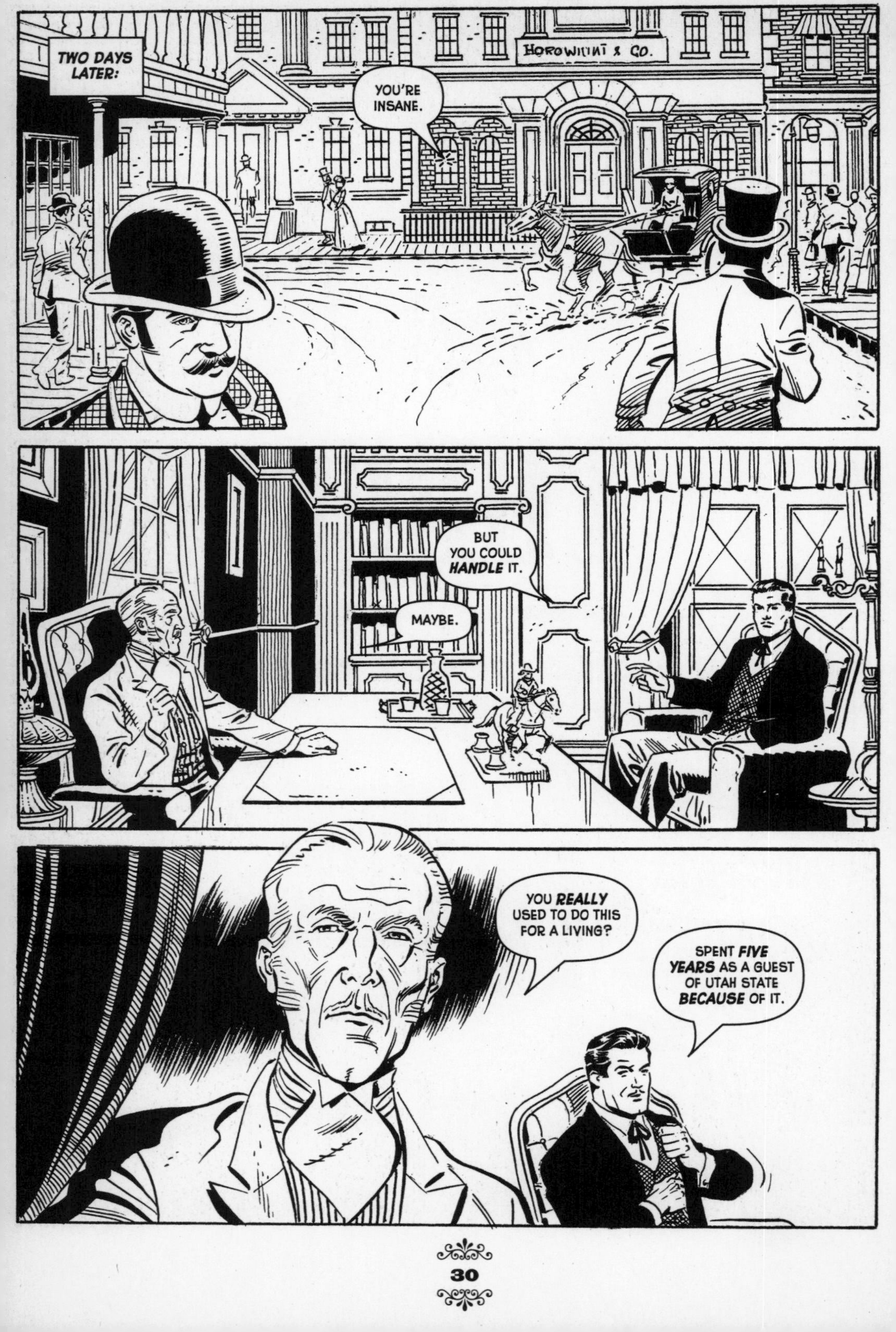
TWO DAYS LATER:
YOU'RE INSANE.
BUT YOU COULD ***HANDLE*** IT.
MAYBE.
YOU ***REALLY*** USED TO DO THIS FOR A LIVING?
SPENT ***FIVE YEARS*** AS A GUEST OF UTAH STATE ***BECAUSE*** OF IT.

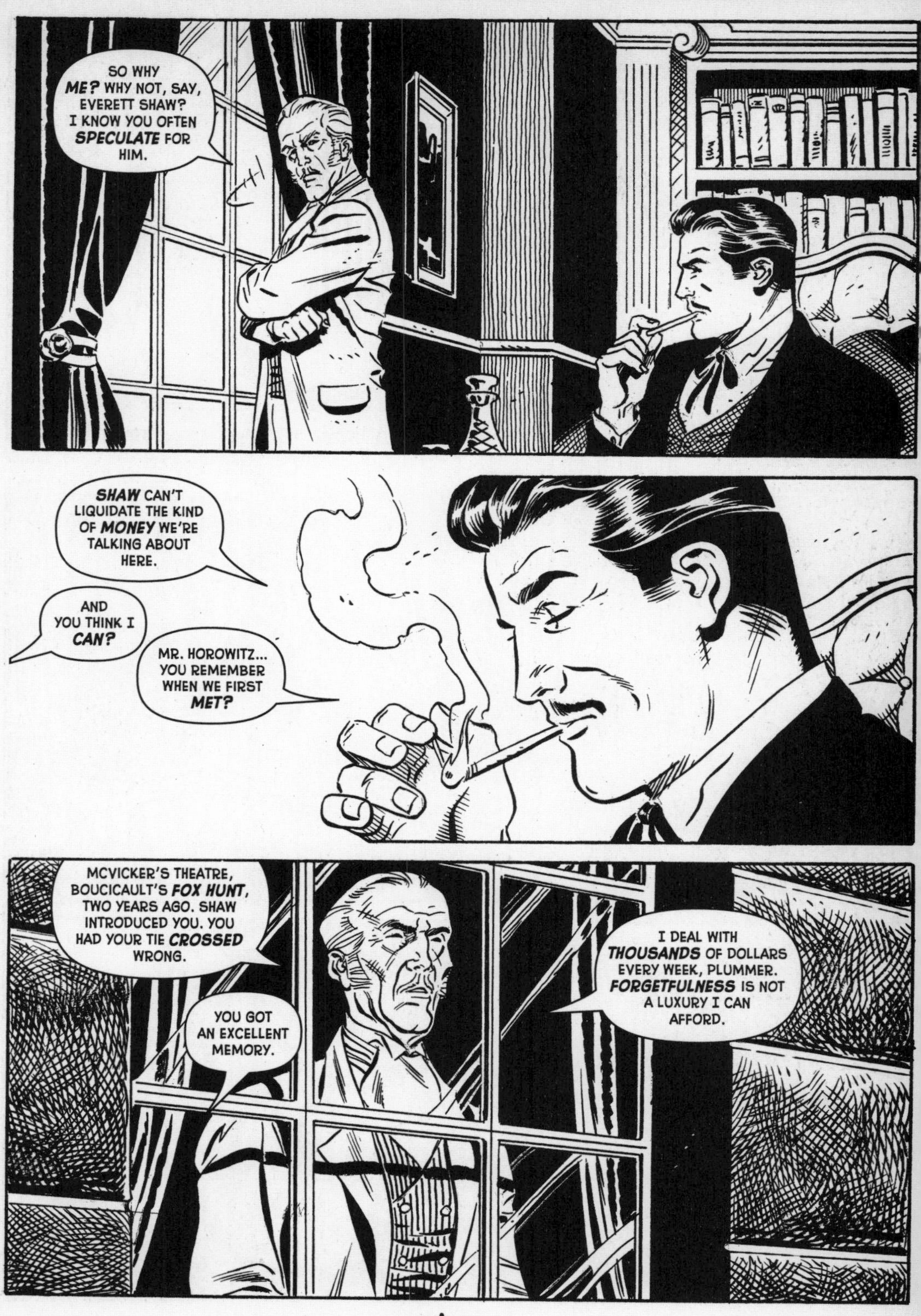
SO WHY ME? WHY NOT, SAY, EVERETT SHAW? I KNOW YOU OFTEN SPECULATE FOR HIM.
SHAW CAN'T LIQUIDATE THE KIND OF MONEY WE'RE TALKING ABOUT HERE.
AND YOU THINK I CAN?
MR. HOROWITZ... YOU REMEMBER WHEN WE FIRST MET?
MCVICKER'S THEATRE, BOUCICAULT'S FOX HUNT, TWO YEARS AGO. SHAW INTRODUCED YOU. YOU HAD YOUR TIE CROSSED WRONG.
YOU GOT AN EXCELLENT MEMORY.
I DEAL WITH THOUSANDS OF DOLLARS EVERY WEEK, PLUMMER. FORGETFULNESS IS NOT A LUXURY I CAN AFFORD.

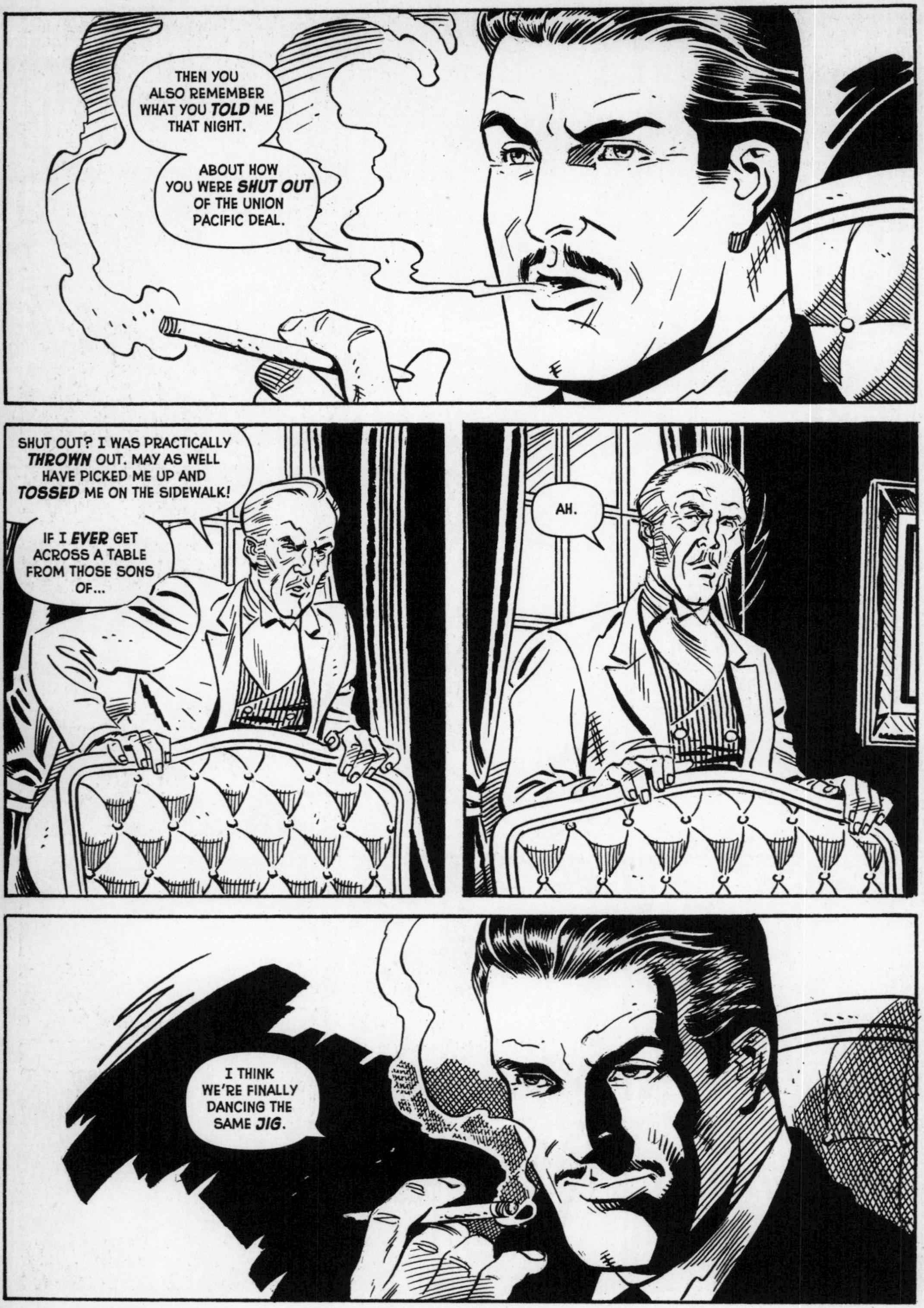
THEN YOU ALSO REMEMBER WHAT YOU *TOLD* ME THAT NIGHT.
ABOUT HOW YOU WERE *SHUT OUT* OF THE UNION PACIFIC DEAL.
SHUT OUT? I WAS PRACTICALLY *THROWN* OUT. MAY AS WELL HAVE PICKED ME UP AND *TOSSED* ME ON THE SIDEWALK!
IF I *EVER* GET ACROSS A TABLE FROM THOSE SONS OF...
AH.
I THINK WE'RE FINALLY DANCING THE SAME *JIG*.

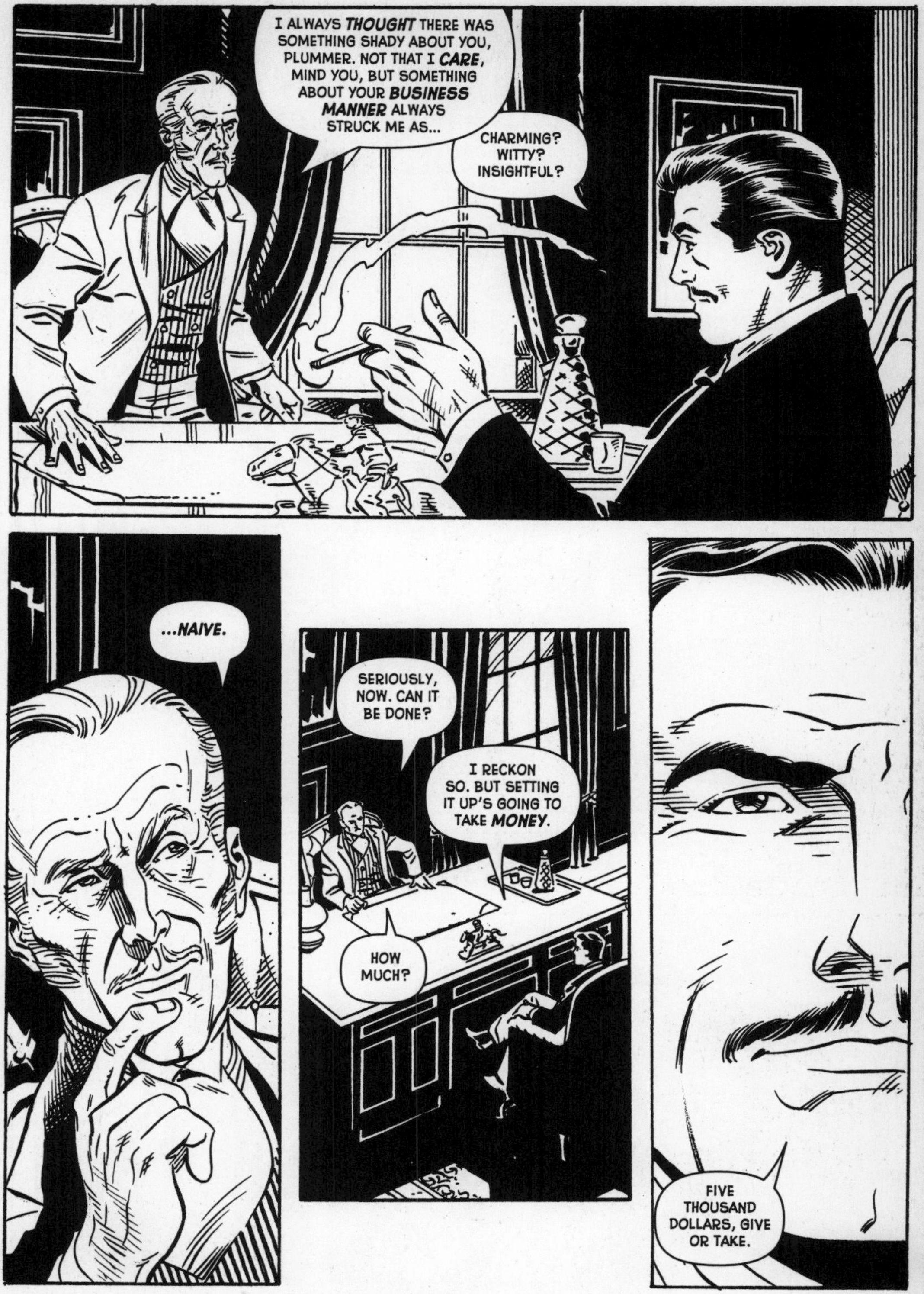
I ALWAYS THOUGHT THERE WAS SOMETHING SHADY ABOUT YOU, PLUMMER. NOT THAT I CARE, MIND YOU, BUT SOMETHING ABOUT YOUR BUSINESS MANNER ALWAYS STRUCK ME AS...
CHARMING? WITTY? INSIGHTFUL?
...NAIVE.
SERIOUSLY, NOW. CAN IT BE DONE?
I RECKON SO. BUT SETTING IT UP'S GOING TO TAKE MONEY.
HOW MUCH?
FIVE THOUSAND DOLLARS, GIVE OR TAKE.

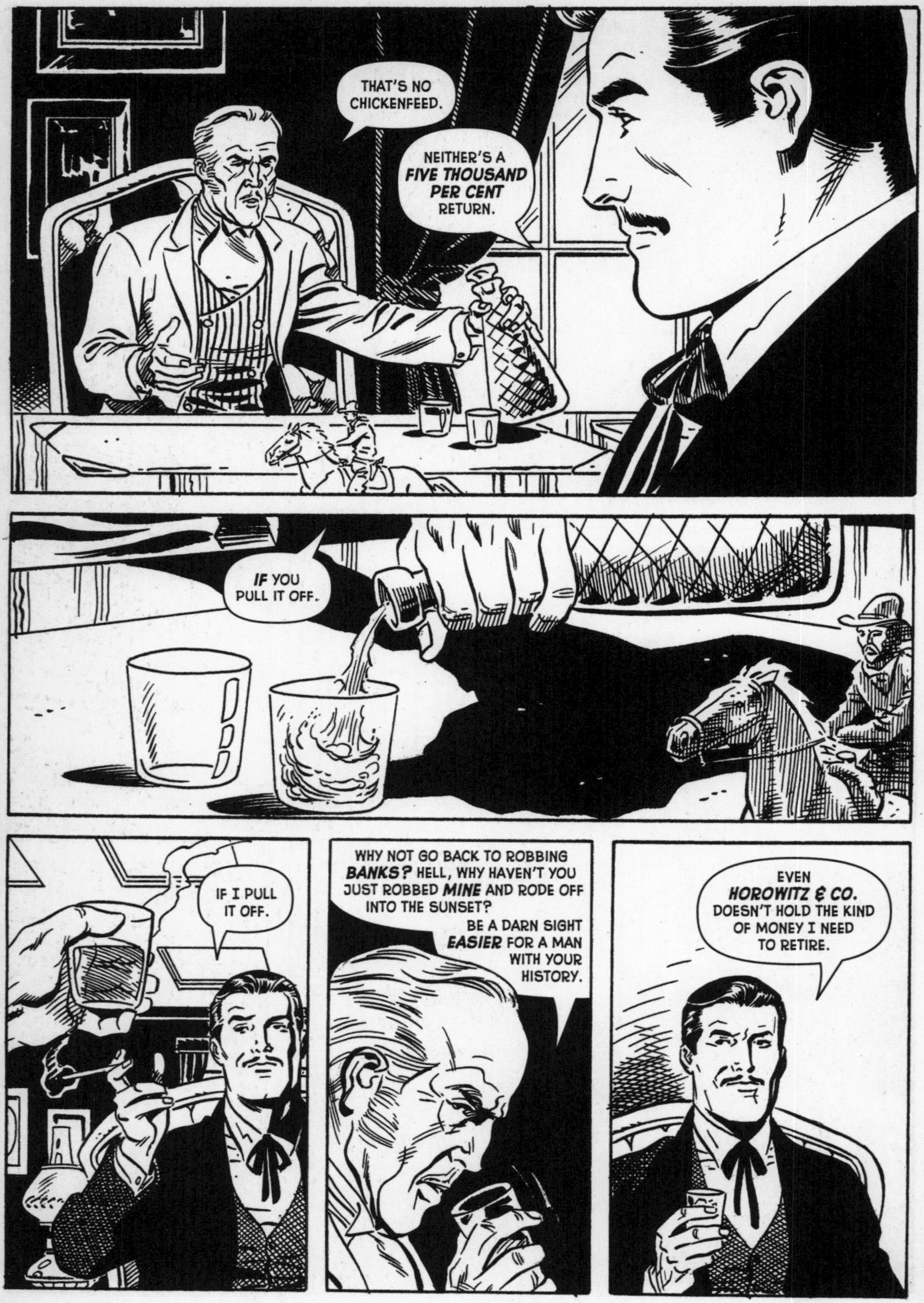
THAT'S NO CHICKENFEED.
NEITHER'S A FIVE THOUSAND PER CENT RETURN.
IF YOU PULL IT OFF.
IF I PULL IT OFF.
WHY NOT GO BACK TO ROBBING BANKS? HELL, WHY HAVEN'T YOU JUST ROBBED MINE AND RODE OFF INTO THE SUNSET?
BE A DARN SIGHT EASIER FOR A MAN WITH YOUR HISTORY.
EVEN HOROWITZ & CO. DOESN'T HOLD THE KIND OF MONEY I NEED TO RETIRE.

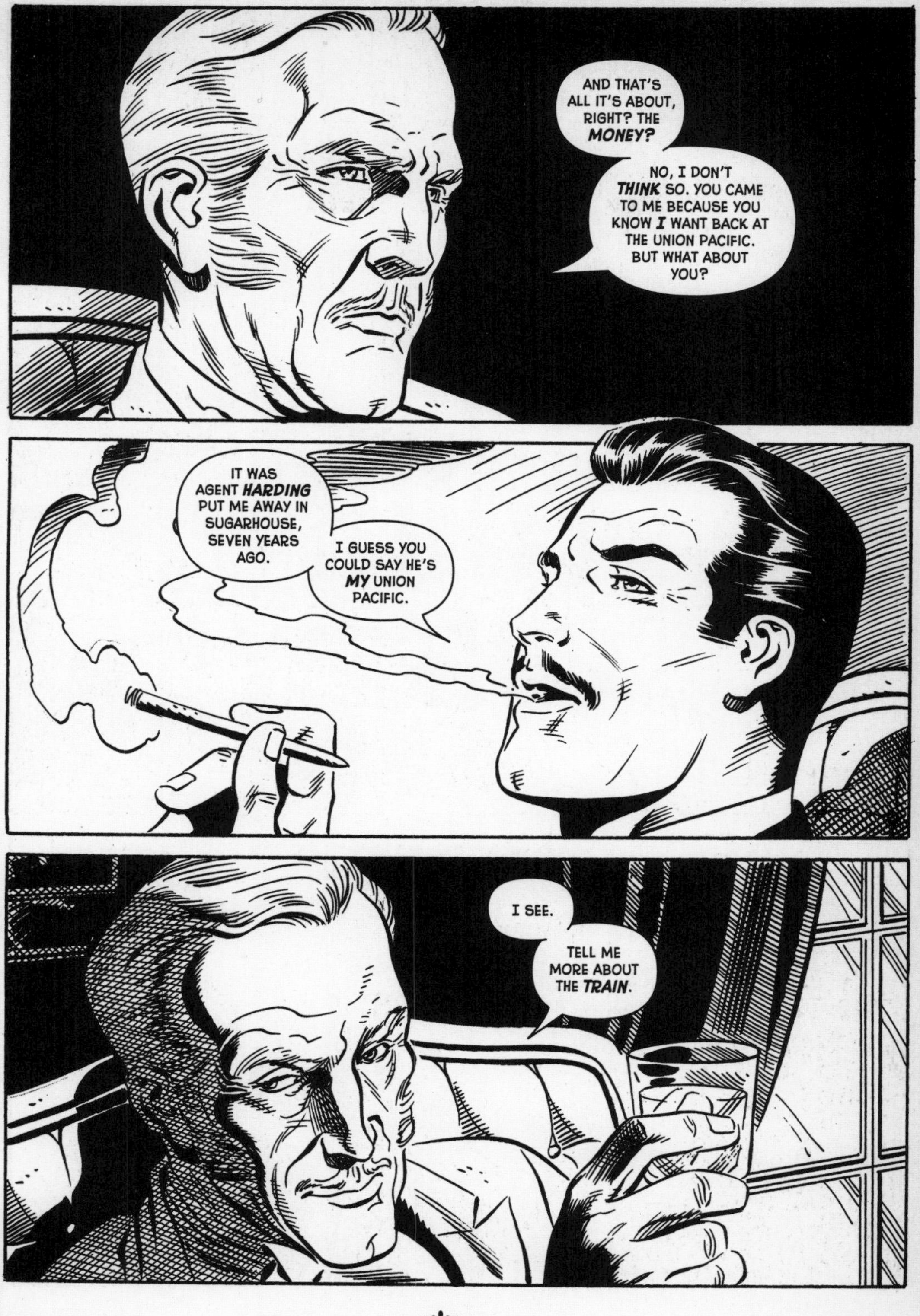
AND THAT'S ALL IT'S ABOUT, RIGHT? THE MONEY?
NO, I DON'T THINK SO. YOU CAME TO ME BECAUSE YOU KNOW I WANT BACK AT THE UNION PACIFIC. BUT WHAT ABOUT YOU?
IT WAS AGENT HARDING PUT ME AWAY IN SUGARHOUSE, SEVEN YEARS AGO.
I GUESS YOU COULD SAY HE'S MY UNION PACIFIC.
I SEE.
TELL ME MORE ABOUT THE TRAIN.

FOUR

★

"THE GENIUS"

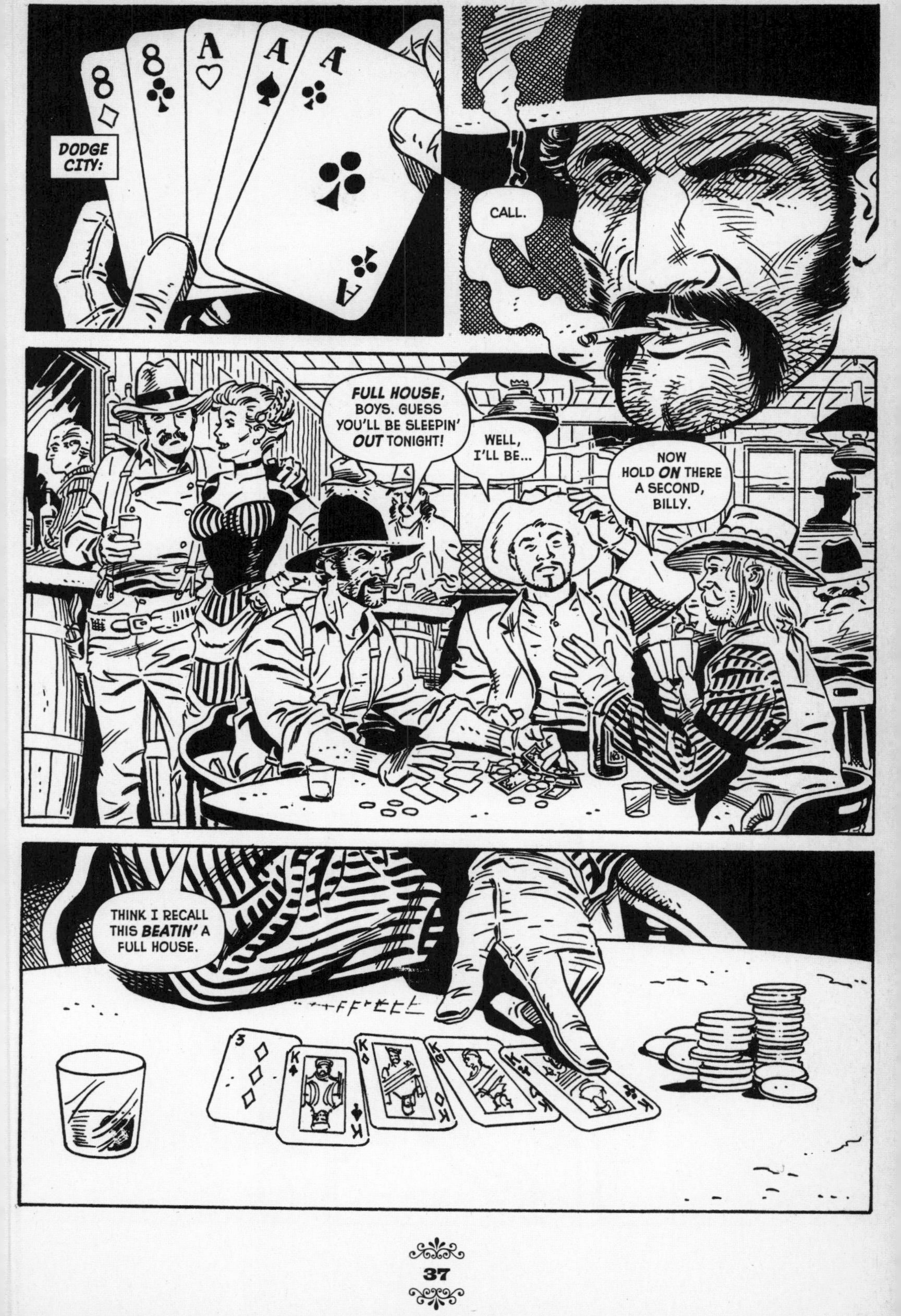
DODGE CITY:
CALL.
FULL HOUSE, BOYS. GUESS YOU'LL BE SLEEPIN' OUT TONIGHT!
WELL, I'LL BE...
NOW HOLD ON THERE A SECOND, BILLY.
THINK I RECALL THIS BEATIN' A FULL HOUSE.

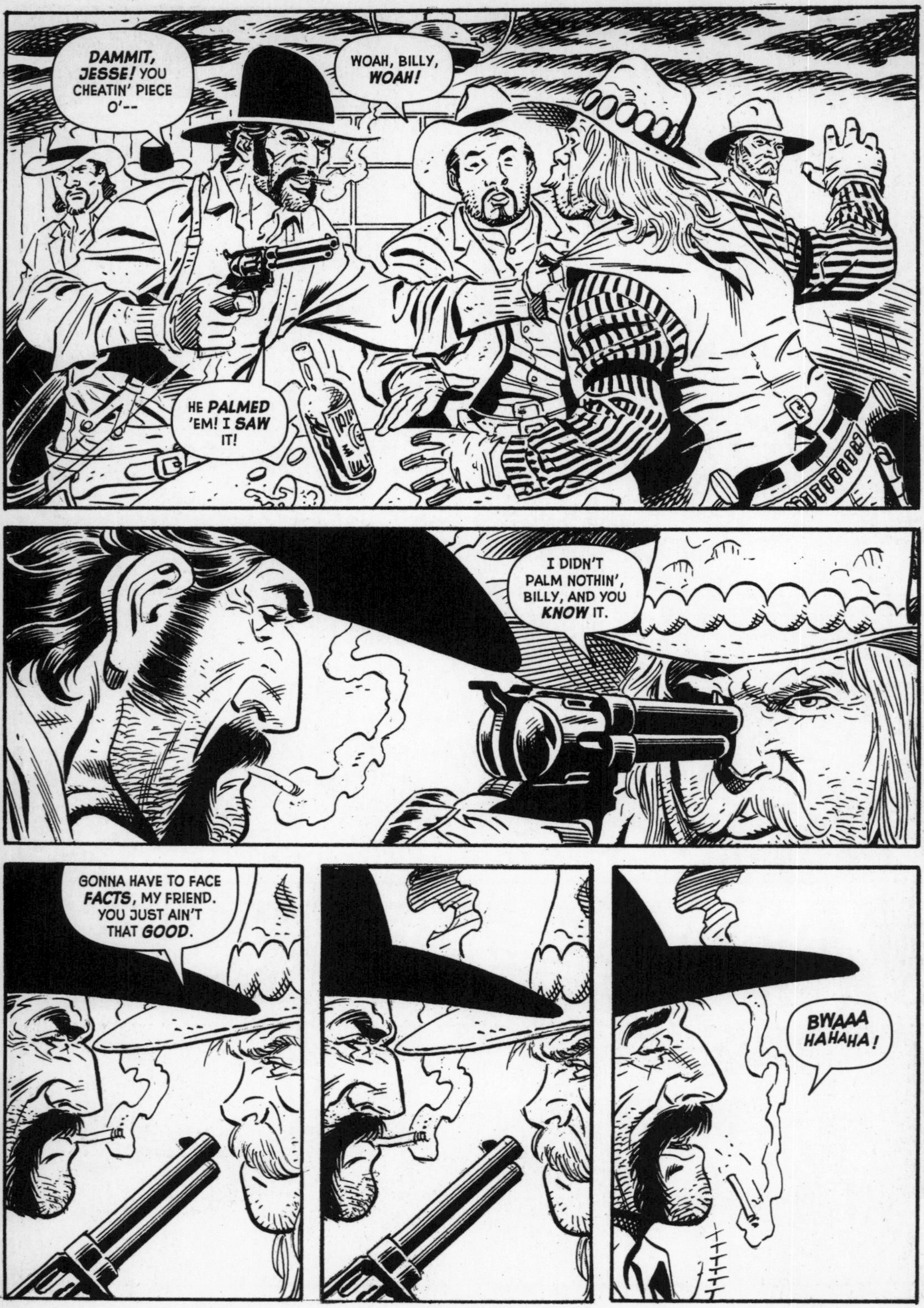
DAMMIT, JESSE! YOU CHEATIN' PIECE O'--
WOAH, BILLY, WOAH!
HE PALMED 'EM! I SAW IT!
I DIDN'T PALM NOTHIN', BILLY, AND YOU KNOW IT.
GONNA HAVE TO FACE FACTS, MY FRIEND. YOU JUST AIN'T THAT GOOD.
BWAAA HAHAHA!

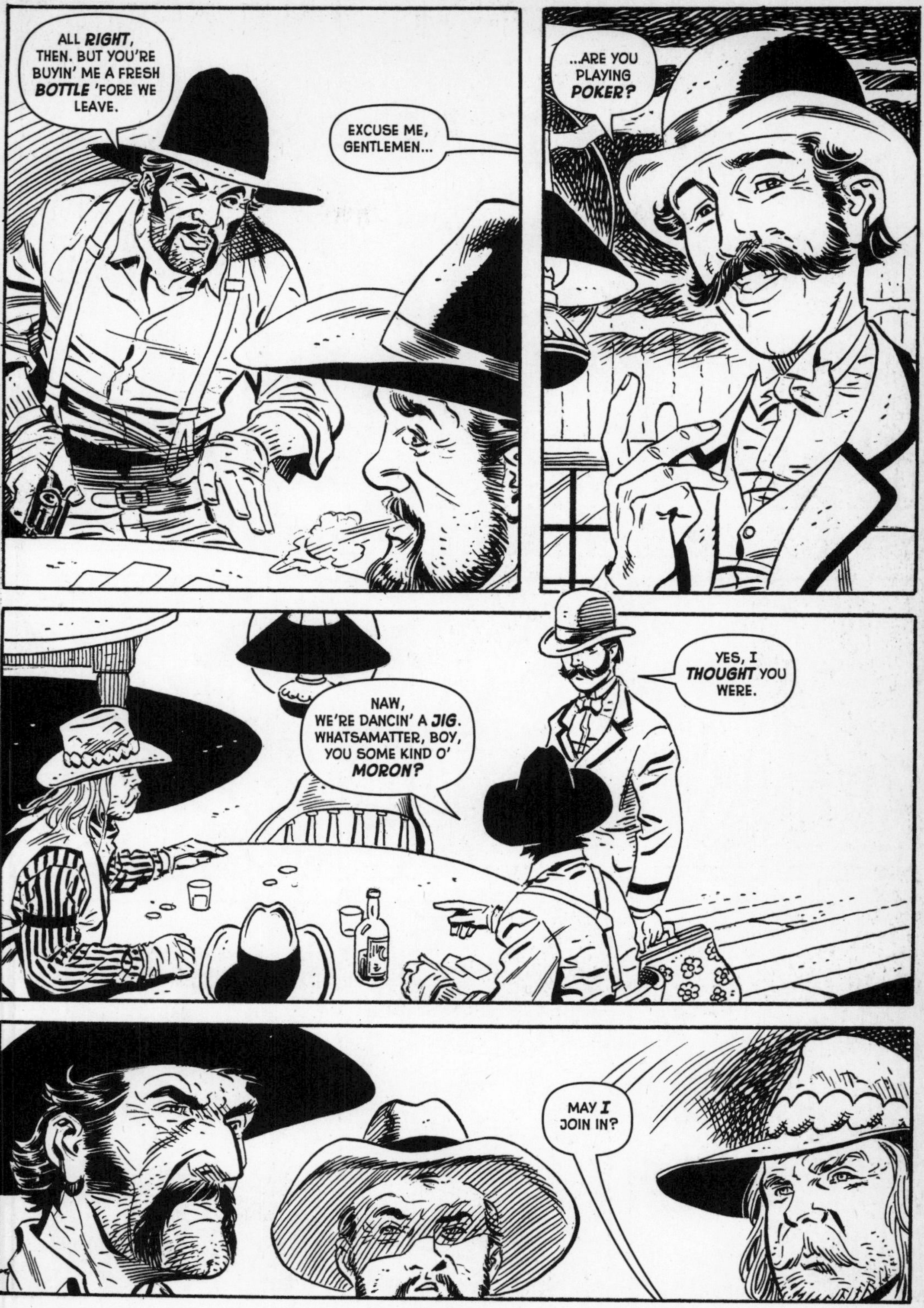
ALL RIGHT, THEN. BUT YOU'RE BUYIN' ME A FRESH BOTTLE 'FORE WE LEAVE.
EXCUSE ME, GENTLEMEN...
...ARE YOU PLAYING POKER?
NAW, WE'RE DANCIN' A JIG. WHATSAMATTER, BOY, YOU SOME KIND O' MORON?
YES, I THOUGHT YOU WERE.
MAY I JOIN IN?

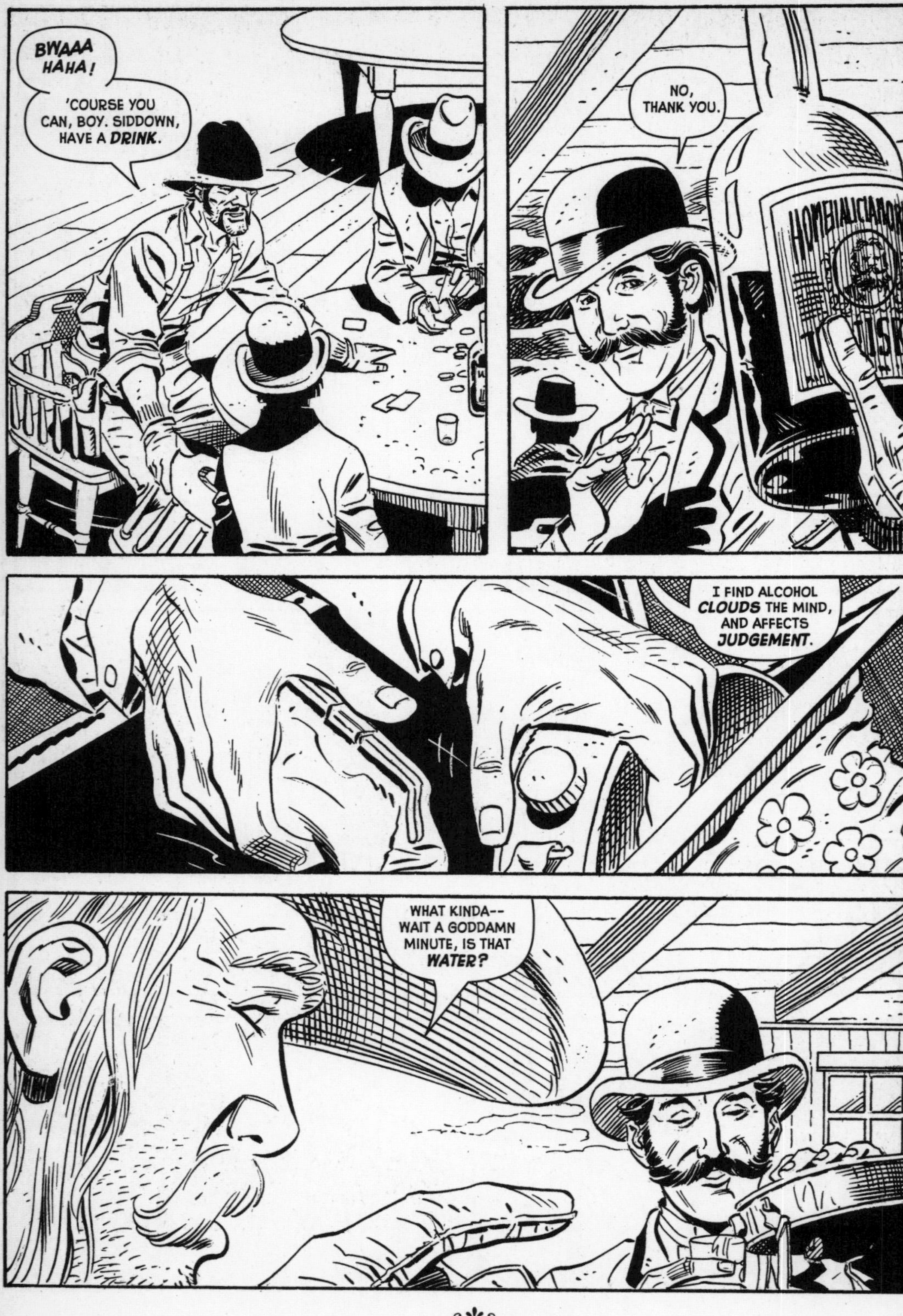
BWAAA HAHA!
'COURSE YOU CAN, BOY. SIDDOWN, HAVE A DRINK.
NO, THANK YOU.
I FIND ALCOHOL CLOUDS THE MIND, AND AFFECTS JUDGEMENT.
WHAT KINDA-- WAIT A GODDAMN MINUTE, IS THAT WATER?

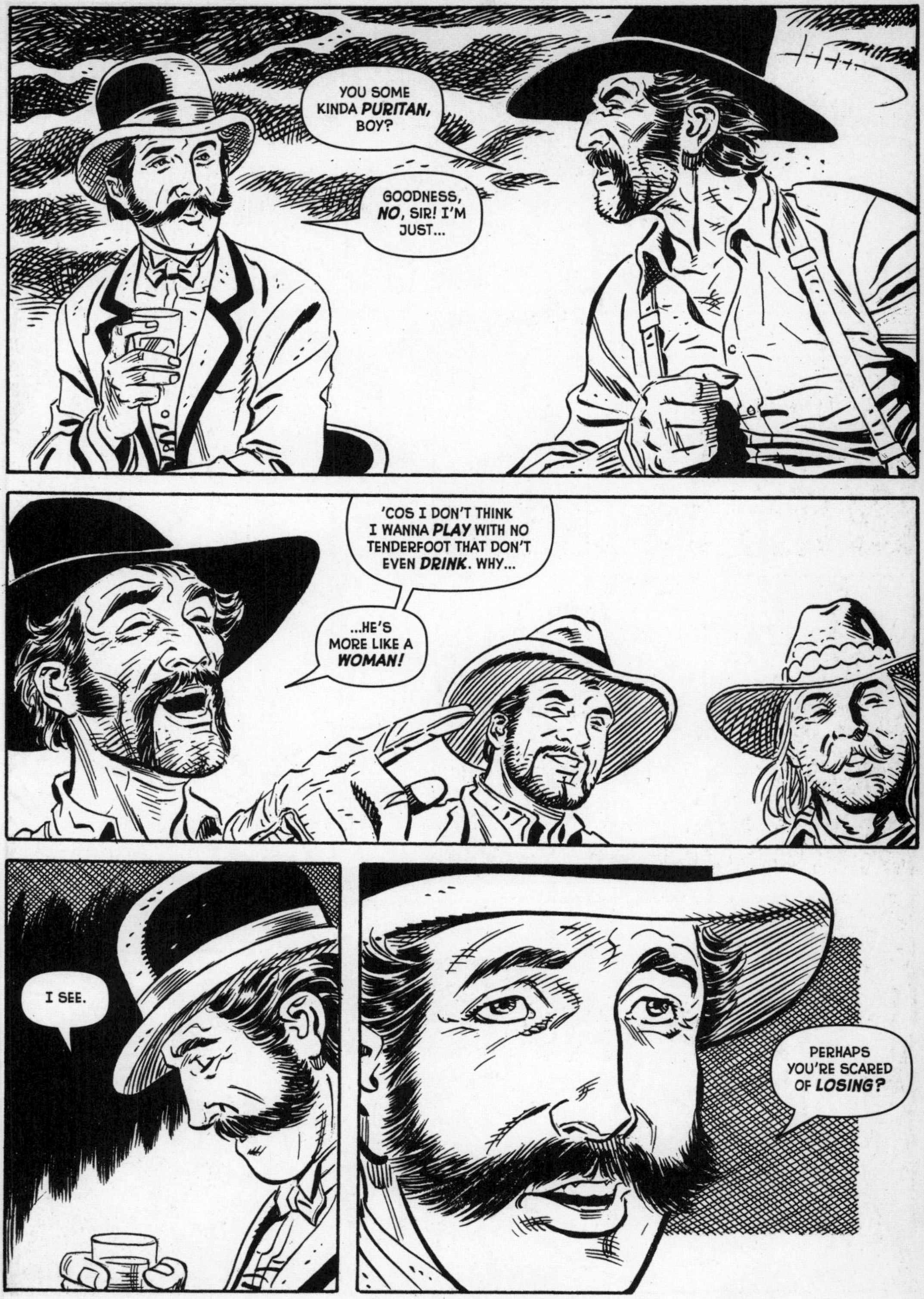
YOU SOME KINDA PURITAN, BOY?
GOODNESS, NO, SIR! I'M JUST...
'COS I DON'T THINK I WANNA PLAY WITH NO TENDERFOOT THAT DON'T EVEN DRINK. WHY...
...HE'S MORE LIKE A WOMAN!
I SEE.
PERHAPS YOU'RE SCARED OF LOSING?

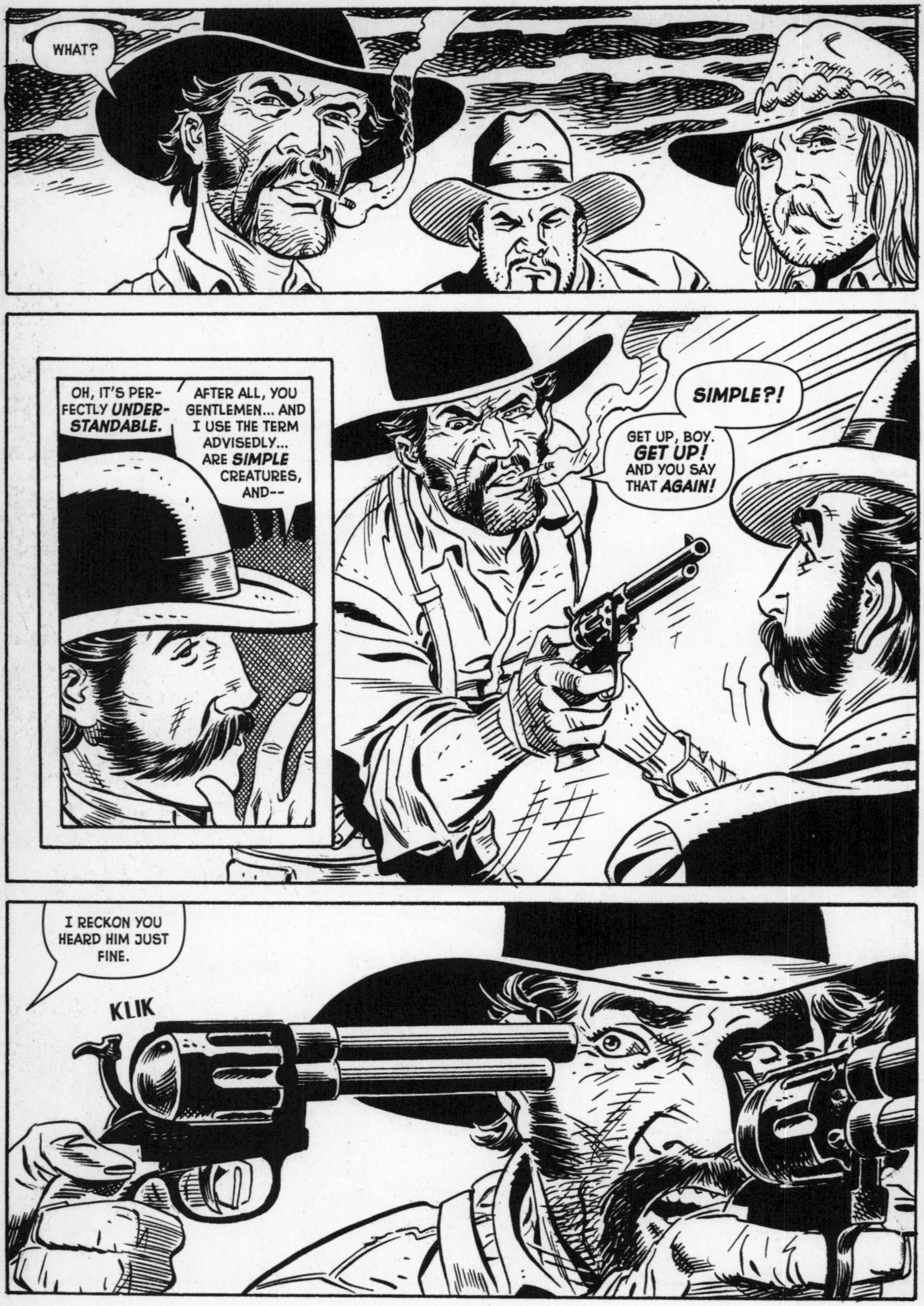
WHAT?
OH, IT'S PERFECTLY UNDERSTANDABLE.
AFTER ALL, YOU GENTLEMEN... AND I USE THE TERM ADVISEDLY... ARE SIMPLE CREATURES, AND--
SIMPLE?!
GET UP, BOY. GET UP! AND YOU SAY THAT AGAIN!
I RECKON YOU HEARD HIM JUST FINE.
KLIK

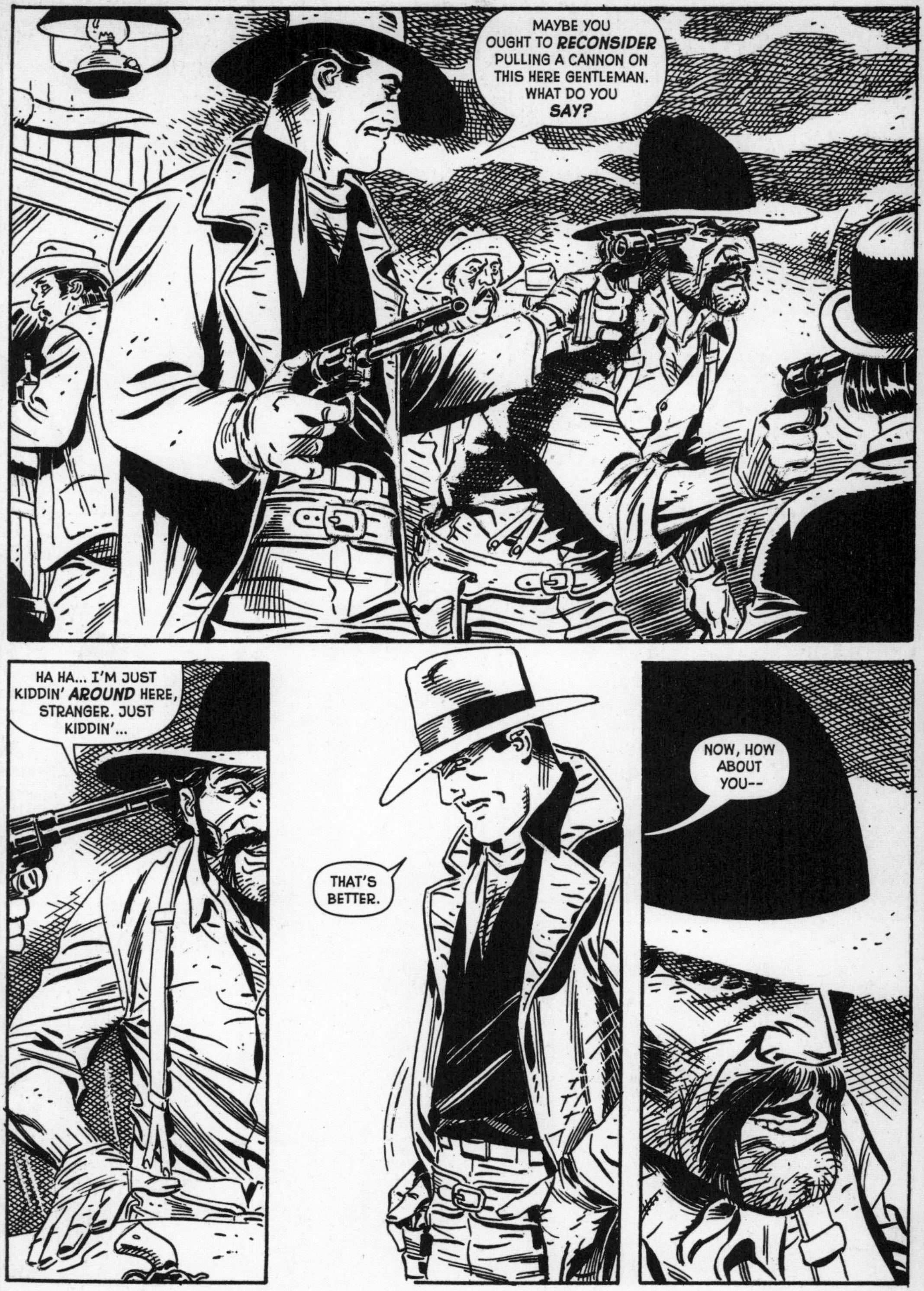
MAYBE YOU OUGHT TO RECONSIDER PULLING A CANNON ON THIS HERE GENTLEMAN. WHAT DO YOU SAY?
HA HA... I'M JUST KIDDIN' AROUND HERE, STRANGER. JUST KIDDIN'...
THAT'S BETTER.
NOW, HOW ABOUT YOU--

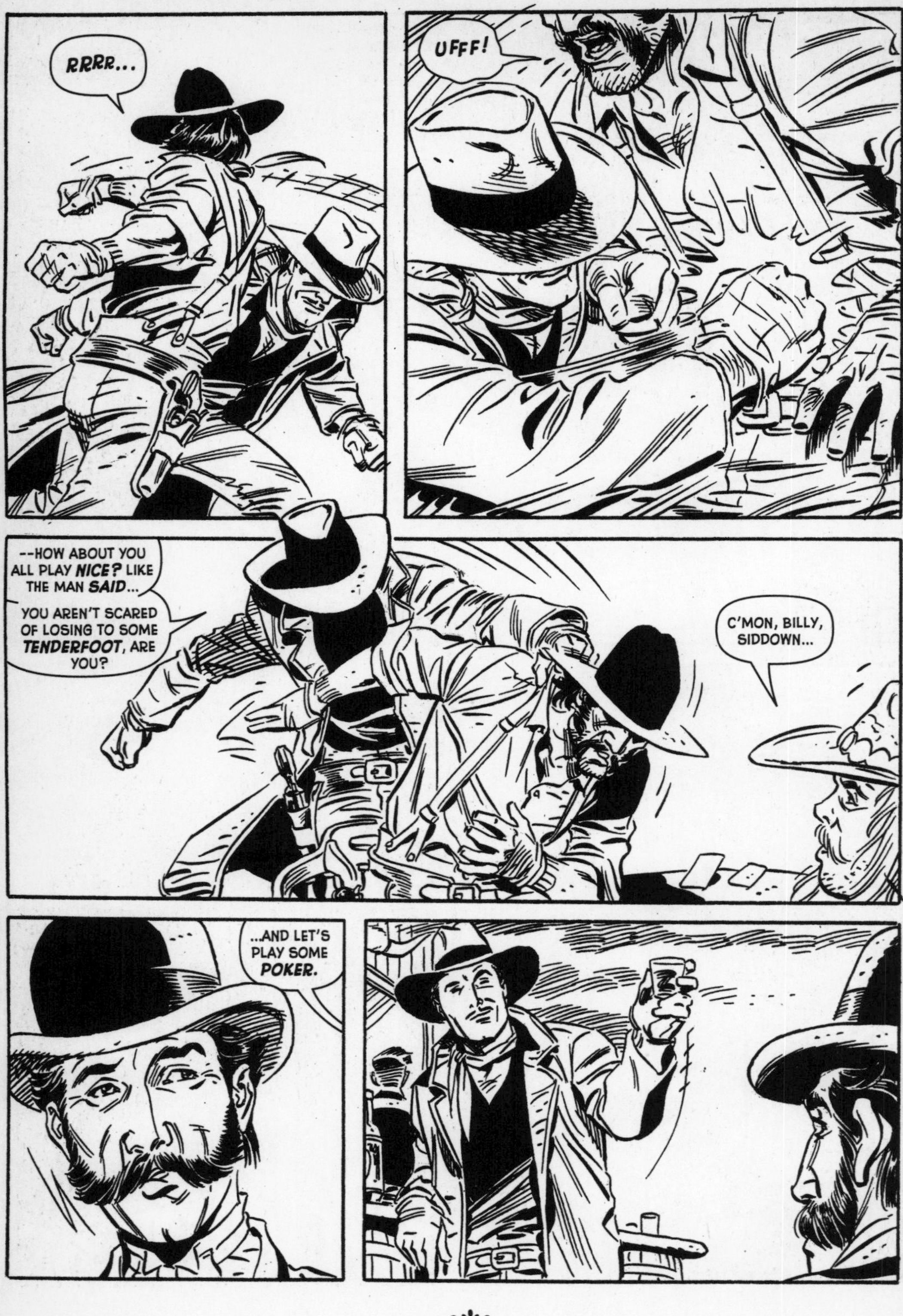
RRRR...
UFFF!
--HOW ABOUT YOU ALL PLAY NICE? LIKE THE MAN SAID...
YOU AREN'T SCARED OF LOSING TO SOME TENDERFOOT, ARE YOU?
C'MON, BILLY, SIDDOWN...
...AND LET'S PLAY SOME POKER.

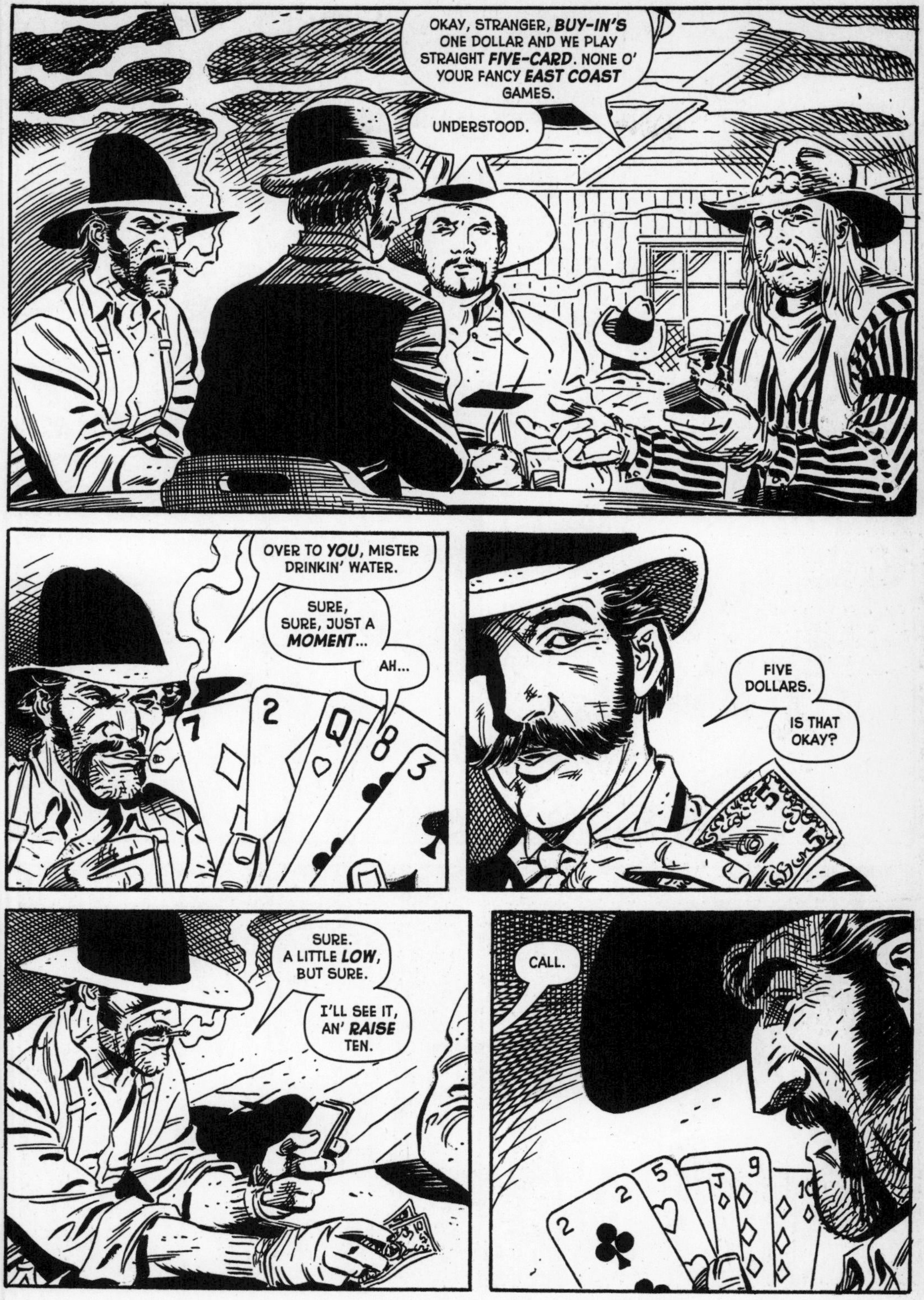
OKAY, STRANGER, BUY-IN'S ONE DOLLAR AND WE PLAY STRAIGHT FIVE-CARD. NONE O' YOUR FANCY EAST COAST GAMES.
UNDERSTOOD.
OVER TO YOU, MISTER DRINKIN' WATER.
SURE, SURE, JUST A MOMENT...
AH...
FIVE DOLLARS.
IS THAT OKAY?
SURE. A LITTLE LOW, BUT SURE.
I'LL SEE IT, AN' RAISE TEN.
CALL.

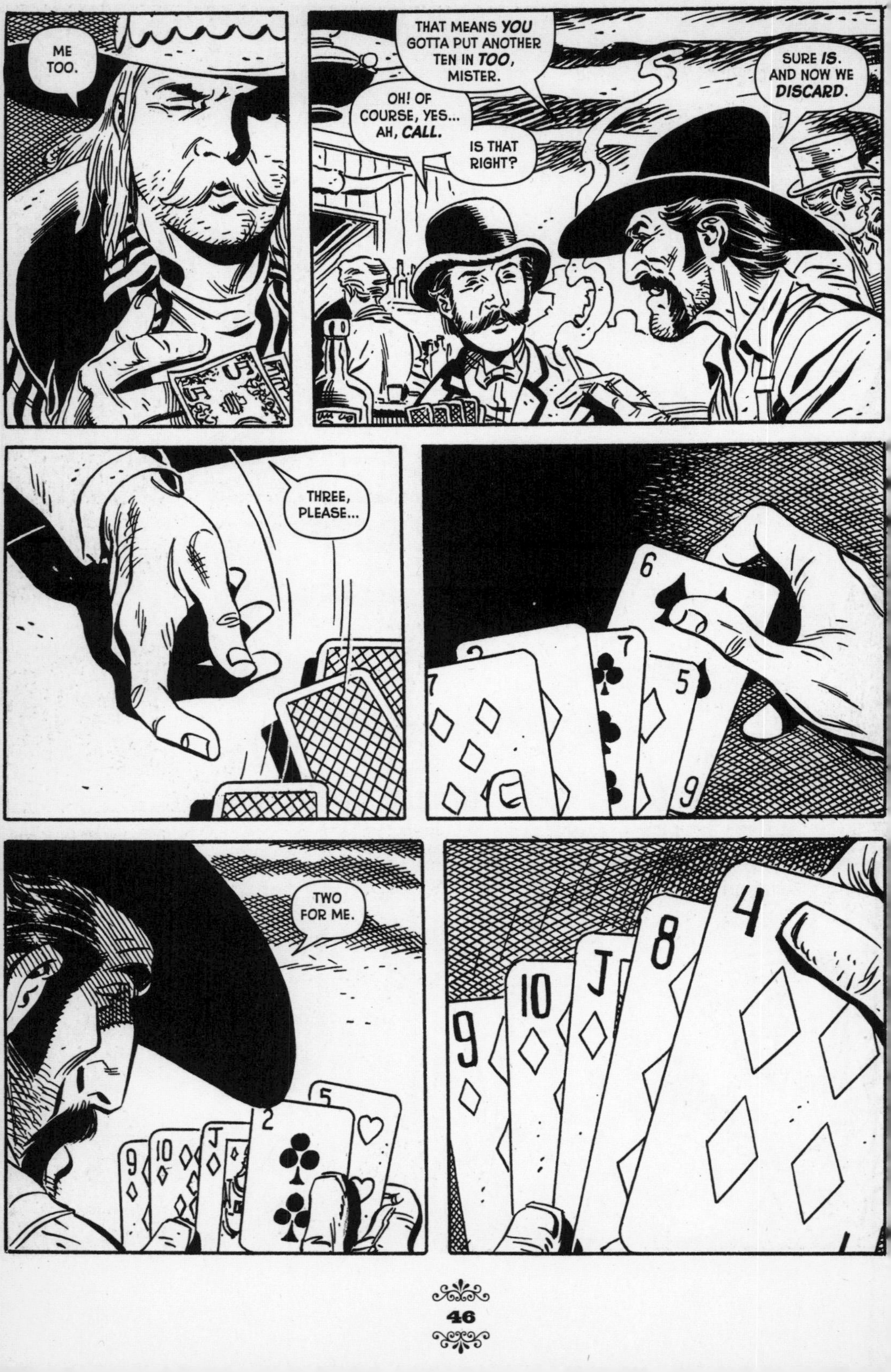
ME TOO.
THAT MEANS *YOU* GOTTA PUT ANOTHER TEN IN *TOO*, MISTER.
OH! OF COURSE, YES... AH, *CALL*.
IS THAT RIGHT?
SURE *IS*. AND NOW WE *DISCARD*.
THREE, PLEASE...
TWO FOR ME.

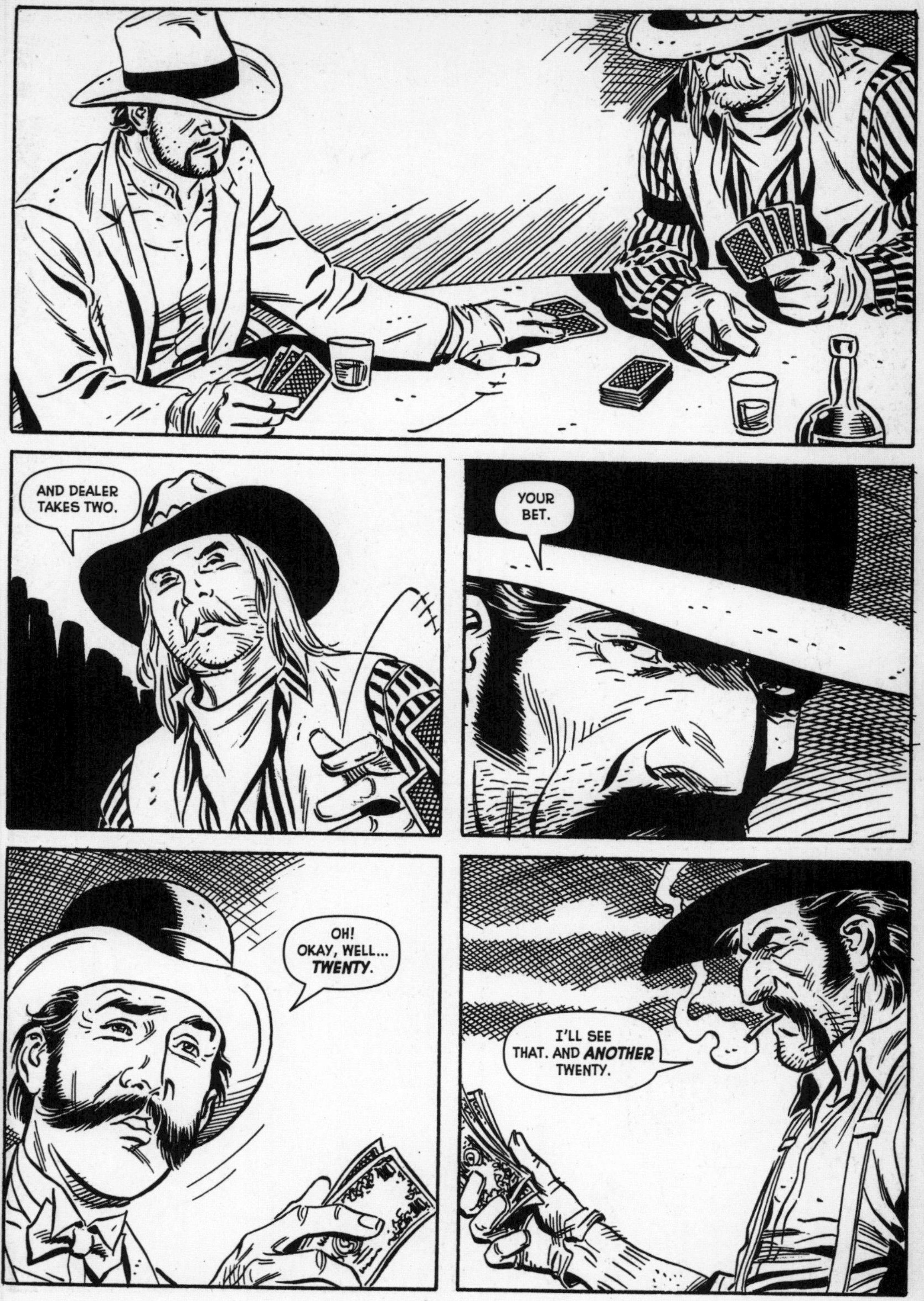
AND DEALER TAKES TWO.
YOUR BET.
OH! OKAY, WELL... TWENTY.
I'LL SEE THAT. AND ANOTHER TWENTY.

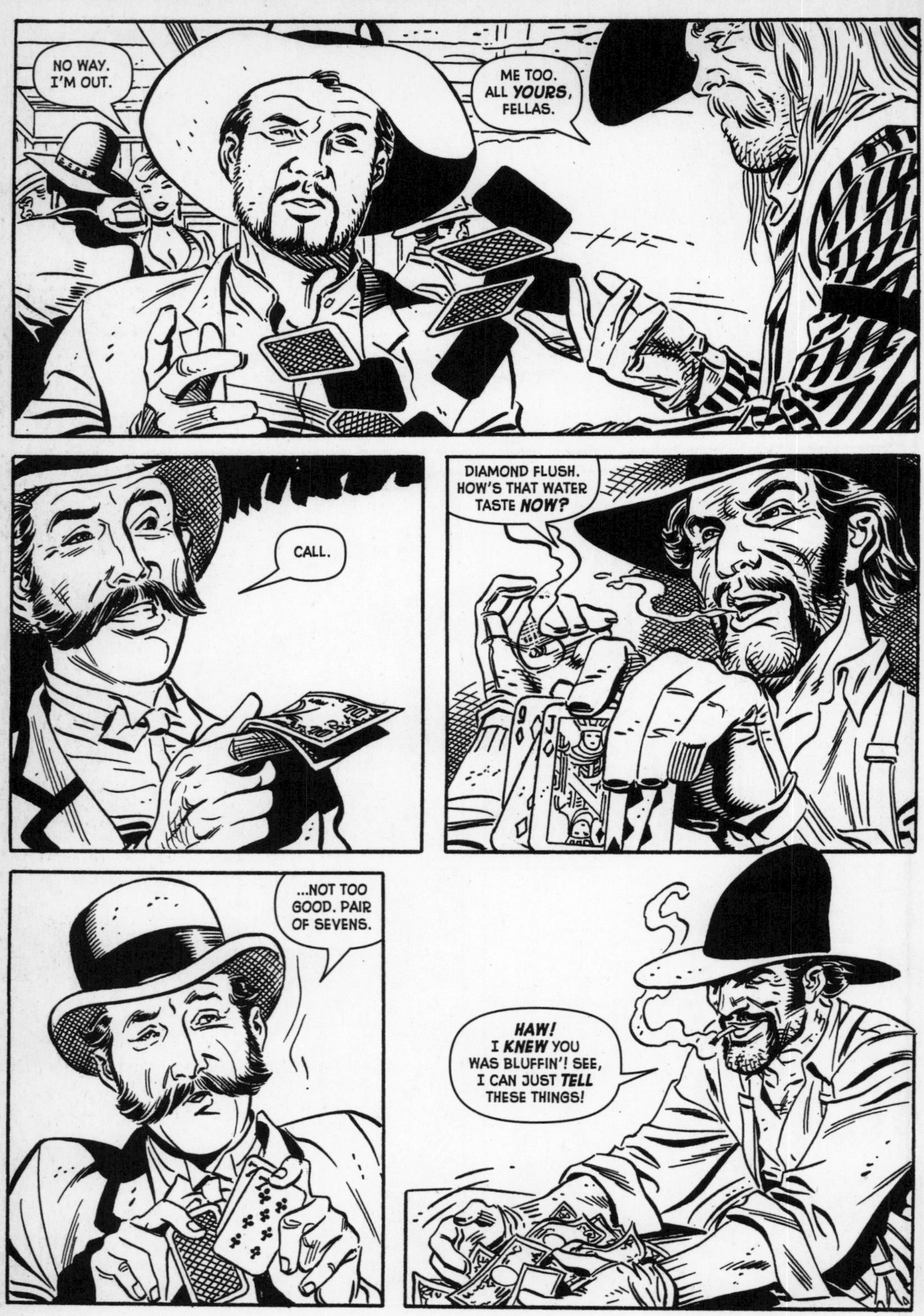
NO WAY. I'M OUT.
ME TOO. ALL YOURS, FELLAS.
CALL.
DIAMOND FLUSH. HOW'S THAT WATER TASTE NOW?
...NOT TOO GOOD. PAIR OF SEVENS.
HAW! I KNEW YOU WAS BLUFFIN'! SEE, I CAN JUST TELL THESE THINGS!

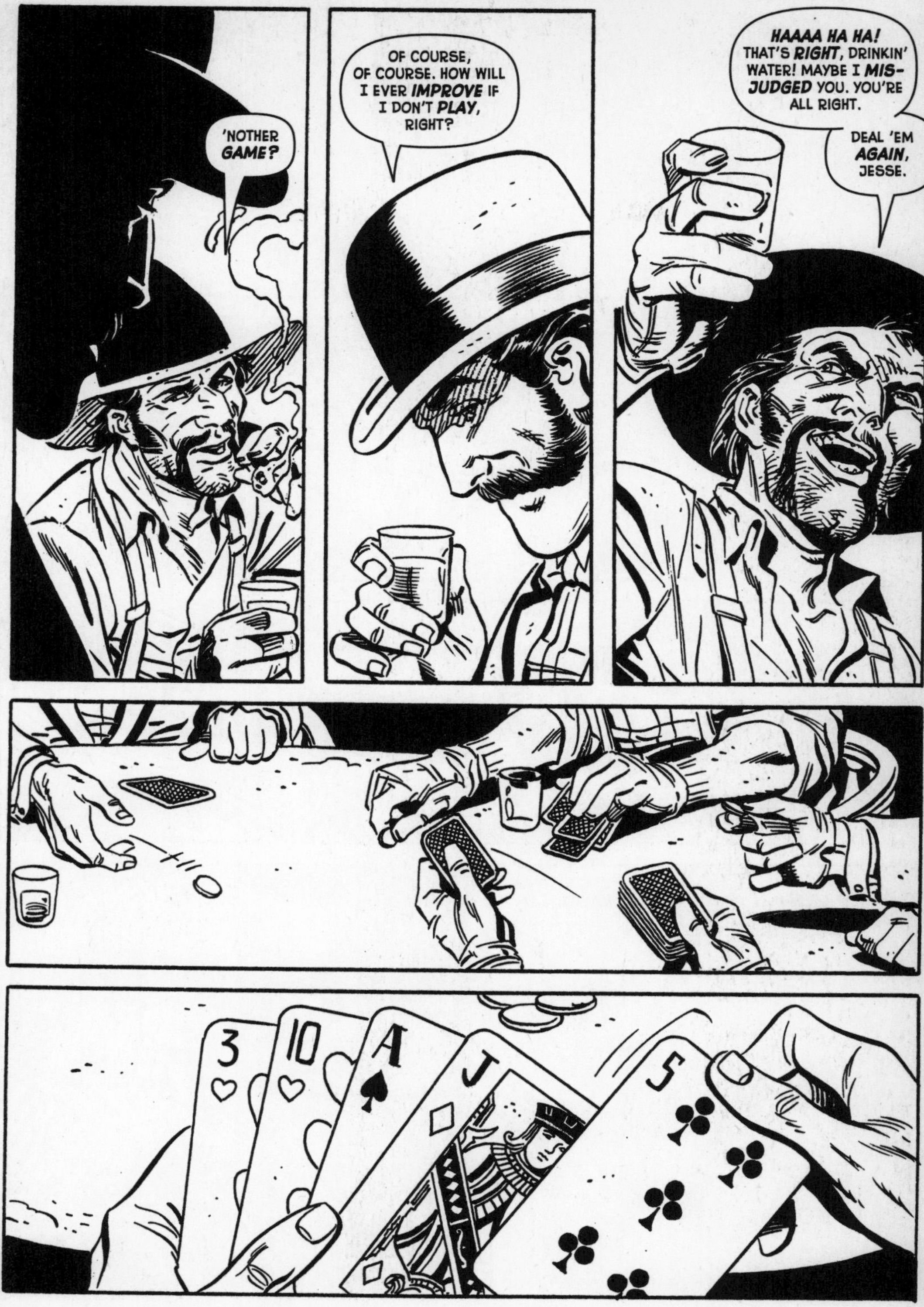
'NOTHER GAME?
OF COURSE, OF COURSE. HOW WILL I EVER IMPROVE IF I DON'T PLAY, RIGHT?
HAAAA HA HA! THAT'S RIGHT, DRINKIN' WATER! MAYBE I MIS-JUDGED YOU. YOU'RE ALL RIGHT.
DEAL 'EM AGAIN, JESSE.
3
10
A
J
5

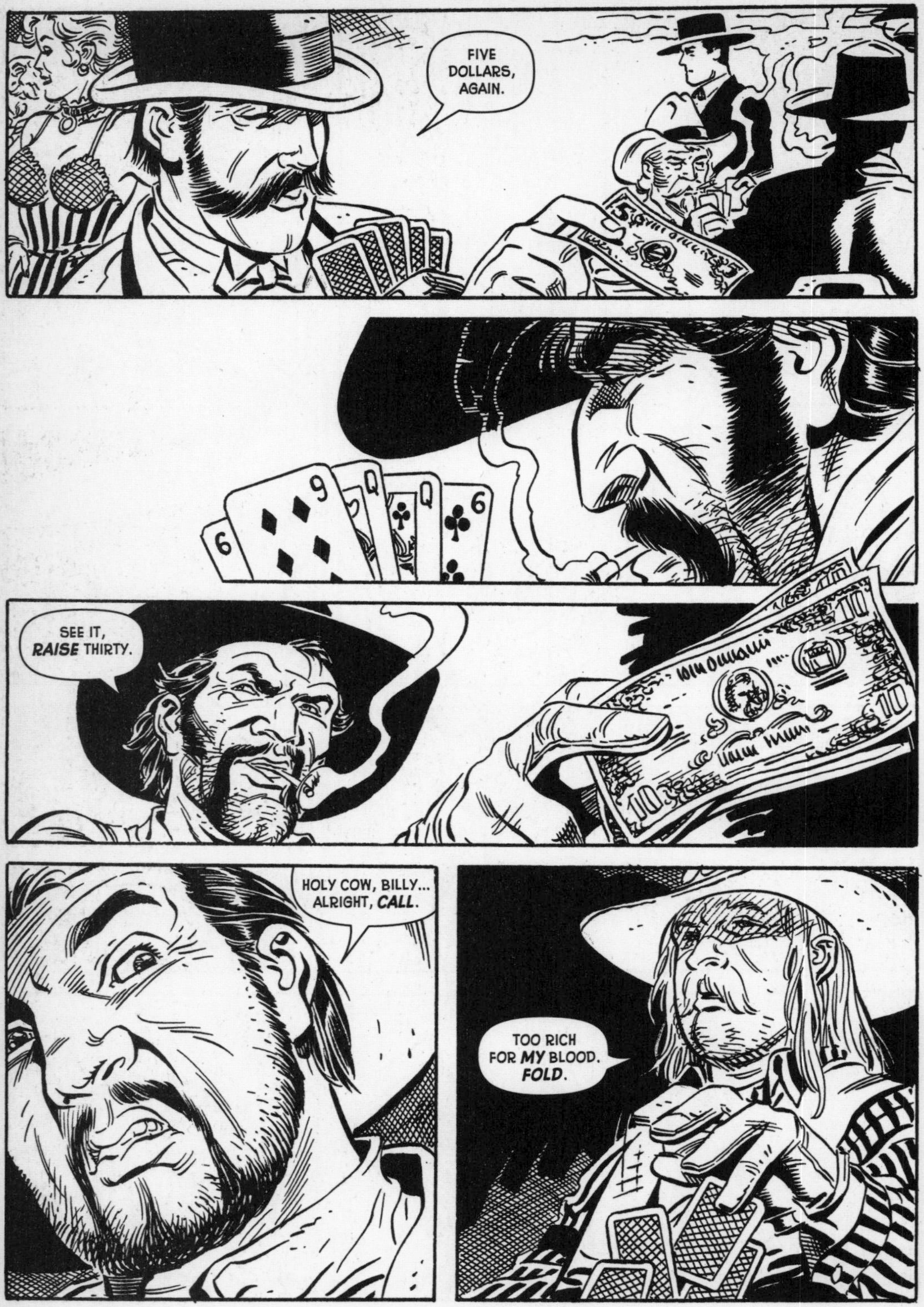
FIVE DOLLARS, AGAIN.
SEE IT, *RAISE* THIRTY.
HOLY COW, BILLY... ALRIGHT, *CALL*.
TOO RICH FOR *MY* BLOOD. *FOLD*.

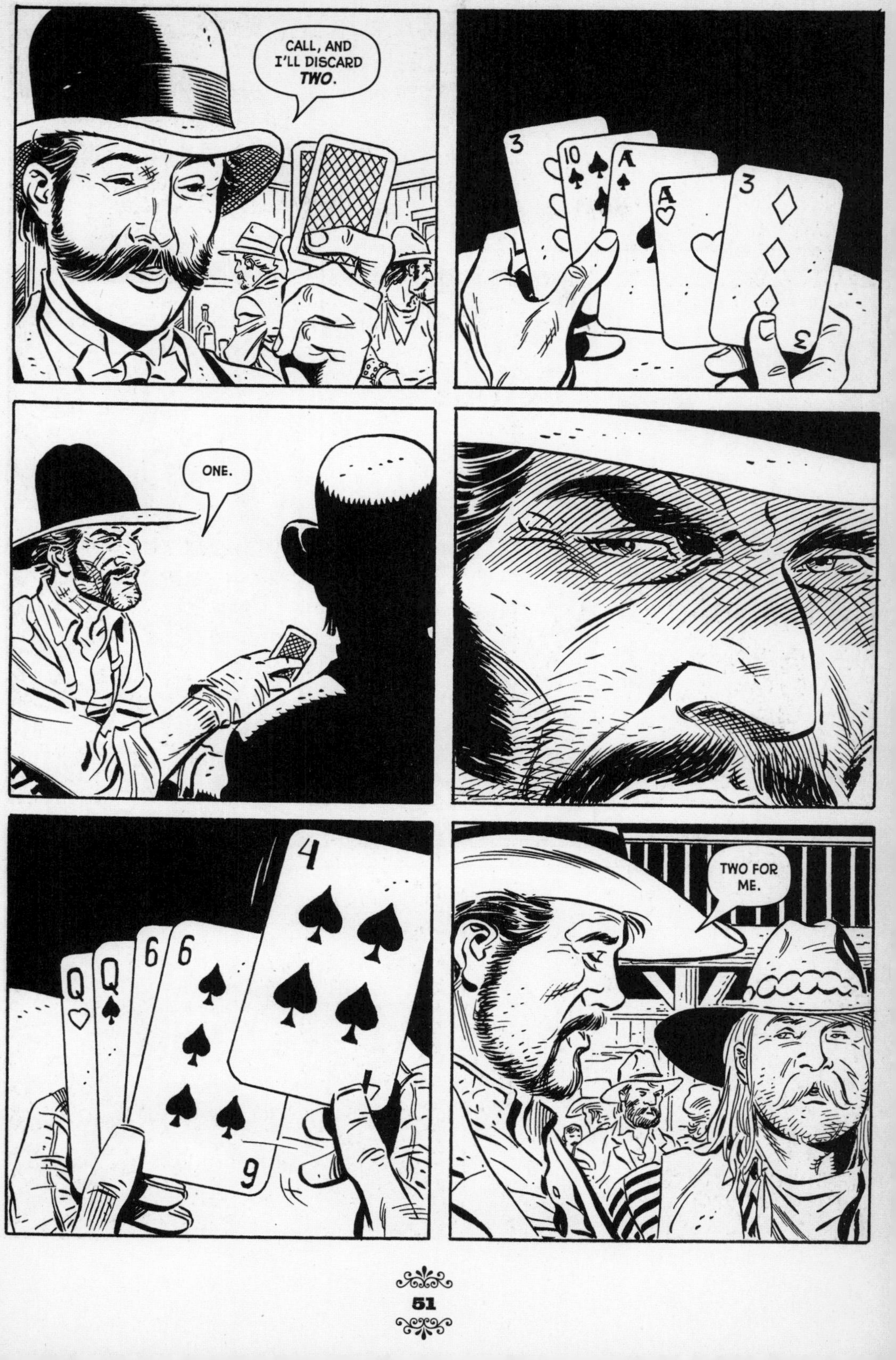
CALL, AND I'LL DISCARD **TWO**.
ONE.
TWO FOR ME.

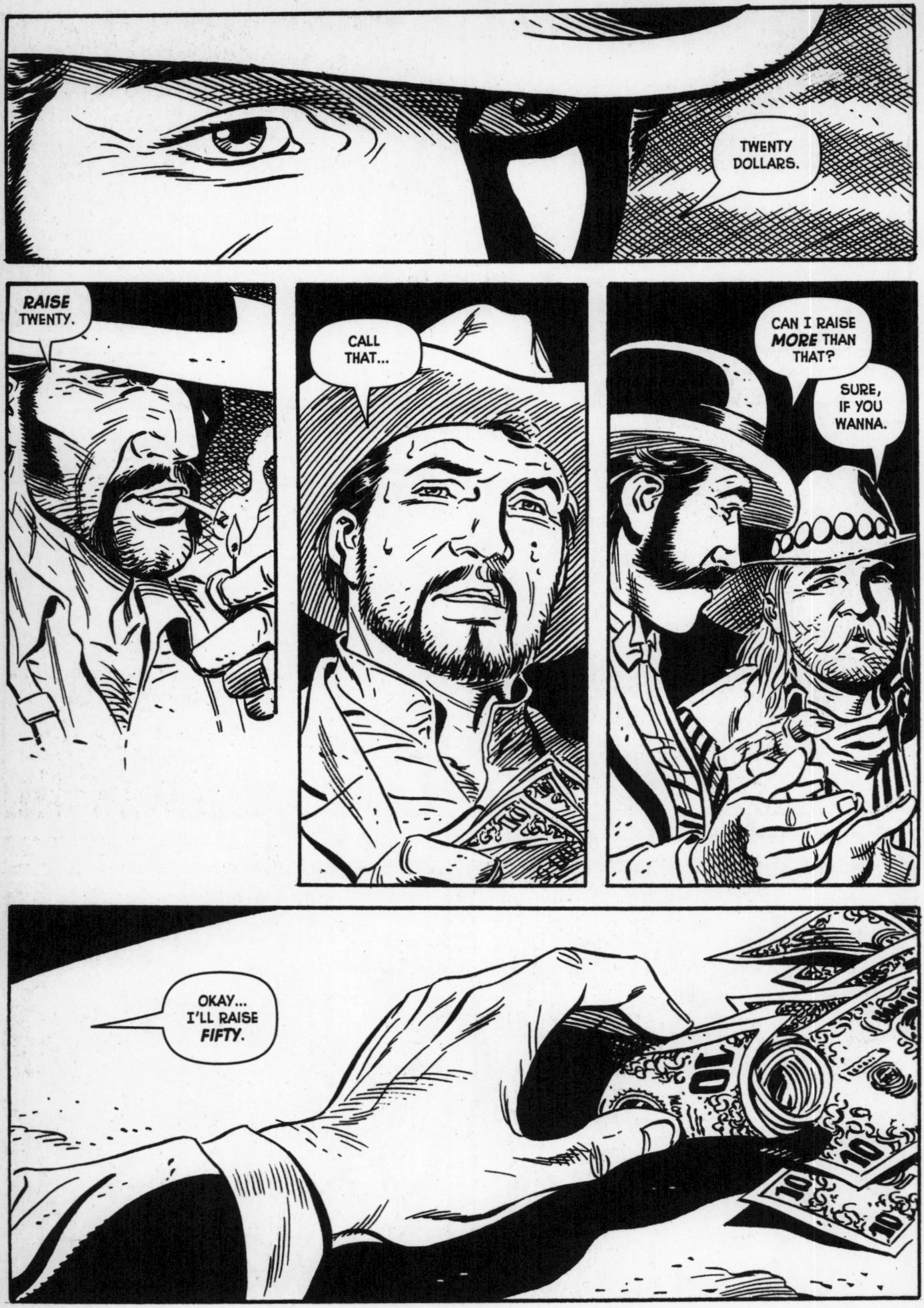
TWENTY DOLLARS.
RAISE TWENTY.
CALL THAT...
CAN I RAISE MORE THAN THAT?
SURE, IF YOU WANNA.
OKAY... I'LL RAISE FIFTY.

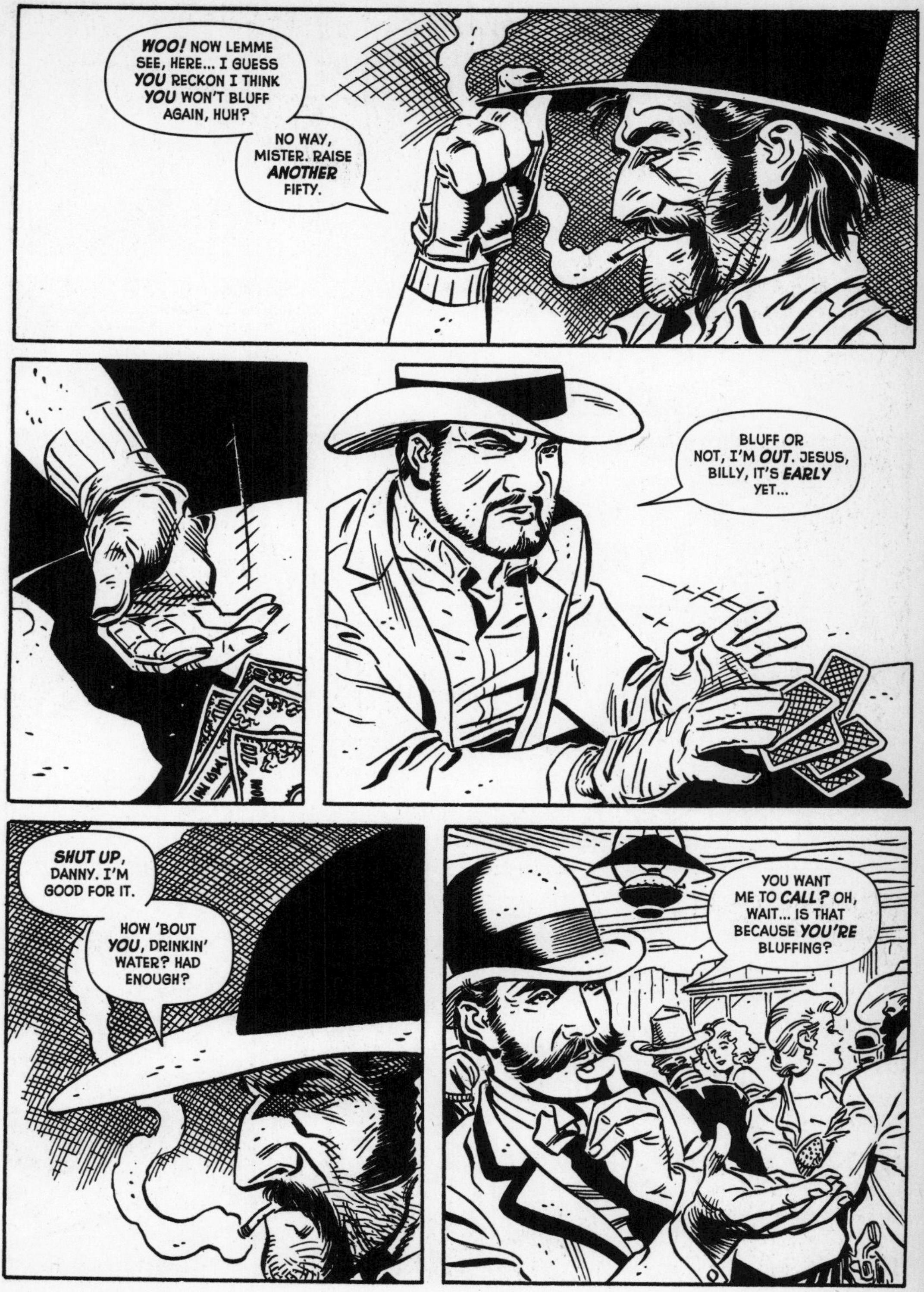
WOO! NOW LEMME SEE, HERE... I GUESS YOU RECKON I THINK YOU WON'T BLUFF AGAIN, HUH?
NO WAY, MISTER. RAISE ANOTHER FIFTY.
BLUFF OR NOT, I'M OUT. JESUS, BILLY, IT'S EARLY YET...
SHUT UP, DANNY. I'M GOOD FOR IT.
HOW 'BOUT YOU, DRINKIN' WATER? HAD ENOUGH?
YOU WANT ME TO CALL? OH, WAIT... IS THAT BECAUSE YOU'RE BLUFFING?

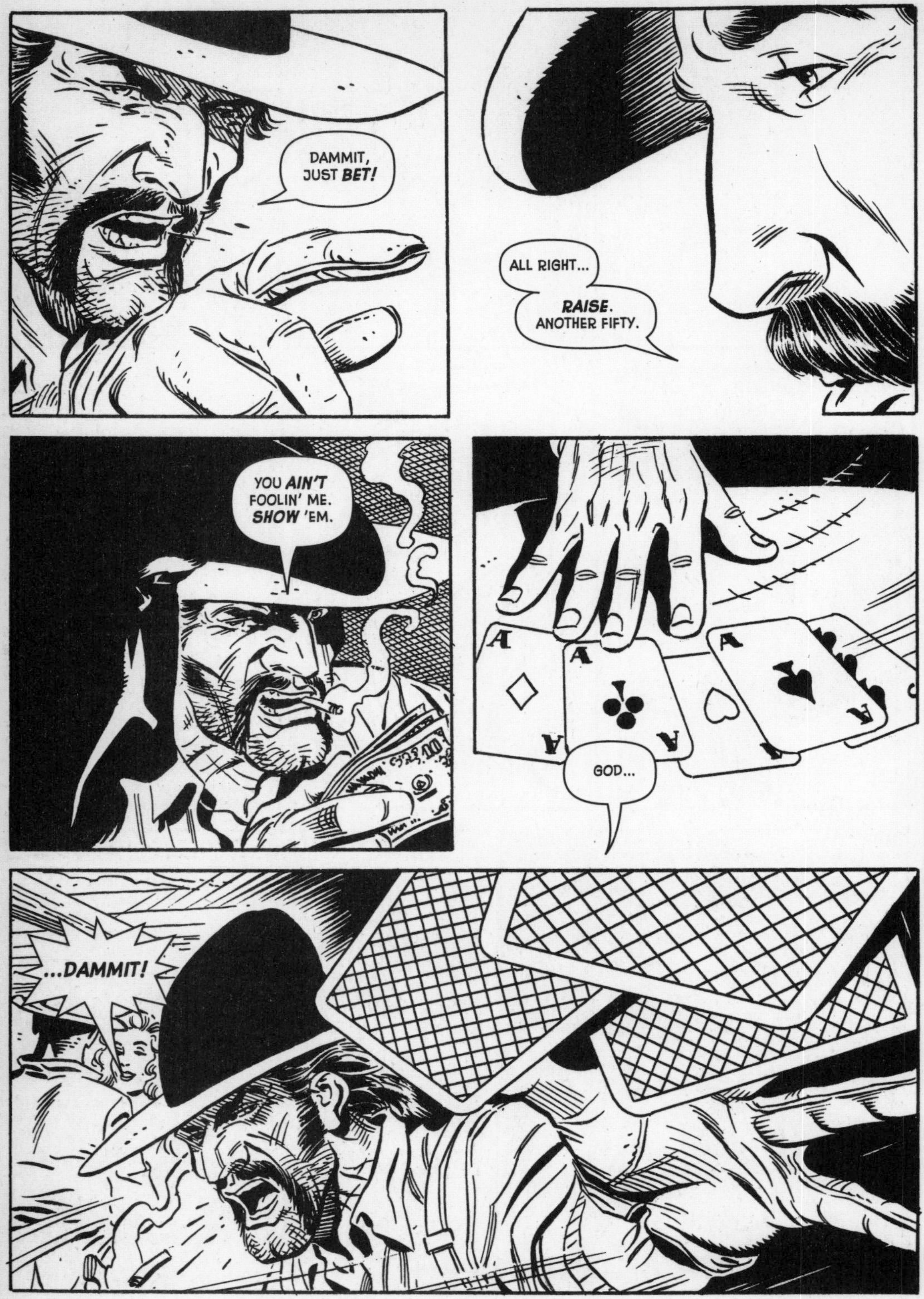
DAMMIT, JUST BET!
ALL RIGHT...
RAISE. ANOTHER FIFTY.
YOU AIN'T FOOLIN' ME. SHOW 'EM.
GOD...
...DAMMIT!

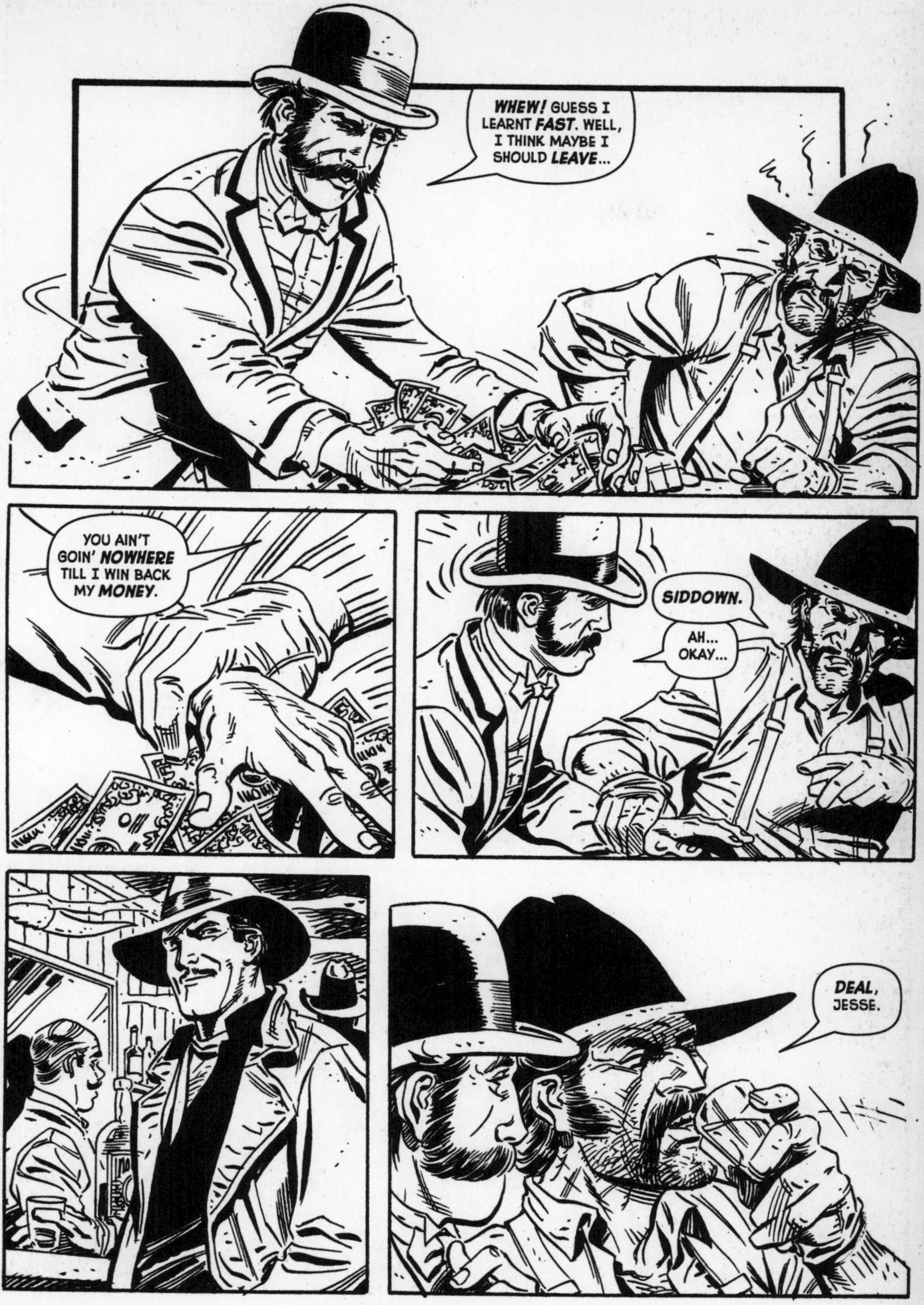
WHEW! GUESS I LEARNT FAST. WELL, I THINK MAYBE I SHOULD LEAVE...
YOU AIN'T GOIN' NOWHERE TILL I WIN BACK MY MONEY.
SIDDOWN.
AH... OKAY...
DEAL, JESSE.

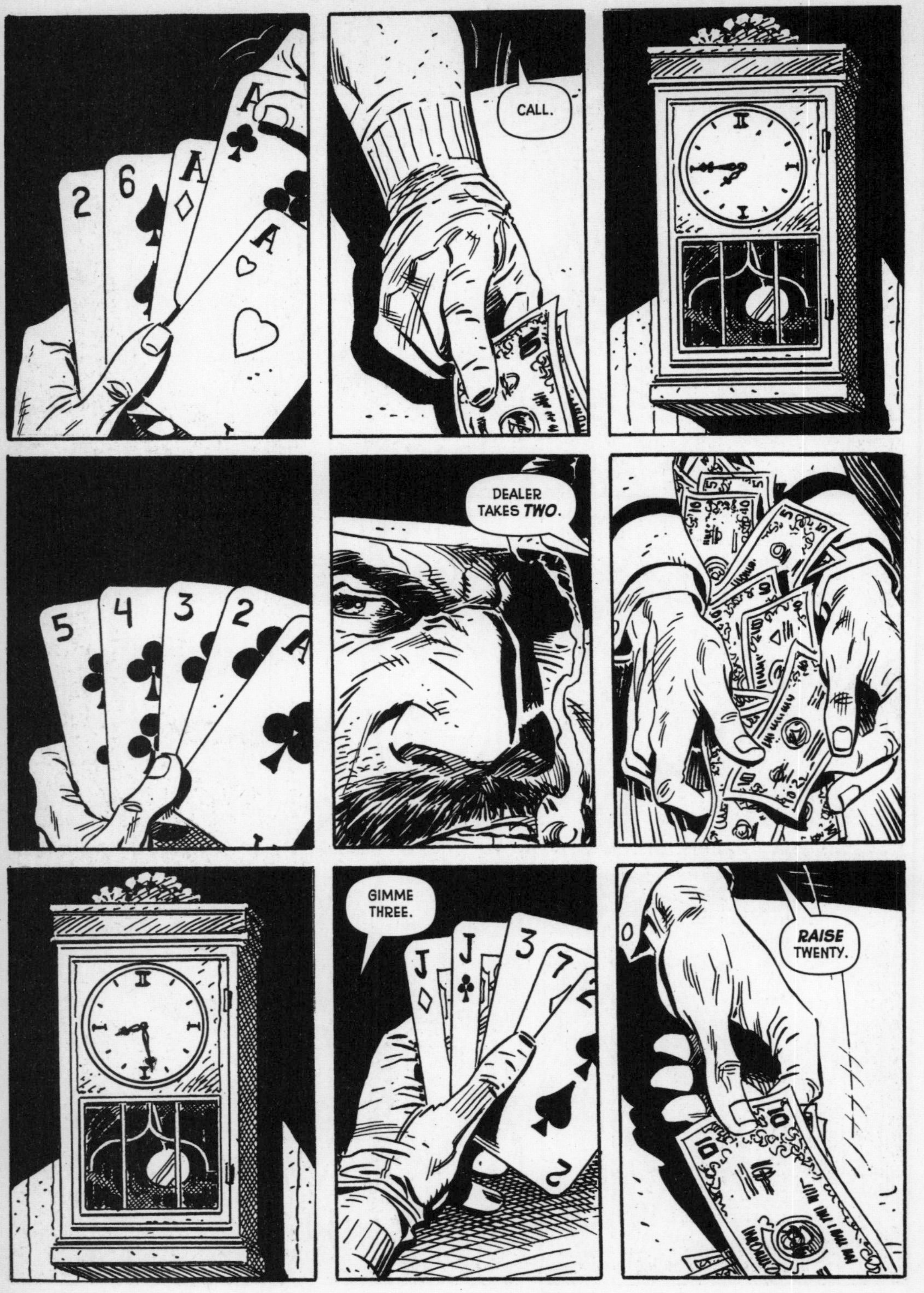
CALL.
DEALER TAKES *TWO*.
GIMME THREE.
RAISE TWENTY.

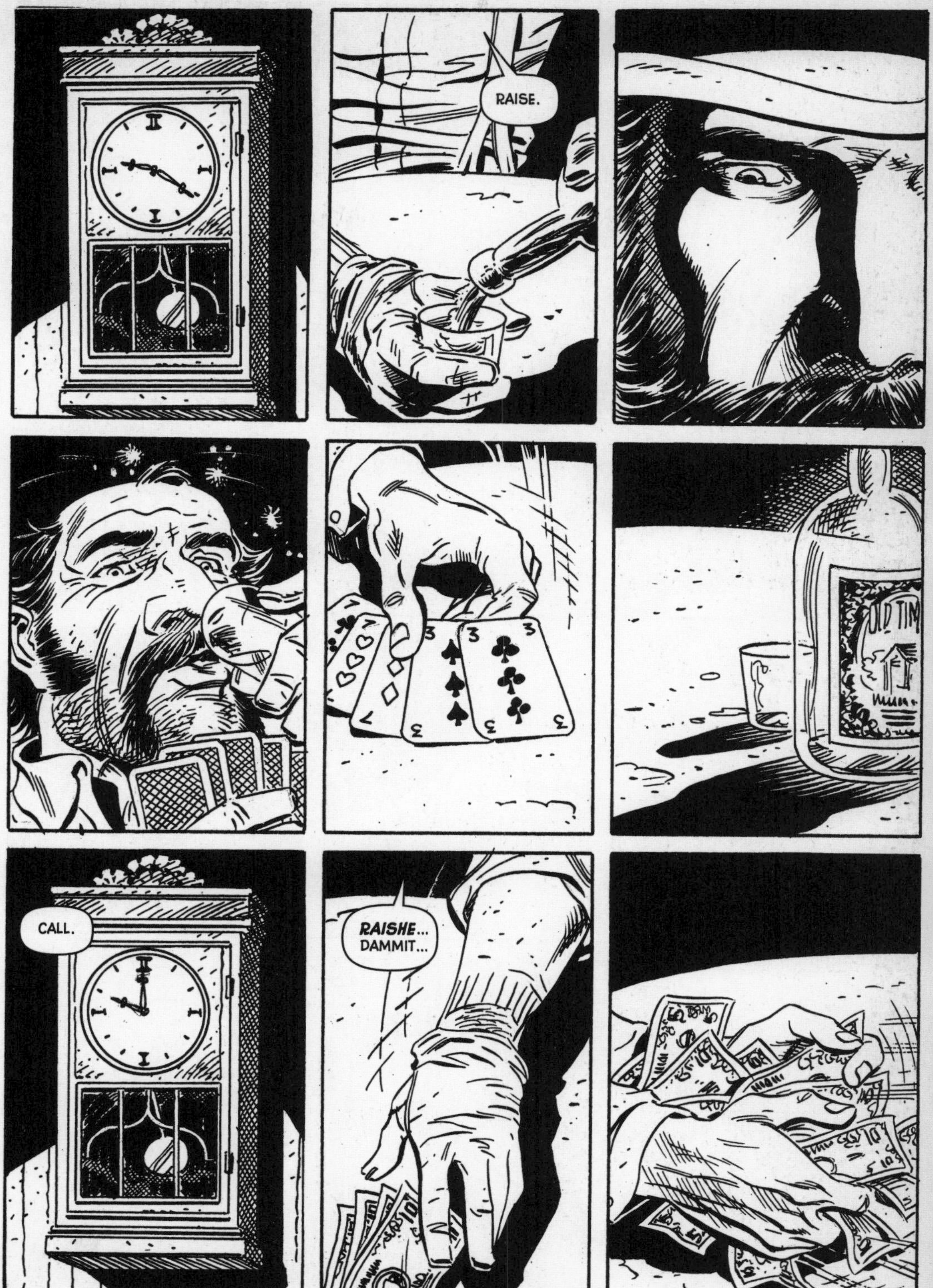
RAISE.
OLD TIM
CALL.
RAISHE...
DAMMIT...

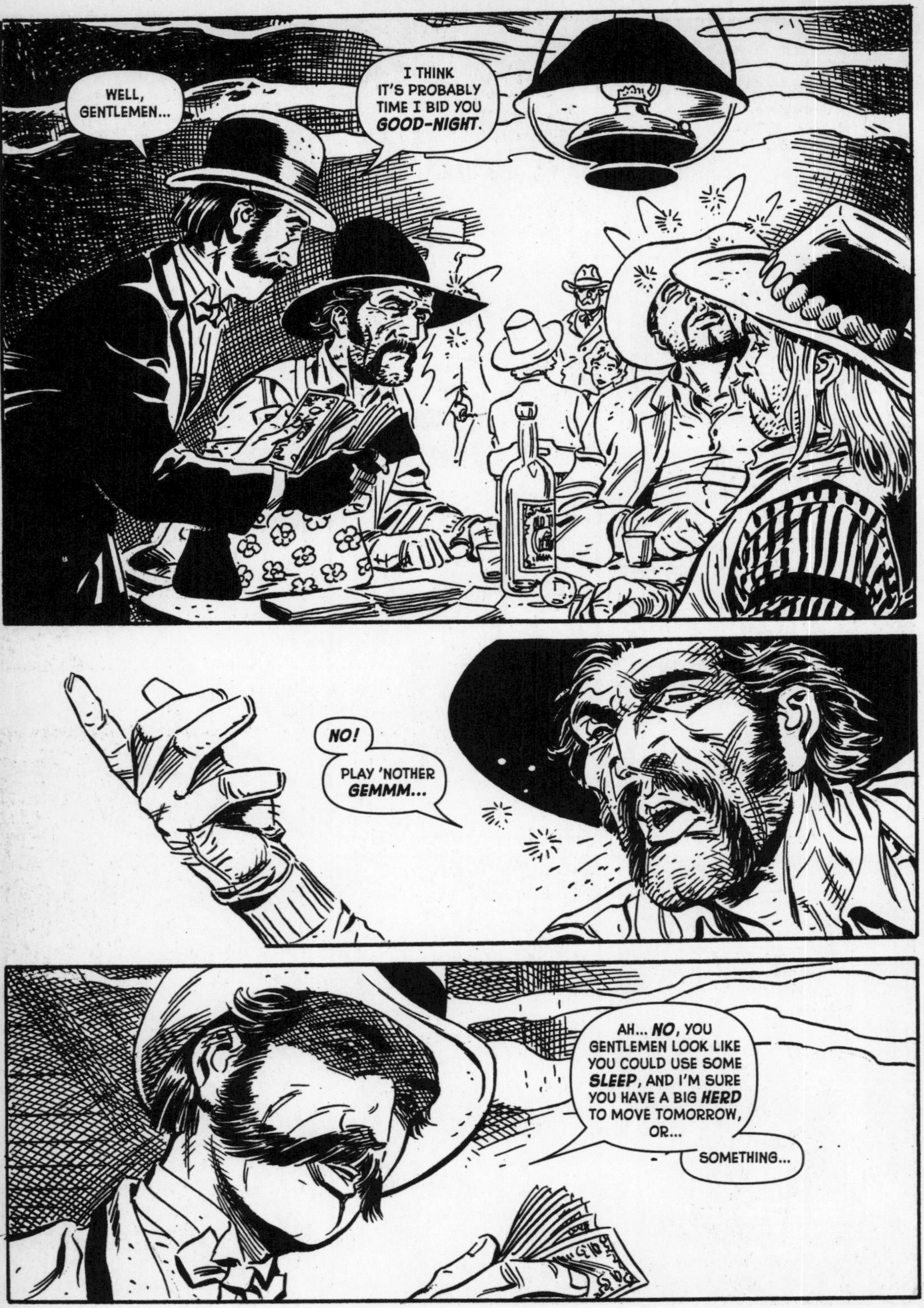
WELL, GENTLEMEN...
I THINK IT'S PROBABLY TIME I BID YOU GOOD-NIGHT.
NO!
PLAY 'NOTHER GEMMM...
AH... NO, YOU GENTLEMEN LOOK LIKE YOU COULD USE SOME SLEEP, AND I'M SURE YOU HAVE A BIG HERD TO MOVE TOMORROW, OR...
SOMETHING...

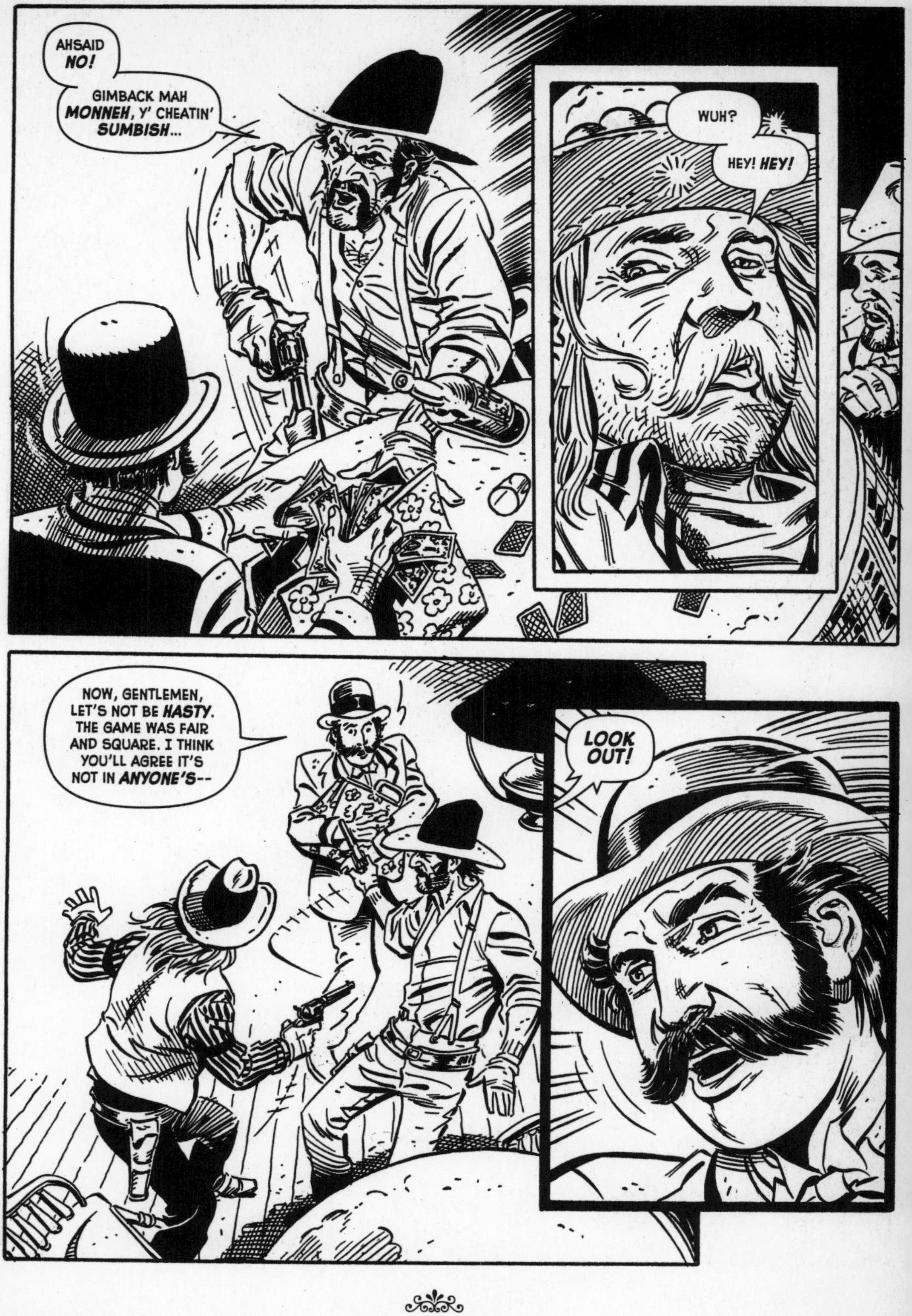
AHSAID NO!
GIMBACK MAH MONNEH, Y' CHEATIN' SUMBISH...
WUH?
HEY! HEY!
NOW, GENTLEMEN, LET'S NOT BE HASTY. THE GAME WAS FAIR AND SQUARE. I THINK YOU'LL AGREE IT'S NOT IN ANYONE'S--
LOOK OUT!

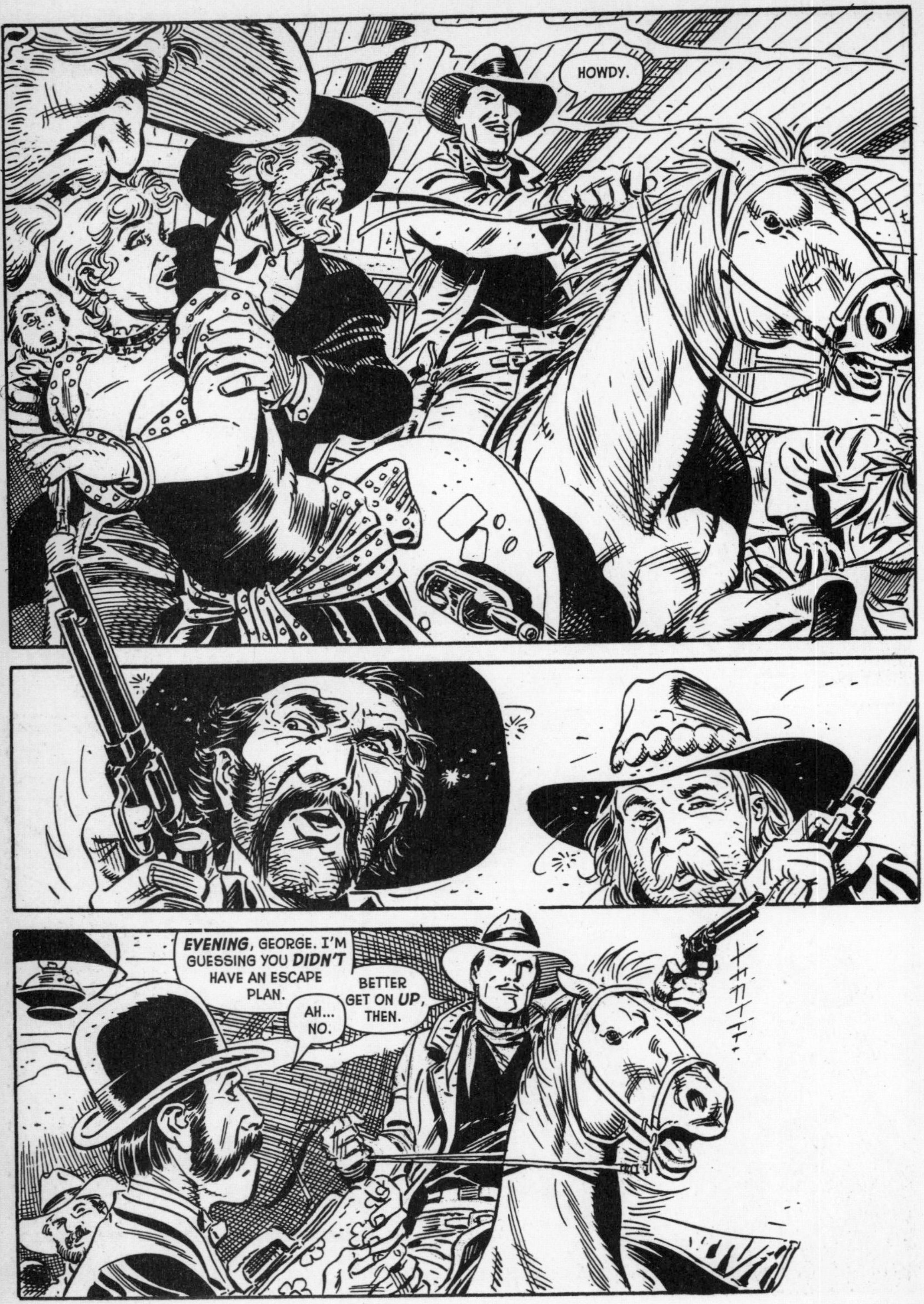
HOWDY.
EVENING, GEORGE. I'M GUESSING YOU *DIDN'T* HAVE AN ESCAPE PLAN.
AH... NO.
BETTER GET ON *UP*, THEN.

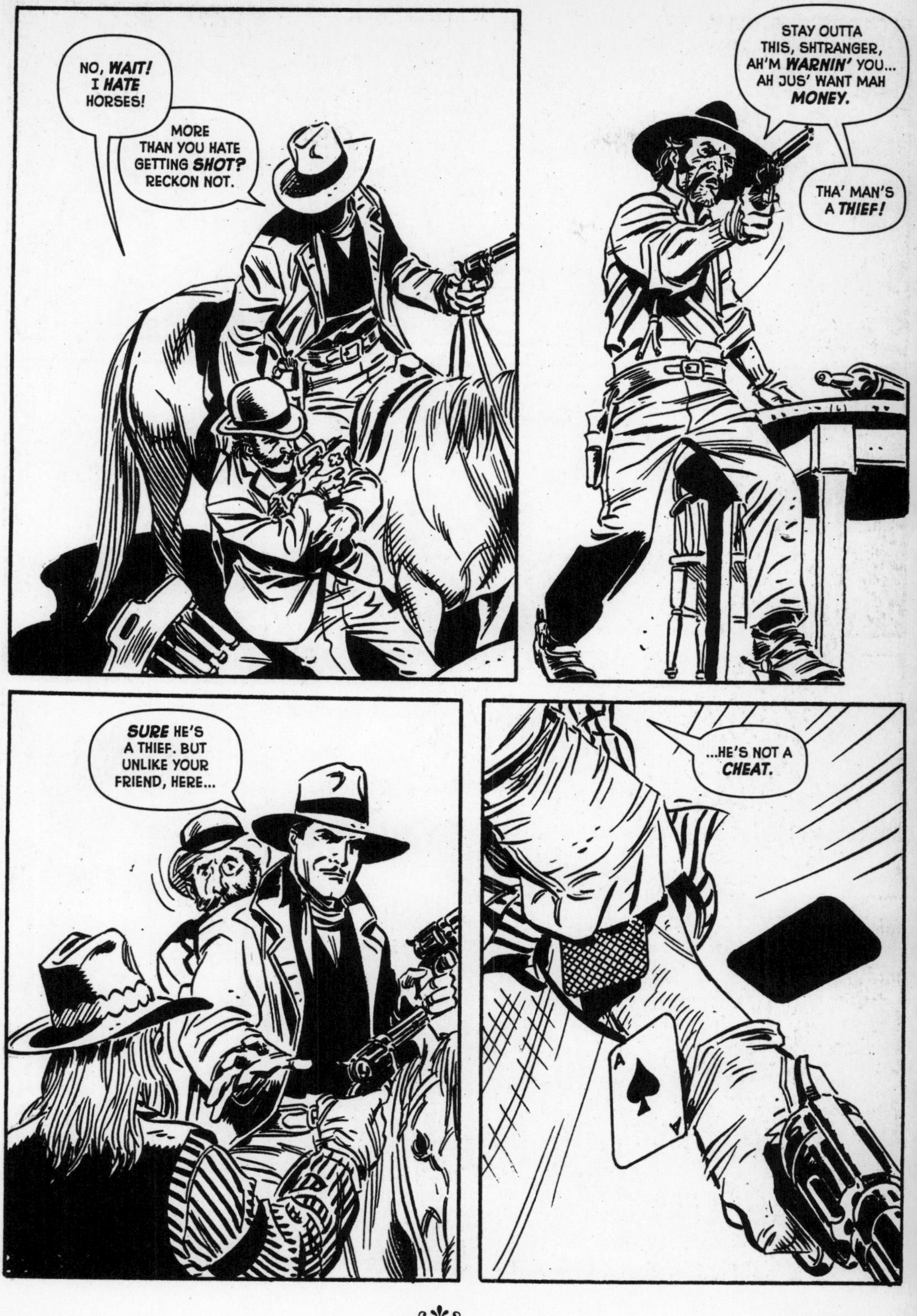
NO, WAIT! I HATE HORSES!
MORE THAN YOU HATE GETTING SHOT? RECKON NOT.
STAY OUTTA THIS, SHTRANGER, AH'M WARNIN' YOU... AH JUS' WANT MAH MONEY.
THA' MAN'S A THIEF!
SURE HE'S A THIEF. BUT UNLIKE YOUR FRIEND, HERE...
...HE'S NOT A CHEAT.

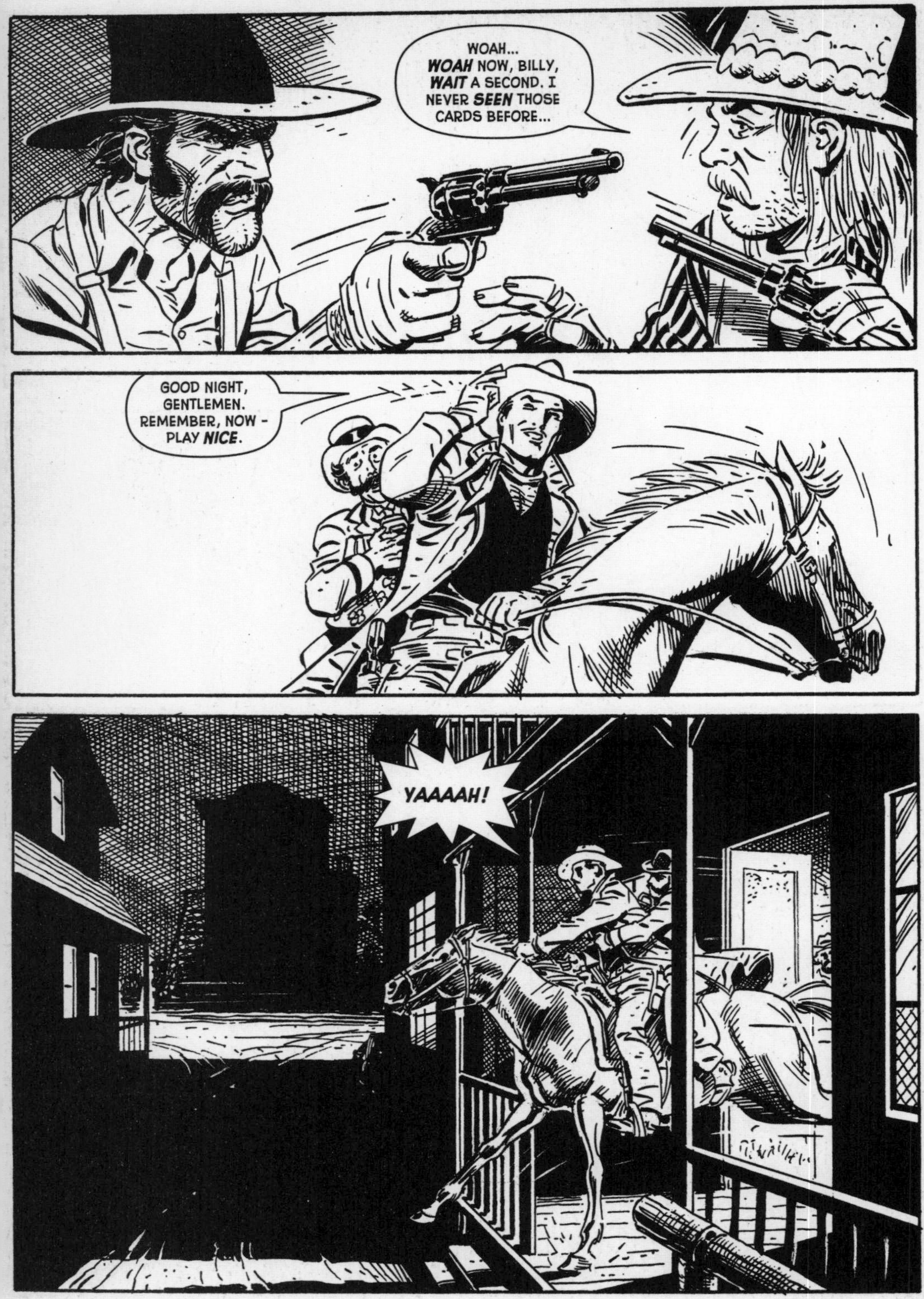
WOAH... **WOAH** NOW, BILLY, **WAIT** A SECOND. I NEVER **SEEN** THOSE CARDS BEFORE...
GOOD NIGHT, GENTLEMEN. REMEMBER, NOW - PLAY **NICE**.
YAAAAH!

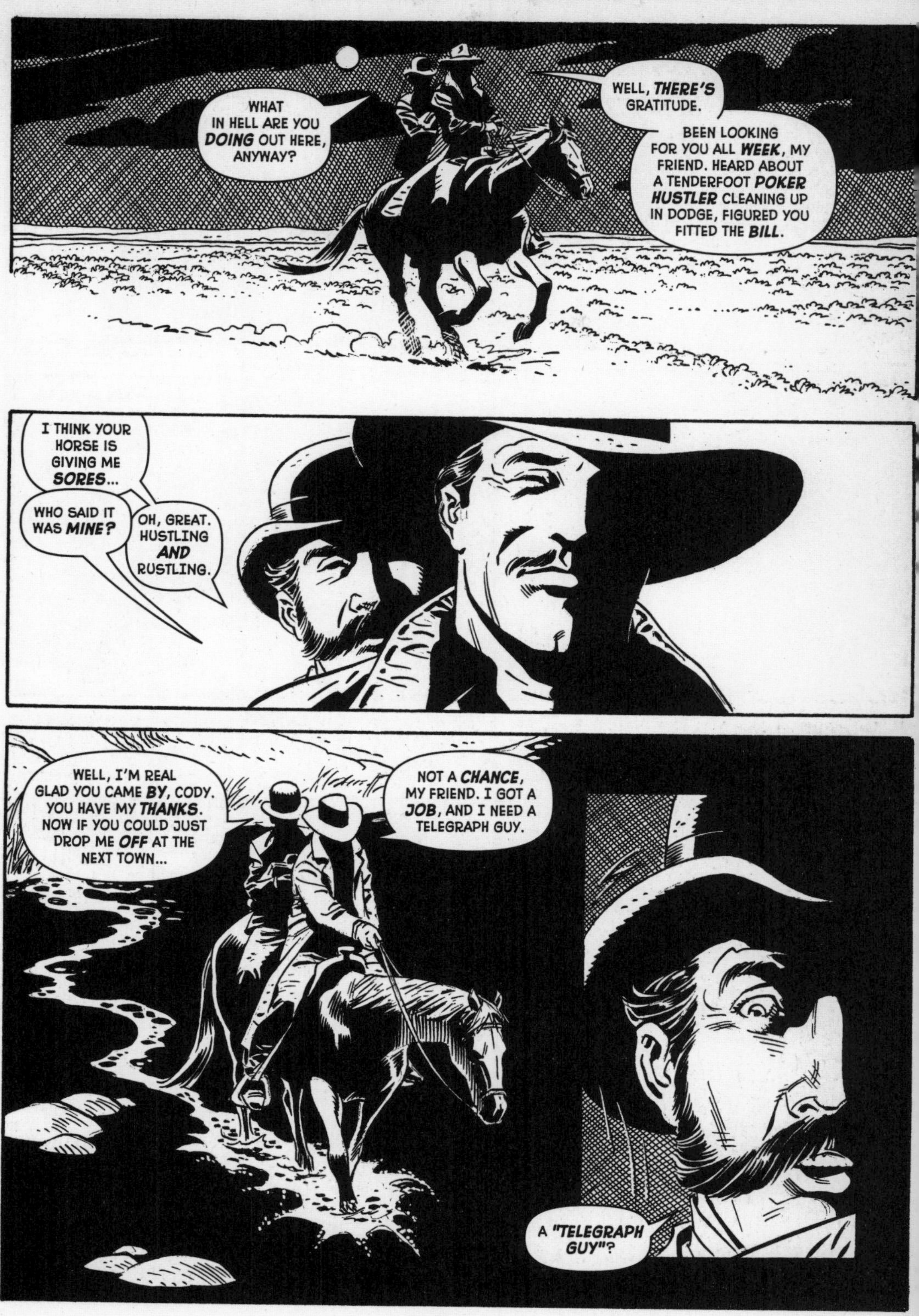
WHAT IN HELL ARE YOU DOING OUT HERE, ANYWAY?
WELL, THERE'S GRATITUDE.
BEEN LOOKING FOR YOU ALL WEEK, MY FRIEND. HEARD ABOUT A TENDERFOOT POKER HUSTLER CLEANING UP IN DODGE, FIGURED YOU FITTED THE BILL.
I THINK YOUR HORSE IS GIVING ME SORES...
WHO SAID IT WAS MINE?
OH, GREAT. HUSTLING AND RUSTLING.
WELL, I'M REAL GLAD YOU CAME BY, CODY. YOU HAVE MY THANKS. NOW IF YOU COULD JUST DROP ME OFF AT THE NEXT TOWN...
NOT A CHANCE, MY FRIEND. I GOT A JOB, AND I NEED A TELEGRAPH GUY.
A "TELEGRAPH GUY"?

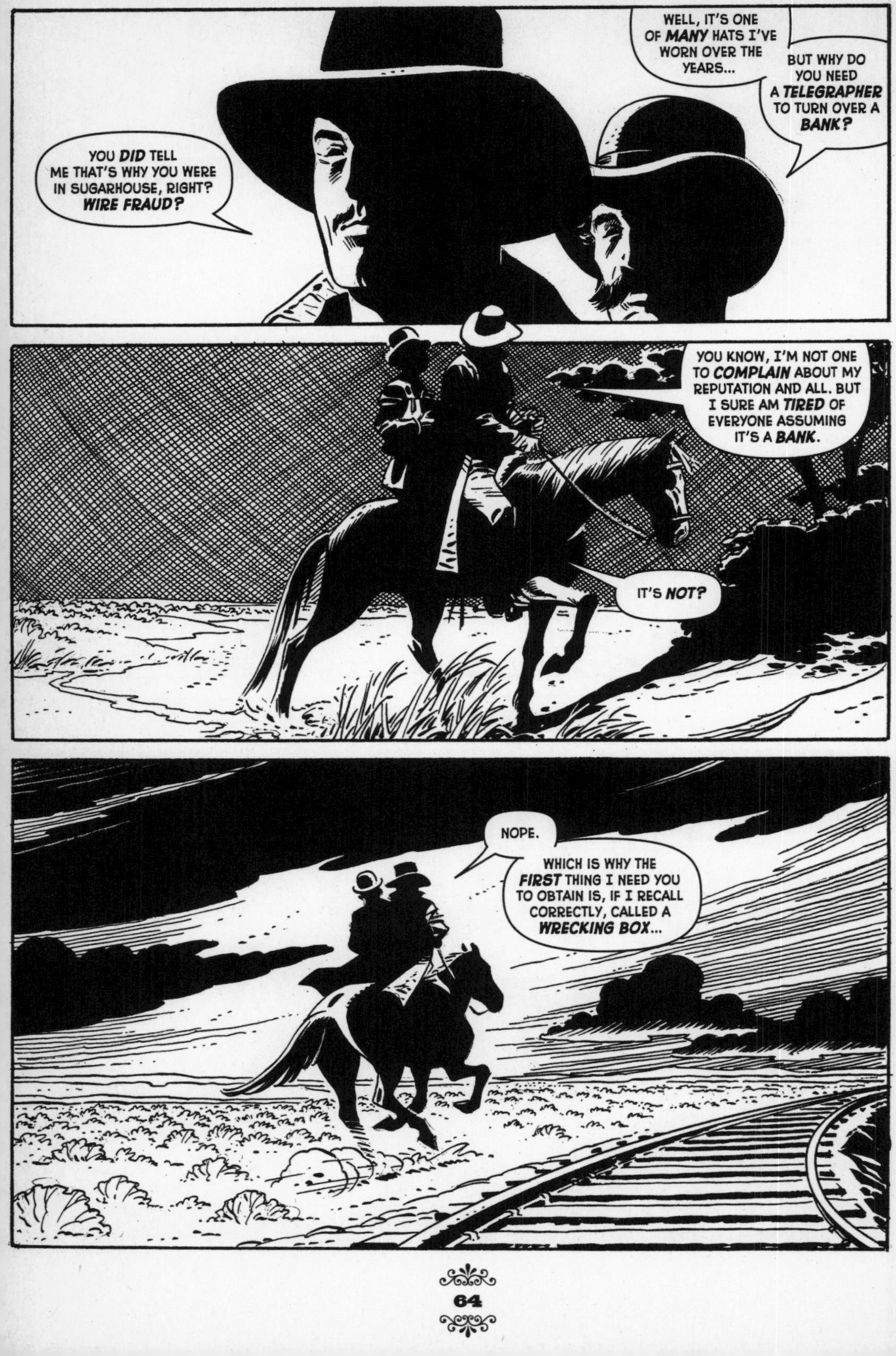
YOU DID TELL ME THAT'S WHY YOU WERE IN SUGARHOUSE, RIGHT? WIRE FRAUD?
WELL, IT'S ONE OF MANY HATS I'VE WORN OVER THE YEARS...
BUT WHY DO YOU NEED A TELEGRAPHER TO TURN OVER A BANK?
YOU KNOW, I'M NOT ONE TO COMPLAIN ABOUT MY REPUTATION AND ALL. BUT I SURE AM TIRED OF EVERYONE ASSUMING IT'S A BANK.
IT'S NOT?
NOPE.
WHICH IS WHY THE FIRST THING I NEED YOU TO OBTAIN IS, IF I RECALL CORRECTLY, CALLED A WRECKING BOX...

FIVE

★

"THE LOCKBREAKER"

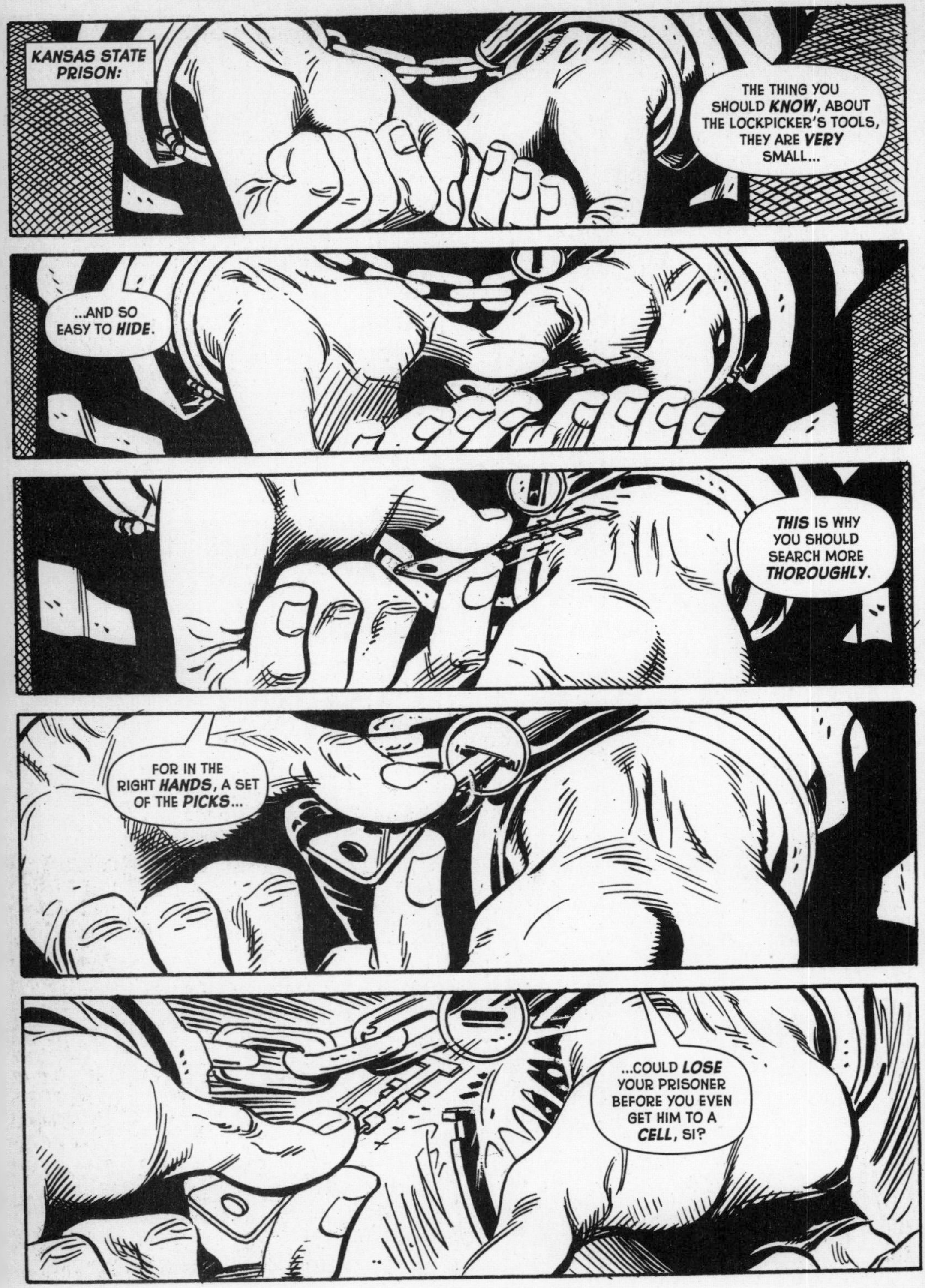
KANSAS STATE PRISON:
THE THING YOU SHOULD KNOW, ABOUT THE LOCKPICKER'S TOOLS, THEY ARE VERY SMALL...
...AND SO EASY TO HIDE.
THIS IS WHY YOU SHOULD SEARCH MORE THOROUGHLY.
FOR IN THE RIGHT HANDS, A SET OF THE PICKS...
...COULD LOSE YOUR PRISONER BEFORE YOU EVEN GET HIM TO A CELL, SI?

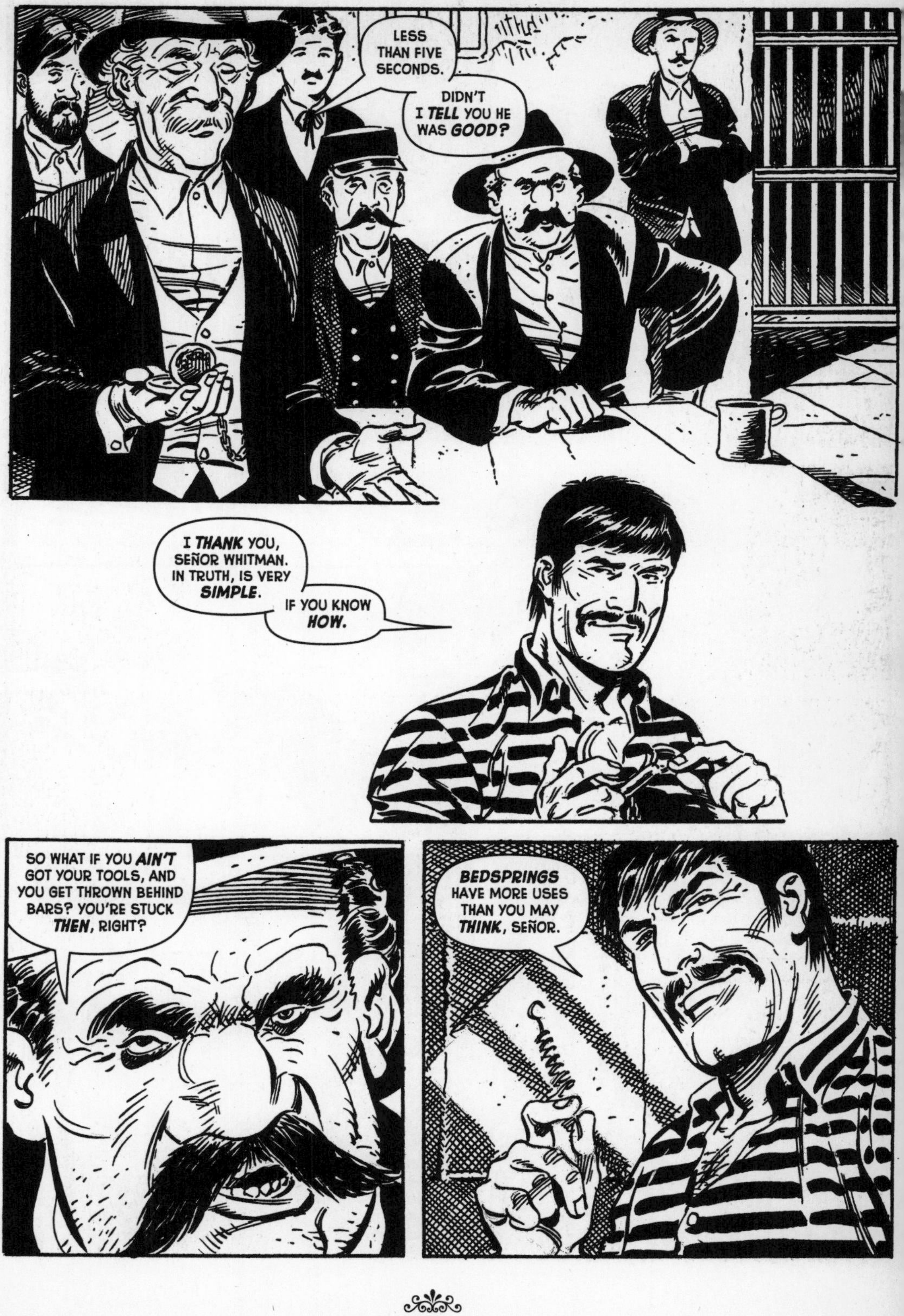
LESS THAN FIVE SECONDS.
DIDN'T I TELL YOU HE WAS GOOD?
I THANK YOU, SEÑOR WHITMAN. IN TRUTH, IS VERY SIMPLE.
IF YOU KNOW HOW.
SO WHAT IF YOU AIN'T GOT YOUR TOOLS, AND YOU GET THROWN BEHIND BARS? YOU'RE STUCK THEN, RIGHT?
BEDSPRINGS HAVE MORE USES THAN YOU MAY THINK, SEÑOR.

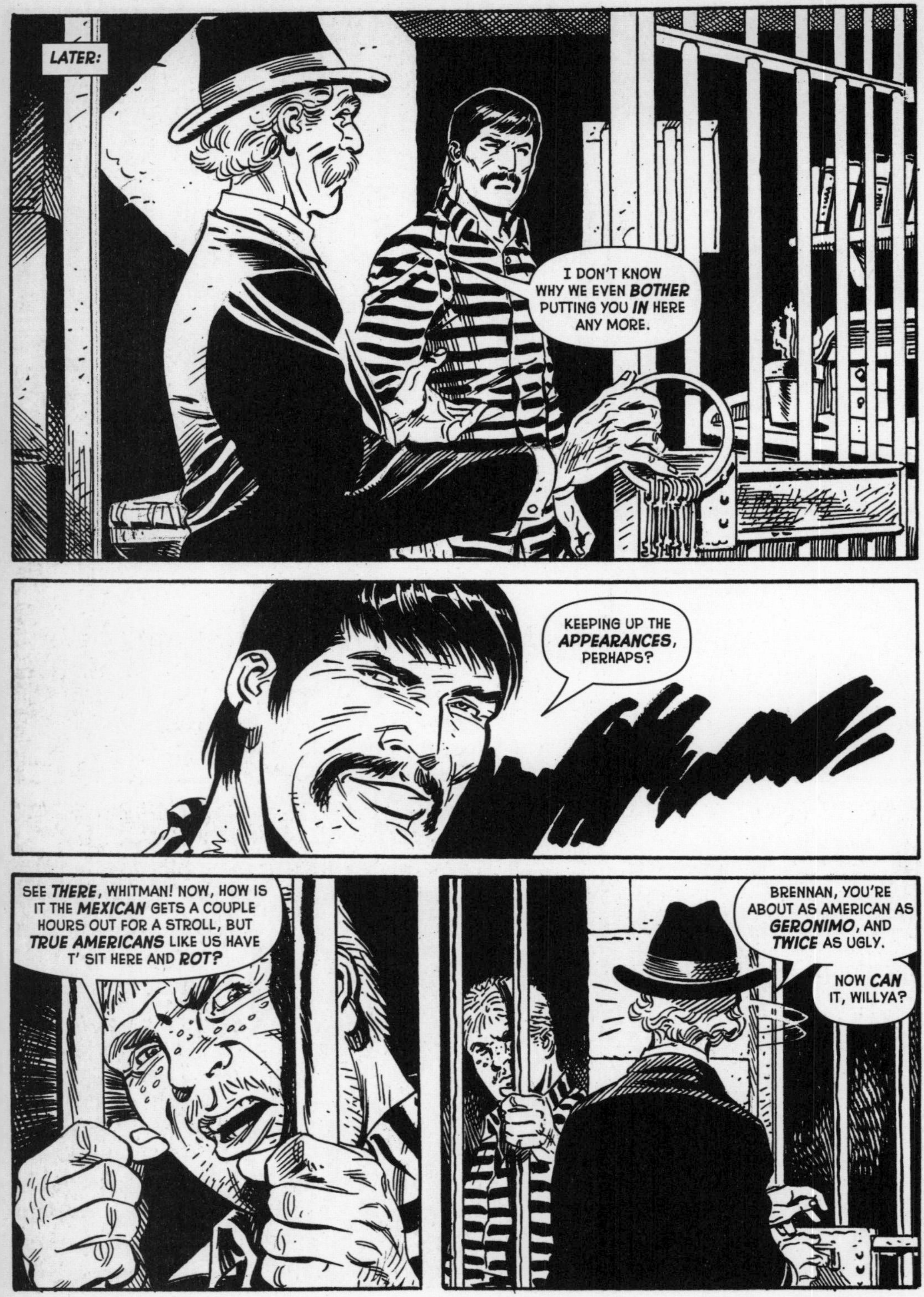
LATER:
I DON'T KNOW WHY WE EVEN BOTHER PUTTING YOU IN HERE ANY MORE.
KEEPING UP THE APPEARANCES, PERHAPS?
SEE THERE, WHITMAN! NOW, HOW IS IT THE MEXICAN GETS A COUPLE HOURS OUT FOR A STROLL, BUT TRUE AMERICANS LIKE US HAVE T' SIT HERE AND ROT?
BRENNAN, YOU'RE ABOUT AS AMERICAN AS GERONIMO, AND TWICE AS UGLY.
NOW CAN IT, WILLYA?

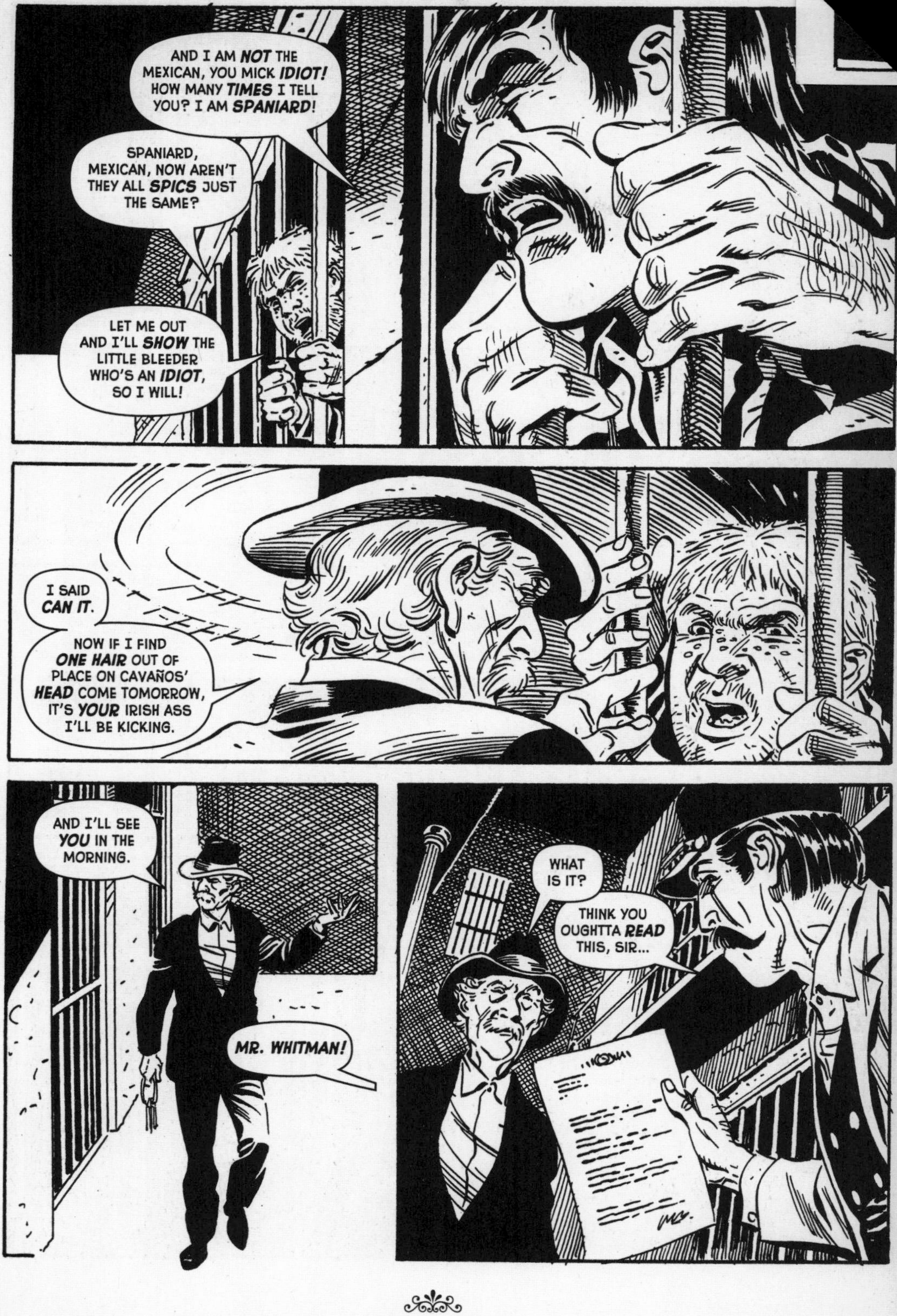
AND I AM NOT THE MEXICAN, YOU MICK IDIOT! HOW MANY TIMES I TELL YOU? I AM SPANIARD!
SPANIARD, MEXICAN, NOW AREN'T THEY ALL SPICS JUST THE SAME?
LET ME OUT AND I'LL SHOW THE LITTLE BLEEDER WHO'S AN IDIOT, SO I WILL!
I SAID CAN IT.
NOW IF I FIND ONE HAIR OUT OF PLACE ON CAVAÑOS' HEAD COME TOMORROW, IT'S YOUR IRISH ASS I'LL BE KICKING.
AND I'LL SEE YOU IN THE MORNING.
MR. WHITMAN!
WHAT IS IT?
THINK YOU OUGHTTA READ THIS, SIR...

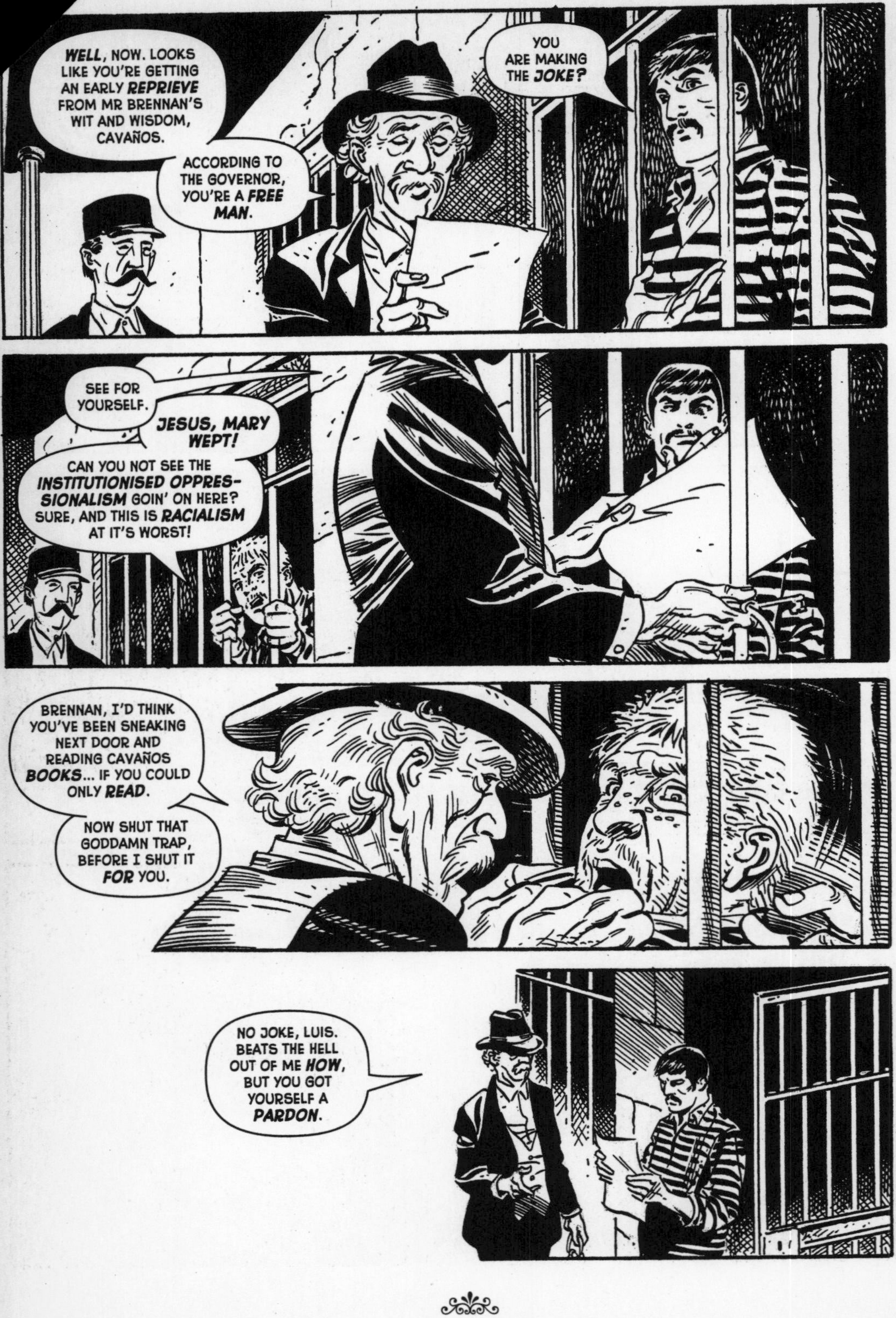
WELL, NOW. LOOKS LIKE YOU'RE GETTING AN EARLY REPRIEVE FROM MR BRENNAN'S WIT AND WISDOM, CAVAÑOS.
ACCORDING TO THE GOVERNOR, YOU'RE A FREE MAN.
YOU ARE MAKING THE JOKE?
SEE FOR YOURSELF.
JESUS, MARY WEPT!
CAN YOU NOT SEE THE INSTITUTIONISED OPPRES-SIONALISM GOIN' ON HERE? SURE, AND THIS IS RACIALISM AT IT'S WORST!
BRENNAN, I'D THINK YOU'VE BEEN SNEAKING NEXT DOOR AND READING CAVAÑOS BOOKS... IF YOU COULD ONLY READ.
NOW SHUT THAT GODDAMN TRAP, BEFORE I SHUT IT FOR YOU.
NO JOKE, LUIS. BEATS THE HELL OUT OF ME HOW, BUT YOU GOT YOURSELF A PARDON.

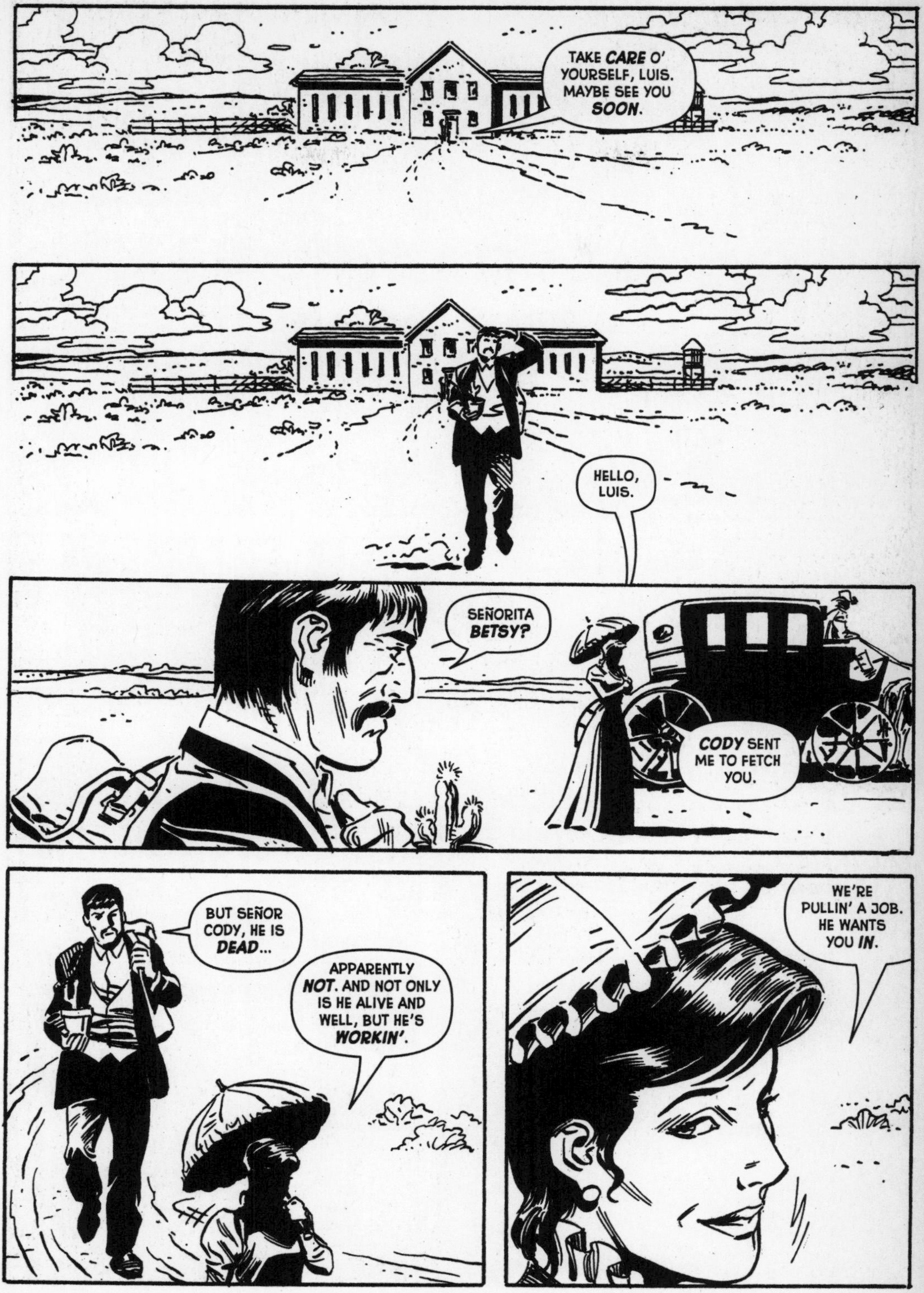
TAKE CARE O' YOURSELF, LUIS. MAYBE SEE YOU SOON.
HELLO, LUIS.
SEÑORITA BETSY?
CODY SENT ME TO FETCH YOU.
BUT SEÑOR CODY, HE IS DEAD...
APPARENTLY NOT. AND NOT ONLY IS HE ALIVE AND WELL, BUT HE'S WORKIN'.
WE'RE PULLIN' A JOB. HE WANTS YOU IN.

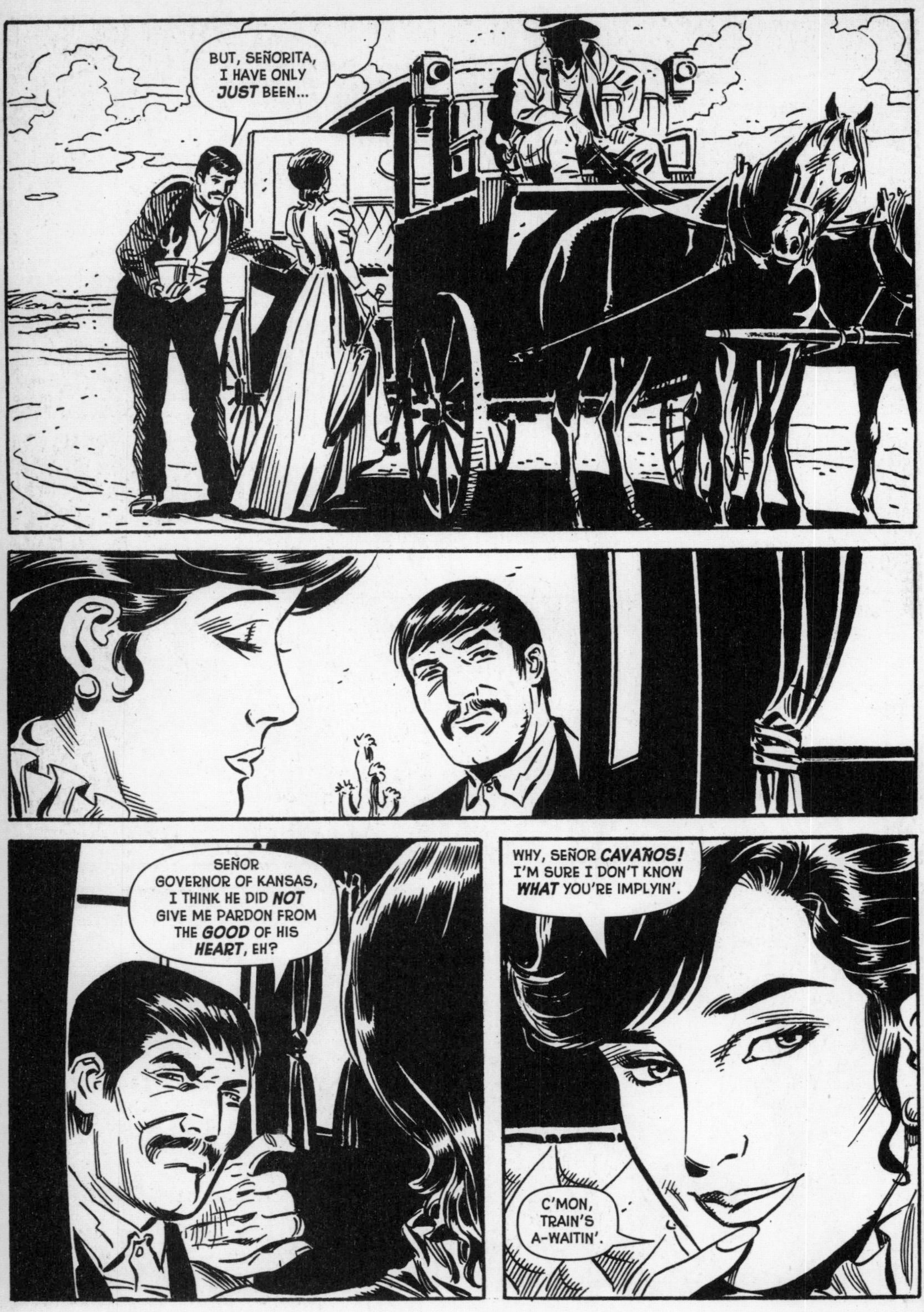
BUT, SEÑORITA, I HAVE ONLY JUST BEEN...
SEÑOR GOVERNOR OF KANSAS, I THINK HE DID NOT GIVE ME PARDON FROM THE GOOD OF HIS HEART, EH?
WHY, SEÑOR CAVAÑOS! I'M SURE I DON'T KNOW WHAT YOU'RE IMPLYIN'.
C'MON, TRAIN'S A-WAITIN'.

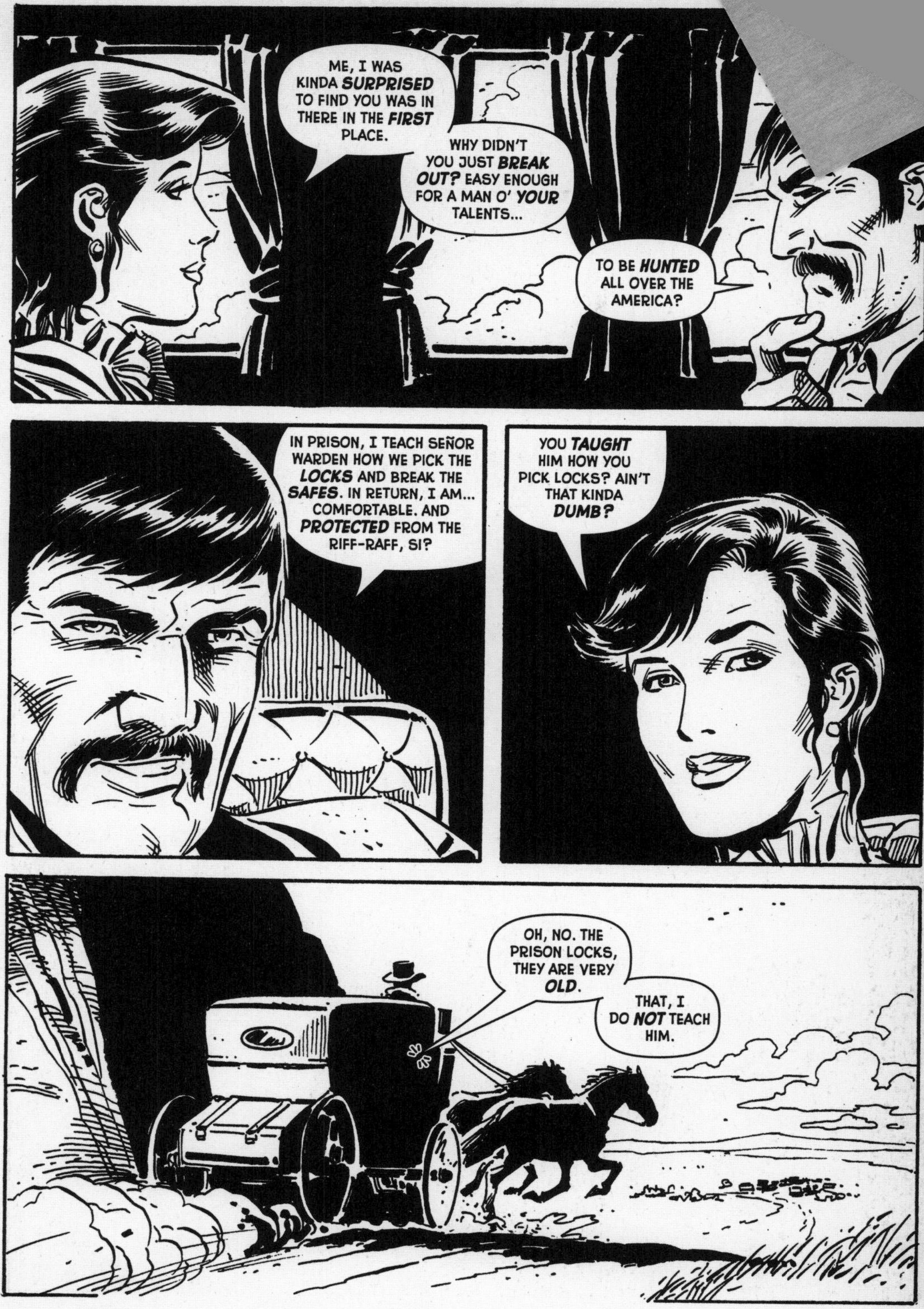
ME, I WAS KINDA SURPRISED TO FIND YOU WAS IN THERE IN THE FIRST PLACE.
WHY DIDN'T YOU JUST BREAK OUT? EASY ENOUGH FOR A MAN O' YOUR TALENTS...
TO BE HUNTED ALL OVER THE AMERICA?
IN PRISON, I TEACH SEÑOR WARDEN HOW WE PICK THE LOCKS AND BREAK THE SAFES. IN RETURN, I AM... COMFORTABLE. AND PROTECTED FROM THE RIFF-RAFF, SI?
YOU TAUGHT HIM HOW YOU PICK LOCKS? AIN'T THAT KINDA DUMB?
OH, NO. THE PRISON LOCKS, THEY ARE VERY OLD.
THAT, I DO NOT TEACH HIM.

SIX

★

"THE INDIAN"

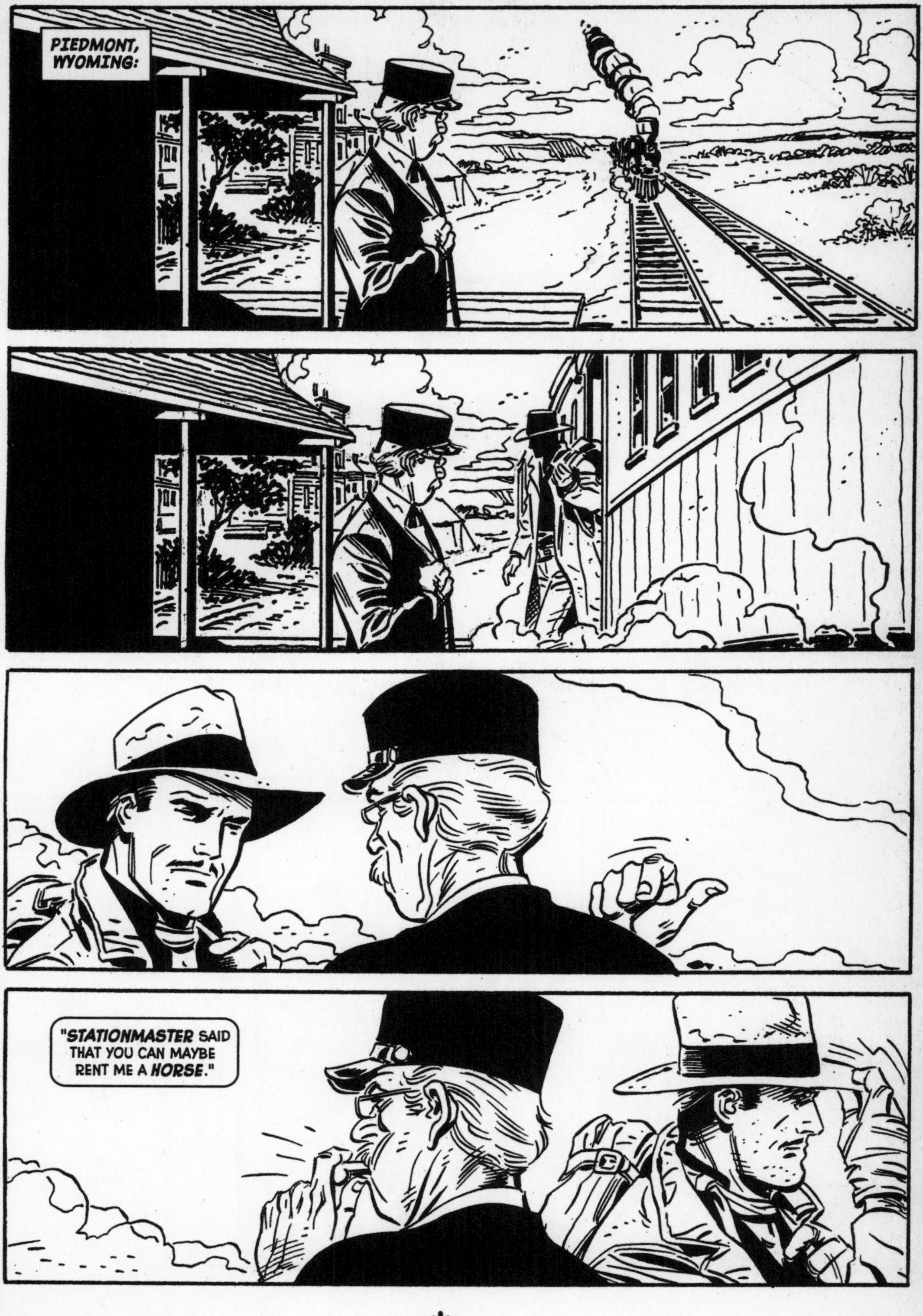
PIEDMONT, WYOMING:
"STATIONMASTER SAID THAT YOU CAN MAYBE RENT ME A HORSE."

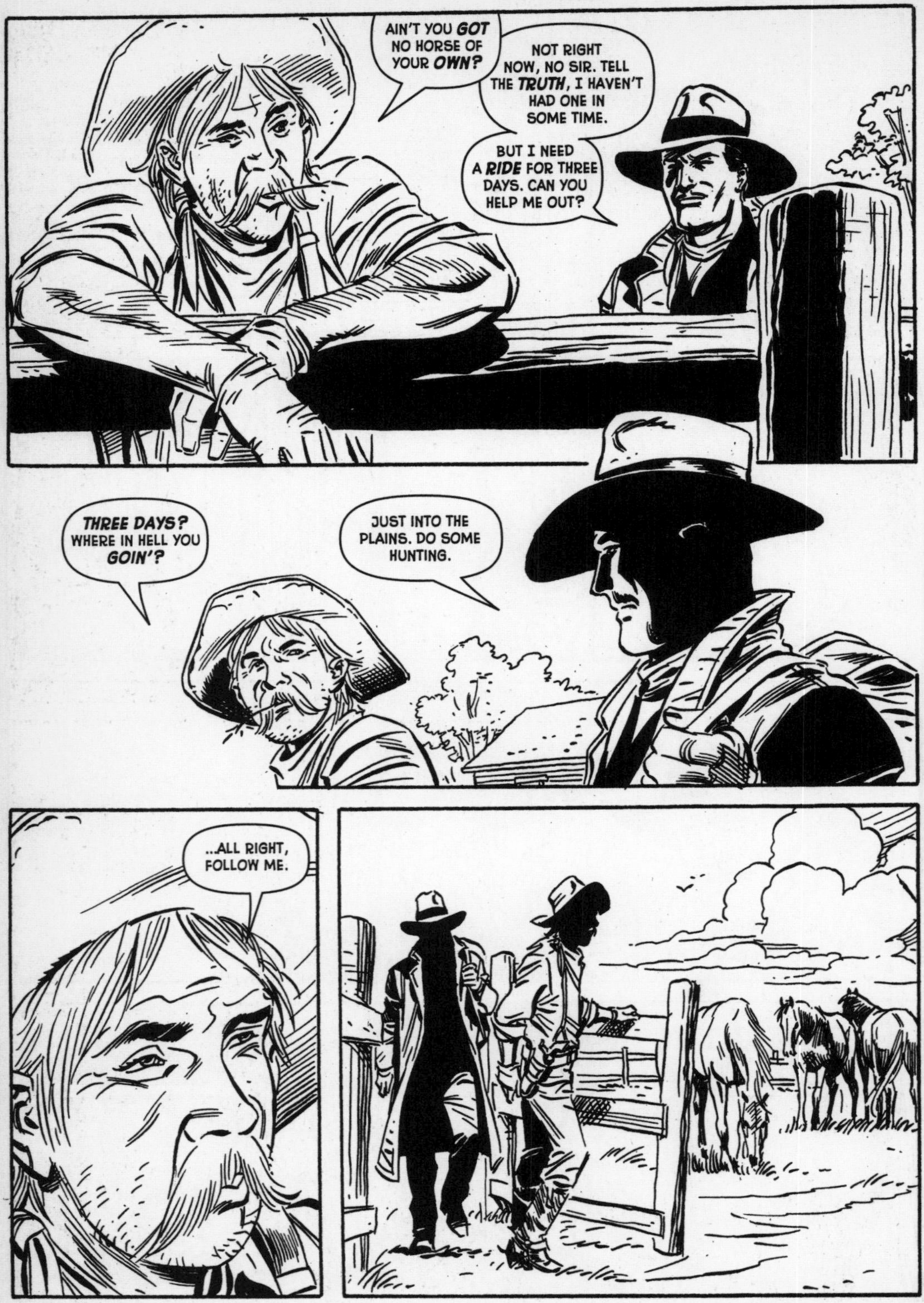
AIN'T YOU GOT NO HORSE OF YOUR OWN?
NOT RIGHT NOW, NO SIR. TELL THE TRUTH, I HAVEN'T HAD ONE IN SOME TIME.
BUT I NEED A RIDE FOR THREE DAYS. CAN YOU HELP ME OUT?
THREE DAYS? WHERE IN HELL YOU GOIN'?
JUST INTO THE PLAINS. DO SOME HUNTING.
...ALL RIGHT, FOLLOW ME.

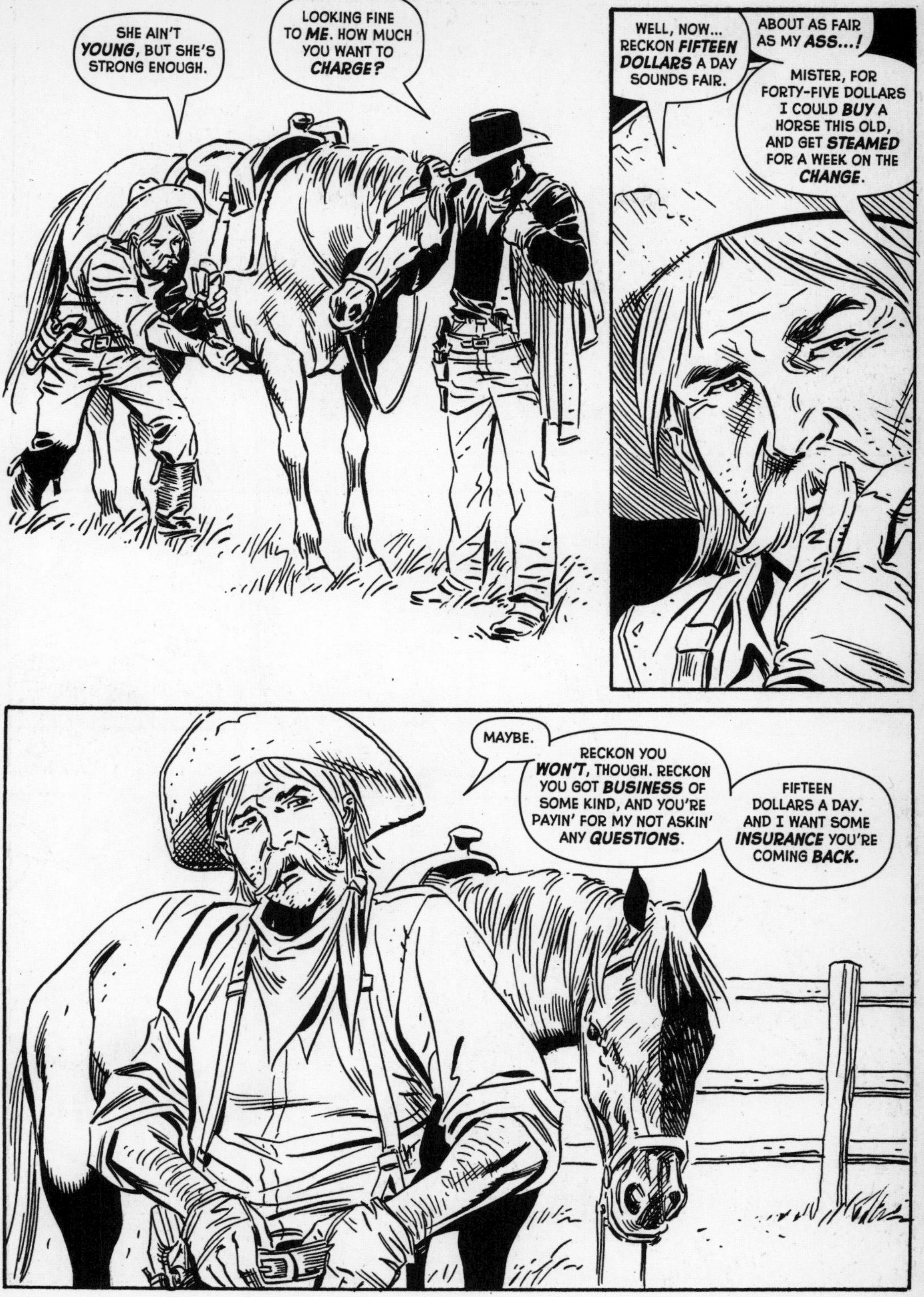
SHE AIN'T YOUNG, BUT SHE'S STRONG ENOUGH.
LOOKING FINE TO ME. HOW MUCH YOU WANT TO CHARGE?
WELL, NOW... RECKON FIFTEEN DOLLARS A DAY SOUNDS FAIR.
ABOUT AS FAIR AS MY ASS...!
MISTER, FOR FORTY-FIVE DOLLARS I COULD BUY A HORSE THIS OLD, AND GET STEAMED FOR A WEEK ON THE CHANGE.
MAYBE.
RECKON YOU WON'T, THOUGH. RECKON YOU GOT BUSINESS OF SOME KIND, AND YOU'RE PAYIN' FOR MY NOT ASKIN' ANY QUESTIONS.
FIFTEEN DOLLARS A DAY. AND I WANT SOME INSURANCE YOU'RE COMING BACK.

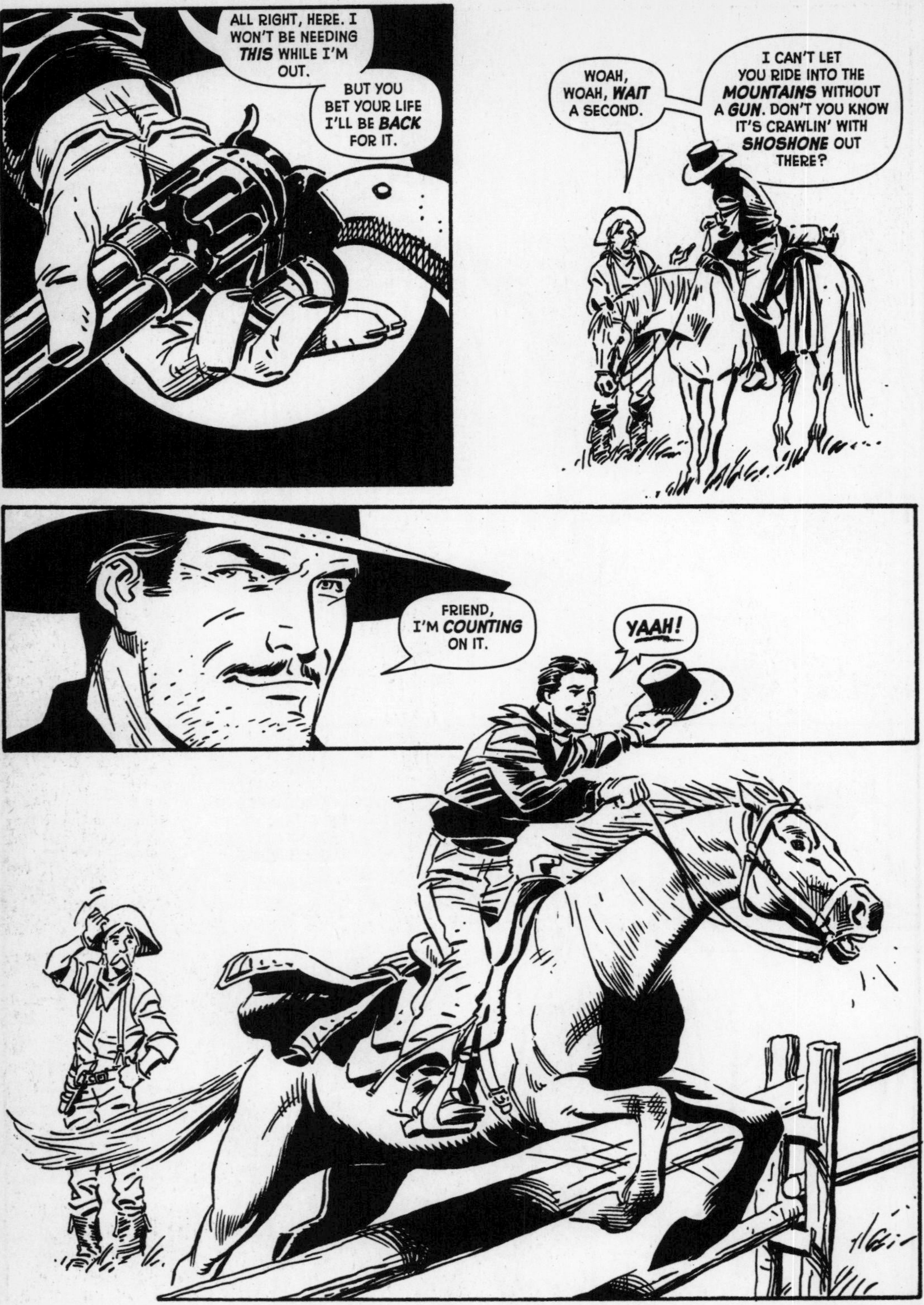
ALL RIGHT, HERE. I WON'T BE NEEDING THIS WHILE I'M OUT.
BUT YOU BET YOUR LIFE I'LL BE BACK FOR IT.
WOAH, WOAH, WAIT A SECOND.
I CAN'T LET YOU RIDE INTO THE MOUNTAINS WITHOUT A GUN. DON'T YOU KNOW IT'S CRAWLIN' WITH SHOSHONE OUT THERE?
FRIEND, I'M COUNTING ON IT.
YAAH!

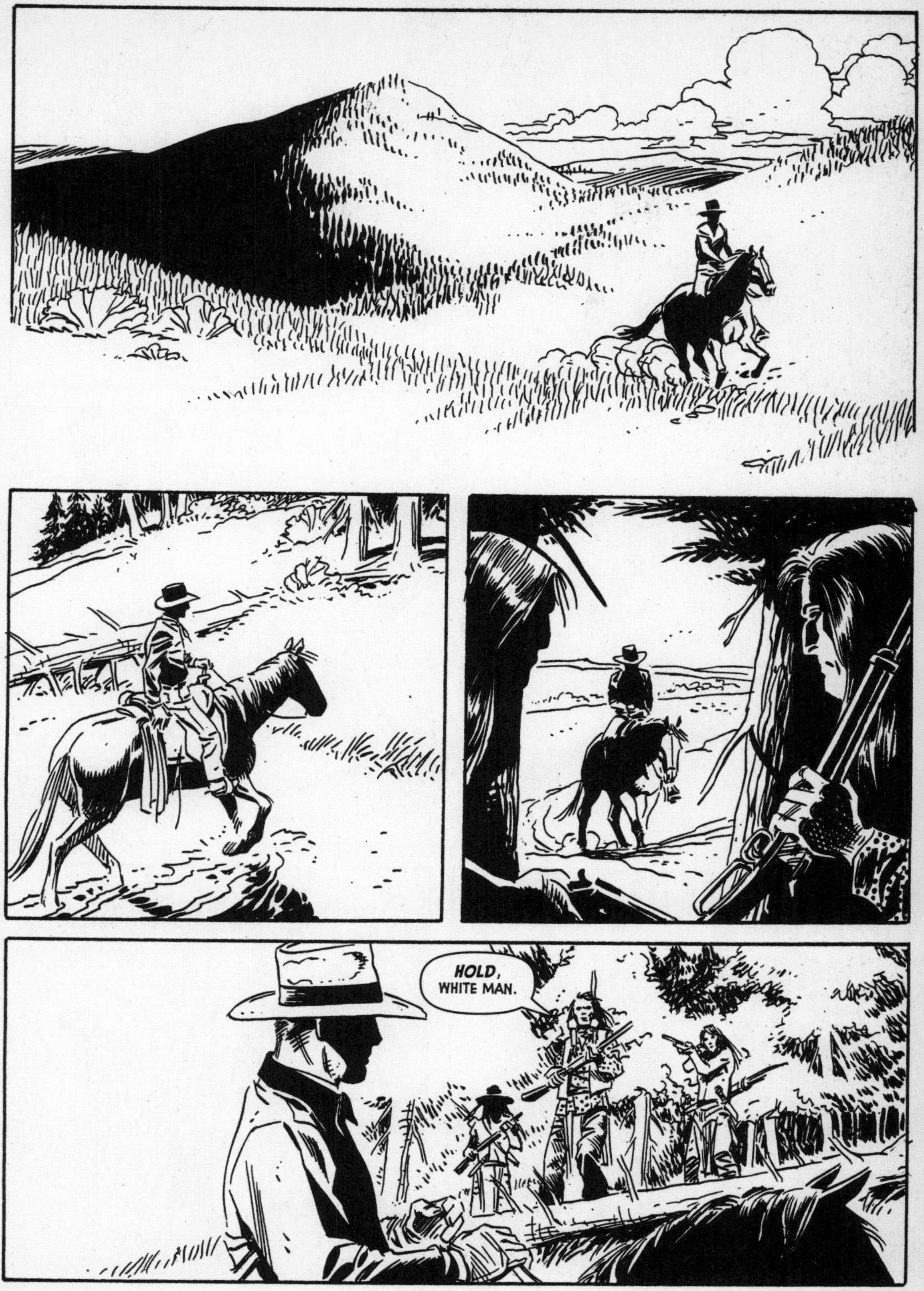
HOLD, WHITE MAN.

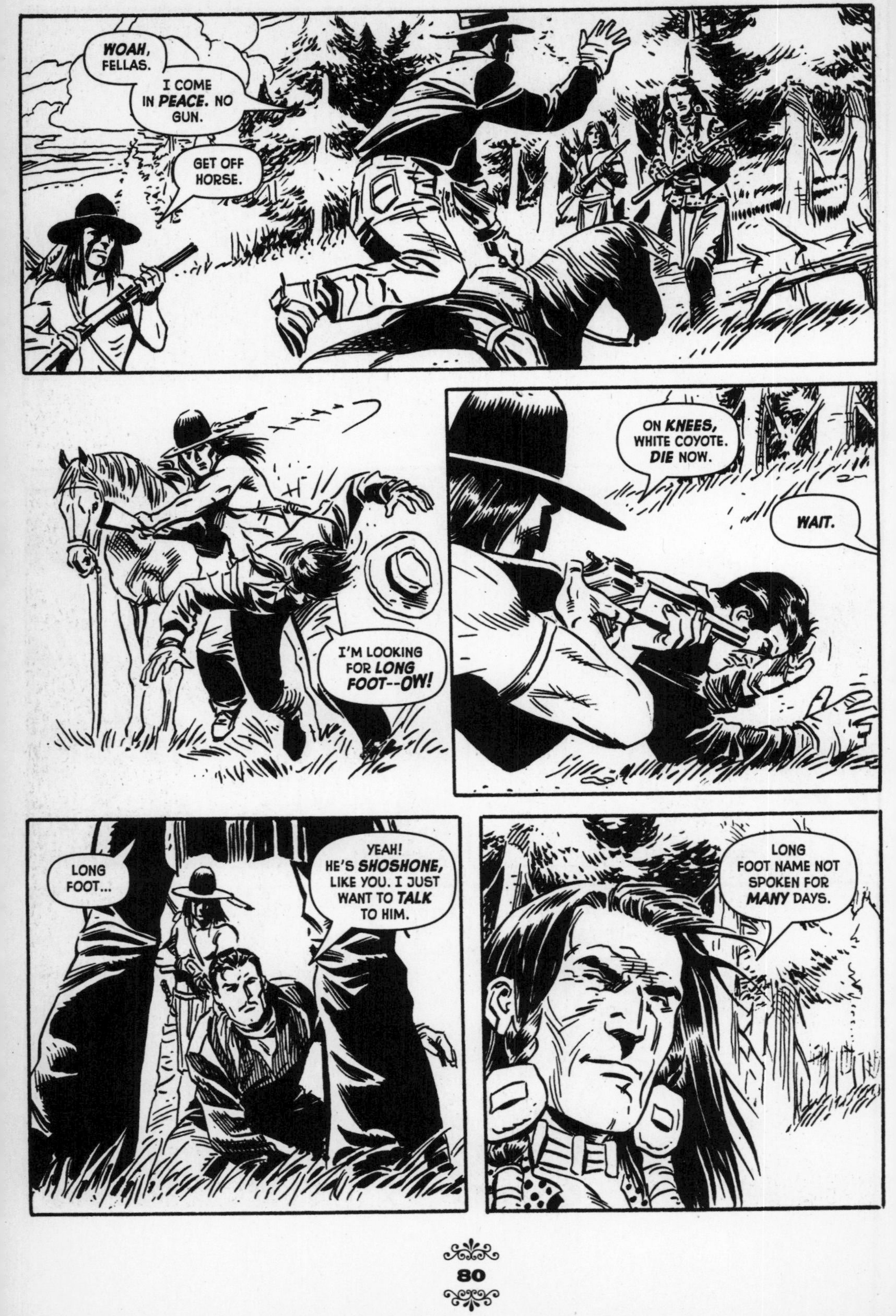
WOAH, FELLAS.
I COME IN PEACE. NO GUN.
GET OFF HORSE.
I'M LOOKING FOR LONG FOOT--OW!
ON KNEES, WHITE COYOTE. DIE NOW.
WAIT.
LONG FOOT...
YEAH! HE'S SHOSHONE, LIKE YOU. I JUST WANT TO TALK TO HIM.
LONG FOOT NAME NOT SPOKEN FOR MANY DAYS.

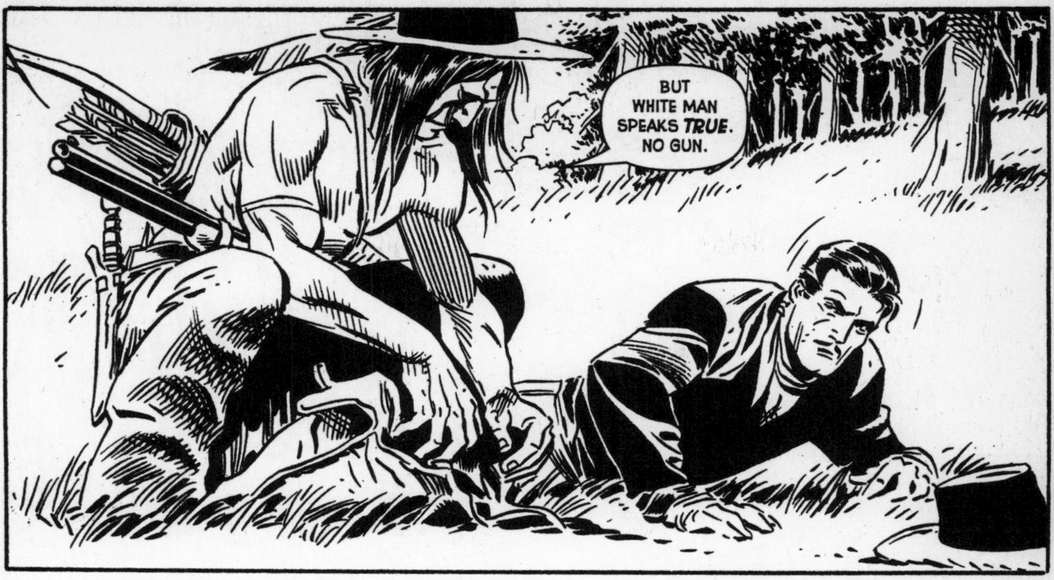
BUT WHITE MAN SPEAKS TRUE. NO GUN.

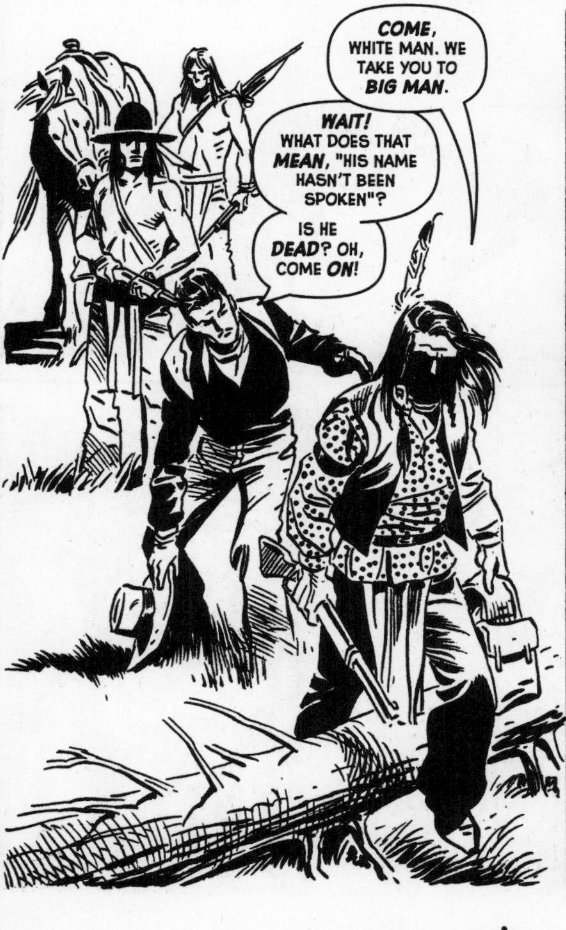
COME, WHITE MAN. WE TAKE YOU TO BIG MAN.
WAIT! WHAT DOES THAT MEAN, "HIS NAME HASN'T BEEN SPOKEN"?
IS HE DEAD? OH, COME ON!

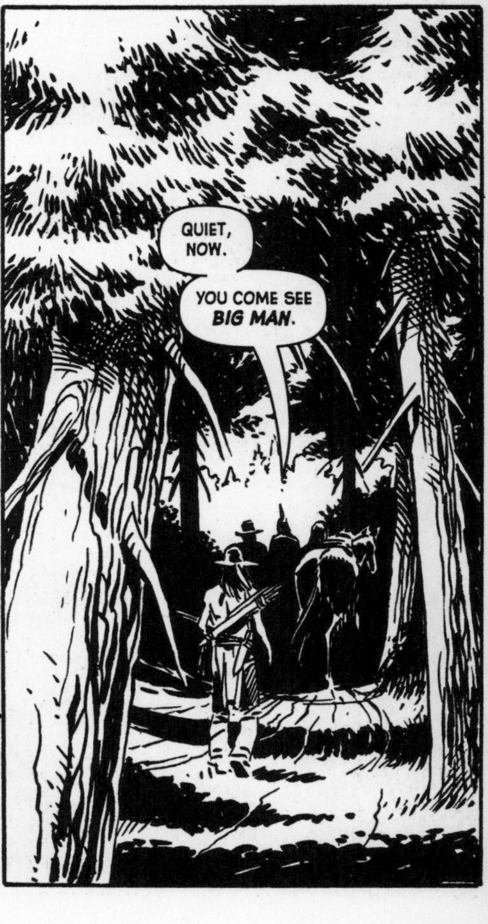
QUIET, NOW.
YOU COME SEE BIG MAN.

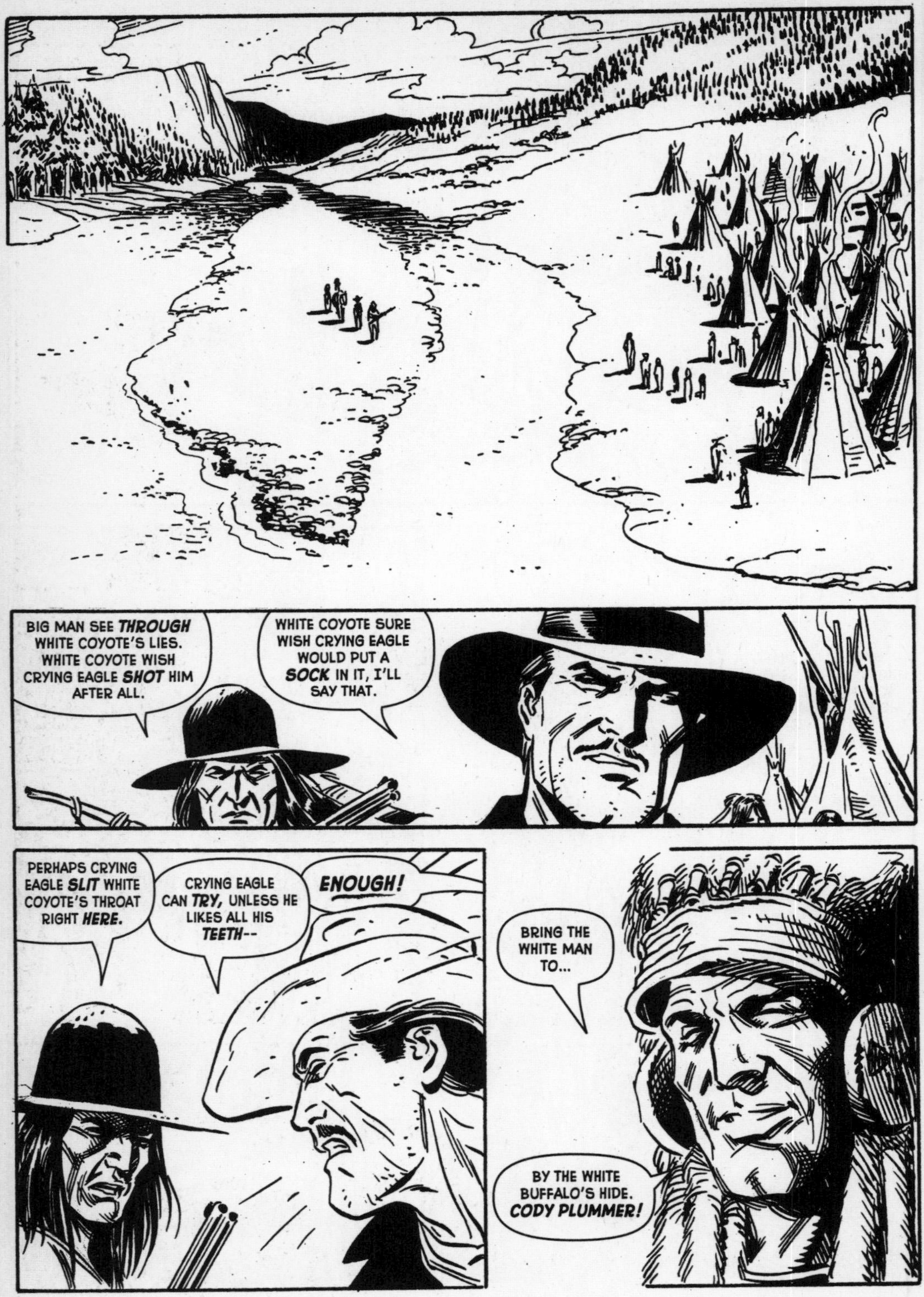
BIG MAN SEE *THROUGH* WHITE COYOTE'S LIES. WHITE COYOTE WISH CRYING EAGLE *SHOT* HIM AFTER ALL.
WHITE COYOTE SURE WISH CRYING EAGLE WOULD PUT A *SOCK* IN IT, I'LL SAY THAT.
PERHAPS CRYING EAGLE *SLIT* WHITE COYOTE'S THROAT RIGHT *HERE.*
CRYING EAGLE CAN *TRY,* UNLESS HE LIKES ALL HIS *TEETH*--
ENOUGH!
BRING THE WHITE MAN TO...
BY THE WHITE BUFFALO'S HIDE. *CODY PLUMMER!*

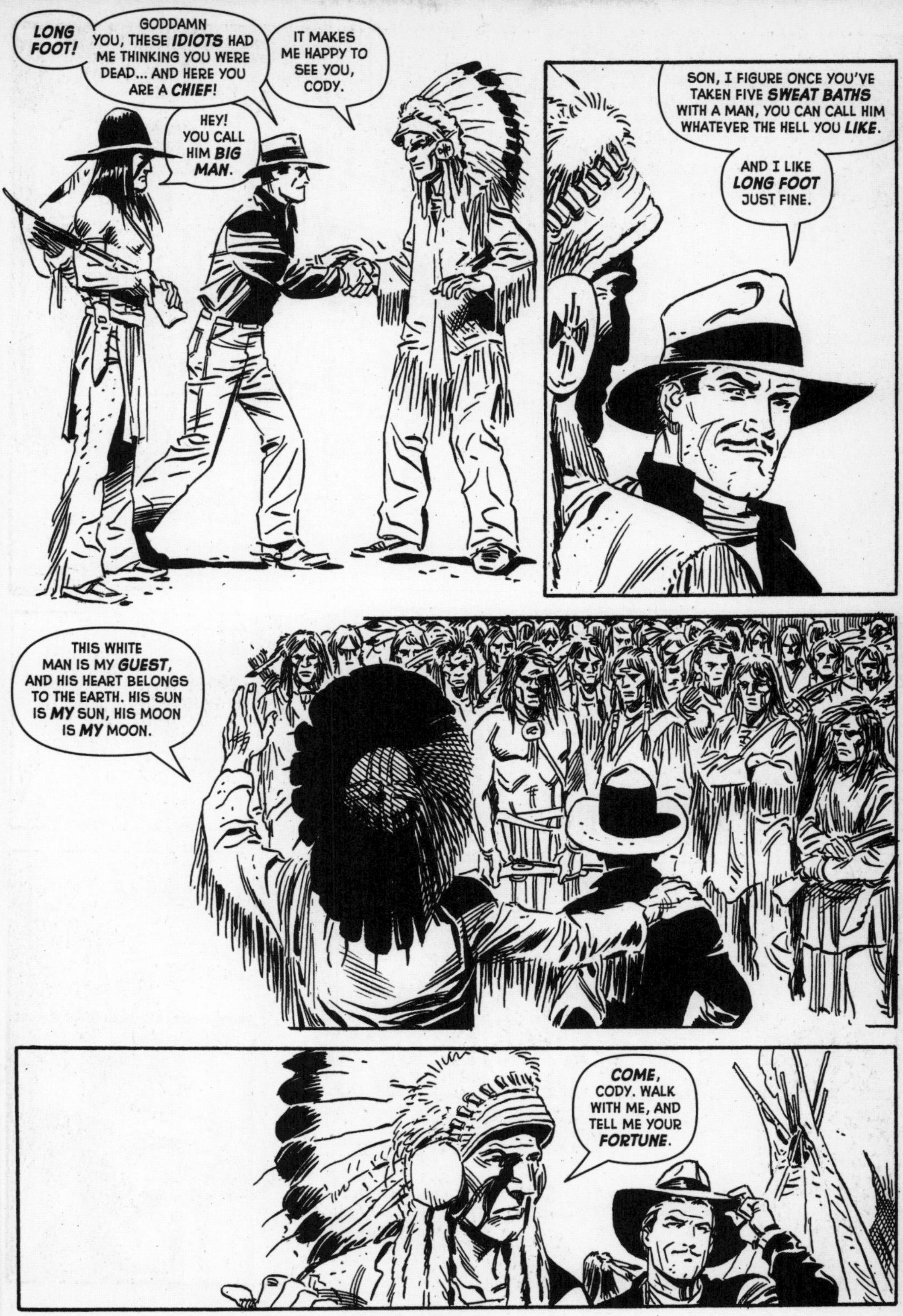
LONG FOOT!
GODDAMN YOU, THESE IDIOTS HAD ME THINKING YOU WERE DEAD... AND HERE YOU ARE A CHIEF!
IT MAKES ME HAPPY TO SEE YOU, CODY.
HEY! YOU CALL HIM BIG MAN.
SON, I FIGURE ONCE YOU'VE TAKEN FIVE SWEAT BATHS WITH A MAN, YOU CAN CALL HIM WHATEVER THE HELL YOU LIKE.
AND I LIKE LONG FOOT JUST FINE.
THIS WHITE MAN IS MY GUEST, AND HIS HEART BELONGS TO THE EARTH. HIS SUN IS MY SUN, HIS MOON IS MY MOON.
COME, CODY. WALK WITH ME, AND TELL ME YOUR FORTUNE.

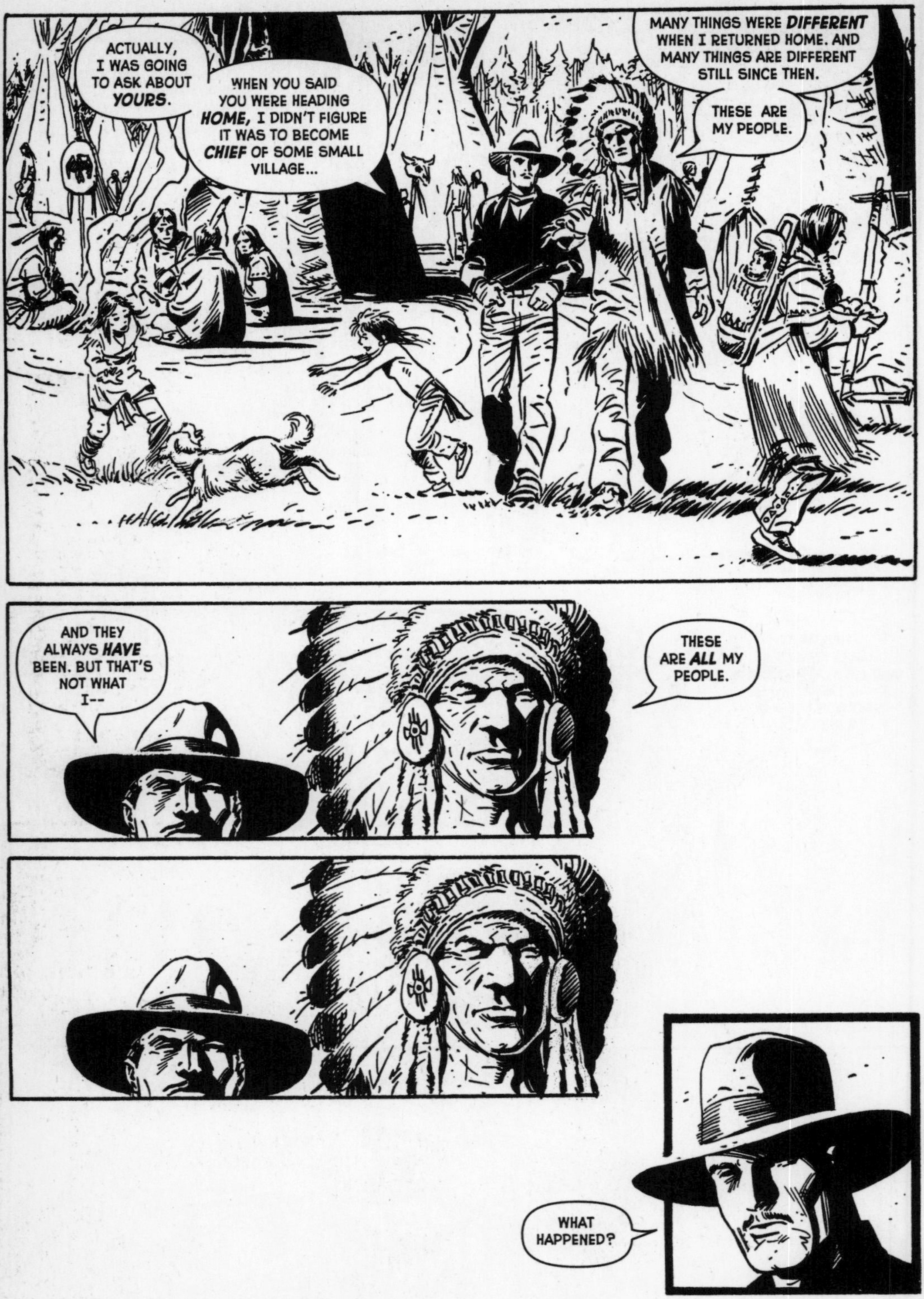
ACTUALLY, I WAS GOING TO ASK ABOUT YOURS.
WHEN YOU SAID YOU WERE HEADING HOME, I DIDN'T FIGURE IT WAS TO BECOME CHIEF OF SOME SMALL VILLAGE...
MANY THINGS WERE DIFFERENT WHEN I RETURNED HOME. AND MANY THINGS ARE DIFFERENT STILL SINCE THEN.
THESE ARE MY PEOPLE.
AND THEY ALWAYS HAVE BEEN. BUT THAT'S NOT WHAT I--
THESE ARE ALL MY PEOPLE.
WHAT HAPPENED?

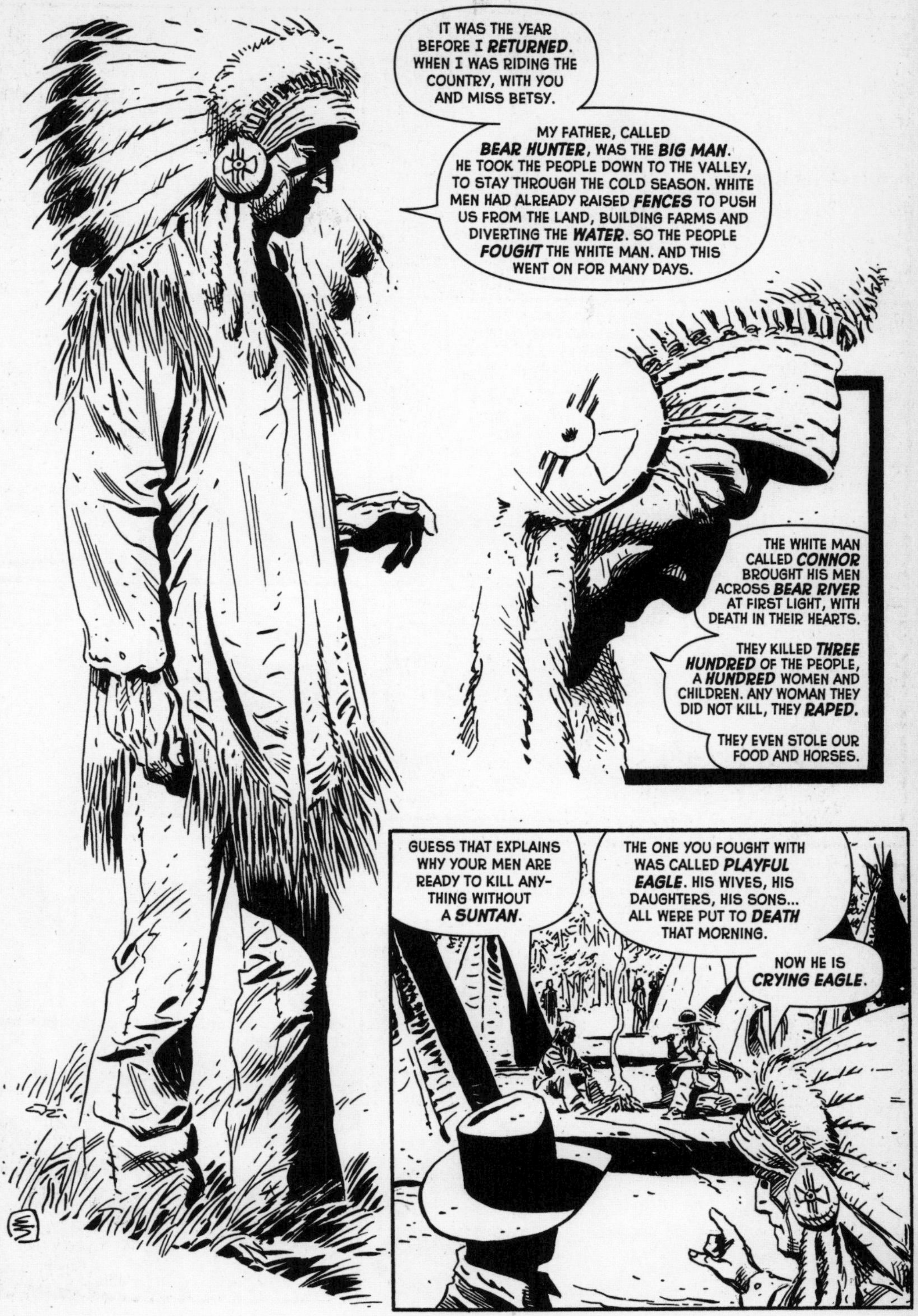
IT WAS THE YEAR BEFORE I RETURNED. WHEN I WAS RIDING THE COUNTRY, WITH YOU AND MISS BETSY.
MY FATHER, CALLED BEAR HUNTER, WAS THE BIG MAN. HE TOOK THE PEOPLE DOWN TO THE VALLEY, TO STAY THROUGH THE COLD SEASON. WHITE MEN HAD ALREADY RAISED FENCES TO PUSH US FROM THE LAND, BUILDING FARMS AND DIVERTING THE WATER. SO THE PEOPLE FOUGHT THE WHITE MAN. AND THIS WENT ON FOR MANY DAYS.
THE WHITE MAN CALLED CONNOR BROUGHT HIS MEN ACROSS BEAR RIVER AT FIRST LIGHT, WITH DEATH IN THEIR HEARTS.
THEY KILLED THREE HUNDRED OF THE PEOPLE, A HUNDRED WOMEN AND CHILDREN. ANY WOMAN THEY DID NOT KILL, THEY RAPED.
THEY EVEN STOLE OUR FOOD AND HORSES.
GUESS THAT EXPLAINS WHY YOUR MEN ARE READY TO KILL ANYTHING WITHOUT A SUNTAN.
THE ONE YOU FOUGHT WITH WAS CALLED PLAYFUL EAGLE. HIS WIVES, HIS DAUGHTERS, HIS SONS... ALL WERE PUT TO DEATH THAT MORNING.
NOW HE IS CRYING EAGLE.

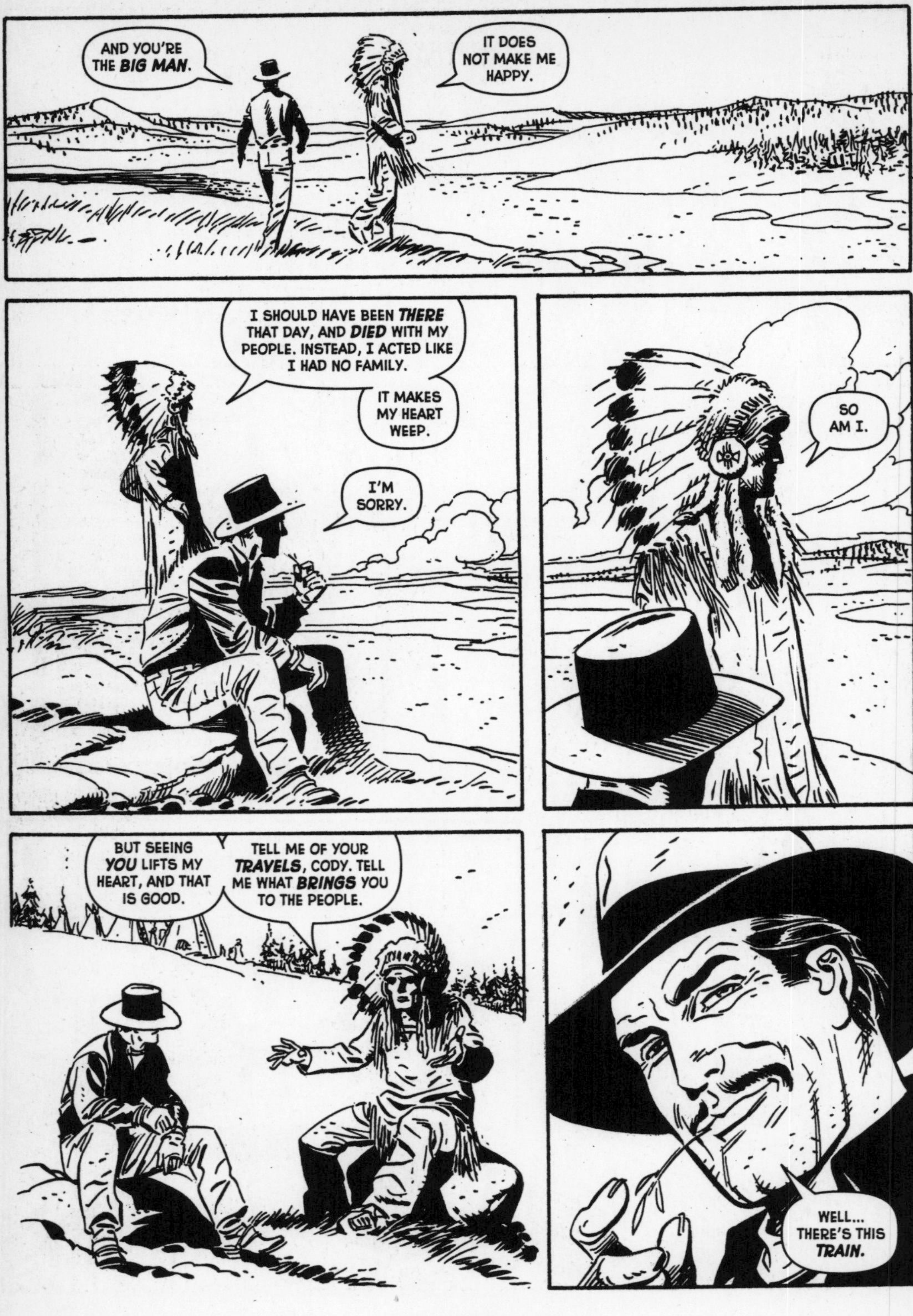
AND YOU'RE THE BIG MAN.
IT DOES NOT MAKE ME HAPPY.
I SHOULD HAVE BEEN THERE THAT DAY, AND DIED WITH MY PEOPLE. INSTEAD, I ACTED LIKE I HAD NO FAMILY.
IT MAKES MY HEART WEEP.
I'M SORRY.
SO AM I.
BUT SEEING YOU LIFTS MY HEART, AND THAT IS GOOD.
TELL ME OF YOUR TRAVELS, CODY. TELL ME WHAT BRINGS YOU TO THE PEOPLE.
WELL... THERE'S THIS TRAIN.

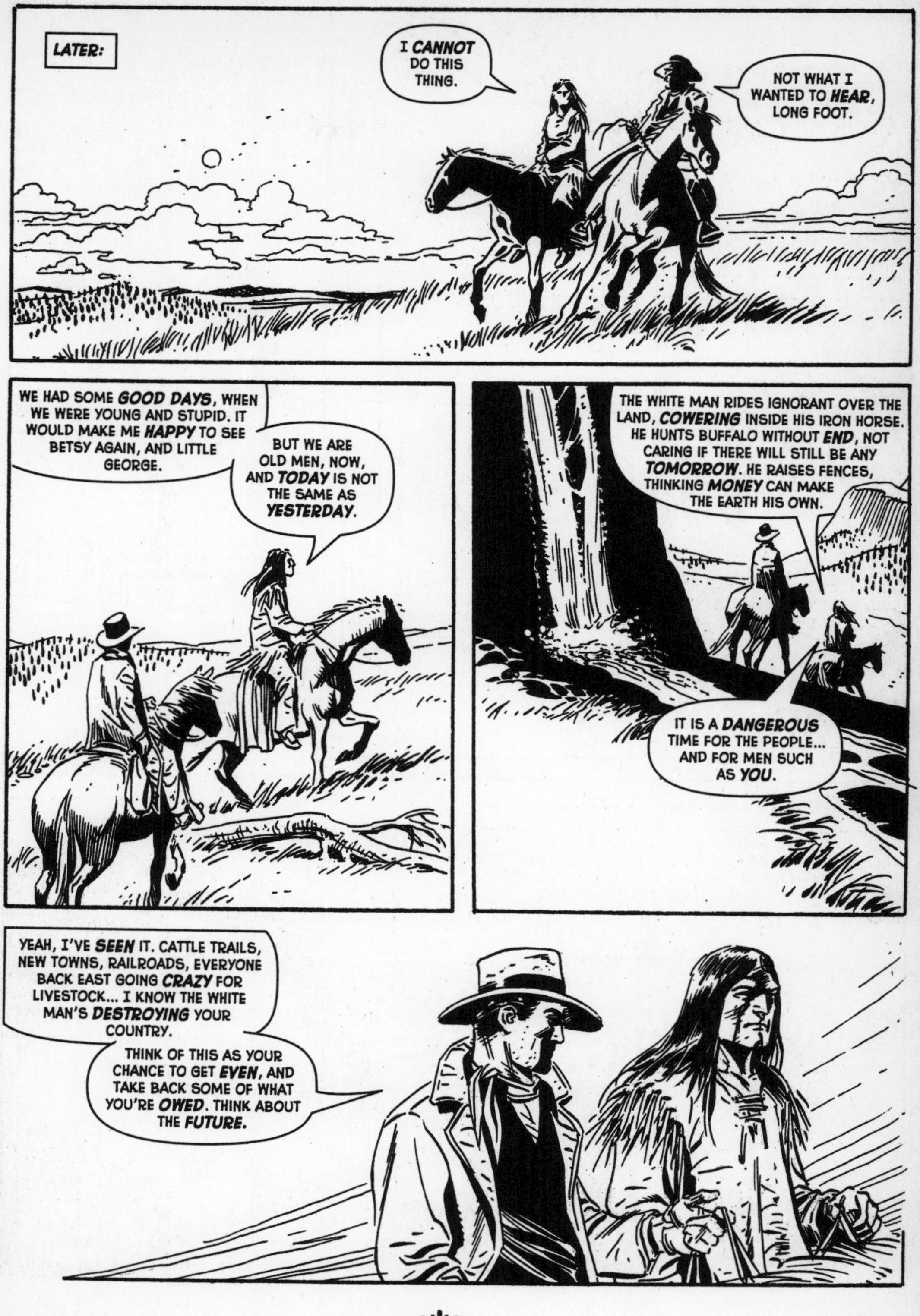
LATER:
I CANNOT DO THIS THING.
NOT WHAT I WANTED TO HEAR, LONG FOOT.
WE HAD SOME GOOD DAYS, WHEN WE WERE YOUNG AND STUPID. IT WOULD MAKE ME HAPPY TO SEE BETSY AGAIN, AND LITTLE GEORGE.
BUT WE ARE OLD MEN, NOW, AND TODAY IS NOT THE SAME AS YESTERDAY.
THE WHITE MAN RIDES IGNORANT OVER THE LAND, COWERING INSIDE HIS IRON HORSE. HE HUNTS BUFFALO WITHOUT END, NOT CARING IF THERE WILL STILL BE ANY TOMORROW. HE RAISES FENCES, THINKING MONEY CAN MAKE THE EARTH HIS OWN.
IT IS A DANGEROUS TIME FOR THE PEOPLE... AND FOR MEN SUCH AS YOU.
YEAH, I'VE SEEN IT. CATTLE TRAILS, NEW TOWNS, RAILROADS, EVERYONE BACK EAST GOING CRAZY FOR LIVESTOCK... I KNOW THE WHITE MAN'S DESTROYING YOUR COUNTRY.
THINK OF THIS AS YOUR CHANCE TO GET EVEN, AND TAKE BACK SOME OF WHAT YOU'RE OWED. THINK ABOUT THE FUTURE.

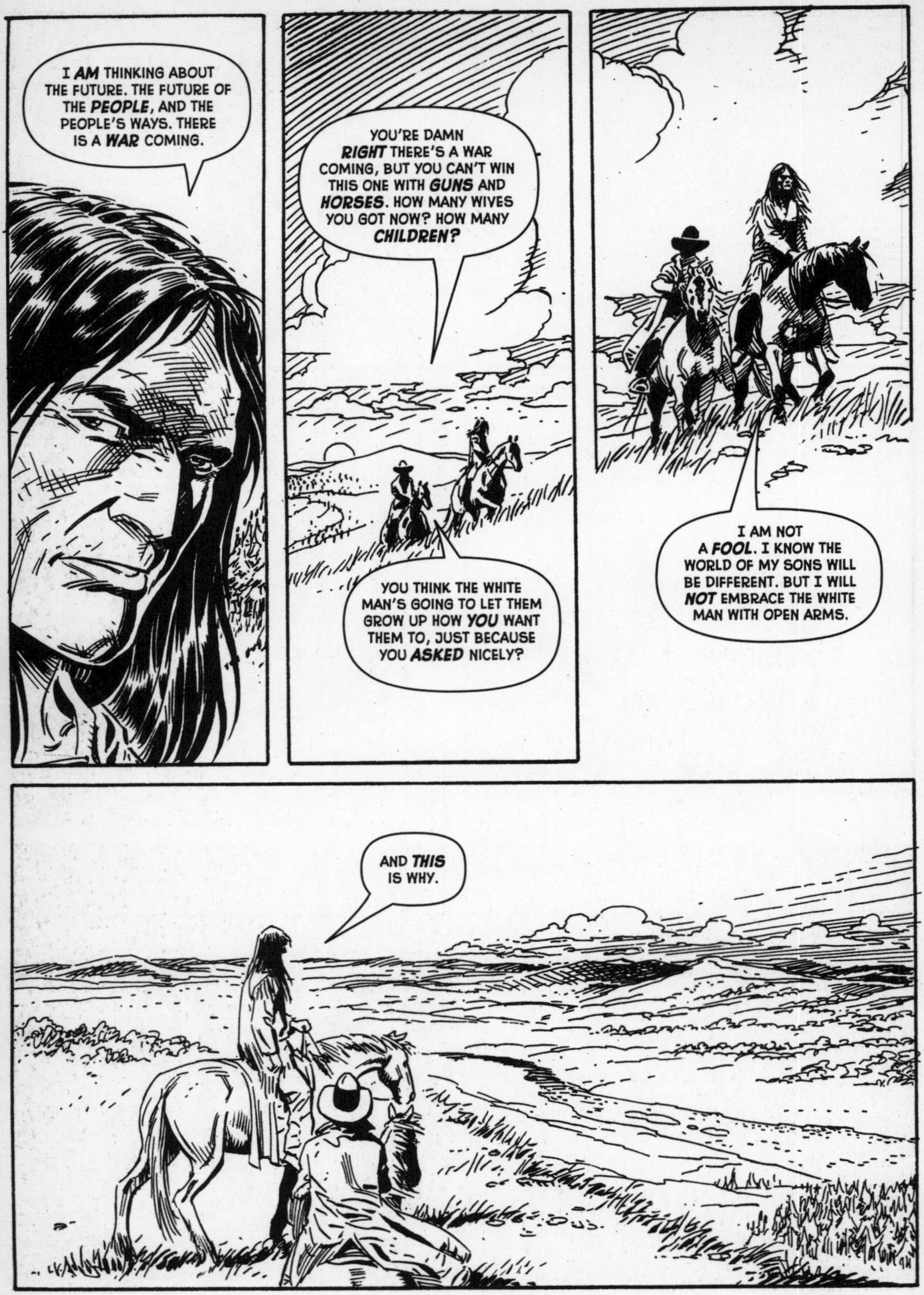
I AM THINKING ABOUT THE FUTURE. THE FUTURE OF THE PEOPLE, AND THE PEOPLE'S WAYS. THERE IS A WAR COMING.
YOU'RE DAMN RIGHT THERE'S A WAR COMING, BUT YOU CAN'T WIN THIS ONE WITH GUNS AND HORSES. HOW MANY WIVES YOU GOT NOW? HOW MANY CHILDREN?
YOU THINK THE WHITE MAN'S GOING TO LET THEM GROW UP HOW YOU WANT THEM TO, JUST BECAUSE YOU ASKED NICELY?
I AM NOT A FOOL. I KNOW THE WORLD OF MY SONS WILL BE DIFFERENT. BUT I WILL NOT EMBRACE THE WHITE MAN WITH OPEN ARMS.
AND THIS IS WHY.

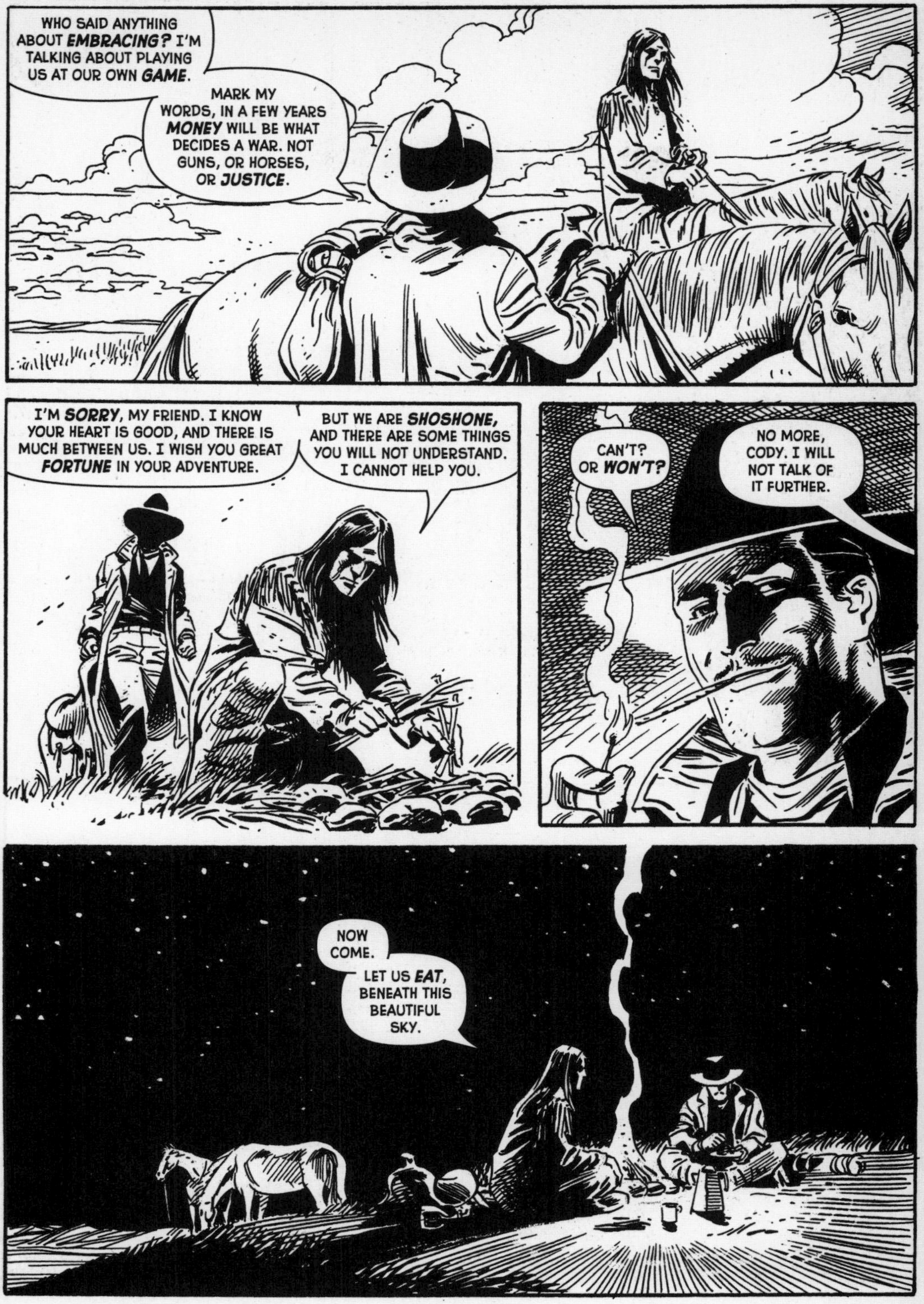
WHO SAID ANYTHING ABOUT EMBRACING? I'M TALKING ABOUT PLAYING US AT OUR OWN GAME.
MARK MY WORDS, IN A FEW YEARS MONEY WILL BE WHAT DECIDES A WAR. NOT GUNS, OR HORSES, OR JUSTICE.
I'M SORRY, MY FRIEND. I KNOW YOUR HEART IS GOOD, AND THERE IS MUCH BETWEEN US. I WISH YOU GREAT FORTUNE IN YOUR ADVENTURE.
BUT WE ARE SHOSHONE, AND THERE ARE SOME THINGS YOU WILL NOT UNDERSTAND. I CANNOT HELP YOU.
CAN'T? OR WON'T?
NO MORE, CODY. I WILL NOT TALK OF IT FURTHER.
NOW COME.
LET US EAT, BENEATH THIS BEAUTIFUL SKY.

SEVEN

★

"THE DRIVER"

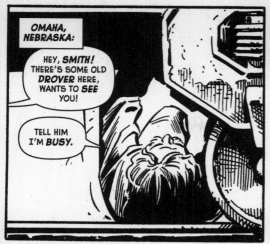

OMAHA, NEBRASKA:

HEY, *SMITH!* THERE'S SOME OLD *DROVER* HERE, WANTS TO *SEE* YOU!

TELL HIM I'M *BUSY.*

NO NEED. I CAN SEE THAT FOR *MYSELF.*

HOW YOU *DOING*, VIRGIL?

WELL, I'LL BE...

CODY PLUMMER.

FIXING TRAIN ENGINES? *SHAME* ON YOU, VIRG. A REAL *WASTE* OF YOUR TALENTS.

HEY, WATCH IT. I *LIKE* TRAINS.

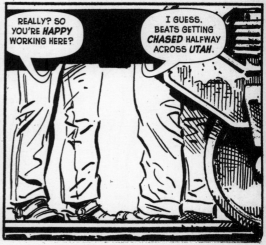

REALLY? SO YOU'RE *HAPPY* WORKING HERE?

I GUESS. BEATS GETTING *CHASED* HALFWAY ACROSS *UTAH.*

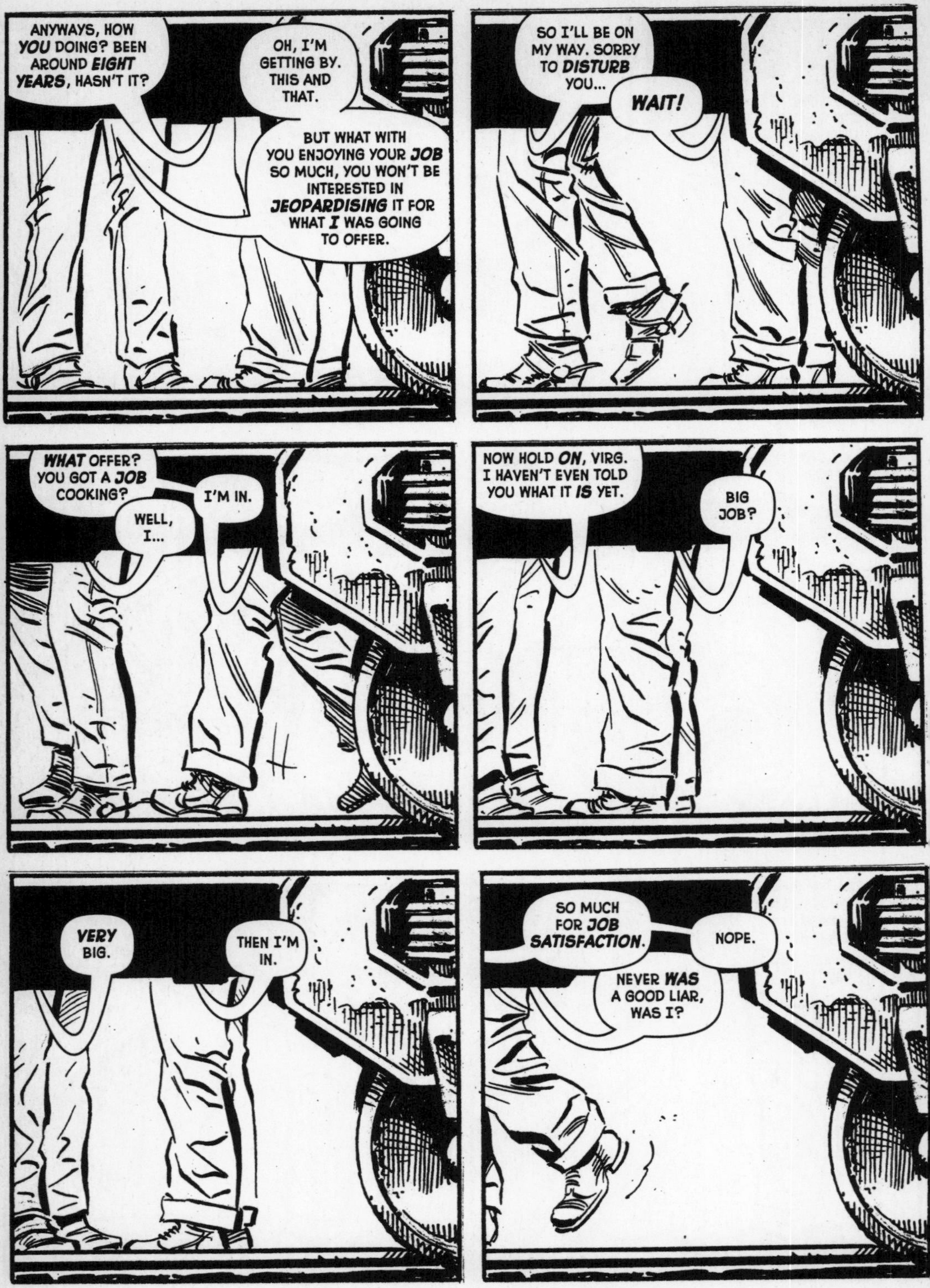
ANYWAYS, HOW YOU DOING? BEEN AROUND EIGHT YEARS, HASN'T IT?
OH, I'M GETTING BY. THIS AND THAT.
BUT WHAT WITH YOU ENJOYING YOUR JOB SO MUCH, YOU WON'T BE INTERESTED IN JEOPARDISING IT FOR WHAT I WAS GOING TO OFFER.
SO I'LL BE ON MY WAY. SORRY TO DISTURB YOU...
WAIT!
WHAT OFFER? YOU GOT A JOB COOKING?
WELL, I...
I'M IN.
NOW HOLD ON, VIRG. I HAVEN'T EVEN TOLD YOU WHAT IT IS YET.
BIG JOB?
VERY BIG.
THEN I'M IN.
SO MUCH FOR JOB SATISFACTION.
NOPE.
NEVER WAS A GOOD LIAR, WAS I?

EIGHT

★

"THE CHALLENGE"

CHICAGO:

EVERYONE HERE? ALL *RIGHT*, THEN.

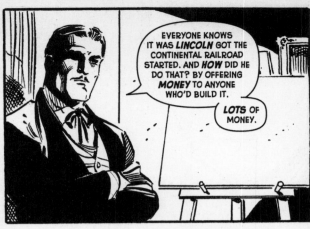

EVERYONE KNOWS IT WAS *LINCOLN* GOT THE CONTINENTAL RAILROAD STARTED. AND *HOW* DID HE DO THAT? BY OFFERING *MONEY* TO ANYONE WHO'D BUILD IT.

LOTS OF MONEY.

THE *RAILWAYS ACT* AUTHORISED *SIXTEEN THOUSAND DOLLARS PER MILE* TO BUILDERS FOR THE RAILROAD ACROSS THE PLAINS. FOR THE MOUNTAINS, THAT WENT UP TO *FORTY-EIGHT THOUSAND* PER MILE.

THE *CENTRAL PACIFIC* COMPANY BUILT *SIX HUNDRED AND NINETY* MILES OF TRACK, ALMOST HALF IT OVER THE MOUNTAINS.

I'M SURE *GEORGE* HAS ALREADY WORKED IT OUT, BUT FOR THE REST OF YOU...

..THAT'S *NINETEEN MILLION DOLLARS.*

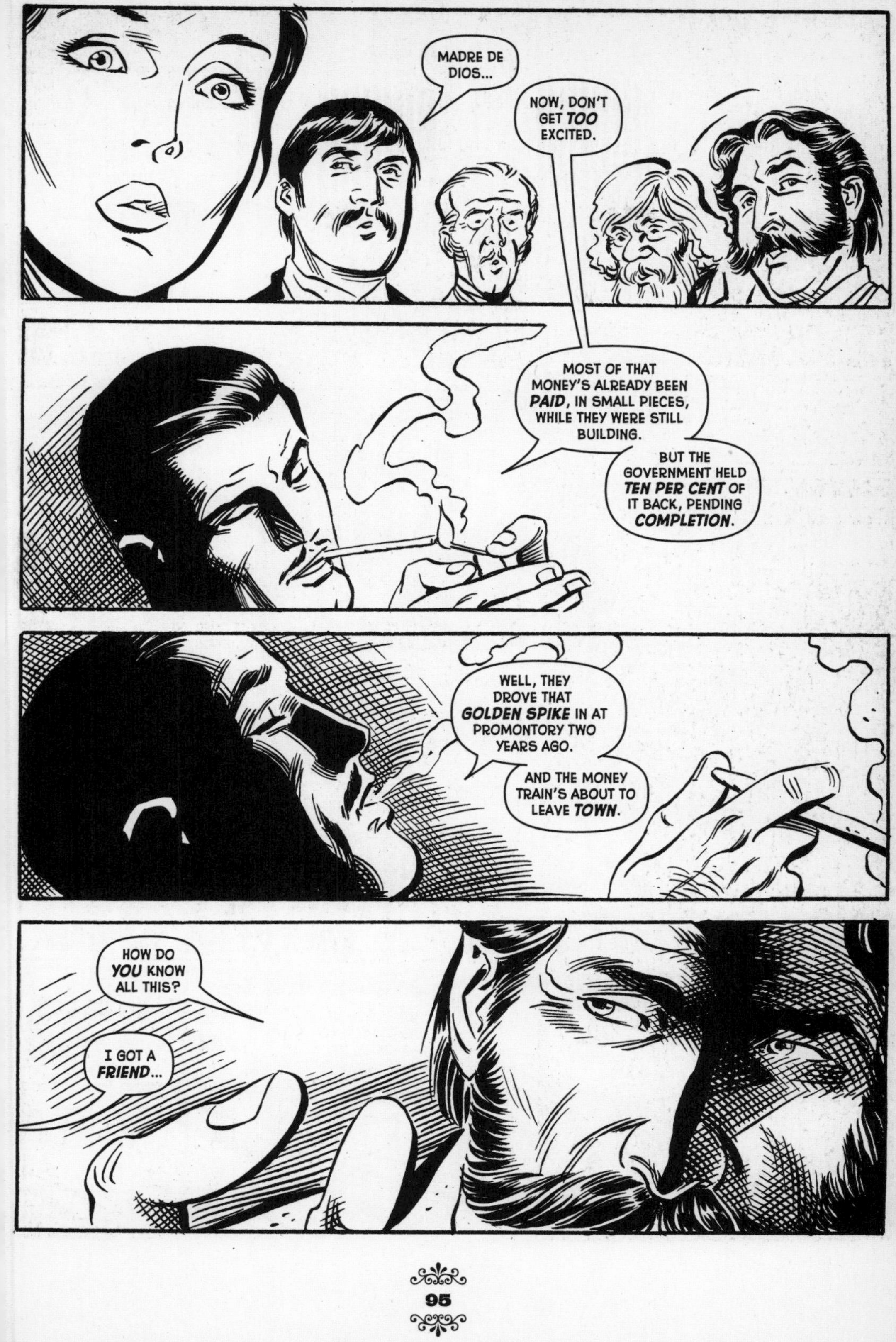
MADRE DE DIOS...
NOW, DON'T GET TOO EXCITED.
MOST OF THAT MONEY'S ALREADY BEEN PAID, IN SMALL PIECES, WHILE THEY WERE STILL BUILDING.
BUT THE GOVERNMENT HELD TEN PER CENT OF IT BACK, PENDING COMPLETION.
WELL, THEY DROVE THAT GOLDEN SPIKE IN AT PROMONTORY TWO YEARS AGO.
AND THE MONEY TRAIN'S ABOUT TO LEAVE TOWN.
HOW DO YOU KNOW ALL THIS?
I GOT A FRIEND...

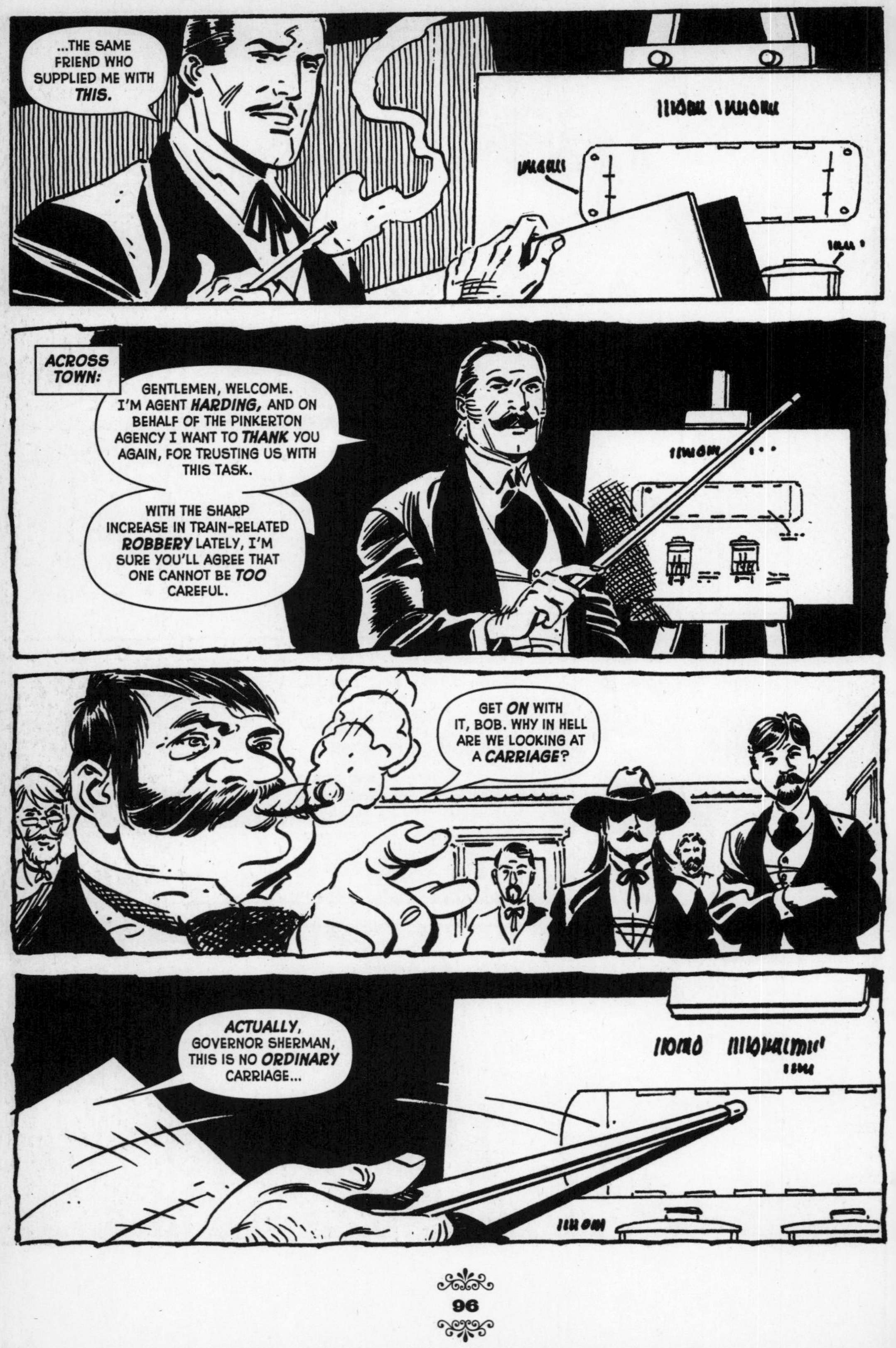
...THE SAME FRIEND WHO SUPPLIED ME WITH THIS.
ACROSS TOWN:
GENTLEMEN, WELCOME. I'M AGENT HARDING, AND ON BEHALF OF THE PINKERTON AGENCY I WANT TO THANK YOU AGAIN, FOR TRUSTING US WITH THIS TASK.
WITH THE SHARP INCREASE IN TRAIN-RELATED ROBBERY LATELY, I'M SURE YOU'LL AGREE THAT ONE CANNOT BE TOO CAREFUL.
GET ON WITH IT, BOB. WHY IN HELL ARE WE LOOKING AT A CARRIAGE?
ACTUALLY, GOVERNOR SHERMAN, THIS IS NO ORDINARY CARRIAGE...

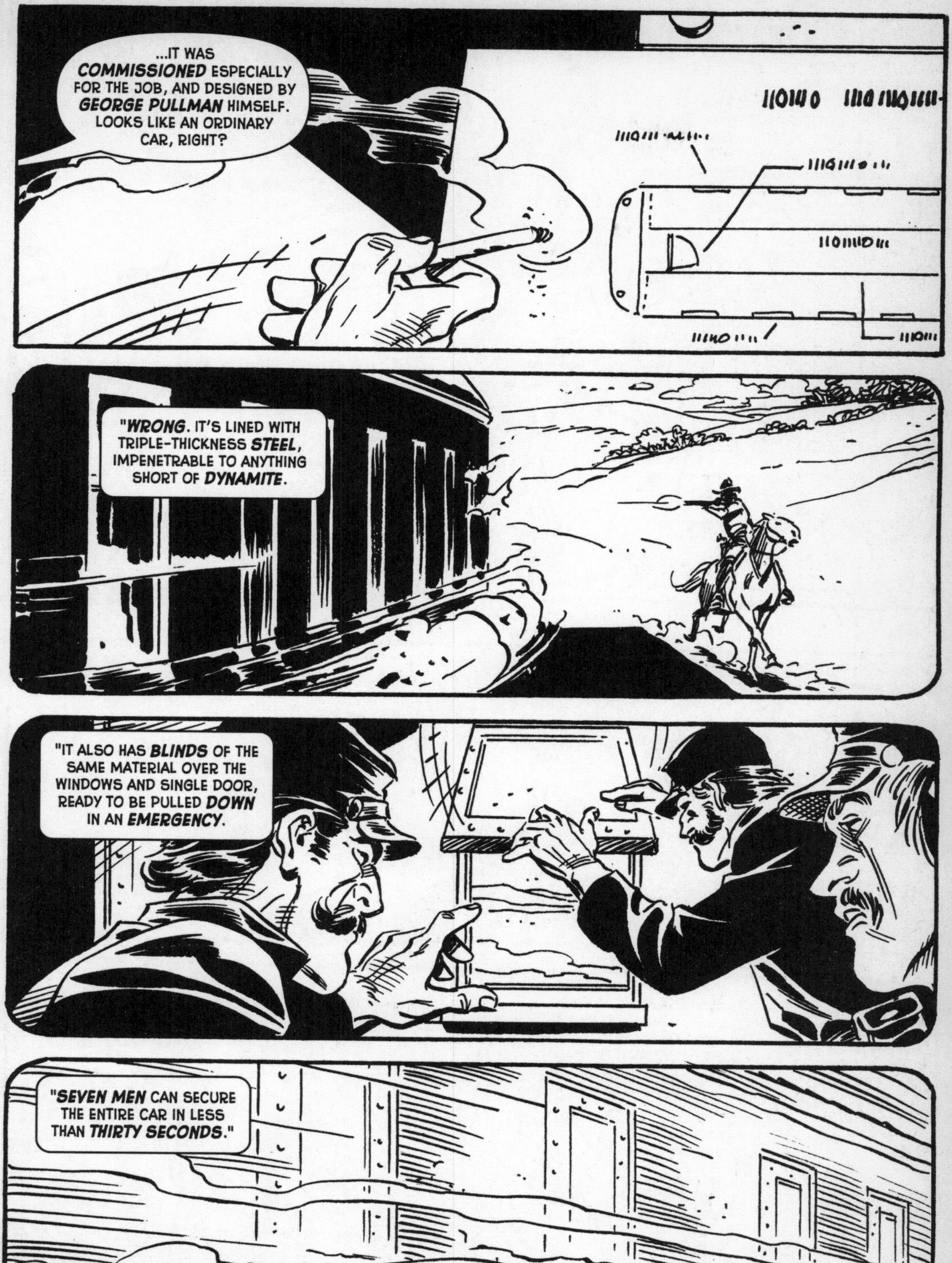

...IT WAS COMMISSIONED ESPECIALLY FOR THE JOB, AND DESIGNED BY GEORGE PULLMAN HIMSELF. LOOKS LIKE AN ORDINARY CAR, RIGHT?
"WRONG. IT'S LINED WITH TRIPLE-THICKNESS STEEL, IMPENETRABLE TO ANYTHING SHORT OF DYNAMITE.
"IT ALSO HAS BLINDS OF THE SAME MATERIAL OVER THE WINDOWS AND SINGLE DOOR, READY TO BE PULLED DOWN IN AN EMERGENCY.
"SEVEN MEN CAN SECURE THE ENTIRE CAR IN LESS THAN THIRTY SECONDS."

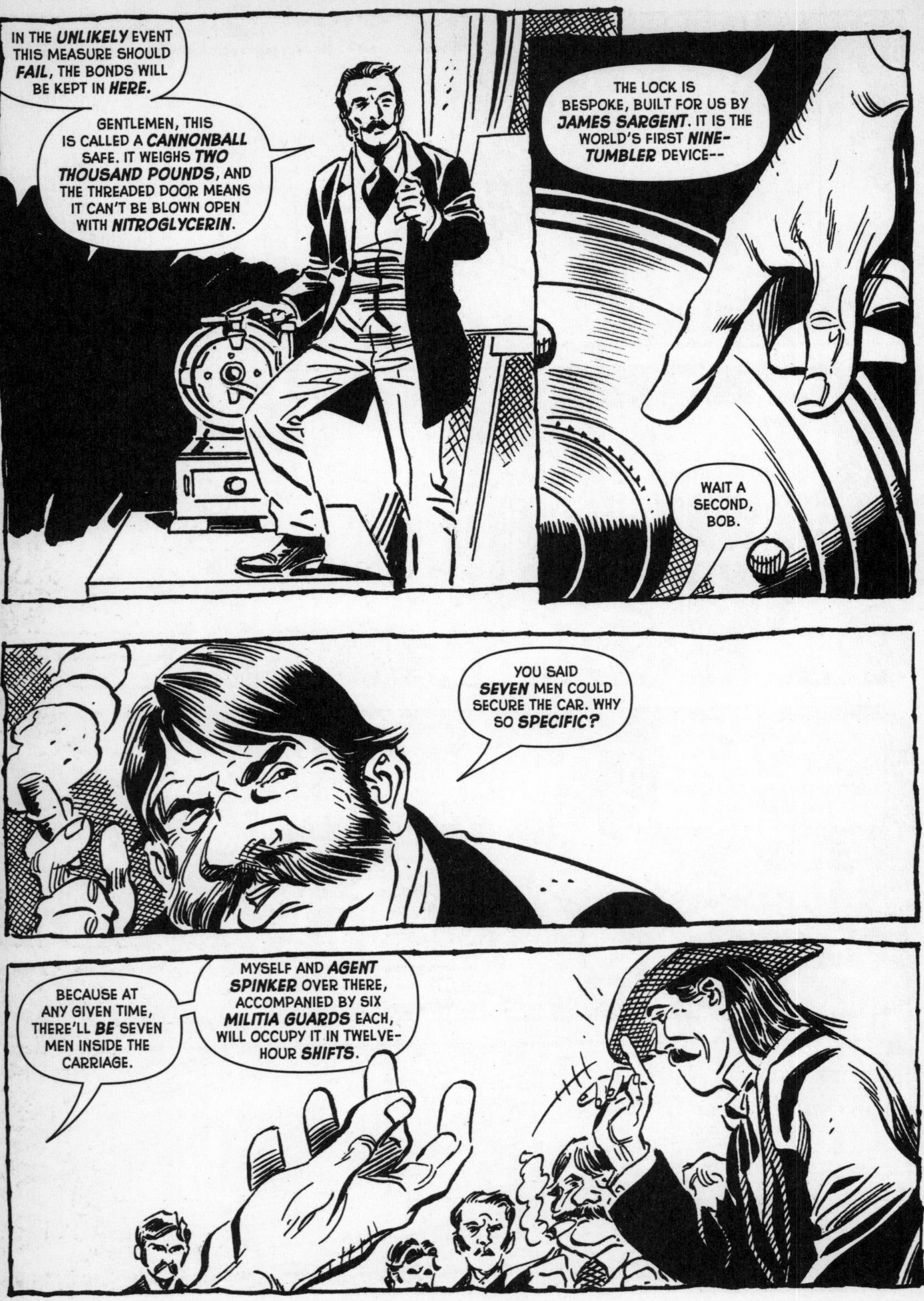
IN THE UNLIKELY EVENT THIS MEASURE SHOULD FAIL, THE BONDS WILL BE KEPT IN HERE.
GENTLEMEN, THIS IS CALLED A CANNONBALL SAFE. IT WEIGHS TWO THOUSAND POUNDS, AND THE THREADED DOOR MEANS IT CAN'T BE BLOWN OPEN WITH NITROGLYCERIN.
THE LOCK IS BESPOKE, BUILT FOR US BY JAMES SARGENT. IT IS THE WORLD'S FIRST NINE-TUMBLER DEVICE--
WAIT A SECOND, BOB.
YOU SAID SEVEN MEN COULD SECURE THE CAR. WHY SO SPECIFIC?
BECAUSE AT ANY GIVEN TIME, THERE'LL BE SEVEN MEN INSIDE THE CARRIAGE.
MYSELF AND AGENT SPINKER OVER THERE, ACCOMPANIED BY SIX MILITIA GUARDS EACH, WILL OCCUPY IT IN TWELVE-HOUR SHIFTS.

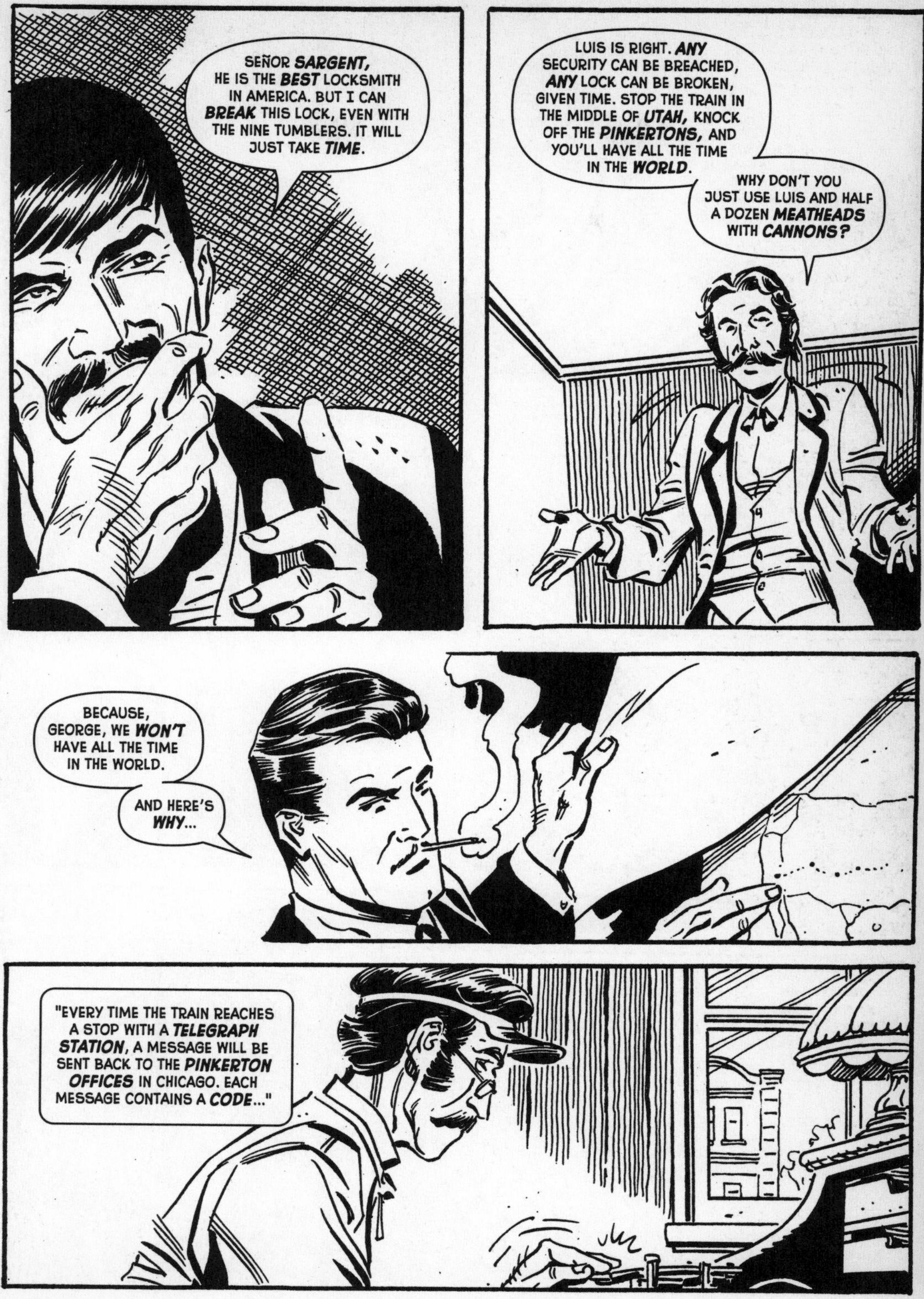
SEÑOR SARGENT, HE IS THE BEST LOCKSMITH IN AMERICA. BUT I CAN BREAK THIS LOCK, EVEN WITH THE NINE TUMBLERS. IT WILL JUST TAKE TIME.
LUIS IS RIGHT. ANY SECURITY CAN BE BREACHED, ANY LOCK CAN BE BROKEN, GIVEN TIME. STOP THE TRAIN IN THE MIDDLE OF UTAH, KNOCK OFF THE PINKERTONS, AND YOU'LL HAVE ALL THE TIME IN THE WORLD.
WHY DON'T YOU JUST USE LUIS AND HALF A DOZEN MEATHEADS WITH CANNONS?
BECAUSE, GEORGE, WE WON'T HAVE ALL THE TIME IN THE WORLD.
AND HERE'S WHY...
"EVERY TIME THE TRAIN REACHES A STOP WITH A TELEGRAPH STATION, A MESSAGE WILL BE SENT BACK TO THE PINKERTON OFFICES IN CHICAGO. EACH MESSAGE CONTAINS A CODE..."

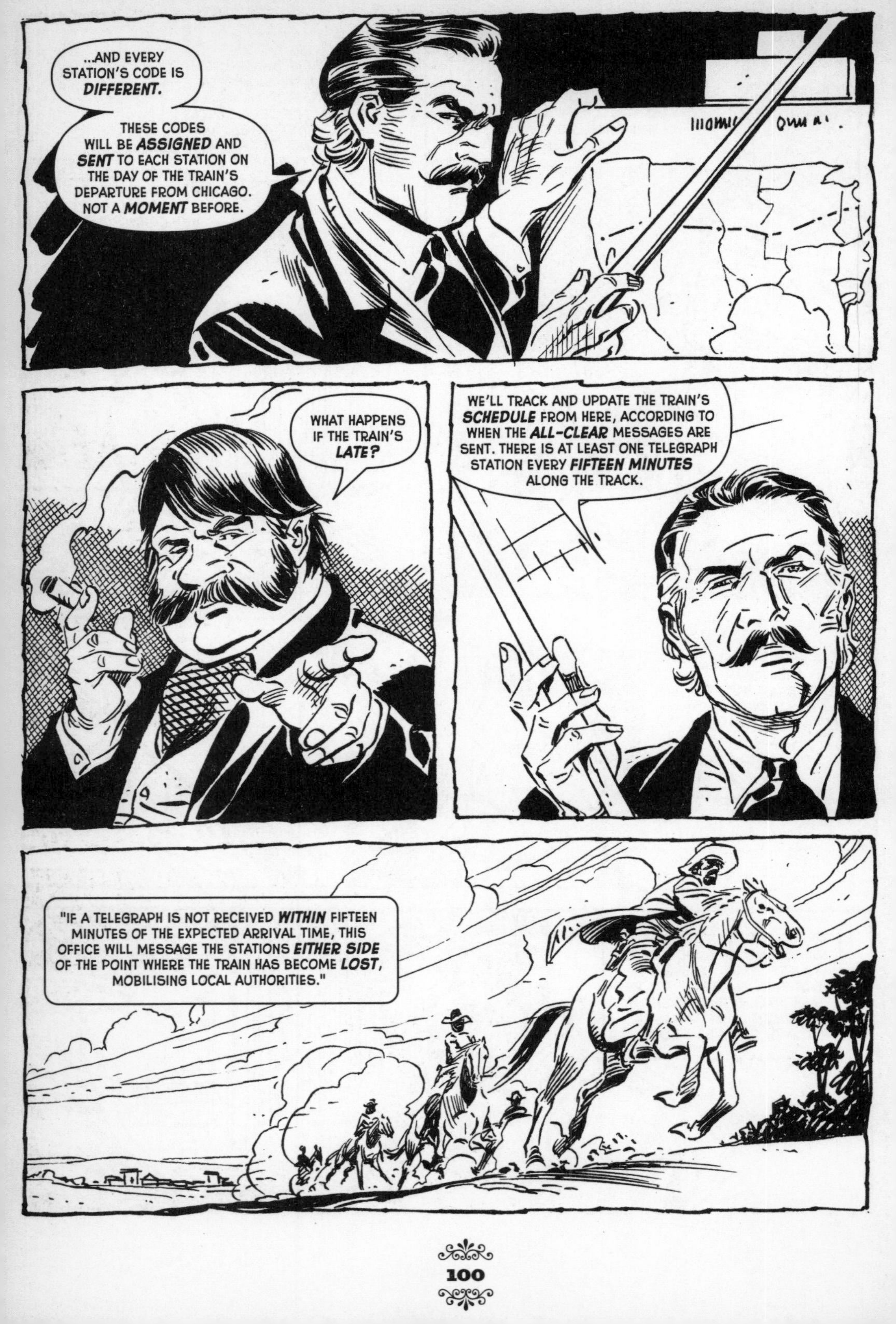
...AND EVERY STATION'S CODE IS DIFFERENT.
THESE CODES WILL BE ASSIGNED AND SENT TO EACH STATION ON THE DAY OF THE TRAIN'S DEPARTURE FROM CHICAGO. NOT A MOMENT BEFORE.
WHAT HAPPENS IF THE TRAIN'S LATE?
WE'LL TRACK AND UPDATE THE TRAIN'S SCHEDULE FROM HERE, ACCORDING TO WHEN THE ALL-CLEAR MESSAGES ARE SENT. THERE IS AT LEAST ONE TELEGRAPH STATION EVERY FIFTEEN MINUTES ALONG THE TRACK.
"IF A TELEGRAPH IS NOT RECEIVED WITHIN FIFTEEN MINUTES OF THE EXPECTED ARRIVAL TIME, THIS OFFICE WILL MESSAGE THE STATIONS EITHER SIDE OF THE POINT WHERE THE TRAIN HAS BECOME LOST, MOBILISING LOCAL AUTHORITIES."

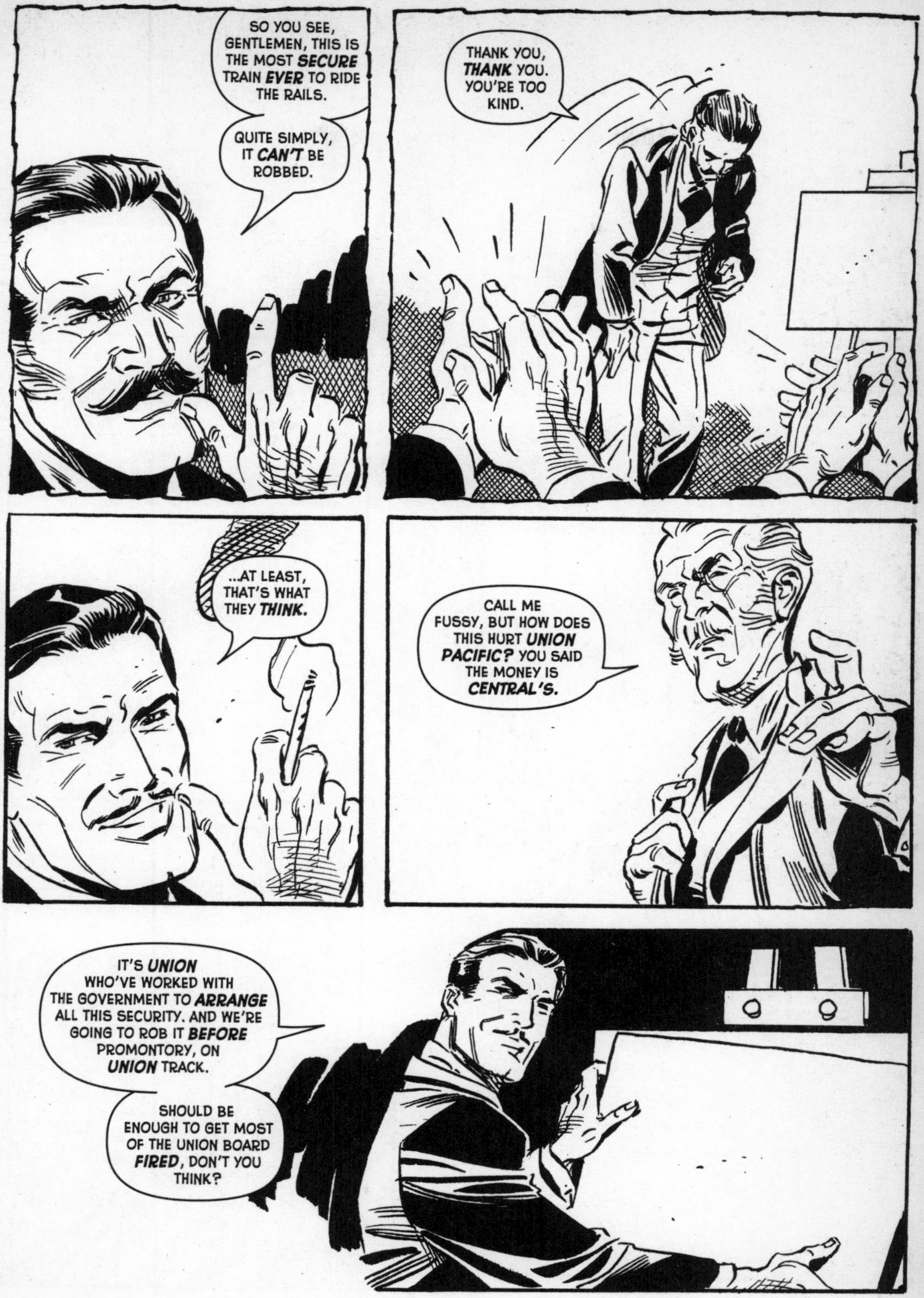
SO YOU SEE, GENTLEMEN, THIS IS THE MOST SECURE TRAIN EVER TO RIDE THE RAILS.
QUITE SIMPLY, IT CAN'T BE ROBBED.
THANK YOU, THANK YOU. YOU'RE TOO KIND.
...AT LEAST, THAT'S WHAT THEY THINK.
CALL ME FUSSY, BUT HOW DOES THIS HURT UNION PACIFIC? YOU SAID THE MONEY IS CENTRAL'S.
IT'S UNION WHO'VE WORKED WITH THE GOVERNMENT TO ARRANGE ALL THIS SECURITY. AND WE'RE GOING TO ROB IT BEFORE PROMONTORY, ON UNION TRACK.
SHOULD BE ENOUGH TO GET MOST OF THE UNION BOARD FIRED, DON'T YOU THINK?

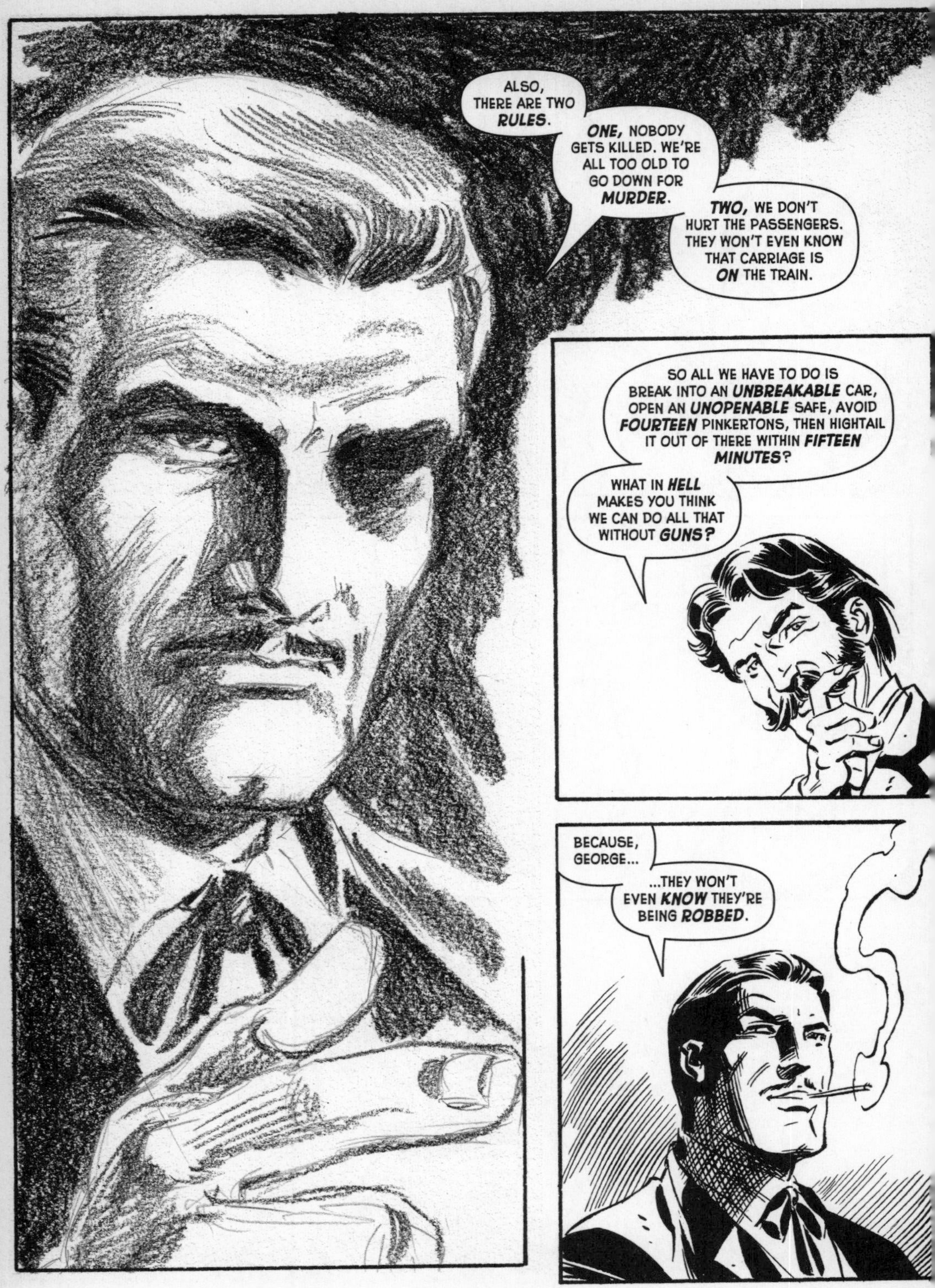
ALSO, THERE ARE TWO RULES.
ONE, NOBODY GETS KILLED. WE'RE ALL TOO OLD TO GO DOWN FOR MURDER.
TWO, WE DON'T HURT THE PASSENGERS. THEY WON'T EVEN KNOW THAT CARRIAGE IS ON THE TRAIN.
SO ALL WE HAVE TO DO IS BREAK INTO AN UNBREAKABLE CAR, OPEN AN UNOPENABLE SAFE, AVOID FOURTEEN PINKERTONS, THEN HIGHTAIL IT OUT OF THERE WITHIN FIFTEEN MINUTES?
WHAT IN HELL MAKES YOU THINK WE CAN DO ALL THAT WITHOUT GUNS?
BECAUSE, GEORGE...
...THEY WON'T EVEN KNOW THEY'RE BEING ROBBED.

NINE

★

"THE JOB"

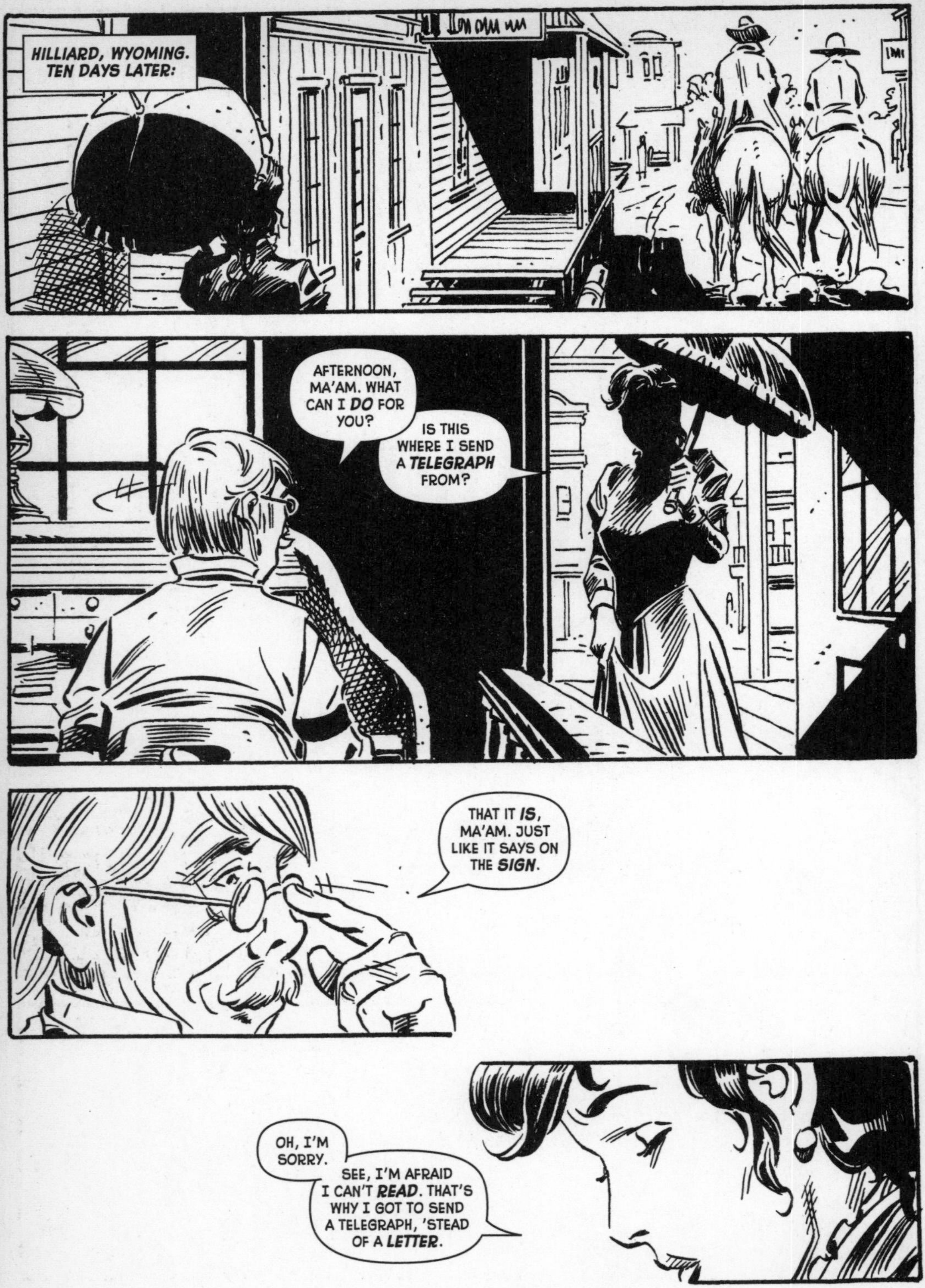
HILLIARD, WYOMING. TEN DAYS LATER:
AFTERNOON, MA'AM. WHAT CAN I DO FOR YOU?
IS THIS WHERE I SEND A TELEGRAPH FROM?
THAT IT IS, MA'AM. JUST LIKE IT SAYS ON THE SIGN.
OH, I'M SORRY.
SEE, I'M AFRAID I CAN'T READ. THAT'S WHY I GOT TO SEND A TELEGRAPH, 'STEAD OF A LETTER.

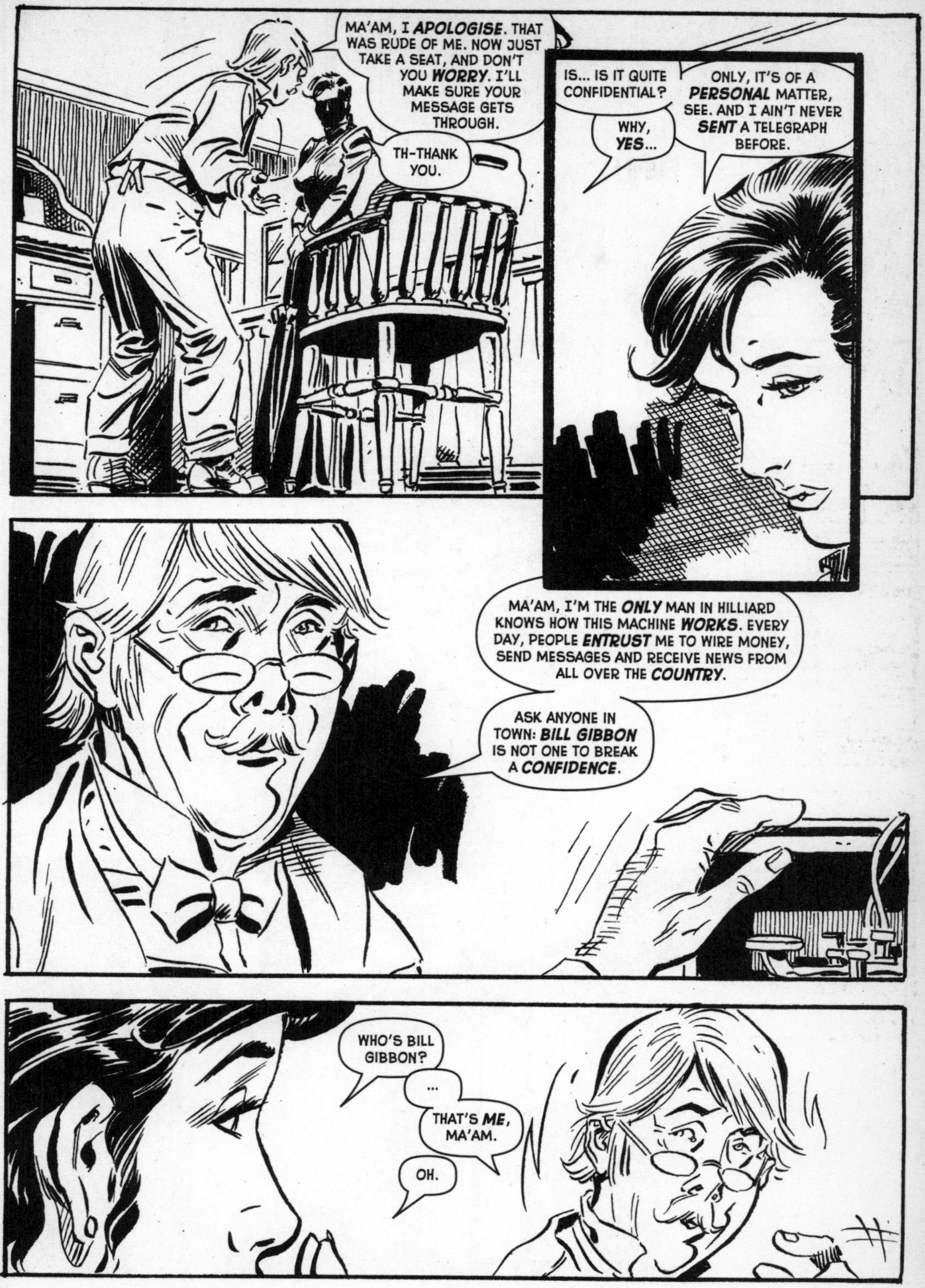
MA'AM, I APOLOGISE. THAT WAS RUDE OF ME. NOW JUST TAKE A SEAT, AND DON'T YOU WORRY. I'LL MAKE SURE YOUR MESSAGE GETS THROUGH.
TH-THANK YOU.
ONLY, IT'S OF A PERSONAL MATTER, SEE. AND I AIN'T NEVER SENT A TELEGRAPH BEFORE.
IS... IS IT QUITE CONFIDENTIAL?
WHY, YES...
MA'AM, I'M THE ONLY MAN IN HILLIARD KNOWS HOW THIS MACHINE WORKS. EVERY DAY, PEOPLE ENTRUST ME TO WIRE MONEY, SEND MESSAGES AND RECEIVE NEWS FROM ALL OVER THE COUNTRY.
ASK ANYONE IN TOWN: BILL GIBBON IS NOT ONE TO BREAK A CONFIDENCE.
WHO'S BILL GIBBON?
...
THAT'S ME, MA'AM.
OH.

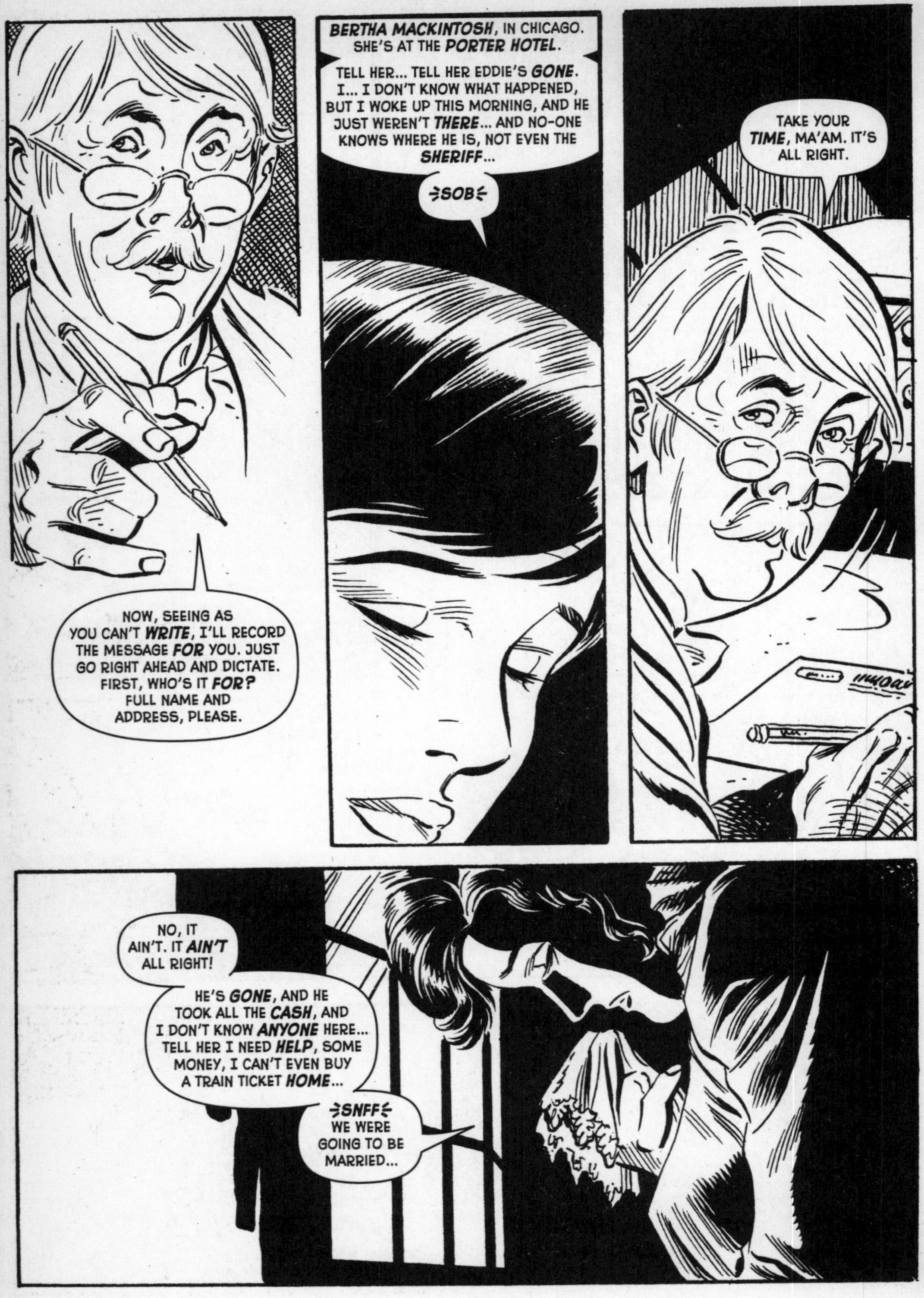
NOW, SEEING AS YOU CAN'T WRITE, I'LL RECORD THE MESSAGE FOR YOU. JUST GO RIGHT AHEAD AND DICTATE. FIRST, WHO'S IT FOR? FULL NAME AND ADDRESS, PLEASE.
BERTHA MACKINTOSH, IN CHICAGO. SHE'S AT THE PORTER HOTEL.
TELL HER... TELL HER EDDIE'S GONE. I... I DON'T KNOW WHAT HAPPENED, BUT I WOKE UP THIS MORNING, AND HE JUST WEREN'T THERE... AND NO-ONE KNOWS WHERE HE IS, NOT EVEN THE SHERIFF...
SOB
TAKE YOUR TIME, MA'AM. IT'S ALL RIGHT.
NO, IT AIN'T. IT AIN'T ALL RIGHT!
HE'S GONE, AND HE TOOK ALL THE CASH, AND I DON'T KNOW ANYONE HERE... TELL HER I NEED HELP, SOME MONEY, I CAN'T EVEN BUY A TRAIN TICKET HOME...
SNFF WE WERE GOING TO BE MARRIED...

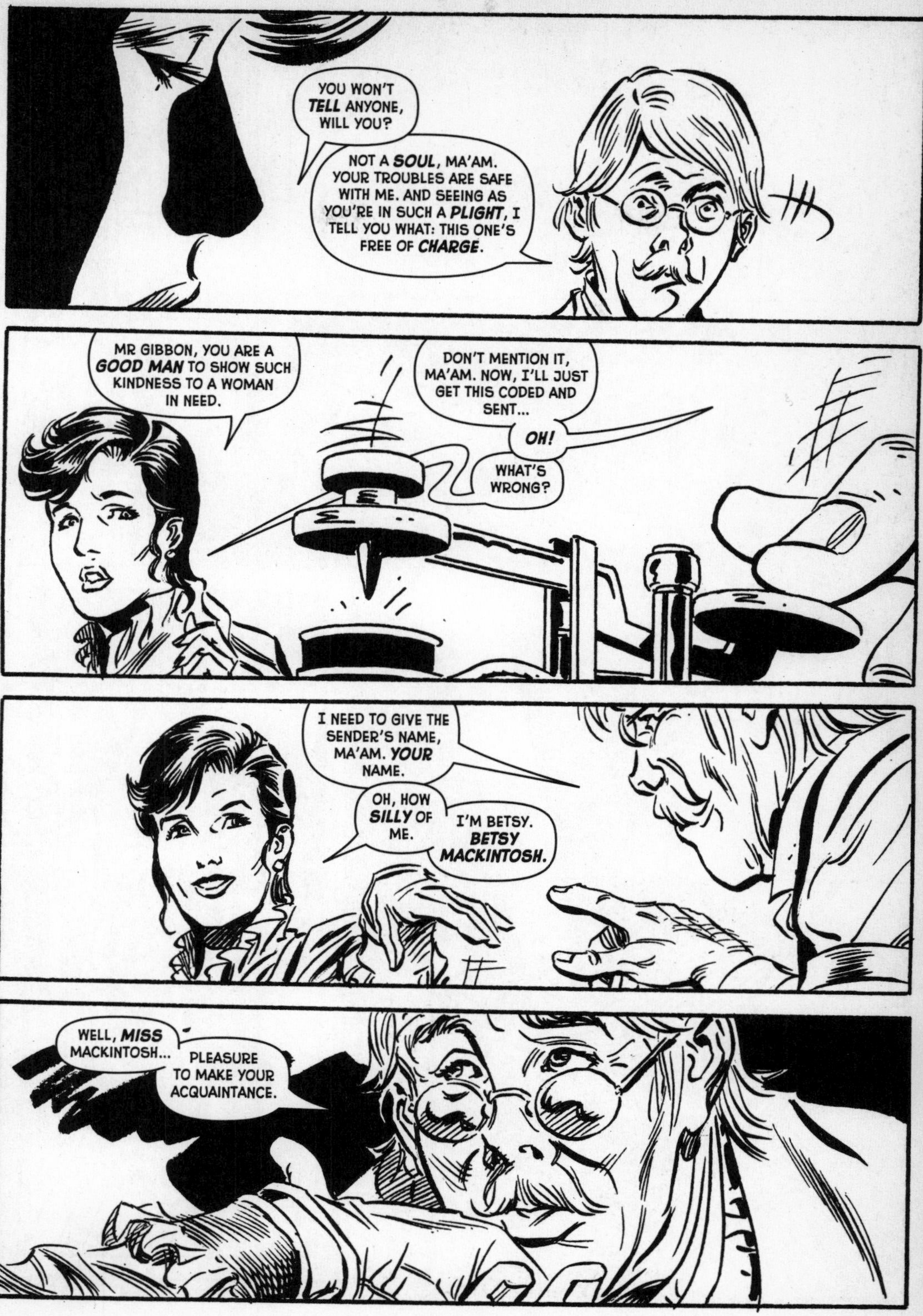

YOU WON'T TELL ANYONE, WILL YOU?
NOT A SOUL, MA'AM. YOUR TROUBLES ARE SAFE WITH ME. AND SEEING AS YOU'RE IN SUCH A PLIGHT, I TELL YOU WHAT: THIS ONE'S FREE OF CHARGE.
MR GIBBON, YOU ARE A GOOD MAN TO SHOW SUCH KINDNESS TO A WOMAN IN NEED.
DON'T MENTION IT, MA'AM. NOW, I'LL JUST GET THIS CODED AND SENT...
OH!
WHAT'S WRONG?
I NEED TO GIVE THE SENDER'S NAME, MA'AM. YOUR NAME.
OH, HOW SILLY OF ME.
I'M BETSY. BETSY MACKINTOSH.
WELL, MISS MACKINTOSH...
PLEASURE TO MAKE YOUR ACQUAINTANCE.

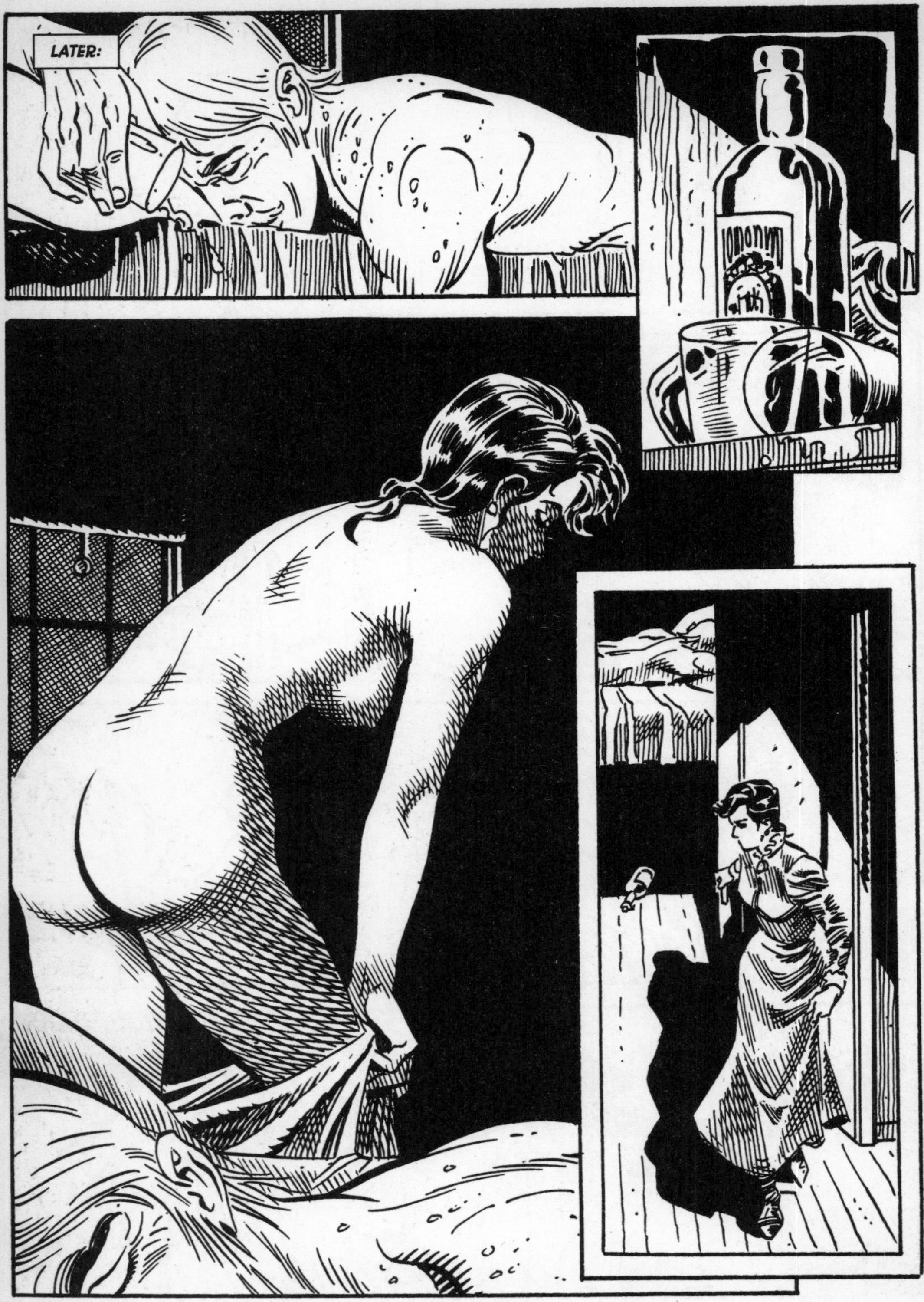
LATER:

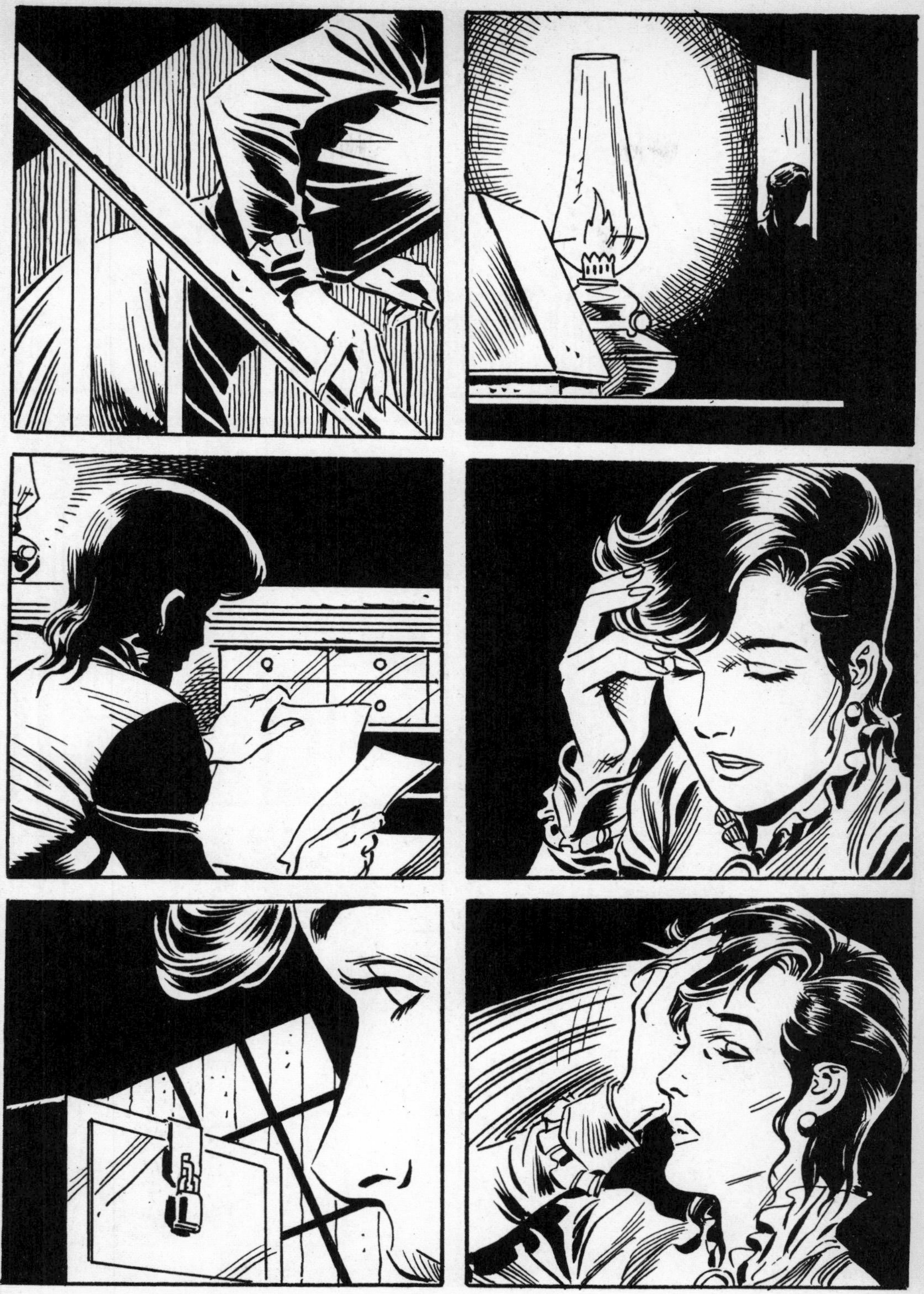

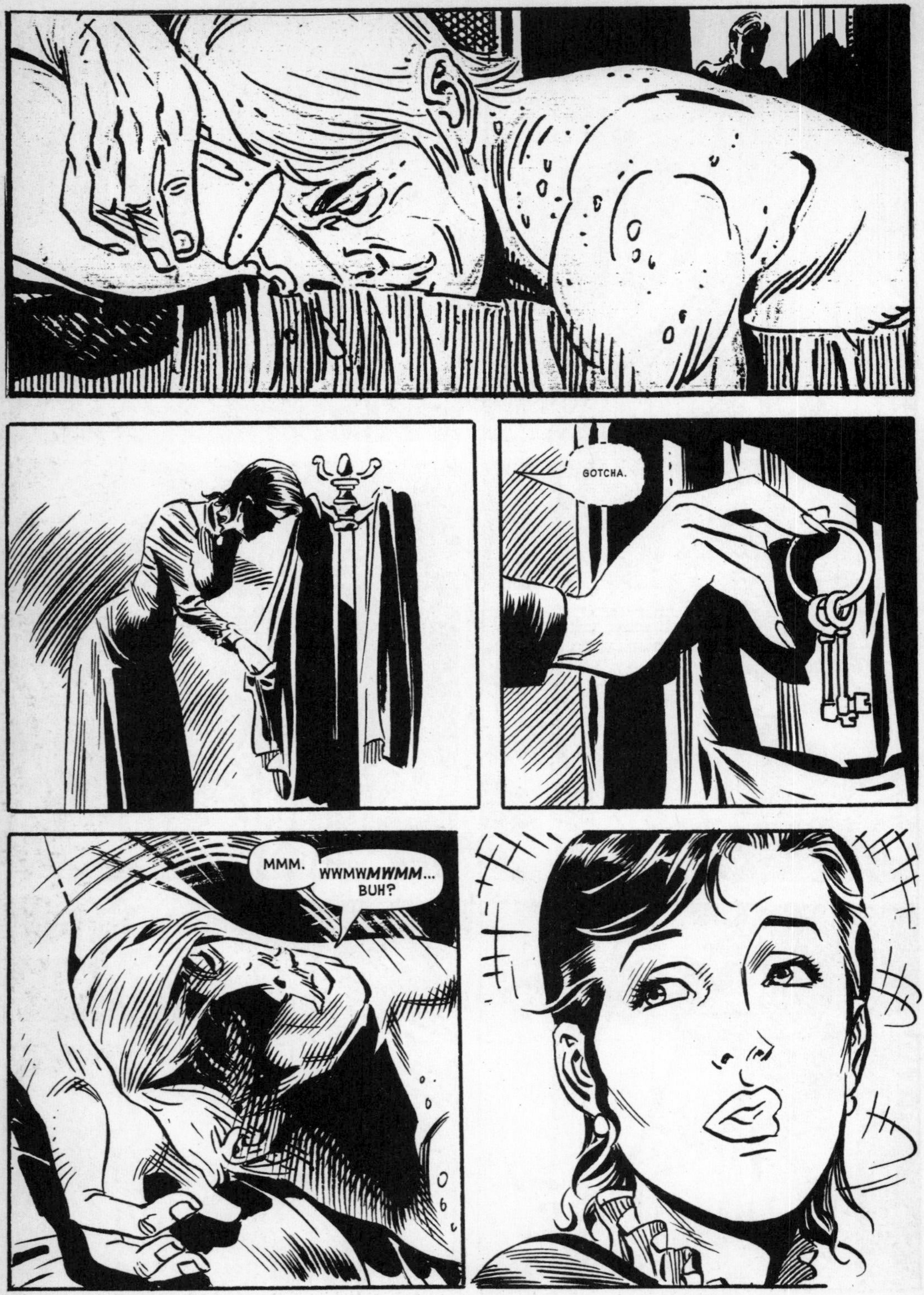
GOTCHA.
MMM.
WWMWMWMM... BUH?

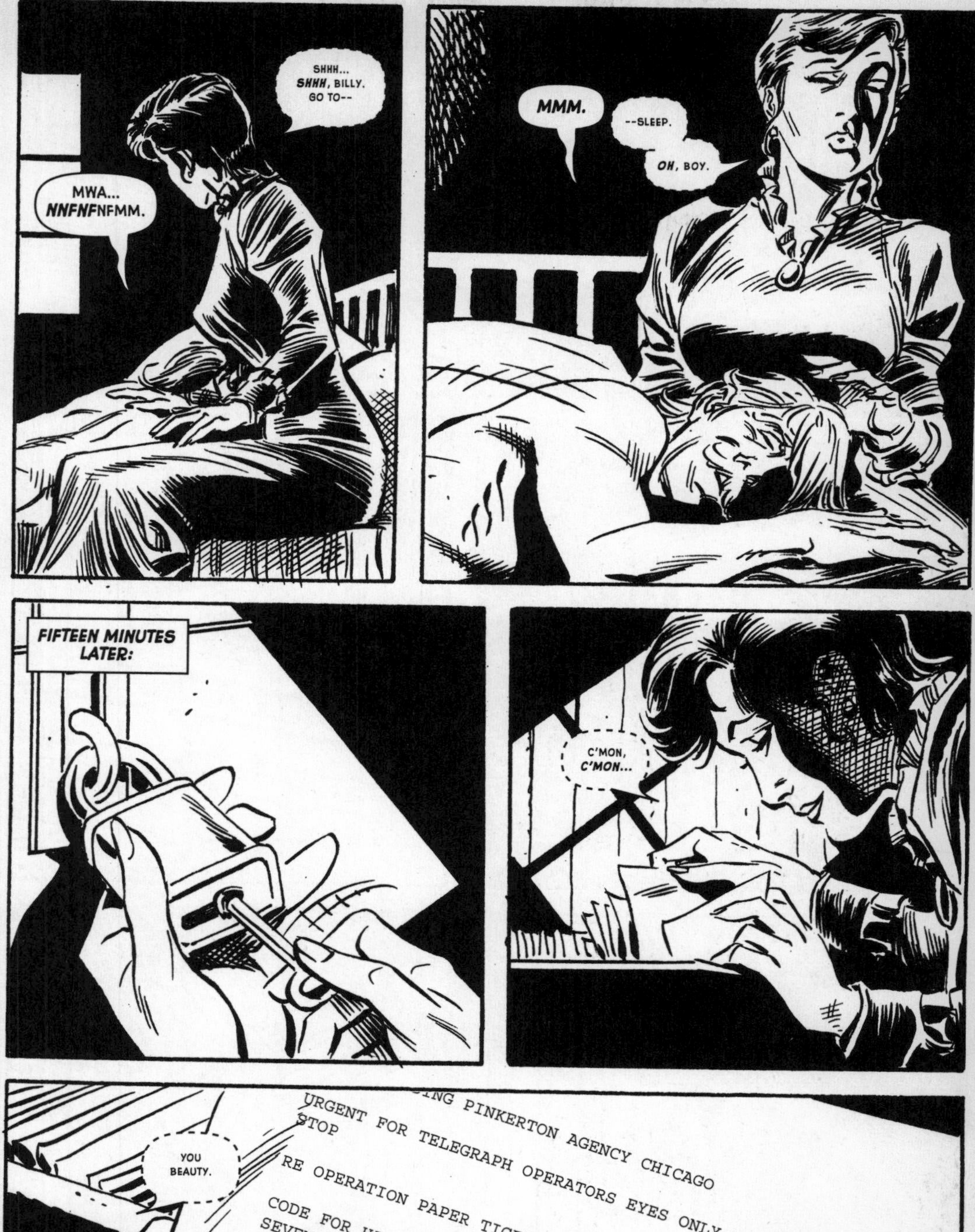

SHHH... SHHH, BILLY. GO TO--
MWA... NNFNFNFMM.
MMM.
--SLEEP.
OH, BOY.
FIFTEEN MINUTES LATER:
C'MON, C'MON...
YOU BEAUTY.
ING PINKERTON AGENCY CHICAGO
URGENT FOR TELEGRAPH OPERATORS EYES ONLY MAXIMUM SECURITY
STOP
RE OPERATION PAPER TIGER STOP
CODE FOR HILLIARD WYOMING STATION IS AITCH ONE
SEVEN OH FOUR ONE FIVE AR AITCH STOP

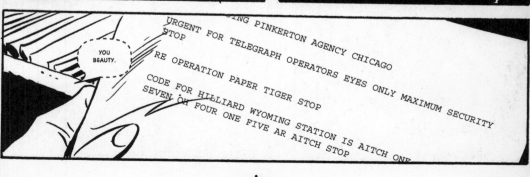

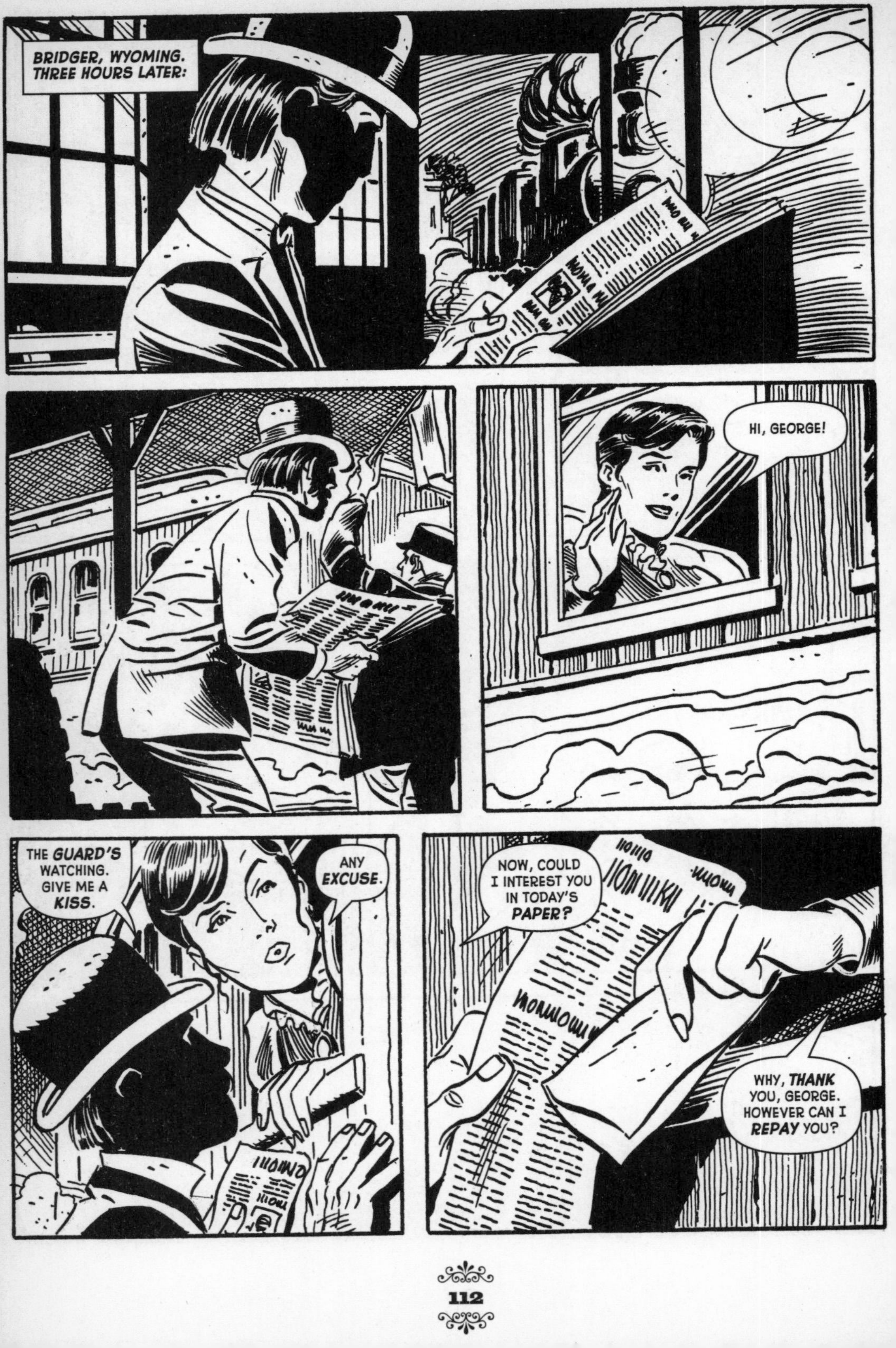
BRIDGER, WYOMING. THREE HOURS LATER:
HI, GEORGE!
THE GUARD'S WATCHING. GIVE ME A KISS.
ANY EXCUSE.
NOW, COULD I INTEREST YOU IN TODAY'S PAPER?
WHY, THANK YOU, GEORGE. HOWEVER CAN I REPAY YOU?

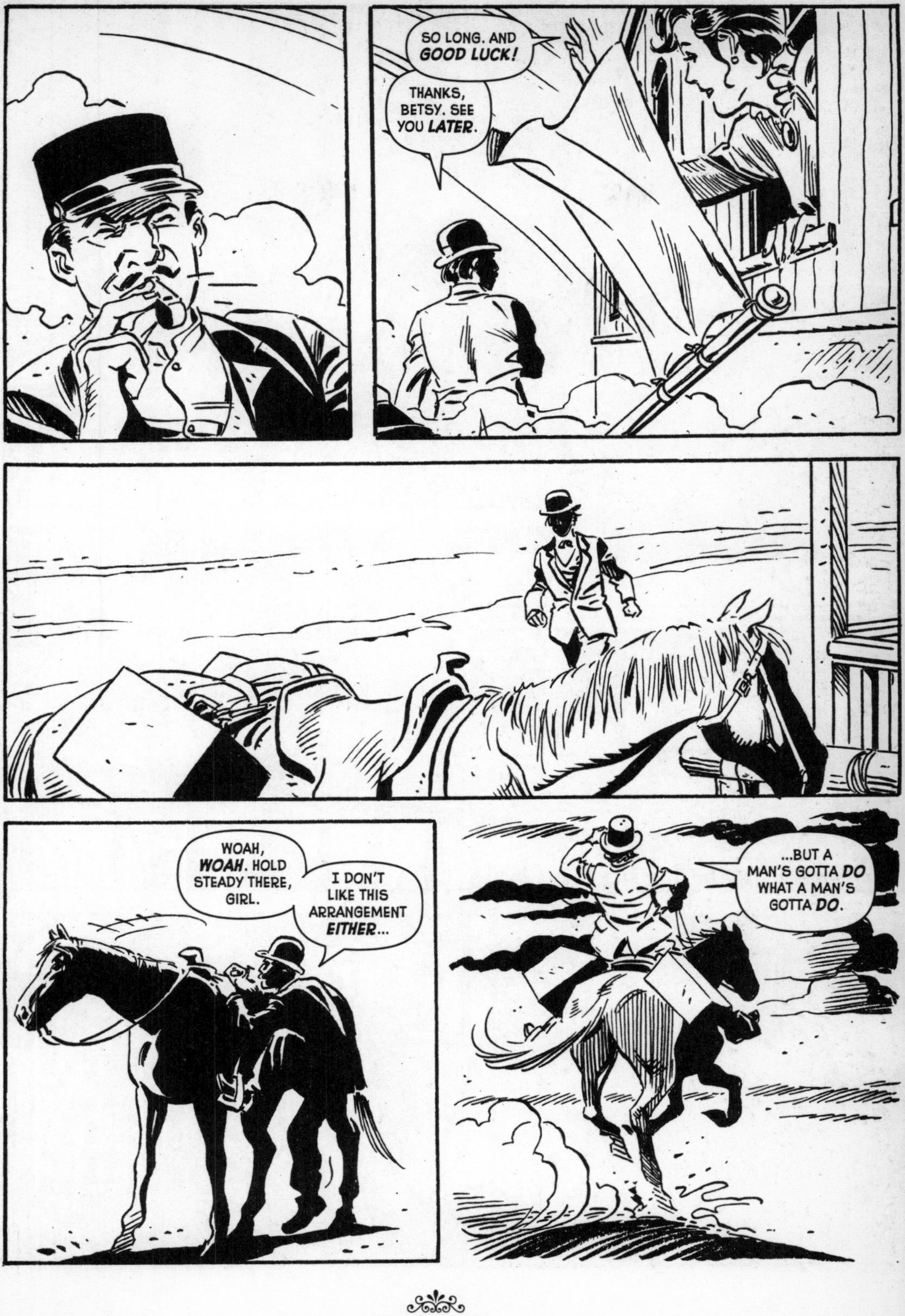
SO LONG. AND GOOD LUCK!
THANKS, BETSY. SEE YOU LATER.
WOAH, WOAH. HOLD STEADY THERE, GIRL.
I DON'T LIKE THIS ARRANGEMENT EITHER...
...BUT A MAN'S GOTTA DO WHAT A MAN'S GOTTA DO.

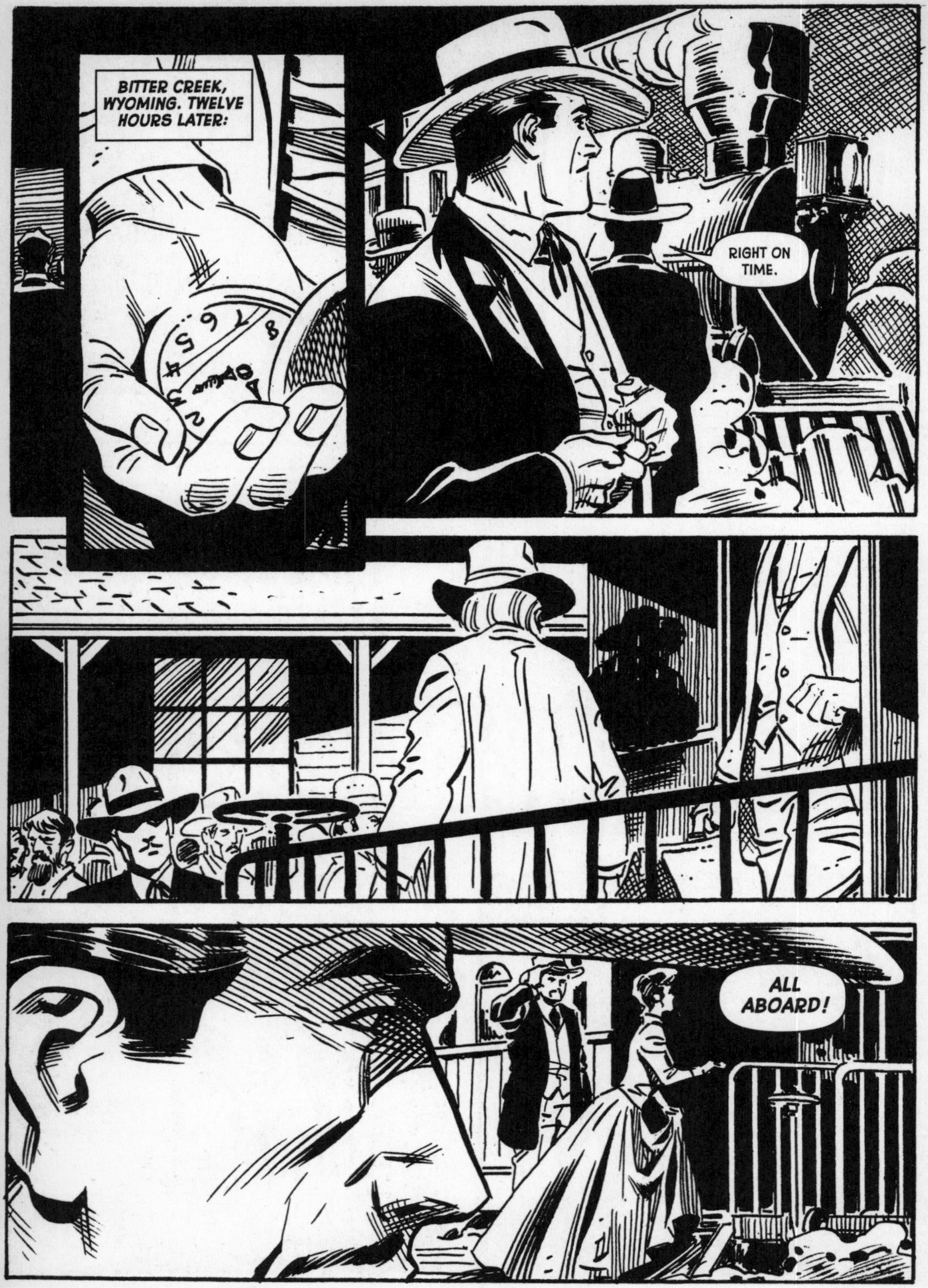
BITTER CREEK, WYOMING. TWELVE HOURS LATER:
RIGHT ON TIME.
ALL ABOARD!

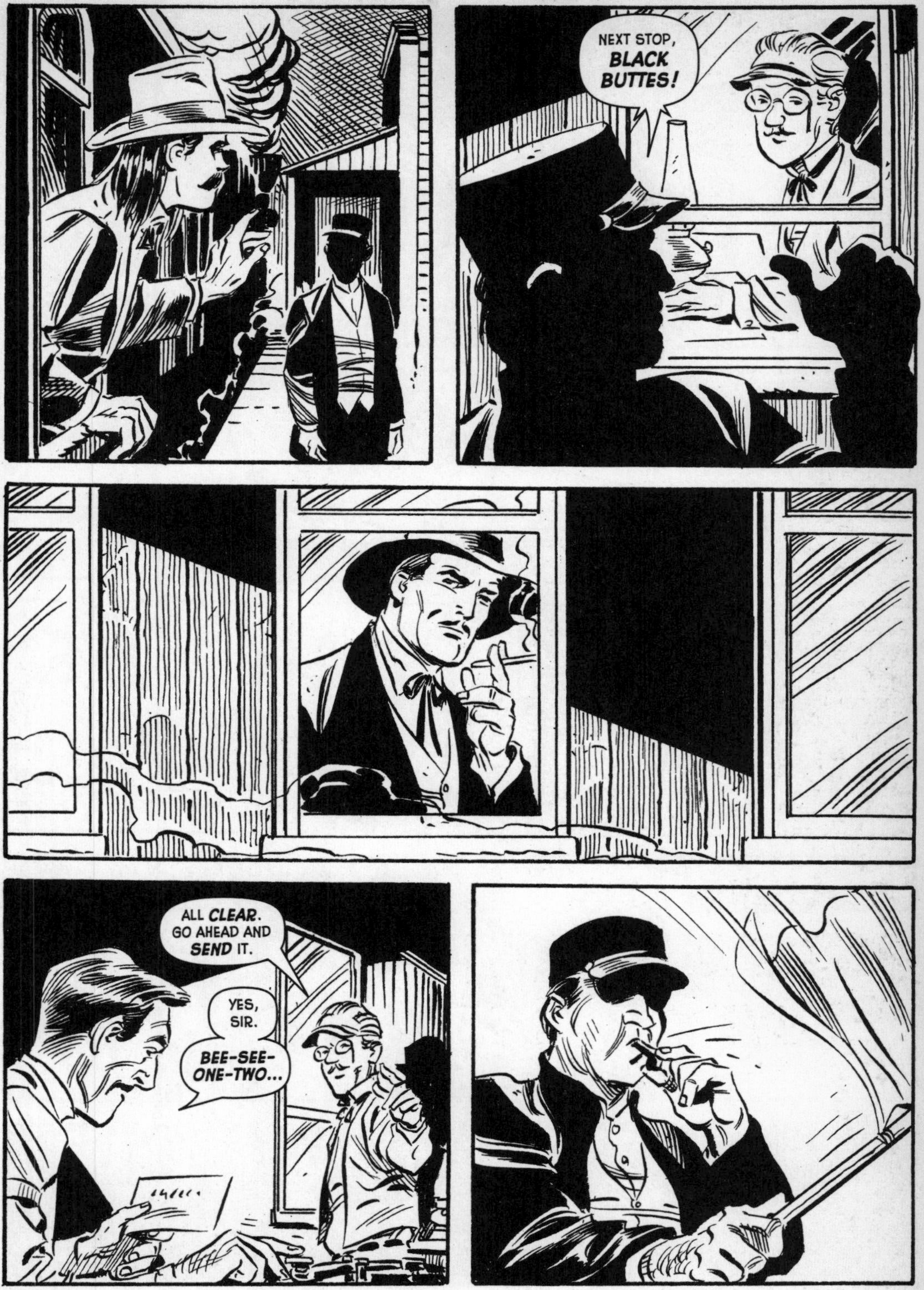
NEXT STOP, BLACK BUTTES!
ALL CLEAR. GO AHEAD AND SEND IT.
YES, SIR.
BEE-SEE-ONE-TWO...

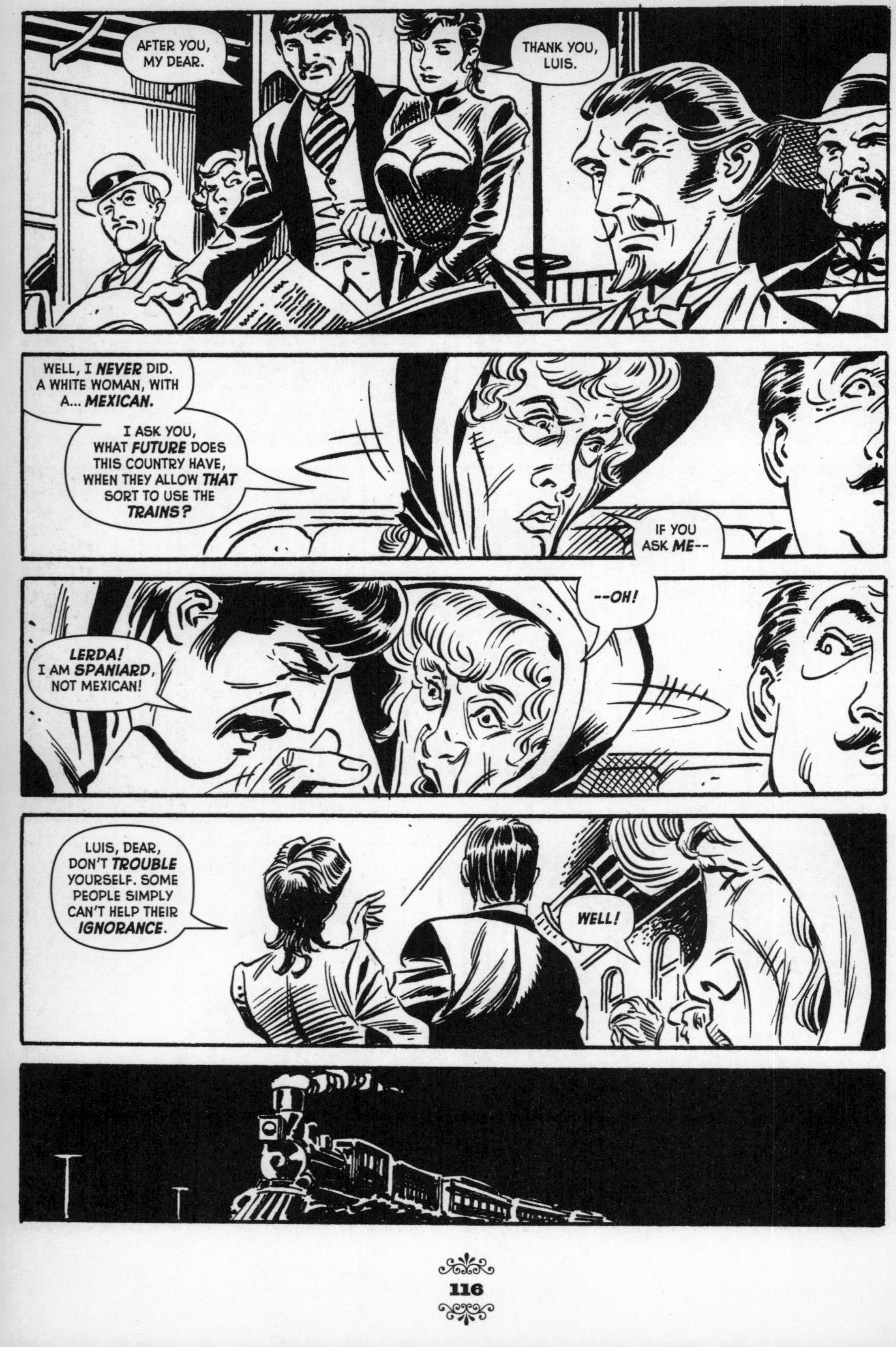
AFTER YOU, MY DEAR.
THANK YOU, LUIS.
WELL, I NEVER DID. A WHITE WOMAN, WITH A... MEXICAN.
I ASK YOU, WHAT FUTURE DOES THIS COUNTRY HAVE, WHEN THEY ALLOW THAT SORT TO USE THE TRAINS?
IF YOU ASK ME--
--OH!
LERDA! I AM SPANIARD, NOT MEXICAN!
LUIS, DEAR, DON'T TROUBLE YOURSELF. SOME PEOPLE SIMPLY CAN'T HELP THEIR IGNORANCE.
WELL!

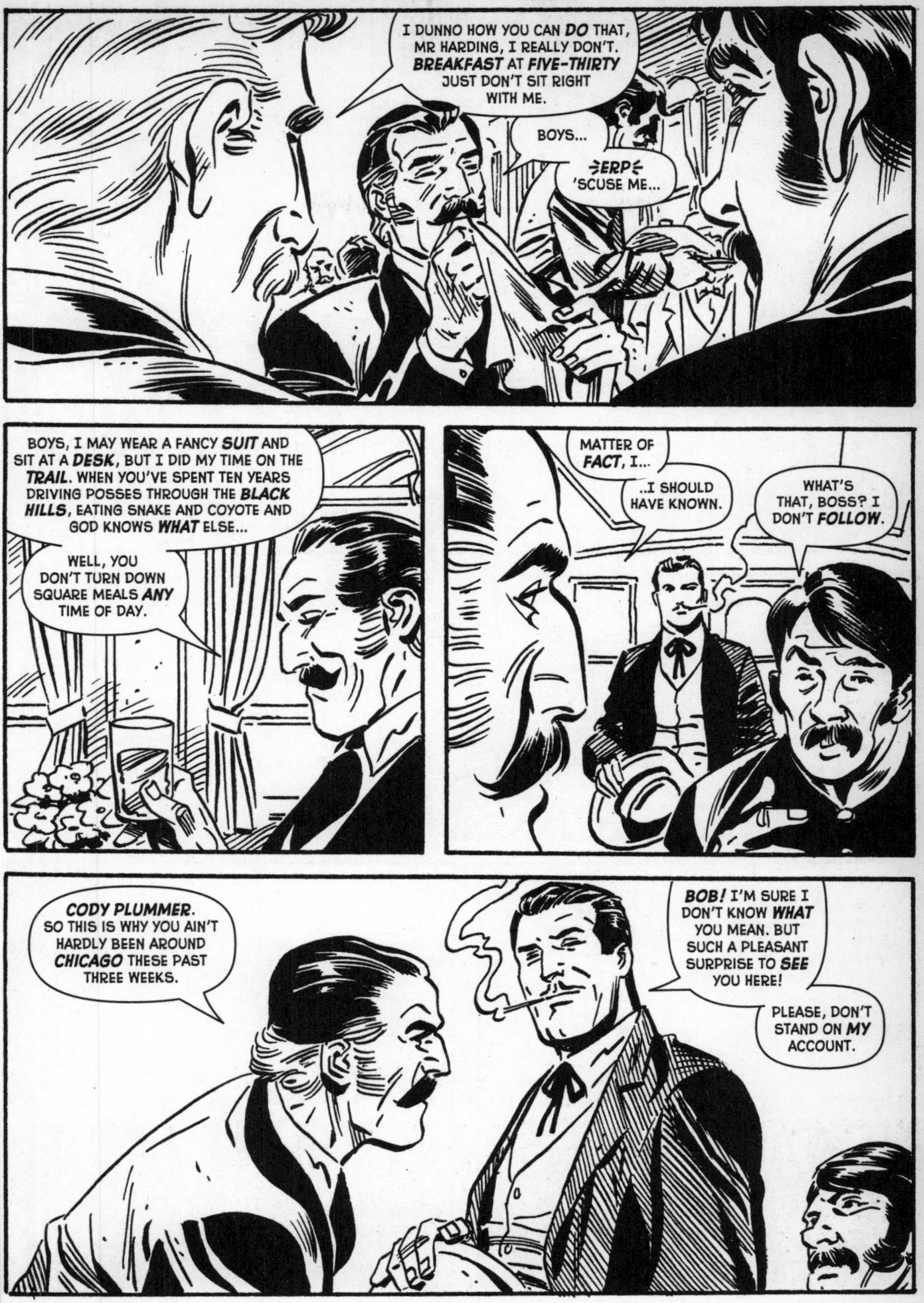
I DUNNO HOW YOU CAN DO THAT, MR HARDING, I REALLY DON'T. BREAKFAST AT FIVE-THIRTY JUST DON'T SIT RIGHT WITH ME.
BOYS...
ERP
'SCUSE ME...
BOYS, I MAY WEAR A FANCY SUIT AND SIT AT A DESK, BUT I DID MY TIME ON THE TRAIL. WHEN YOU'VE SPENT TEN YEARS DRIVING POSSES THROUGH THE BLACK HILLS, EATING SNAKE AND COYOTE AND GOD KNOWS WHAT ELSE...
WELL, YOU DON'T TURN DOWN SQUARE MEALS ANY TIME OF DAY.
MATTER OF FACT, I...
..I SHOULD HAVE KNOWN.
WHAT'S THAT, BOSS? I DON'T FOLLOW.
CODY PLUMMER. SO THIS IS WHY YOU AIN'T HARDLY BEEN AROUND CHICAGO THESE PAST THREE WEEKS.
BOB! I'M SURE I DON'T KNOW WHAT YOU MEAN. BUT SUCH A PLEASANT SURPRISE TO SEE YOU HERE!
PLEASE, DON'T STAND ON MY ACCOUNT.

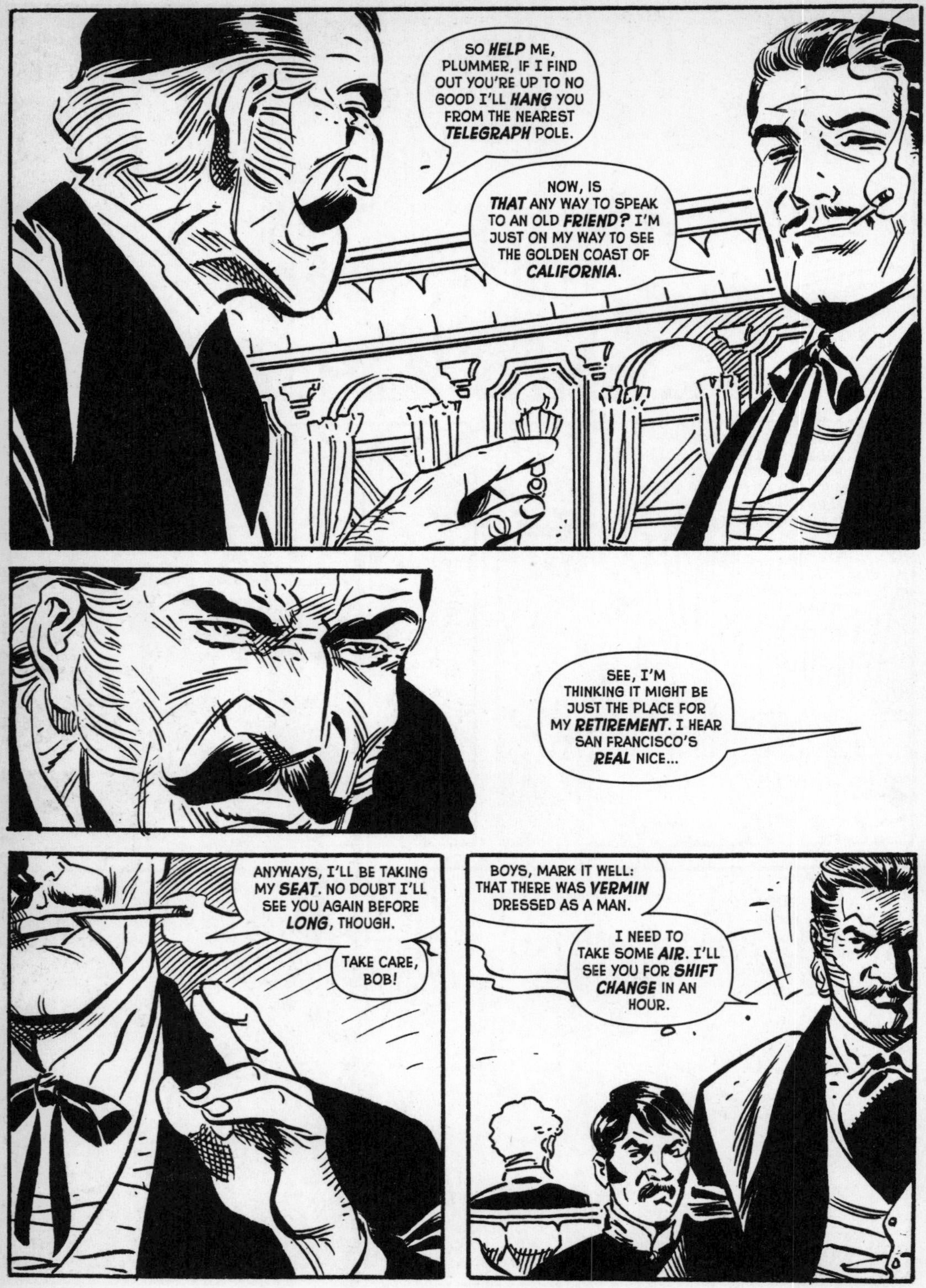
SO HELP ME, PLUMMER, IF I FIND OUT YOU'RE UP TO NO GOOD I'LL HANG YOU FROM THE NEAREST TELEGRAPH POLE.
NOW, IS THAT ANY WAY TO SPEAK TO AN OLD FRIEND? I'M JUST ON MY WAY TO SEE THE GOLDEN COAST OF CALIFORNIA.
SEE, I'M THINKING IT MIGHT BE JUST THE PLACE FOR MY RETIREMENT. I HEAR SAN FRANCISCO'S REAL NICE...
ANYWAYS, I'LL BE TAKING MY SEAT. NO DOUBT I'LL SEE YOU AGAIN BEFORE LONG, THOUGH.
TAKE CARE, BOB!
BOYS, MARK IT WELL: THAT THERE WAS VERMIN DRESSED AS A MAN.
I NEED TO TAKE SOME AIR. I'LL SEE YOU FOR SHIFT CHANGE IN AN HOUR.

HERE HE *COMES*. YOU ALL READY TO GET SOME *SLEEP*?

EVERYBODY HERE?

ALL RIGHT, THEN. LET'S *GO*.

C'MON, C'MON, *MOVE IT!* INTO POSITIONS! LET'S GET THIS DOOR *CLOSED!*

HOW'S IT *GOING*, BEN?

NO PROBLEMS HERE. ANY TROUBLE OUT THERE?

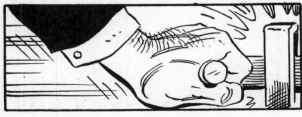

CODY PLUMMER'S ON BOARD. RECKON HE THINKS THIS IS JUST AN *ORDINARY* TRAIN HE CAN HOLD *UP.*

HE'S IN FOR ONE *ALMIGHTY* SHOCK.

ALL RIGHT...

≈YAWN≈

...EVERYBODY *OUT!* MOVE IT, *MOVE IT!* SUPPER'S A-WAITING!

SEE YOU AT *EVANSTON,* BOB.

THAT YOU WILL. GO ON, *REST* AWHILE.

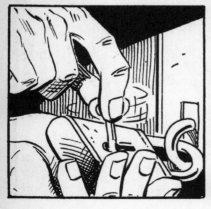

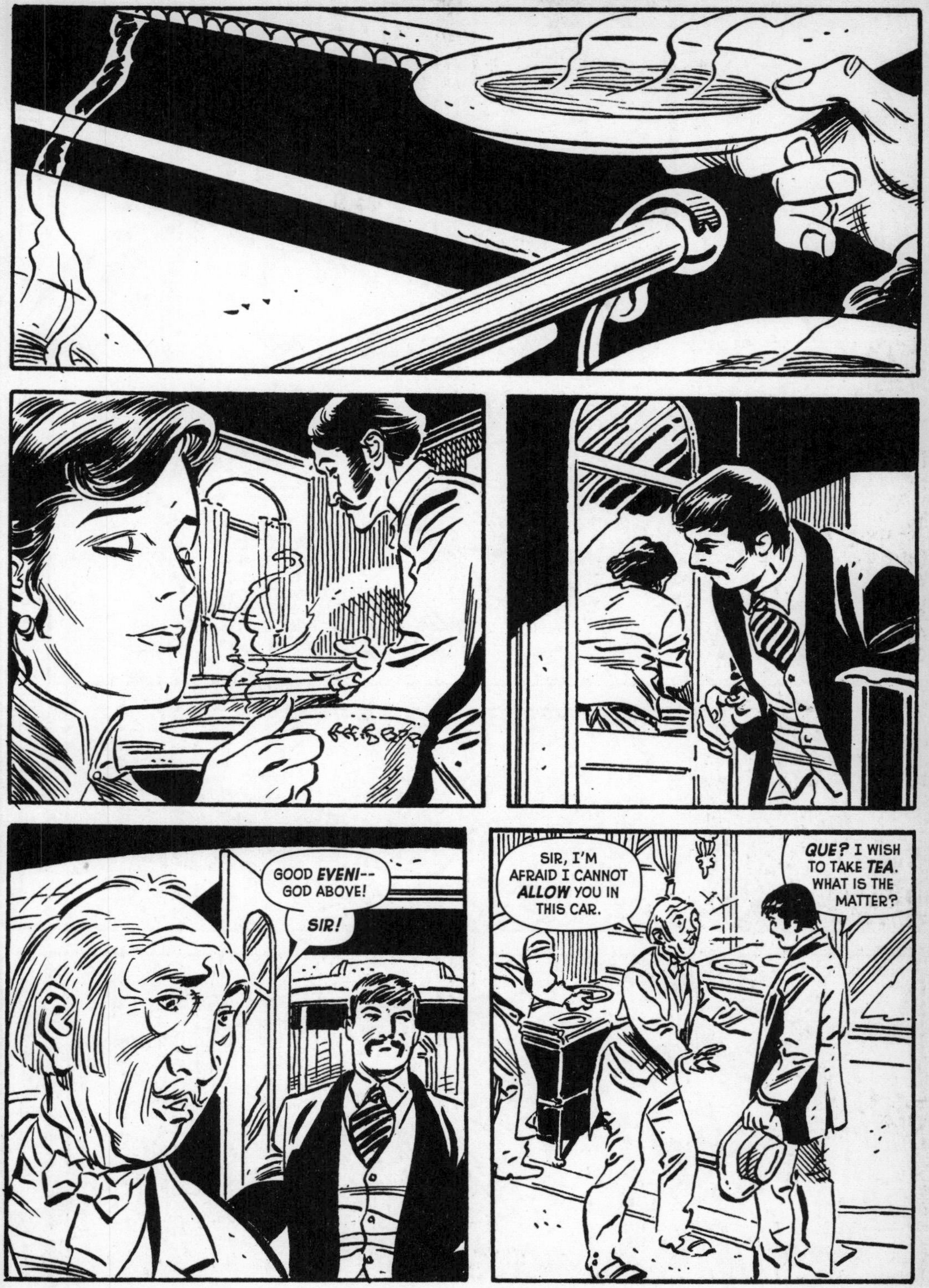
GOOD EVENI-- GOD ABOVE!
SIR!
SIR, I'M AFRAID I CANNOT ALLOW YOU IN THIS CAR.
QUE? I WISH TO TAKE TEA. WHAT IS THE MATTER?

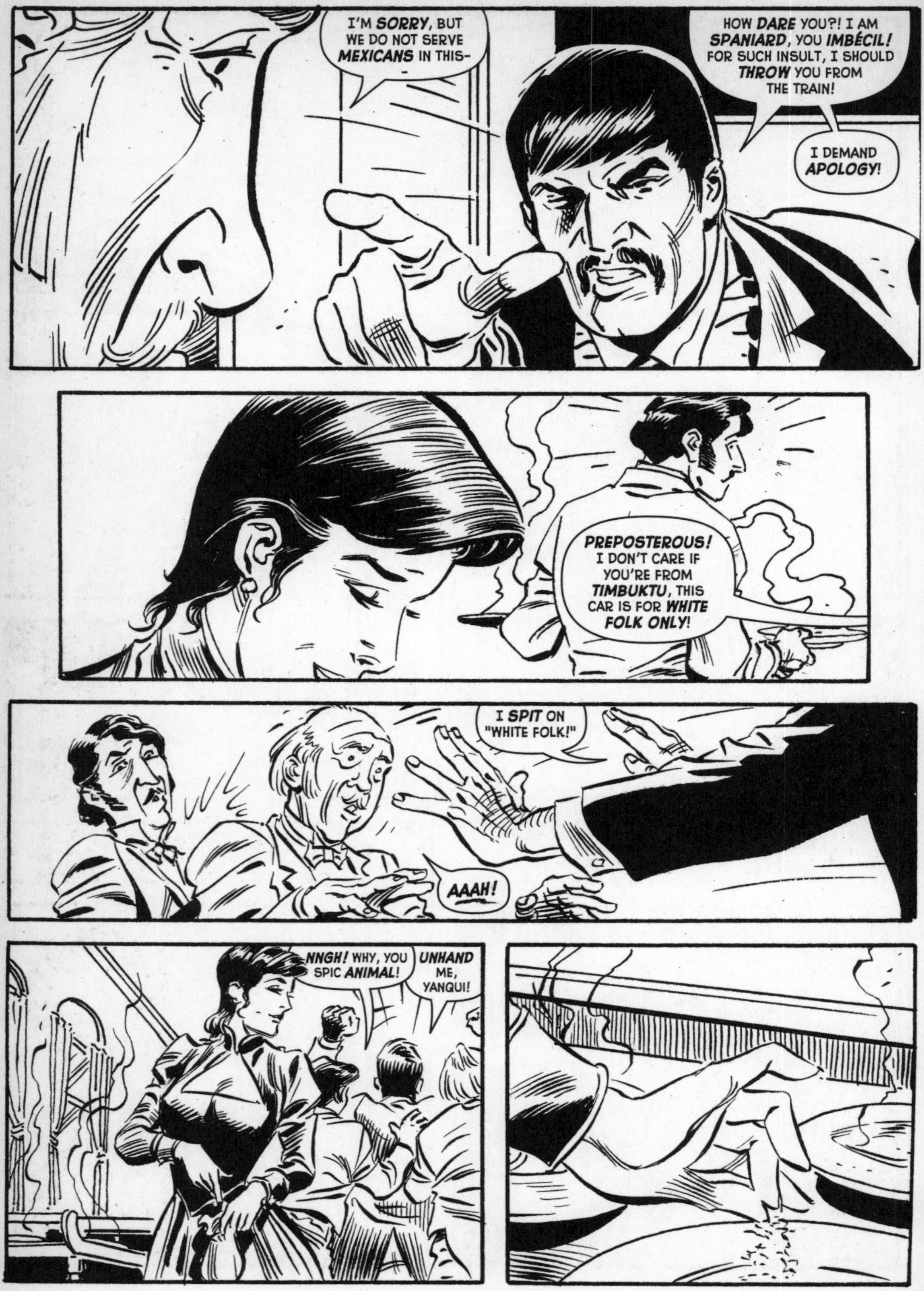
I'M SORRY, BUT WE DO NOT SERVE MEXICANS IN THIS-
HOW DARE YOU?! I AM SPANIARD, YOU IMBÉCIL! FOR SUCH INSULT, I SHOULD THROW YOU FROM THE TRAIN!
I DEMAND APOLOGY!
PREPOSTEROUS! I DON'T CARE IF YOU'RE FROM TIMBUKTU, THIS CAR IS FOR WHITE FOLK ONLY!
I SPIT ON "WHITE FOLK!"
AAAH!
NNGH! WHY, YOU SPIC ANIMAL!
UNHAND ME, YANQUI!

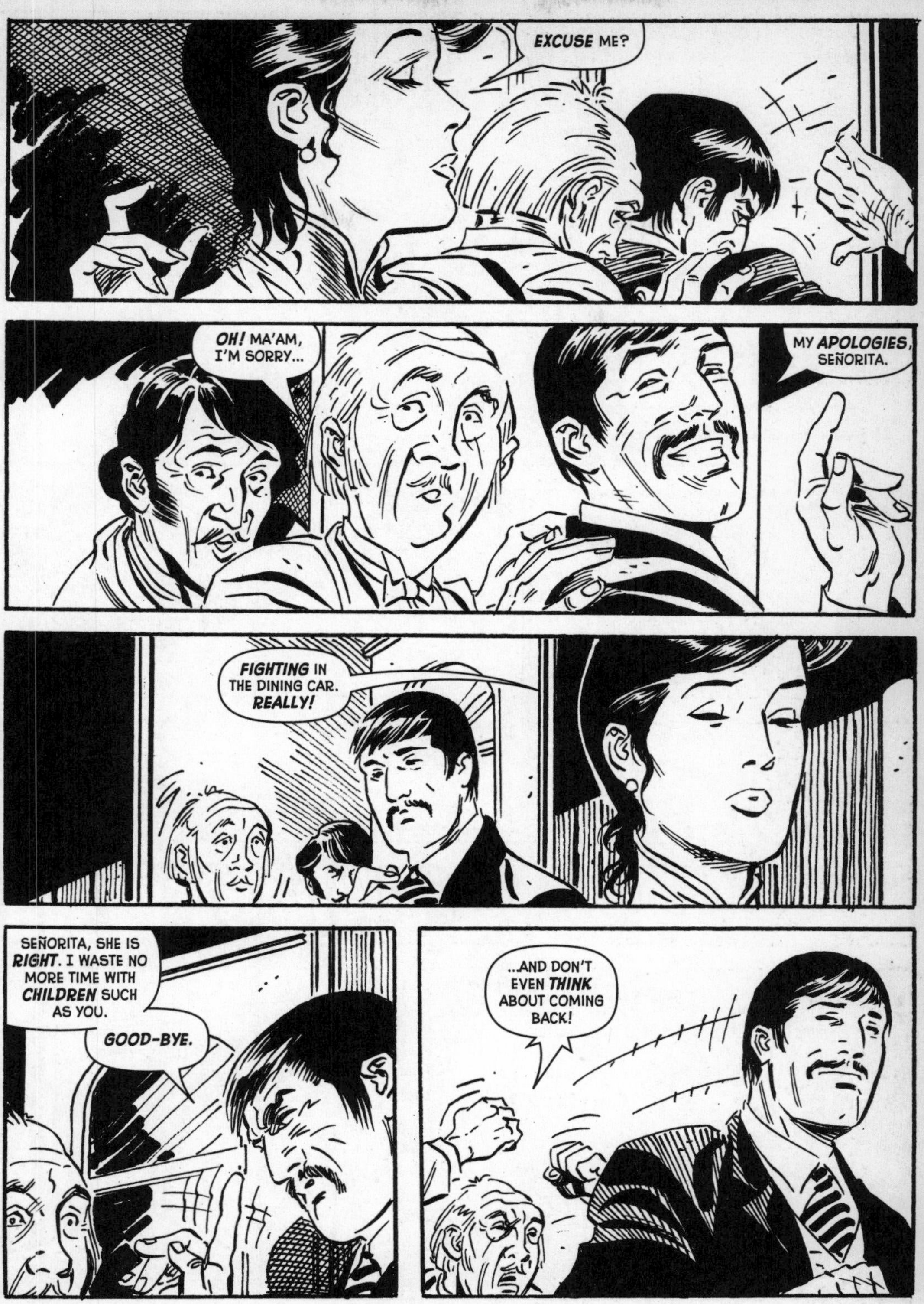
EXCUSE ME?
OH! MA'AM, I'M SORRY...
MY APOLOGIES, SEÑORITA.
FIGHTING IN THE DINING CAR. REALLY!
SEÑORITA, SHE IS RIGHT. I WASTE NO MORE TIME WITH CHILDREN SUCH AS YOU.
GOOD-BYE.
...AND DON'T EVEN THINK ABOUT COMING BACK!

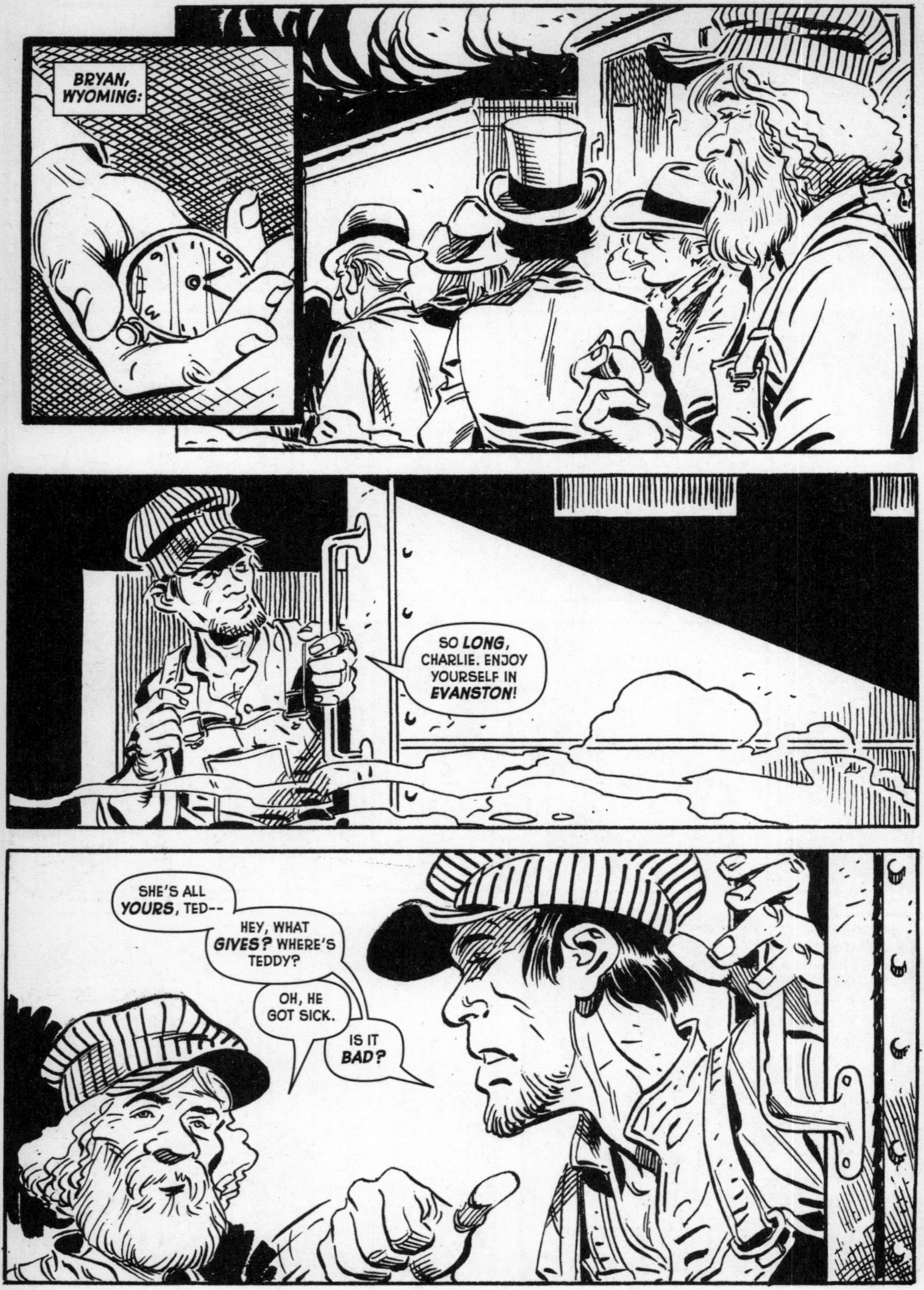
BRYAN, WYOMING:
SO LONG, CHARLIE. ENJOY YOURSELF IN EVANSTON!
SHE'S ALL YOURS, TED--
HEY, WHAT GIVES? WHERE'S TEDDY?
OH, HE GOT SICK.
IS IT BAD?

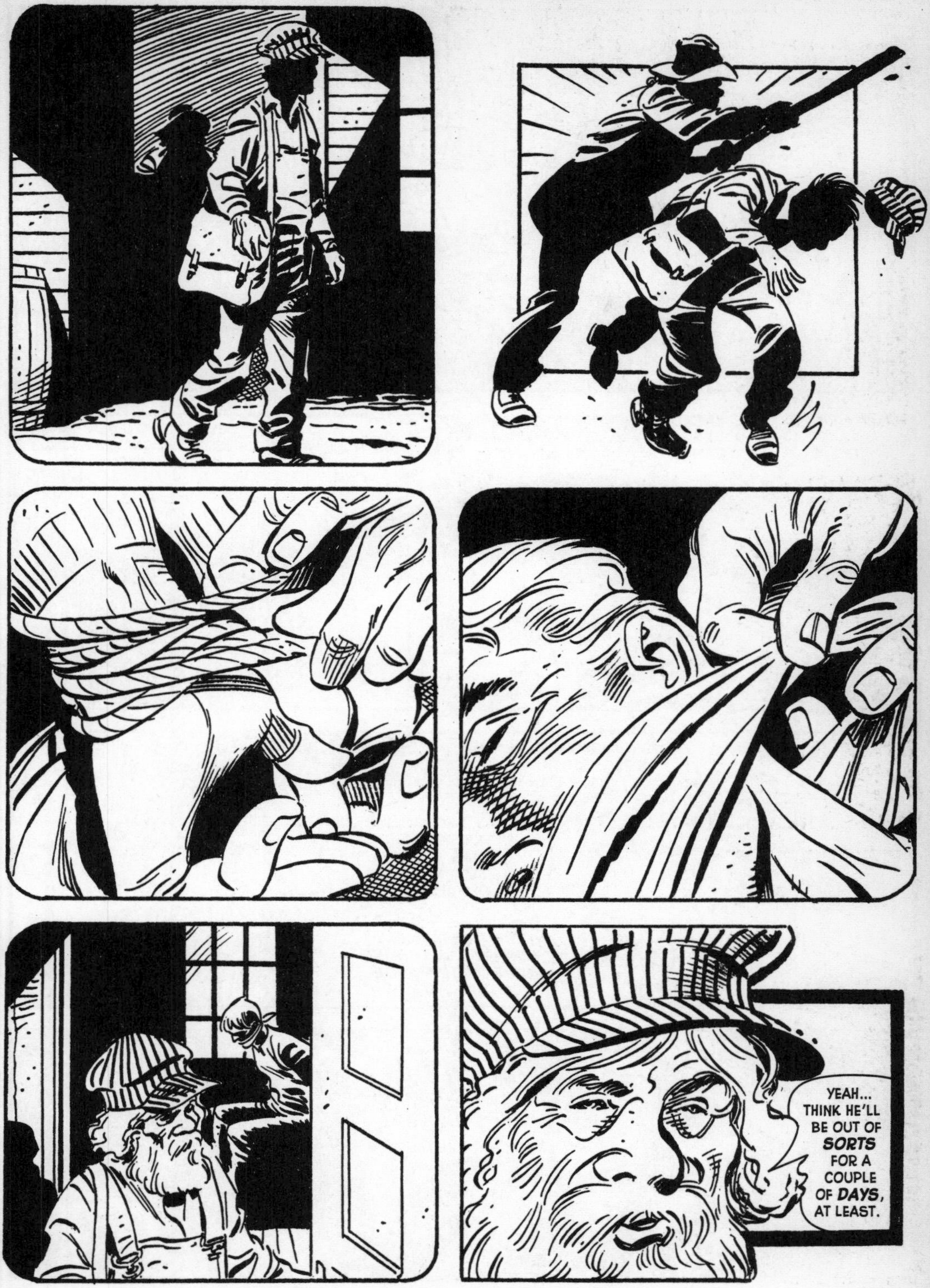
YEAH... THINK HE'LL BE OUT OF SORTS FOR A COUPLE OF DAYS, AT LEAST.

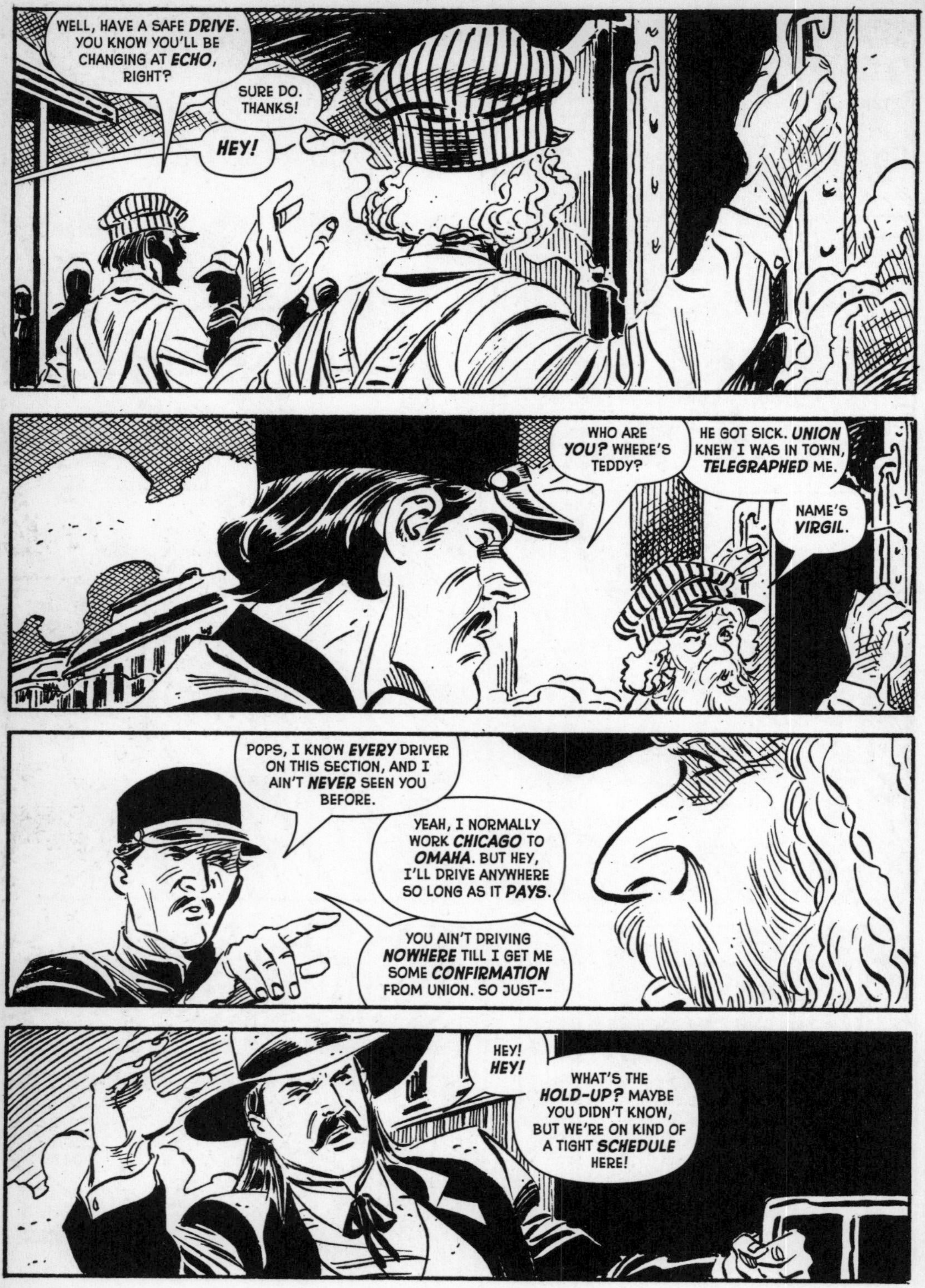
WELL, HAVE A SAFE DRIVE. YOU KNOW YOU'LL BE CHANGING AT ECHO, RIGHT?
SURE DO. THANKS!
HEY!
WHO ARE YOU? WHERE'S TEDDY?
HE GOT SICK. UNION KNEW I WAS IN TOWN, TELEGRAPHED ME.
NAME'S VIRGIL.
POPS, I KNOW EVERY DRIVER ON THIS SECTION, AND I AIN'T NEVER SEEN YOU BEFORE.
YEAH, I NORMALLY WORK CHICAGO TO OMAHA. BUT HEY, I'LL DRIVE ANYWHERE SO LONG AS IT PAYS.
YOU AIN'T DRIVING NOWHERE TILL I GET ME SOME CONFIRMATION FROM UNION. SO JUST--
HEY! HEY!
WHAT'S THE HOLD-UP? MAYBE YOU DIDN'T KNOW, BUT WE'RE ON KIND OF A TIGHT SCHEDULE HERE!

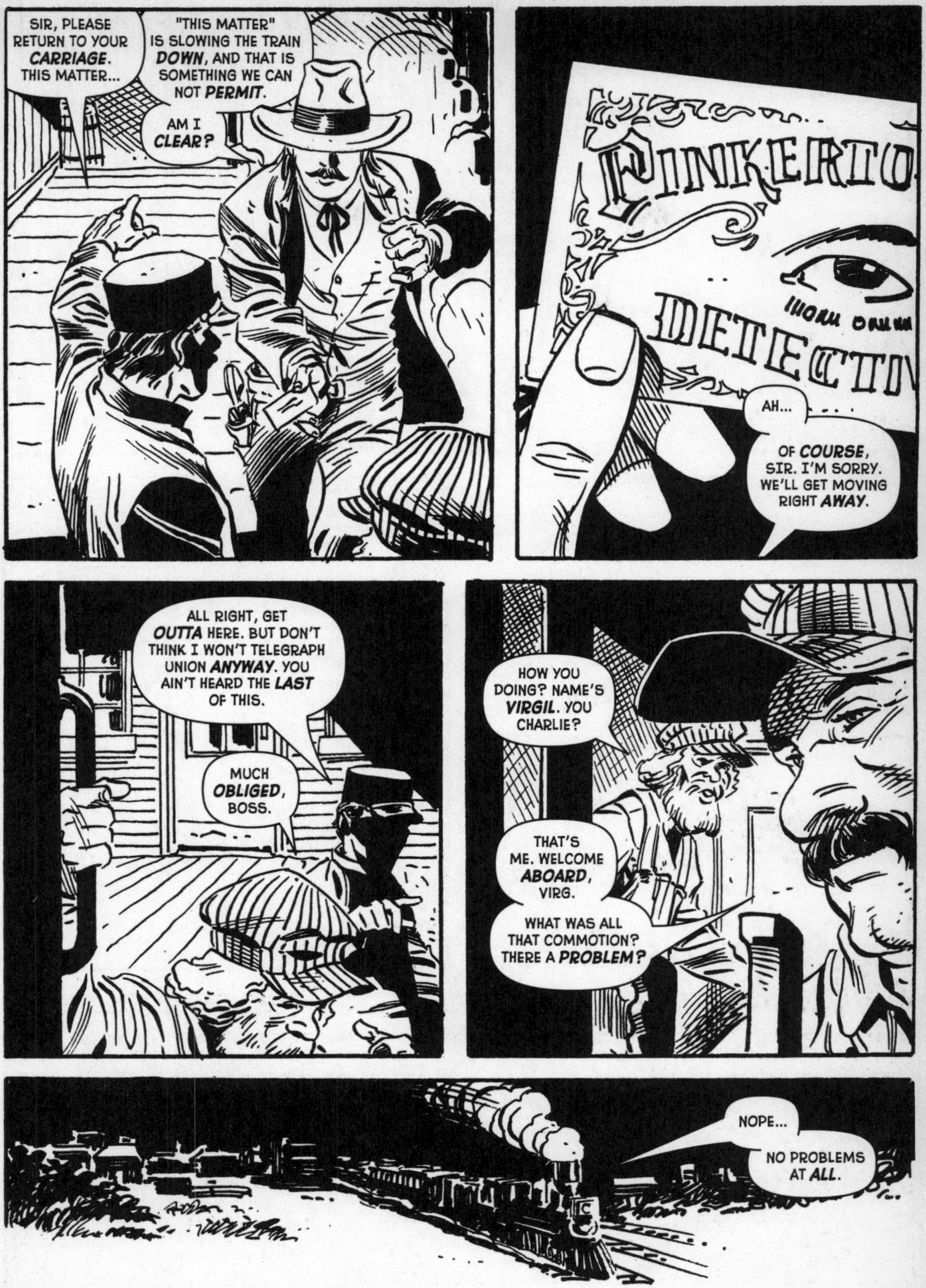
SIR, PLEASE RETURN TO YOUR CARRIAGE. THIS MATTER...
"THIS MATTER" IS SLOWING THE TRAIN DOWN, AND THAT IS SOMETHING WE CAN NOT PERMIT.
AM I CLEAR?
AH...
OF COURSE, SIR. I'M SORRY. WE'LL GET MOVING RIGHT AWAY.
ALL RIGHT, GET OUTTA HERE. BUT DON'T THINK I WON'T TELEGRAPH UNION ANYWAY. YOU AIN'T HEARD THE LAST OF THIS.
MUCH OBLIGED, BOSS.
HOW YOU DOING? NAME'S VIRGIL. YOU CHARLIE?
THAT'S ME. WELCOME ABOARD, VIRG.
WHAT WAS ALL THAT COMMOTION? THERE A PROBLEM?
NOPE...
NO PROBLEMS AT ALL.

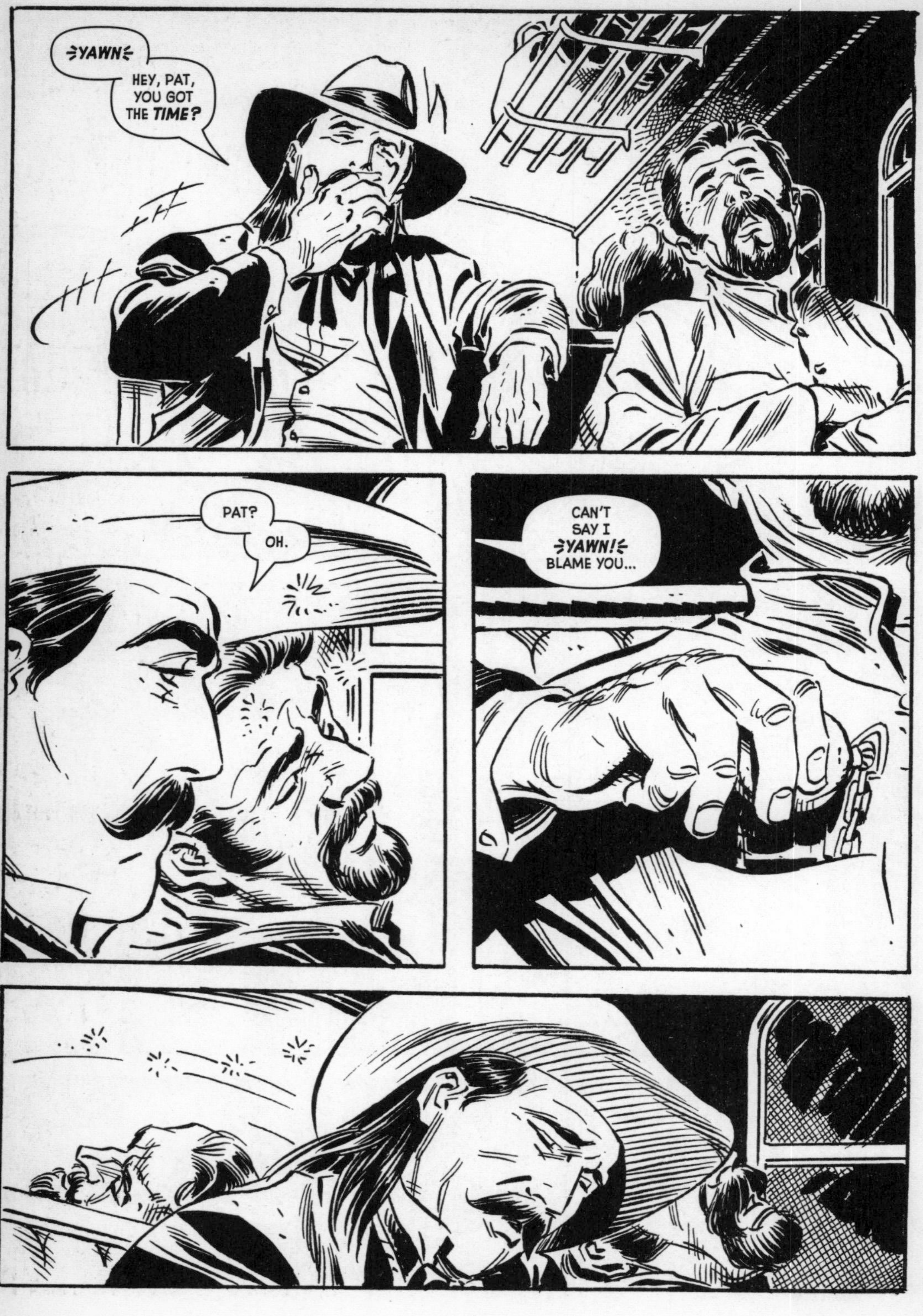

YAWN
HEY, PAT, YOU GOT THE TIME?
PAT?
OH.
CAN'T SAY I YAWN! BLAME YOU...

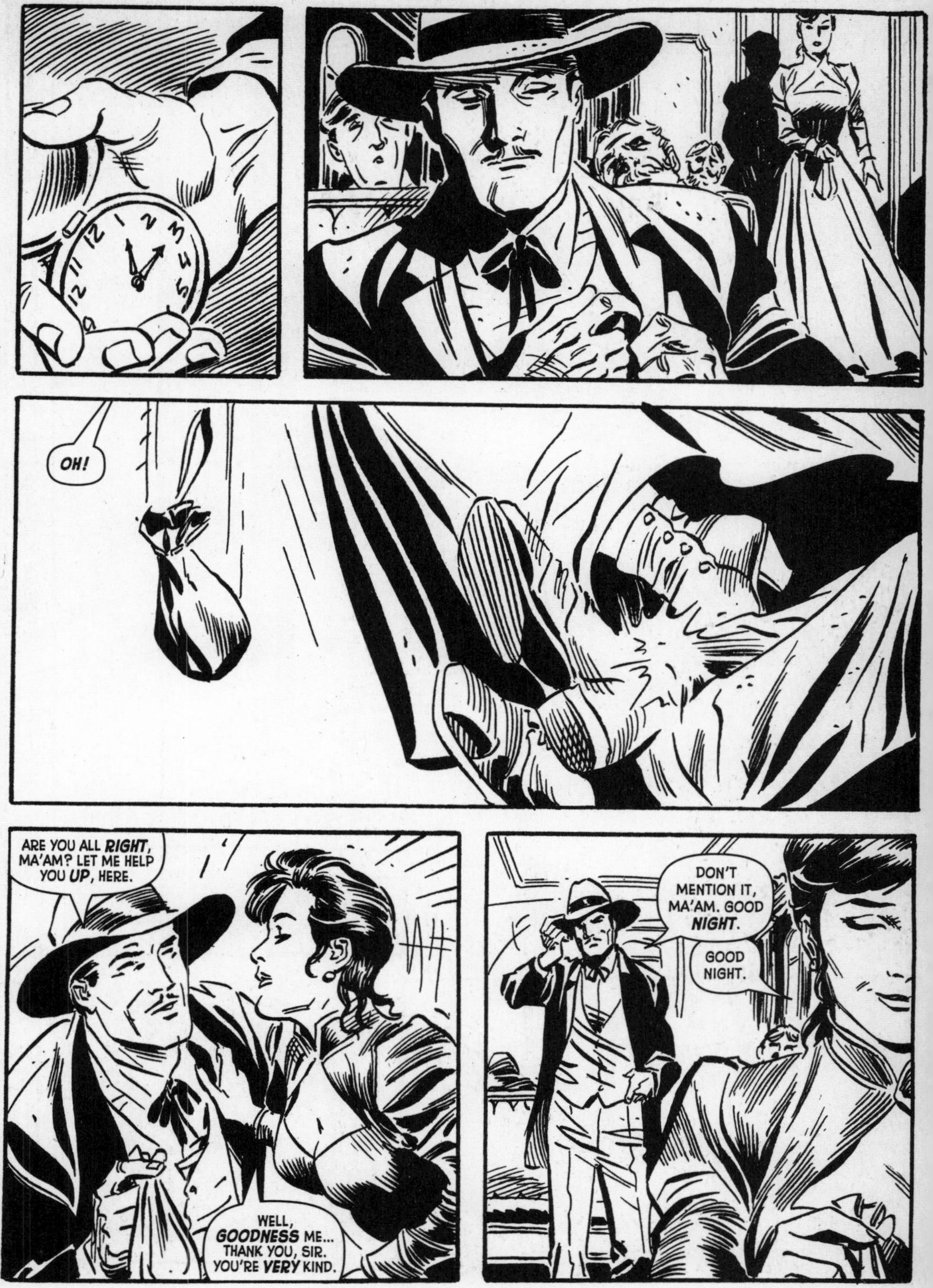
OH!
ARE YOU ALL RIGHT, MA'AM? LET ME HELP YOU UP, HERE.
WELL, GOODNESS ME... THANK YOU, SIR. YOU'RE VERY KIND.
DON'T MENTION IT, MA'AM. GOOD NIGHT.
GOOD NIGHT.

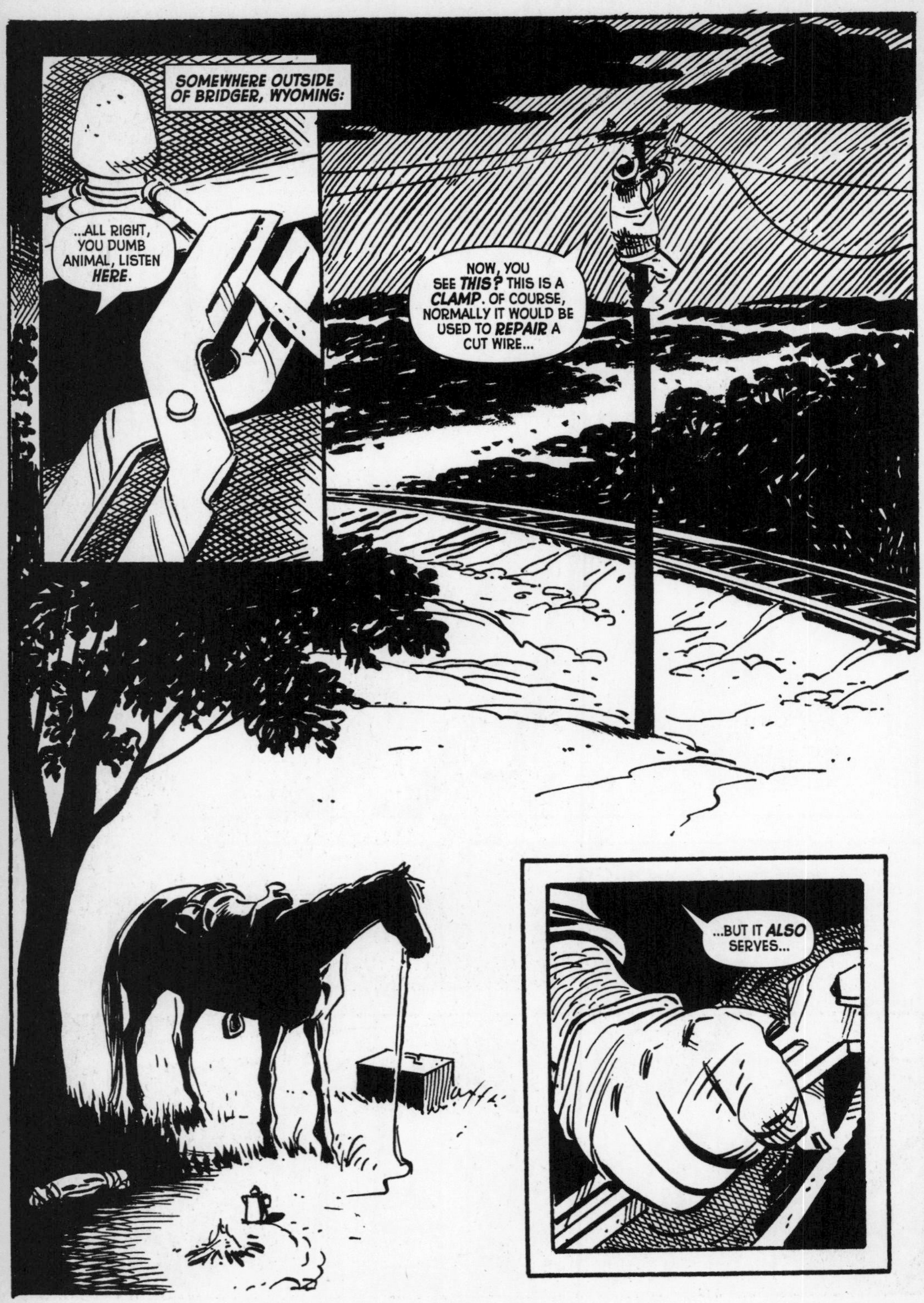
SOMEWHERE OUTSIDE OF BRIDGER, WYOMING:
...ALL RIGHT, YOU DUMB ANIMAL, LISTEN HERE.
NOW, YOU SEE THIS? THIS IS A CLAMP. OF COURSE, NORMALLY IT WOULD BE USED TO REPAIR A CUT WIRE...
...BUT IT ALSO SERVES...

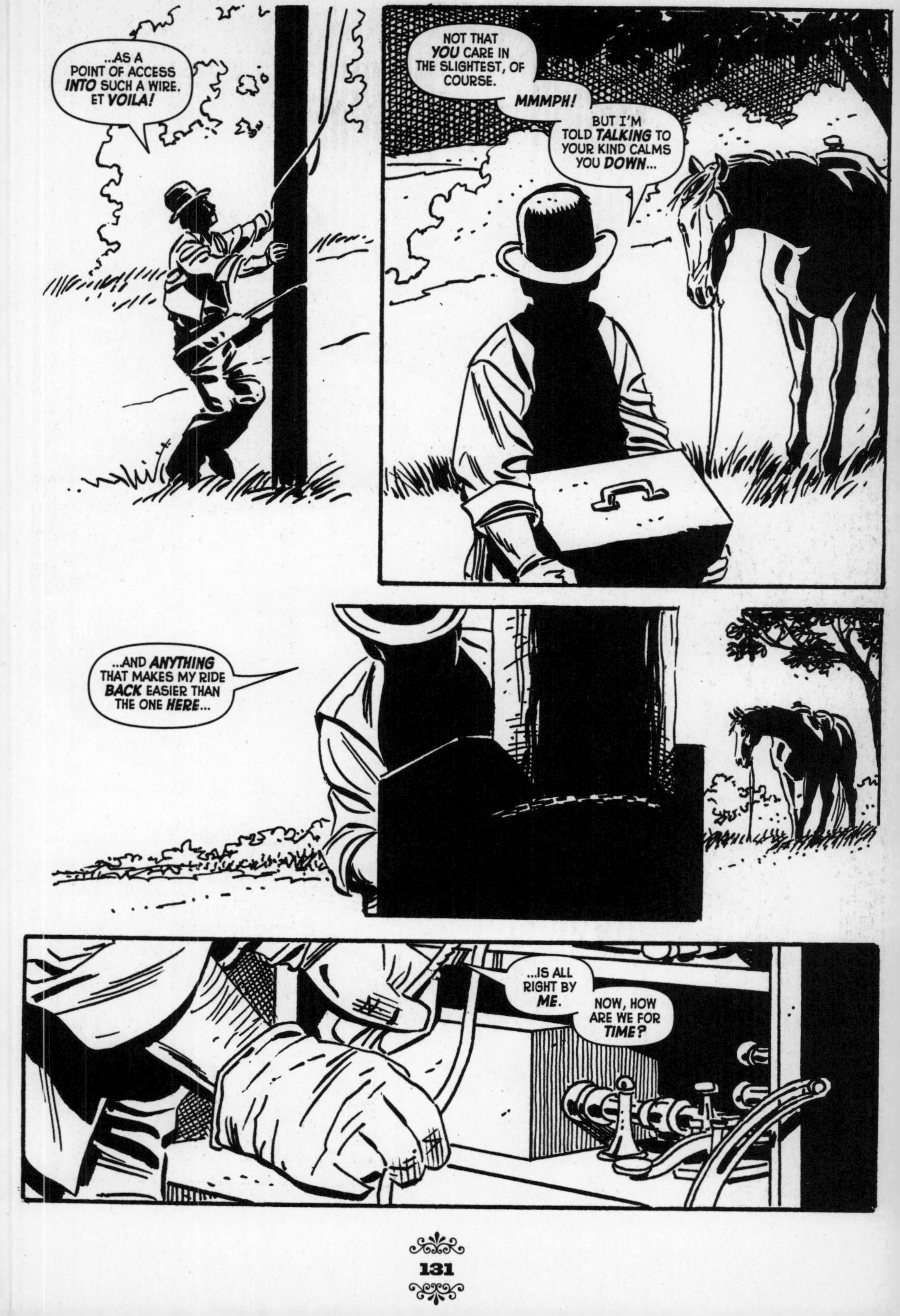
...AS A POINT OF ACCESS INTO SUCH A WIRE. ET VOILA!
NOT THAT YOU CARE IN THE SLIGHTEST, OF COURSE.
MMMPH!
BUT I'M TOLD TALKING TO YOUR KIND CALMS YOU DOWN...
...AND ANYTHING THAT MAKES MY RIDE BACK EASIER THAN THE ONE HERE...
...IS ALL RIGHT BY ME.
NOW, HOW ARE WE FOR TIME?

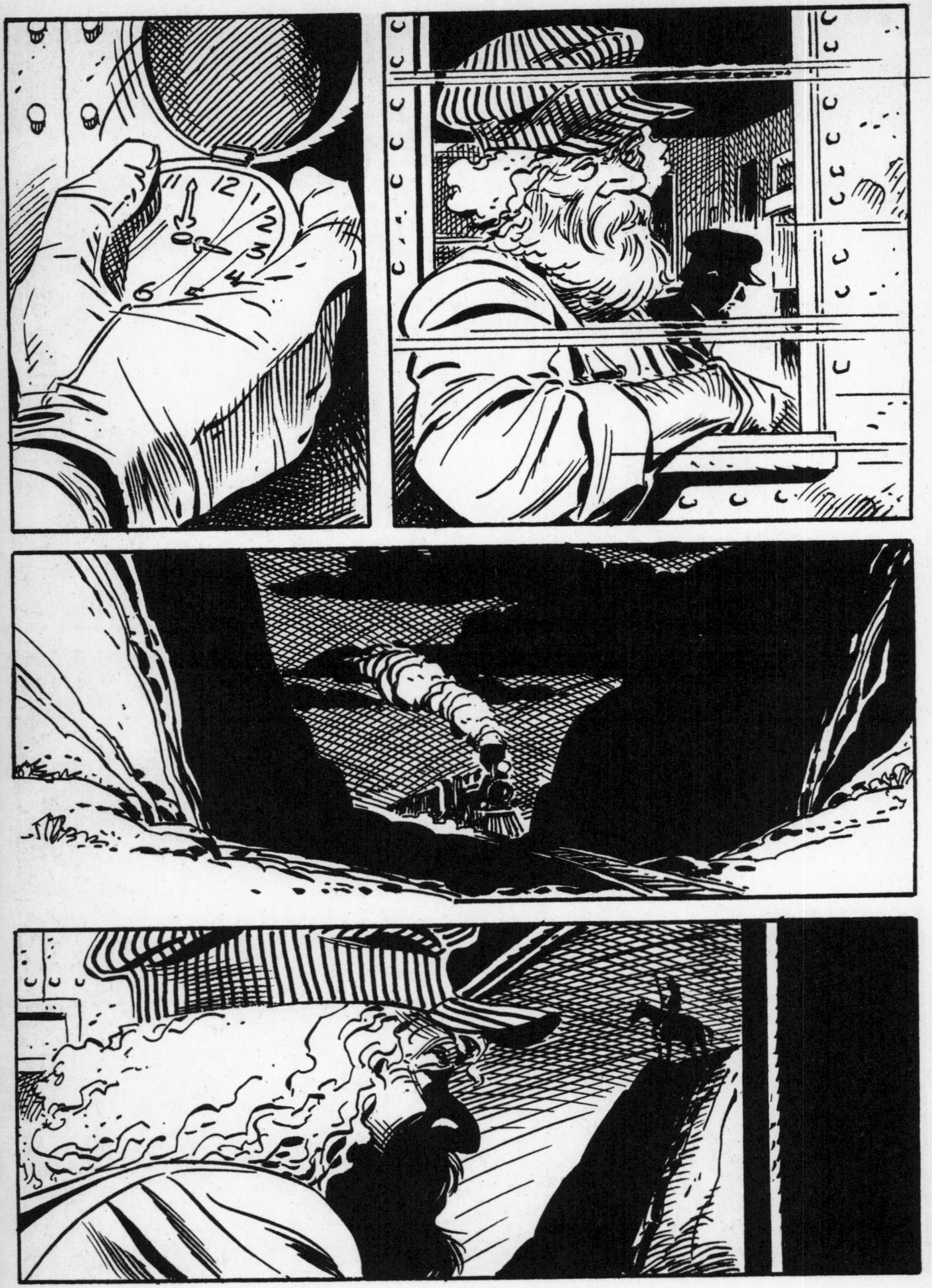

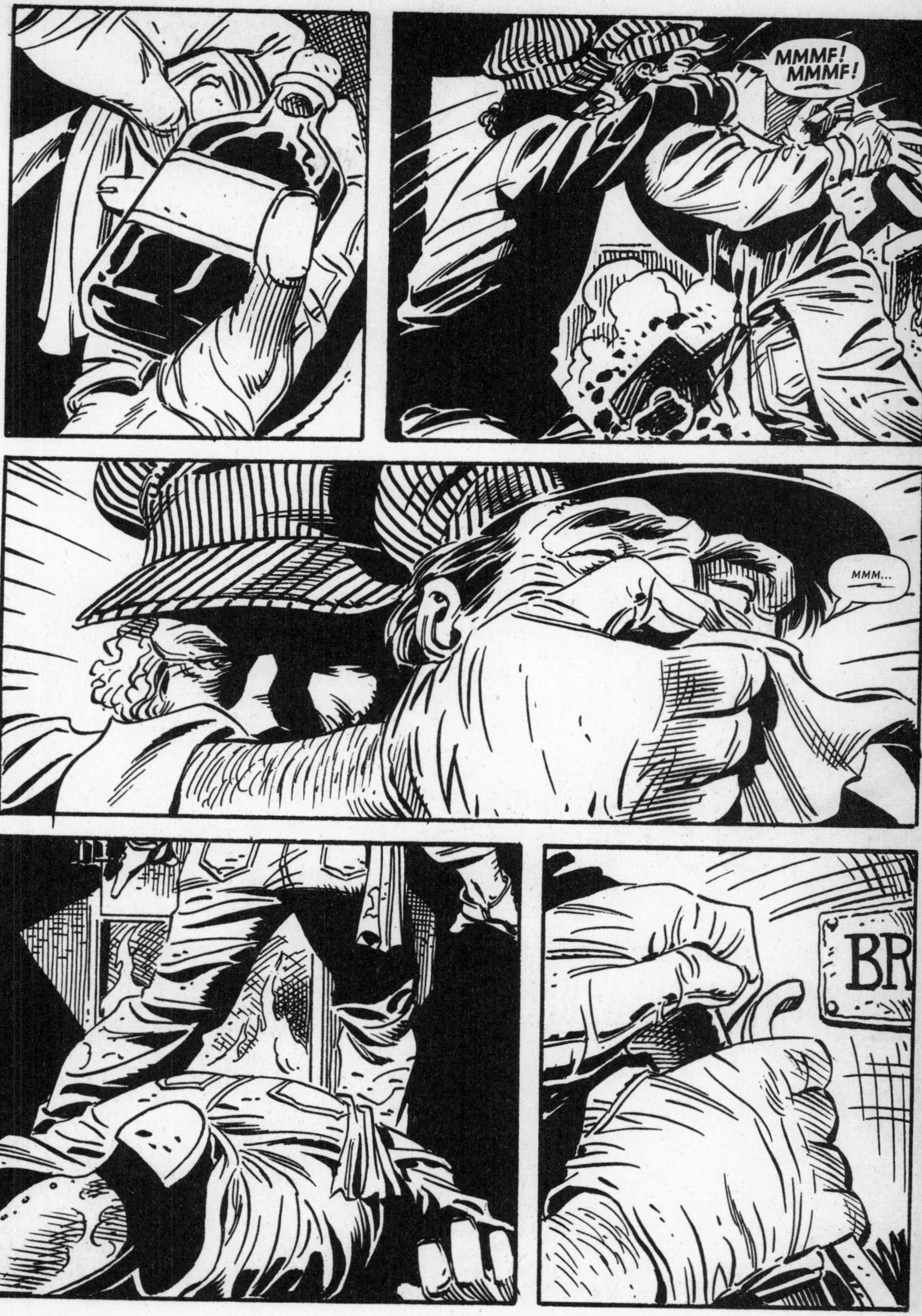
MMMF! MMMF!
MMM...
BR

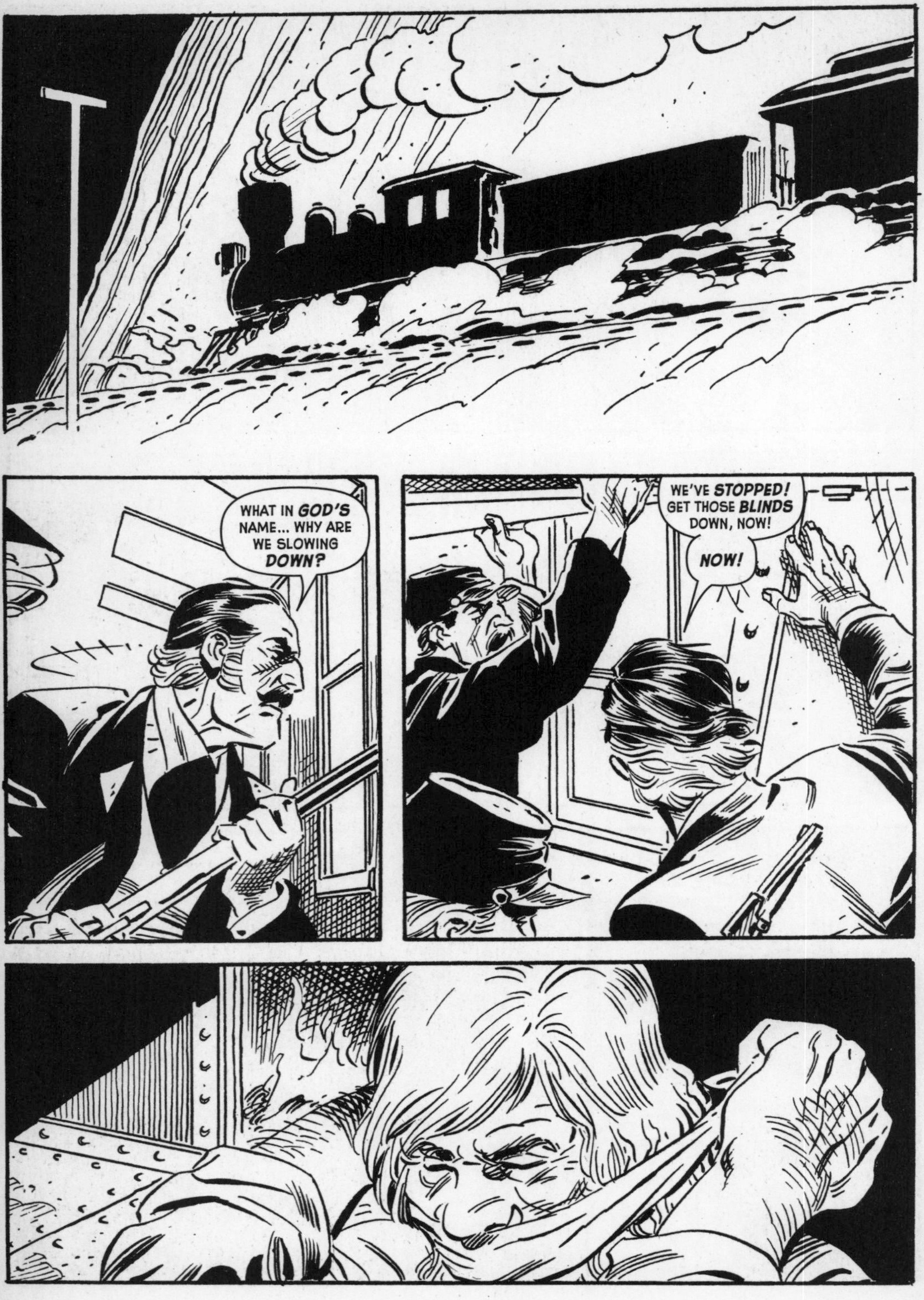
WHAT IN GOD'S NAME... WHY ARE WE SLOWING DOWN?
WE'VE STOPPED! GET THOSE BLINDS DOWN, NOW!
NOW!

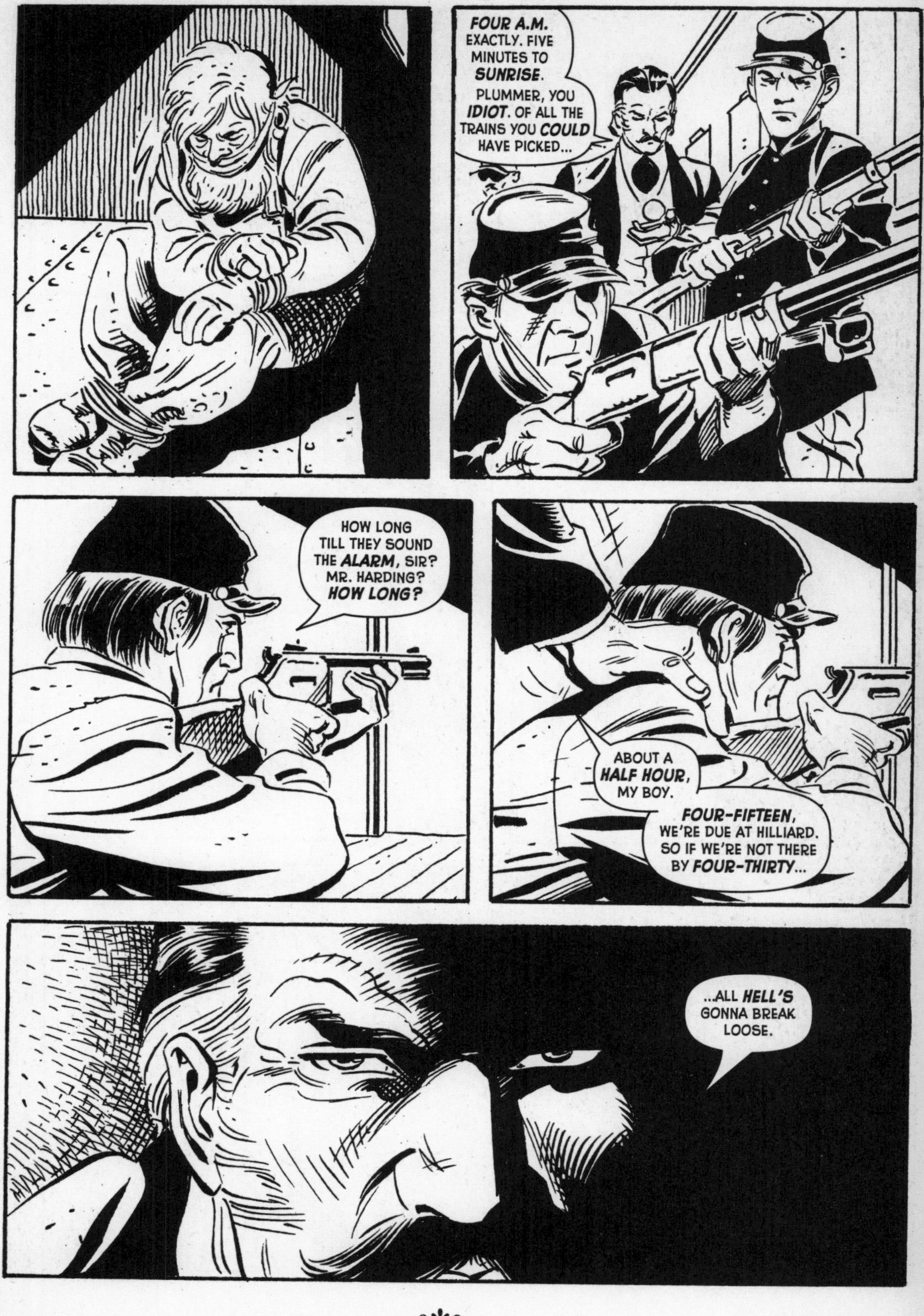
FOUR A.M. EXACTLY. FIVE MINUTES TO SUNRISE.
PLUMMER, YOU IDIOT. OF ALL THE TRAINS YOU COULD HAVE PICKED...
HOW LONG TILL THEY SOUND THE ALARM, SIR? MR. HARDING? HOW LONG?
ABOUT A HALF HOUR, MY BOY.
FOUR-FIFTEEN, WE'RE DUE AT HILLIARD. SO IF WE'RE NOT THERE BY FOUR-THIRTY...
...ALL HELL'S GONNA BREAK LOOSE.

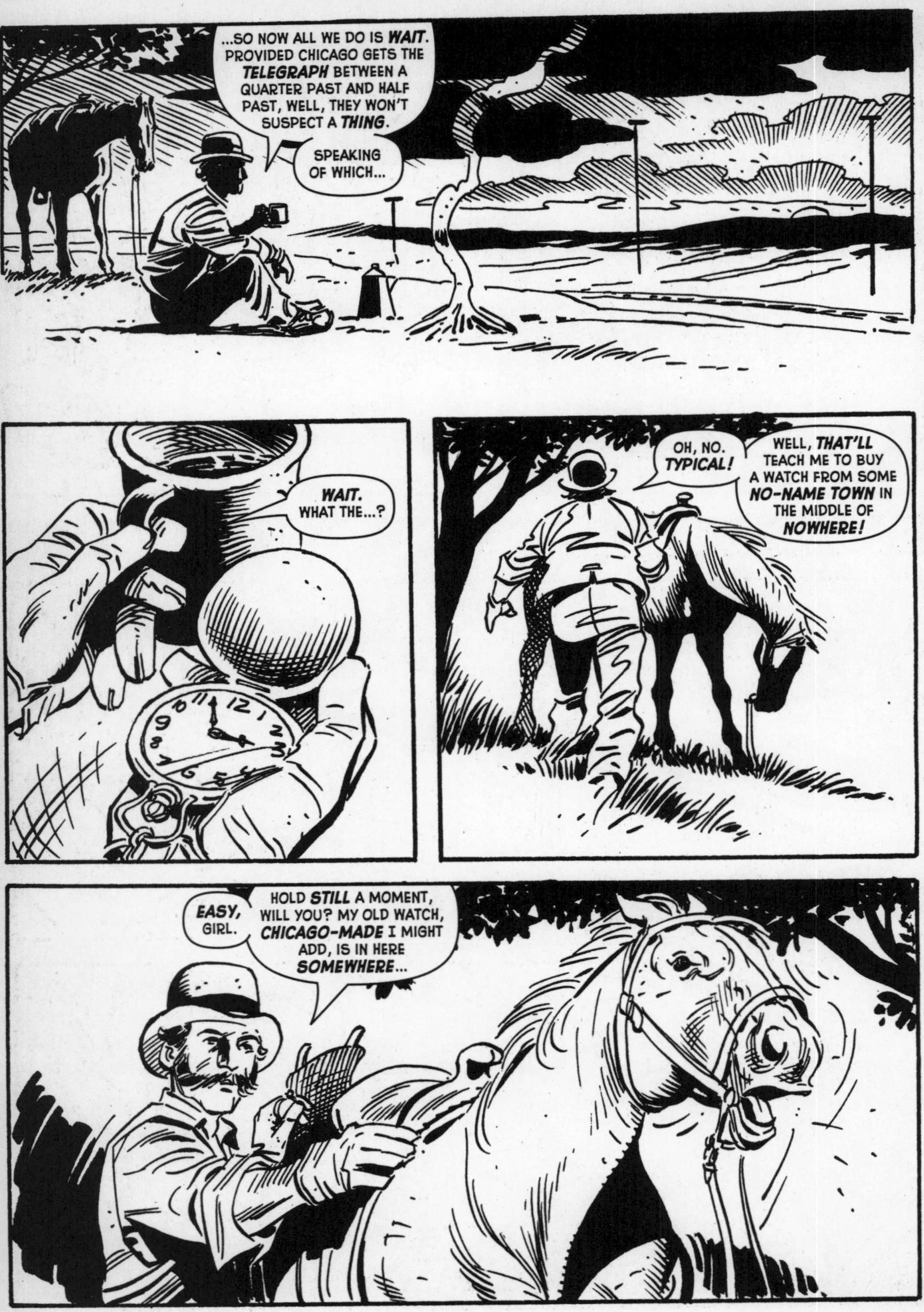
...SO NOW ALL WE DO IS WAIT. PROVIDED CHICAGO GETS THE TELEGRAPH BETWEEN A QUARTER PAST AND HALF PAST, WELL, THEY WON'T SUSPECT A THING.
SPEAKING OF WHICH...
WAIT. WHAT THE...?
OH, NO. TYPICAL!
WELL, THAT'LL TEACH ME TO BUY A WATCH FROM SOME NO-NAME TOWN IN THE MIDDLE OF NOWHERE!
EASY, GIRL.
HOLD STILL A MOMENT, WILL YOU? MY OLD WATCH, CHICAGO-MADE I MIGHT ADD, IS IN HERE SOMEWHERE...

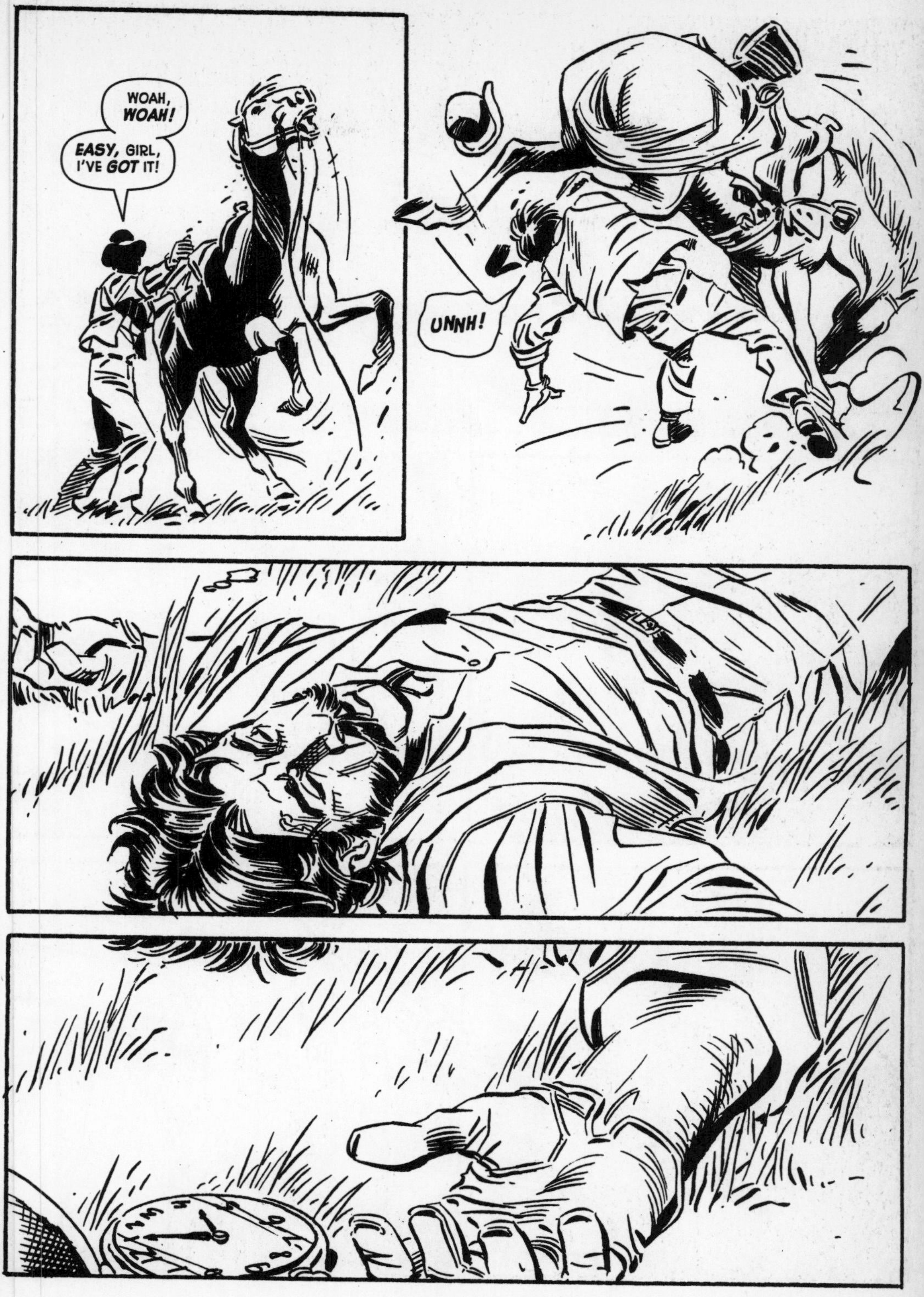
WOAH, WOAH!
EASY, GIRL, I'VE GOT IT!
UNNH!

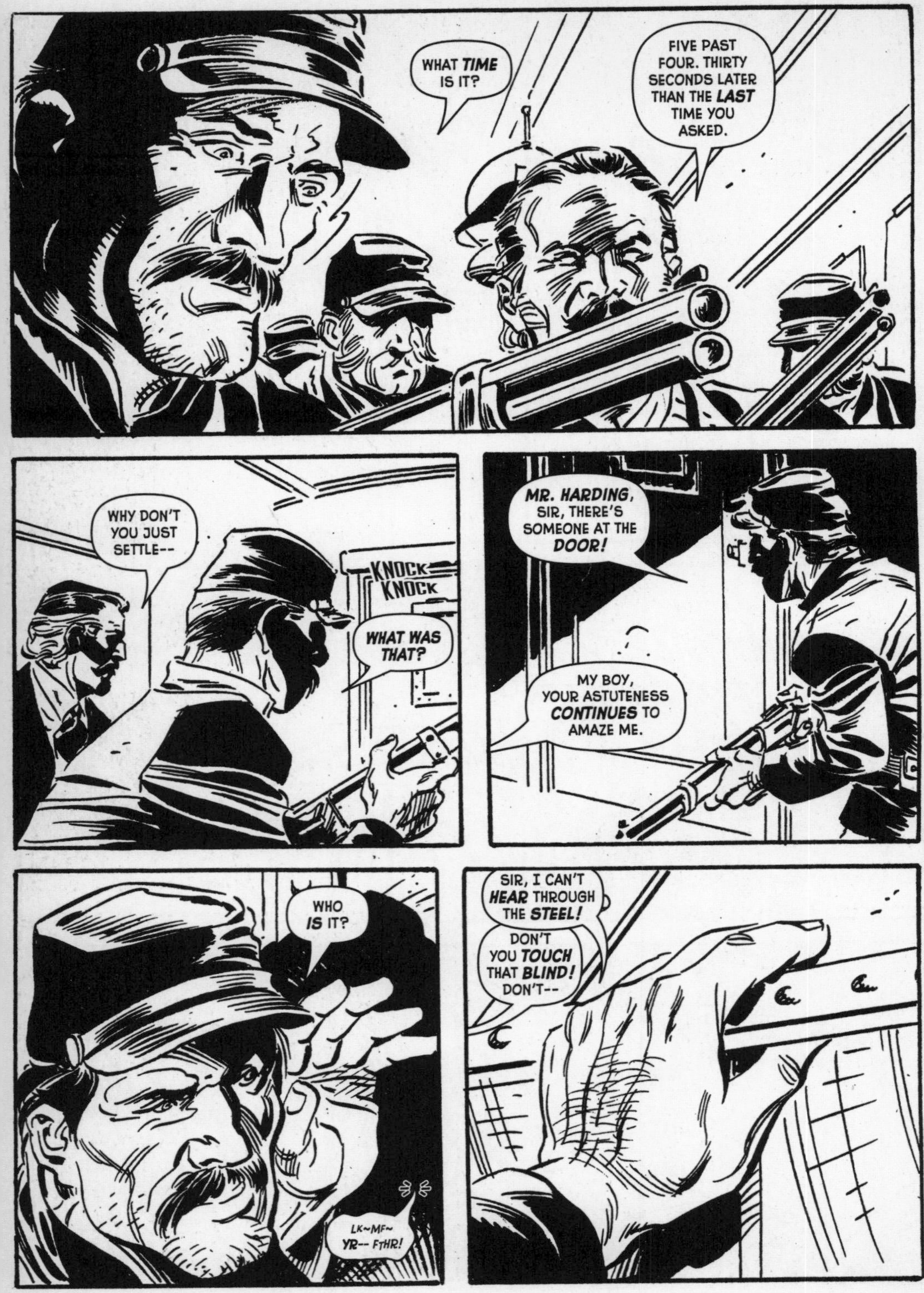
WHAT TIME IS IT?
FIVE PAST FOUR. THIRTY SECONDS LATER THAN THE LAST TIME YOU ASKED.
WHY DON'T YOU JUST SETTLE--
KNOCK KNOCK
WHAT WAS THAT?
MR. HARDING, SIR, THERE'S SOMEONE AT THE DOOR!
MY BOY, YOUR ASTUTENESS CONTINUES TO AMAZE ME.
WHO IS IT?
LK~MF~ YR-- FTHR!
SIR, I CAN'T HEAR THROUGH THE STEEL!
DON'T YOU TOUCH THAT BLIND! DON'T--

I SAID OPEN THE DOOR RIGHT NOW, OR I'LL KILL THIS LOUSY MEXICAN!

...ALL RIGHT.

OPEN THE DOOR.

BUT, MR. HARDING--

OPEN IT.

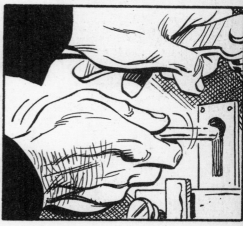

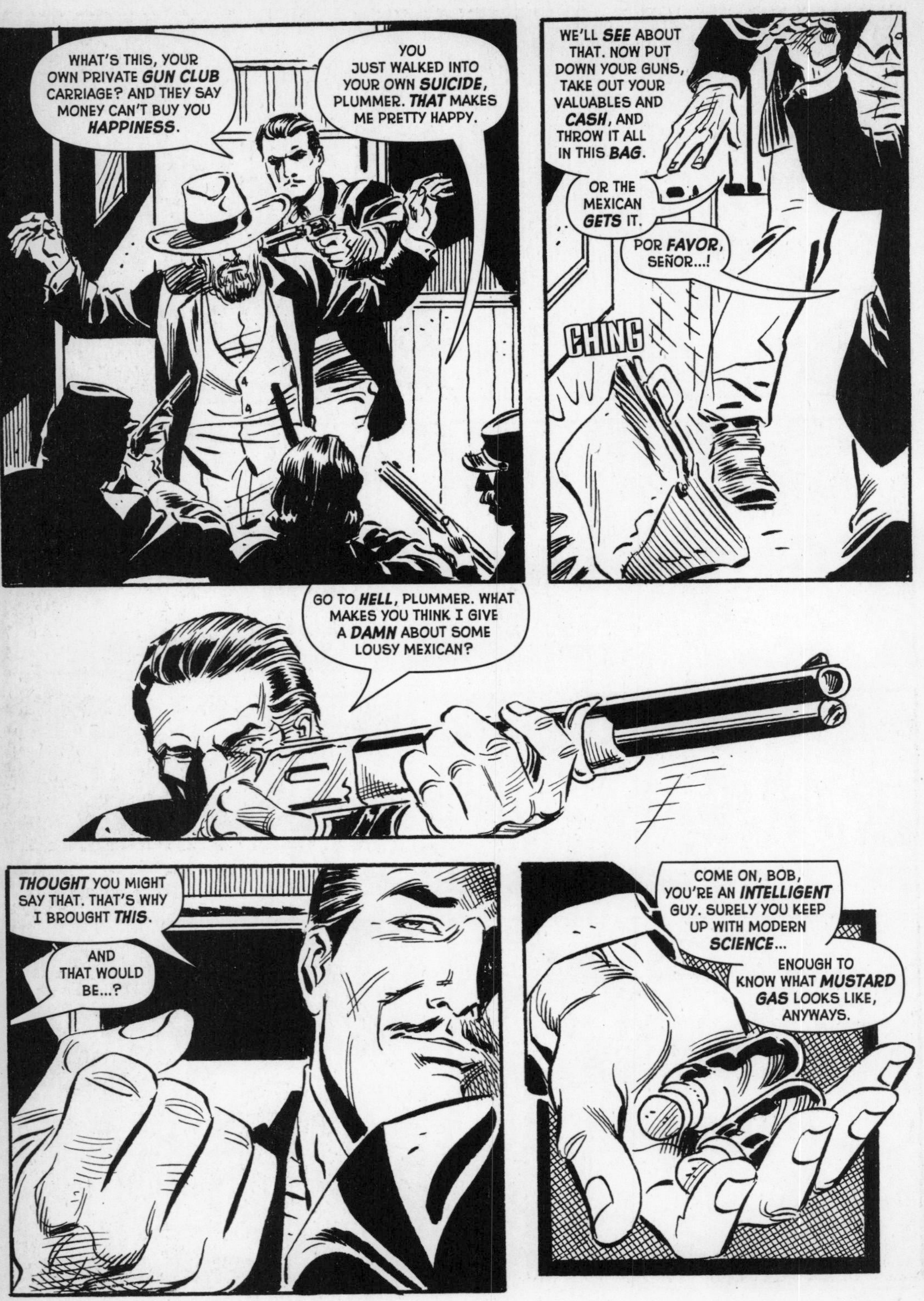
WHAT'S THIS, YOUR OWN PRIVATE GUN CLUB CARRIAGE? AND THEY SAY MONEY CAN'T BUY YOU HAPPINESS.
YOU JUST WALKED INTO YOUR OWN SUICIDE, PLUMMER. THAT MAKES ME PRETTY HAPPY.
WE'LL SEE ABOUT THAT. NOW PUT DOWN YOUR GUNS, TAKE OUT YOUR VALUABLES AND CASH, AND THROW IT ALL IN THIS BAG.
OR THE MEXICAN GETS IT.
POR FAVOR, SEÑOR...!
CHING
GO TO HELL, PLUMMER. WHAT MAKES YOU THINK I GIVE A DAMN ABOUT SOME LOUSY MEXICAN?
THOUGHT YOU MIGHT SAY THAT. THAT'S WHY I BROUGHT THIS.
AND THAT WOULD BE...?
COME ON, BOB, YOU'RE AN INTELLIGENT GUY. SURELY YOU KEEP UP WITH MODERN SCIENCE...
ENOUGH TO KNOW WHAT MUSTARD GAS LOOKS LIKE, ANYWAYS.

YOU'D KILL EVERYONE ON THE *TRAIN*, YOU IDIOT. INCLUDING *YOU*.

LONG AS I CAN TAKE YOU *WITH* ME, I'LL DIE *HAPPY*. HOW ABOUT *YOU*, BOB?

SEÑOR, *NO*... I WORK, I HAVE *FAMILY*...

SHUT UP, PONCHO.

NO! I WILL NOT LET YOU *DO* THIS!

NNGH!

GET *OFF* ME, YOU *STUPID*--

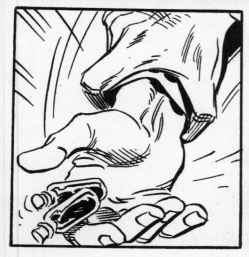

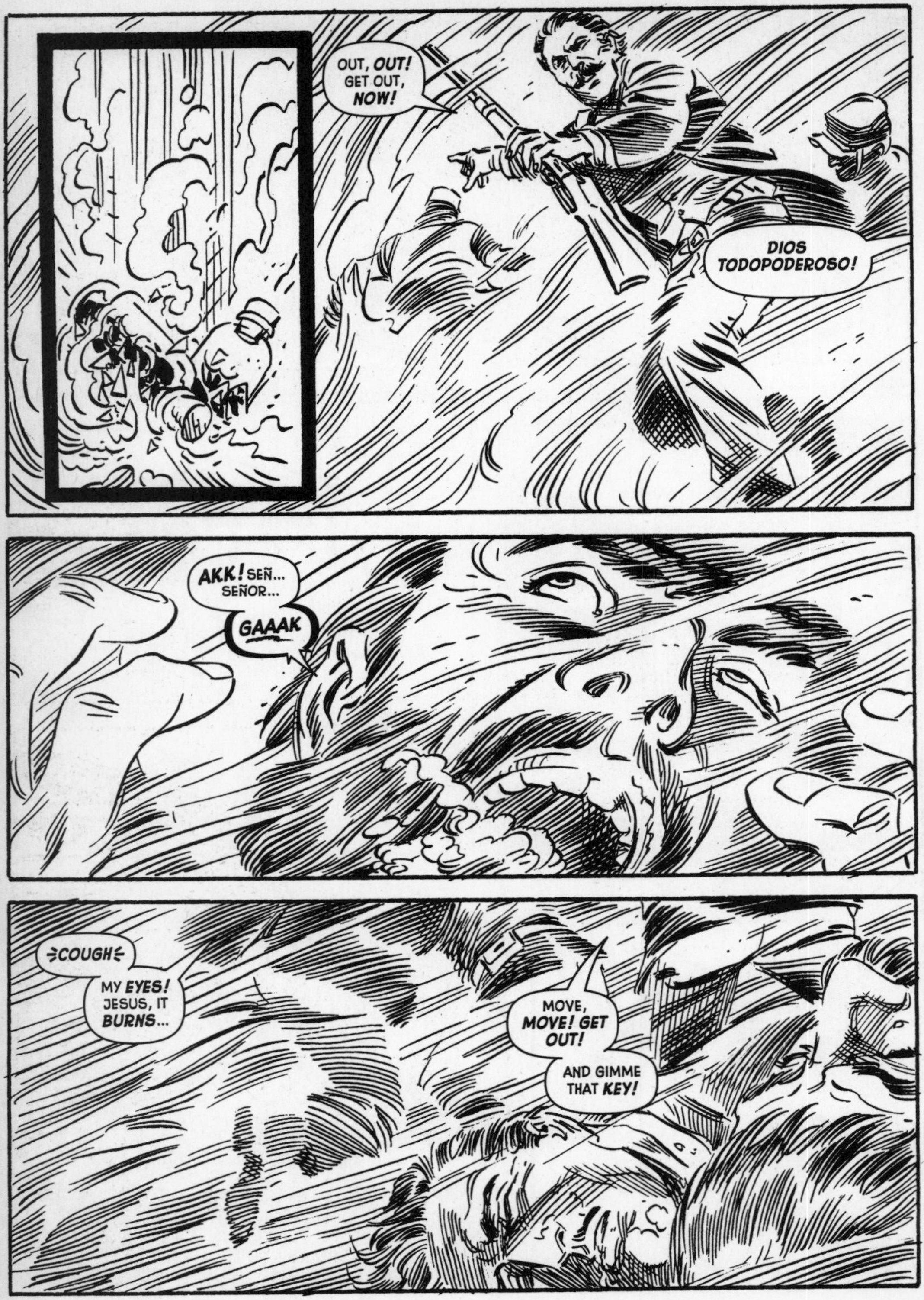
OUT, OUT! GET OUT, NOW!
DIOS TODOPODEROSO!
AKK! SEÑ... SEÑOR...
GAAAK
COUGH
MY EYES! JESUS, IT BURNS...
MOVE, MOVE! GET OUT!
AND GIMME THAT KEY!

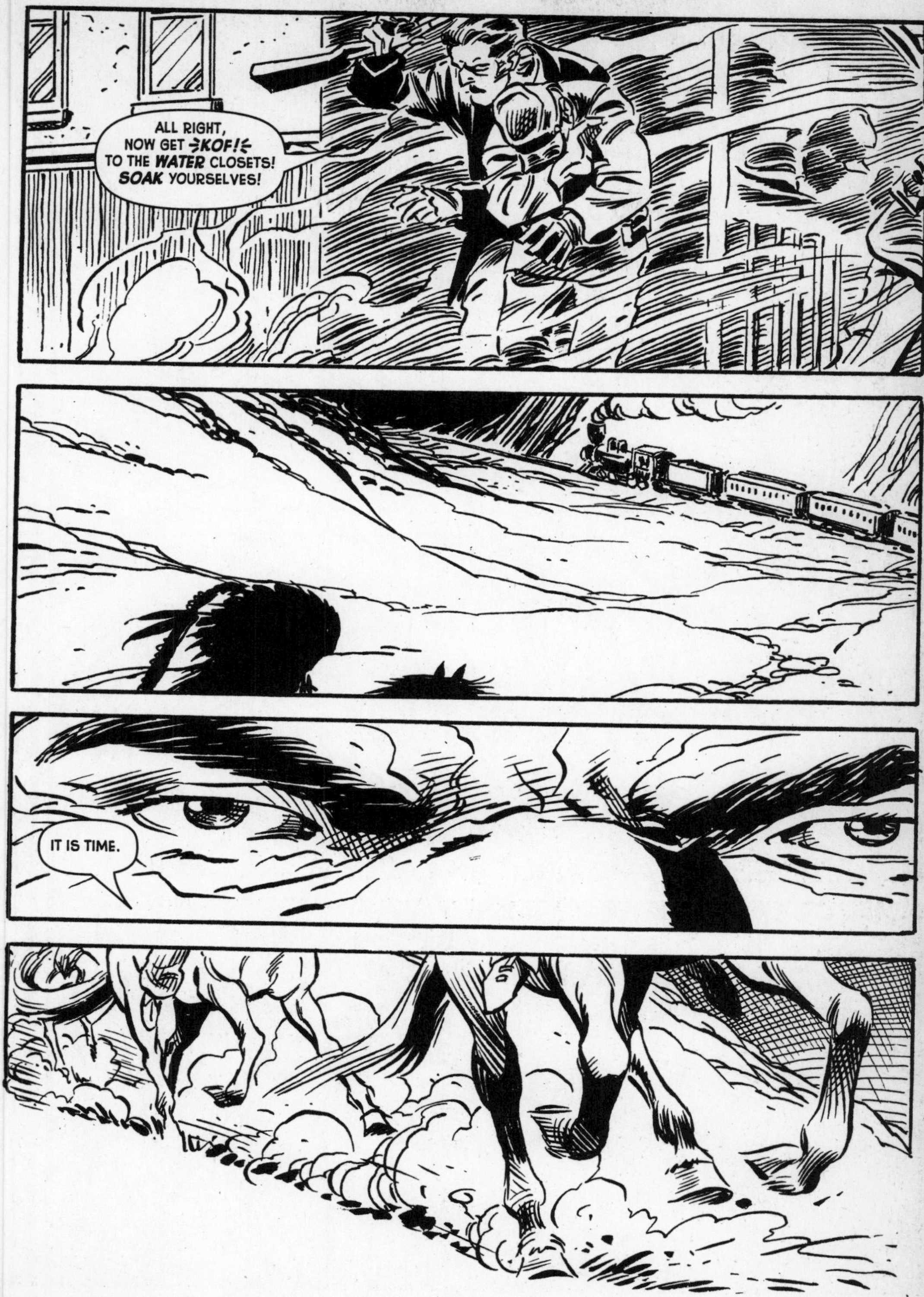
ALL RIGHT, NOW GET ⇒KOF!⇐ TO THE WATER CLOSETS! SOAK YOURSELVES!
IT IS TIME.

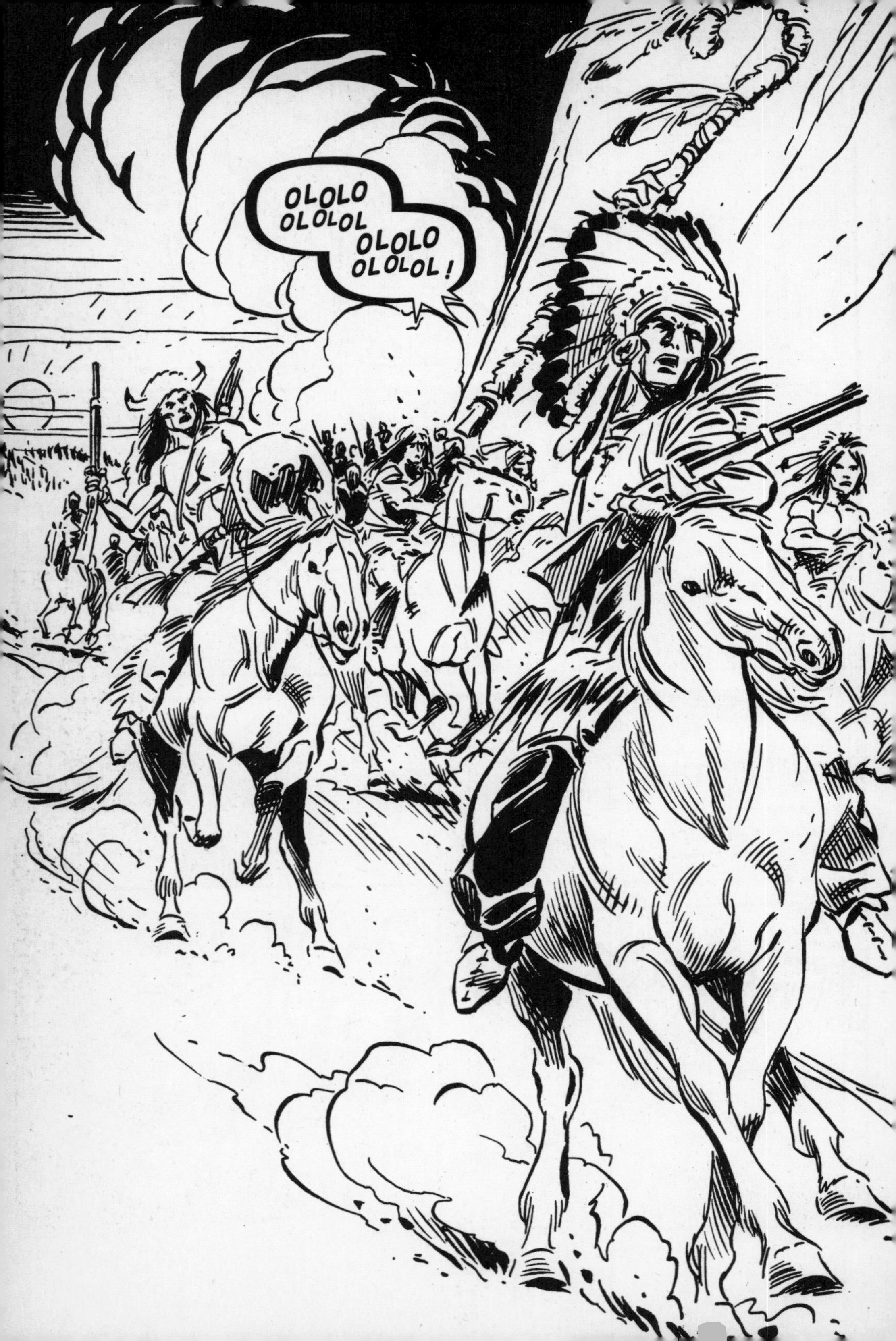
OLOLO OLOLOL OLOLO OLOLOL!

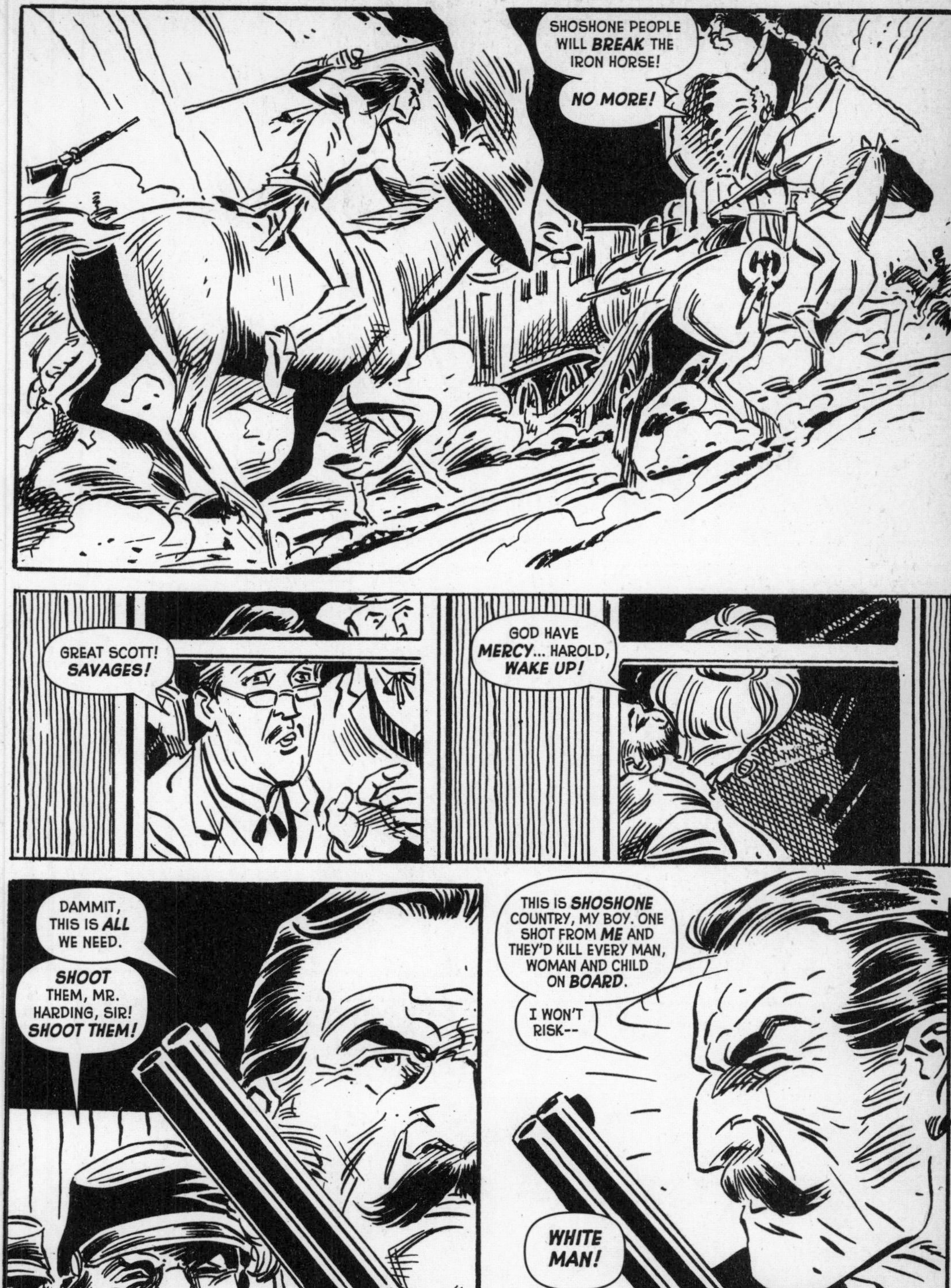
SHOSHONE PEOPLE WILL BREAK THE IRON HORSE!
NO MORE!
GREAT SCOTT! SAVAGES!
GOD HAVE MERCY... HAROLD, WAKE UP!
DAMMIT, THIS IS ALL WE NEED.
SHOOT THEM, MR. HARDING, SIR! SHOOT THEM!
THIS IS SHOSHONE COUNTRY, MY BOY. ONE SHOT FROM ME AND THEY'D KILL EVERY MAN, WOMAN AND CHILD ON BOARD.
I WON'T RISK--
WHITE MAN!

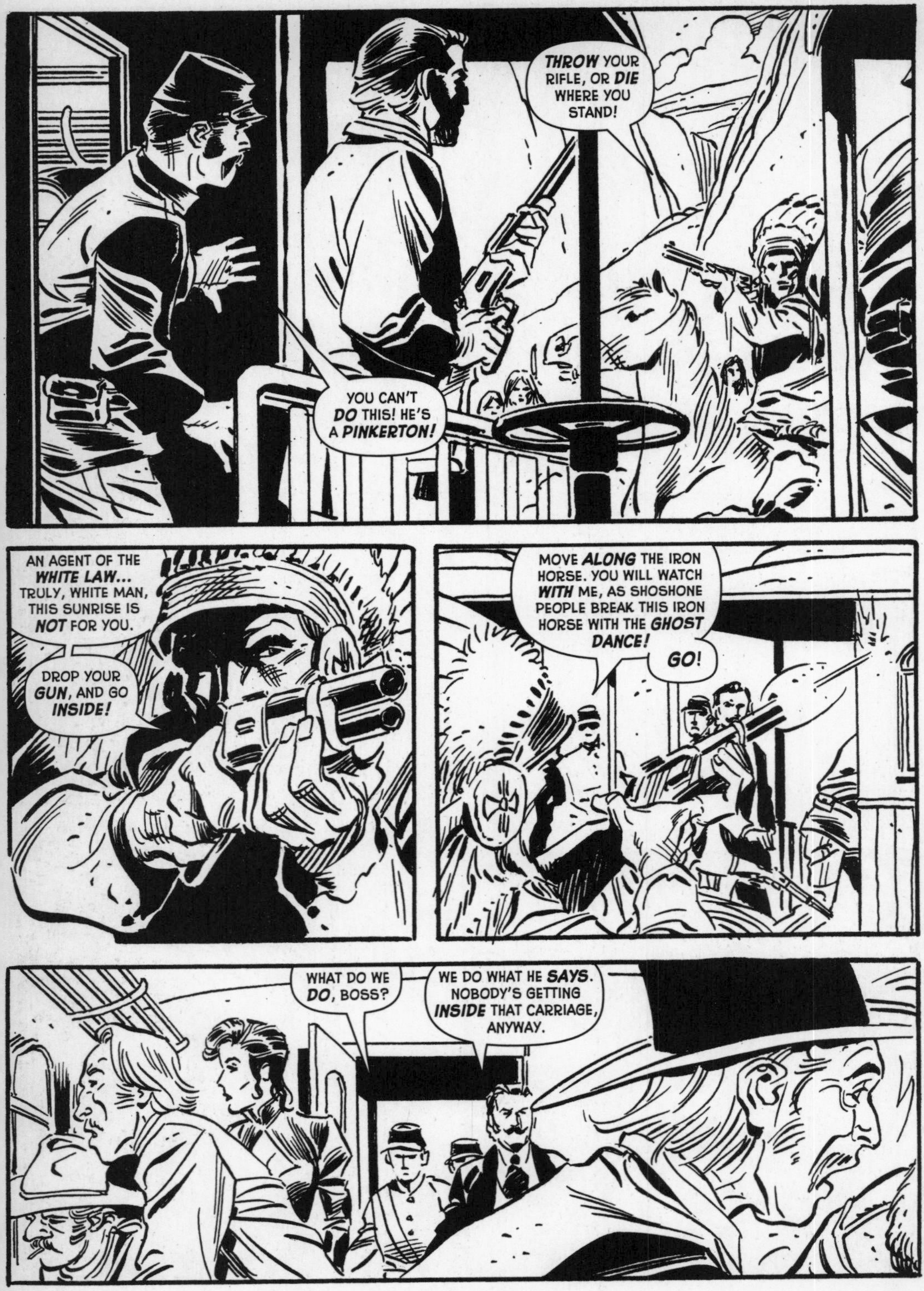
THROW YOUR RIFLE, OR DIE WHERE YOU STAND!
YOU CAN'T DO THIS! HE'S A PINKERTON!
AN AGENT OF THE WHITE LAW... TRULY, WHITE MAN, THIS SUNRISE IS NOT FOR YOU.
DROP YOUR GUN, AND GO INSIDE!
MOVE ALONG THE IRON HORSE. YOU WILL WATCH WITH ME, AS SHOSHONE PEOPLE BREAK THIS IRON HORSE WITH THE GHOST DANCE!
GO!
WHAT DO WE DO, BOSS?
WE DO WHAT HE SAYS. NOBODY'S GETTING INSIDE THAT CARRIAGE, ANYWAY.

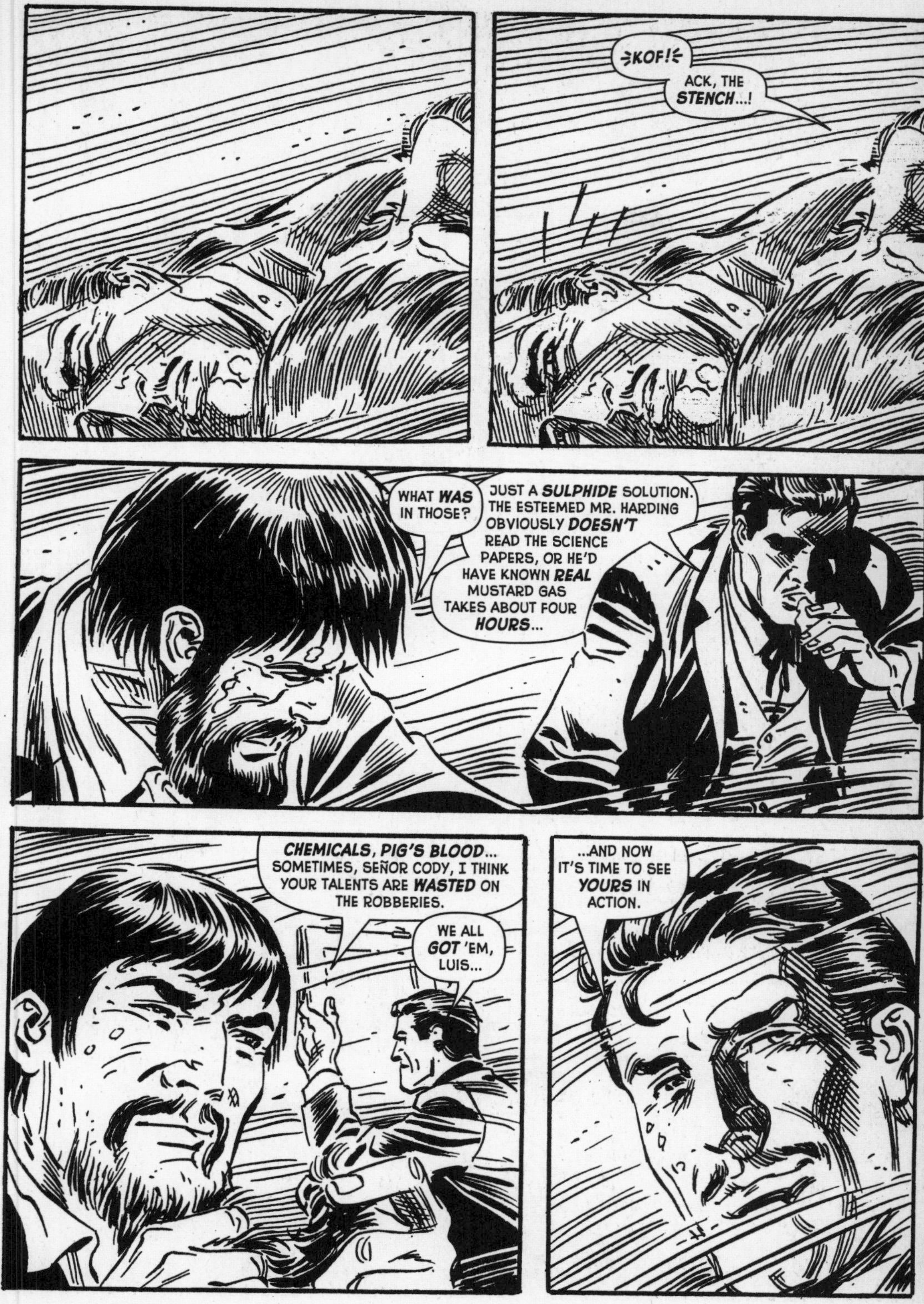
KOF!
ACK, THE STENCH...!
WHAT WAS IN THOSE?
JUST A SULPHIDE SOLUTION. THE ESTEEMED MR. HARDING OBVIOUSLY DOESN'T READ THE SCIENCE PAPERS, OR HE'D HAVE KNOWN REAL MUSTARD GAS TAKES ABOUT FOUR HOURS...
CHEMICALS, PIG'S BLOOD... SOMETIMES, SEÑOR CODY, I THINK YOUR TALENTS ARE WASTED ON THE ROBBERIES.
WE ALL GOT 'EM, LUIS...
...AND NOW IT'S TIME TO SEE YOURS IN ACTION.

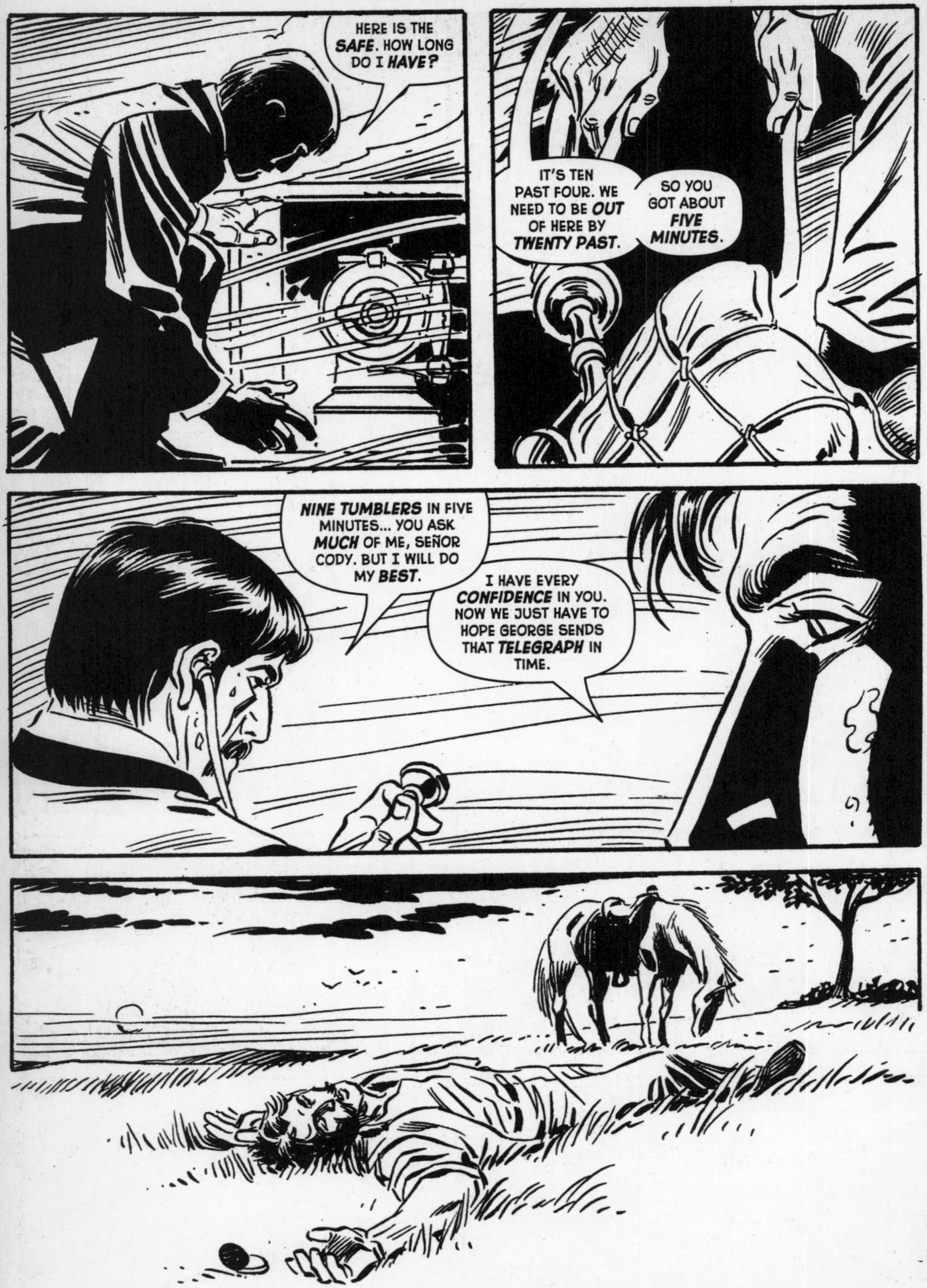
HERE IS THE SAFE. HOW LONG DO I HAVE?
IT'S TEN PAST FOUR. WE NEED TO BE OUT OF HERE BY TWENTY PAST.
SO YOU GOT ABOUT FIVE MINUTES.
NINE TUMBLERS IN FIVE MINUTES... YOU ASK MUCH OF ME, SEÑOR CODY. BUT I WILL DO MY BEST.
I HAVE EVERY CONFIDENCE IN YOU. NOW WE JUST HAVE TO HOPE GEORGE SENDS THAT TELEGRAPH IN TIME.

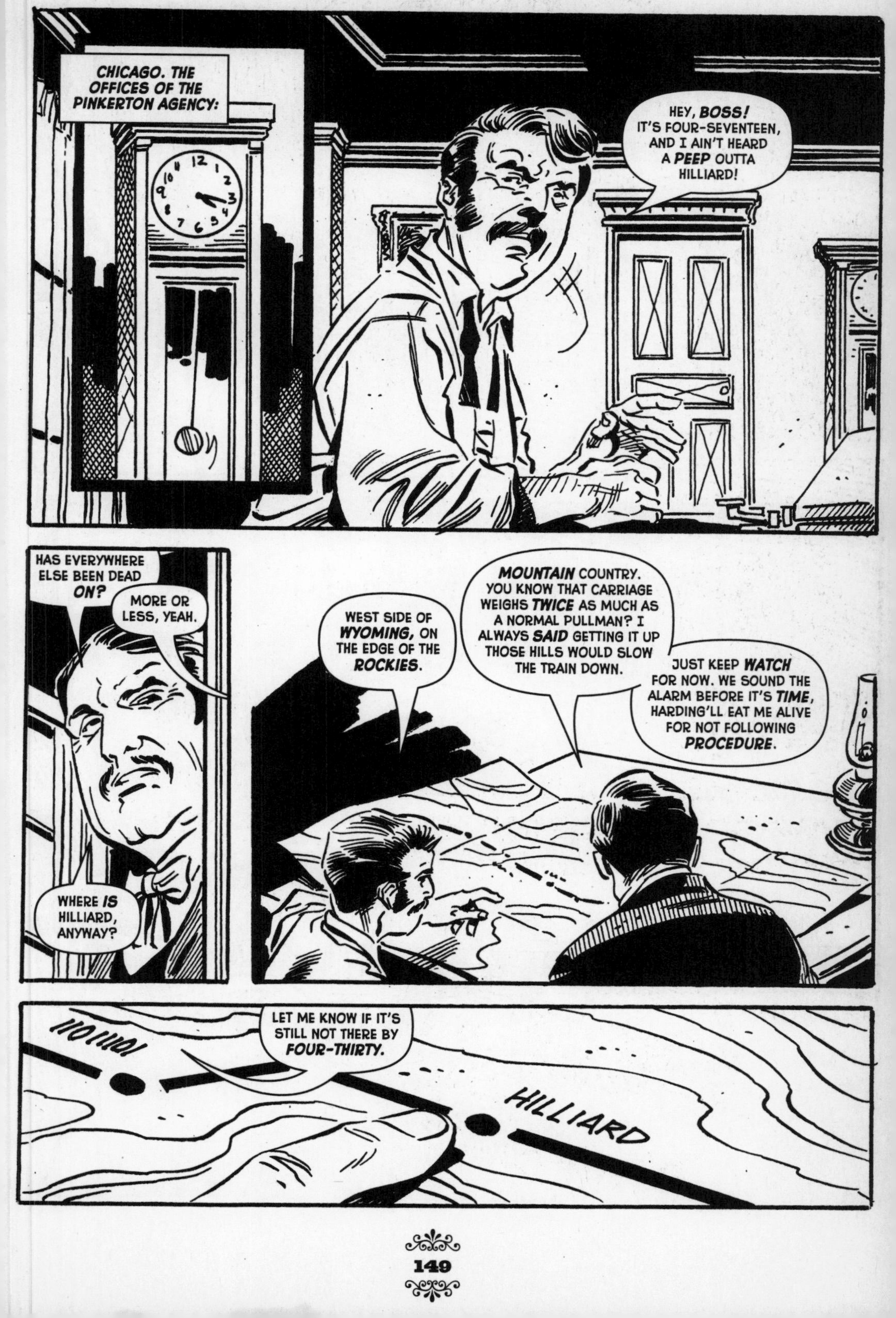
CHICAGO. THE OFFICES OF THE PINKERTON AGENCY:
HEY, BOSS! IT'S FOUR-SEVENTEEN, AND I AIN'T HEARD A PEEP OUTTA HILLIARD!
HAS EVERYWHERE ELSE BEEN DEAD ON?
MORE OR LESS, YEAH.
WHERE IS HILLIARD, ANYWAY?
WEST SIDE OF WYOMING, ON THE EDGE OF THE ROCKIES.
MOUNTAIN COUNTRY. YOU KNOW THAT CARRIAGE WEIGHS TWICE AS MUCH AS A NORMAL PULLMAN? I ALWAYS SAID GETTING IT UP THOSE HILLS WOULD SLOW THE TRAIN DOWN.
JUST KEEP WATCH FOR NOW. WE SOUND THE ALARM BEFORE IT'S TIME, HARDING'LL EAT ME ALIVE FOR NOT FOLLOWING PROCEDURE.
LET ME KNOW IF IT'S STILL NOT THERE BY FOUR-THIRTY.
HILLIARD

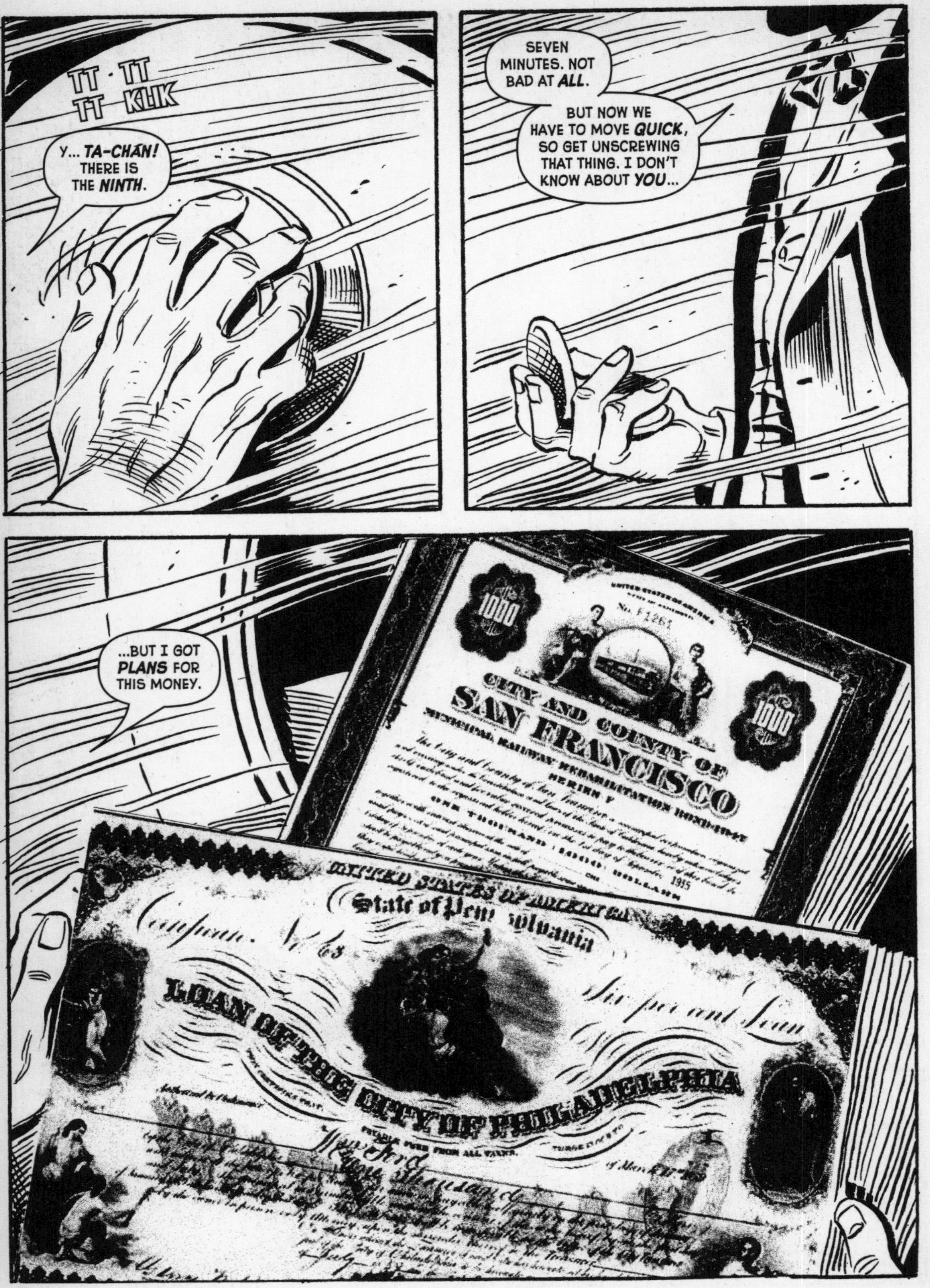
TT · TT
TT KLIK
Y... TA-CHÁN! THERE IS THE NINTH.
SEVEN MINUTES. NOT BAD AT ALL.
BUT NOW WE HAVE TO MOVE QUICK, SO GET UNSCREWING THAT THING. I DON'T KNOW ABOUT YOU...
...BUT I GOT PLANS FOR THIS MONEY.
1000
1000
CITY AND COUNTY OF
SAN FRANCISCO
SERIES F
ONE THOUSAND 1000 DOLLARS
1915
UNITED STATES OF AMERICA
State of Pennsylvania
Six per cent Loan
LOAN OF THE CITY OF PHILADELPHIA
FREE FROM ALL TAXES.

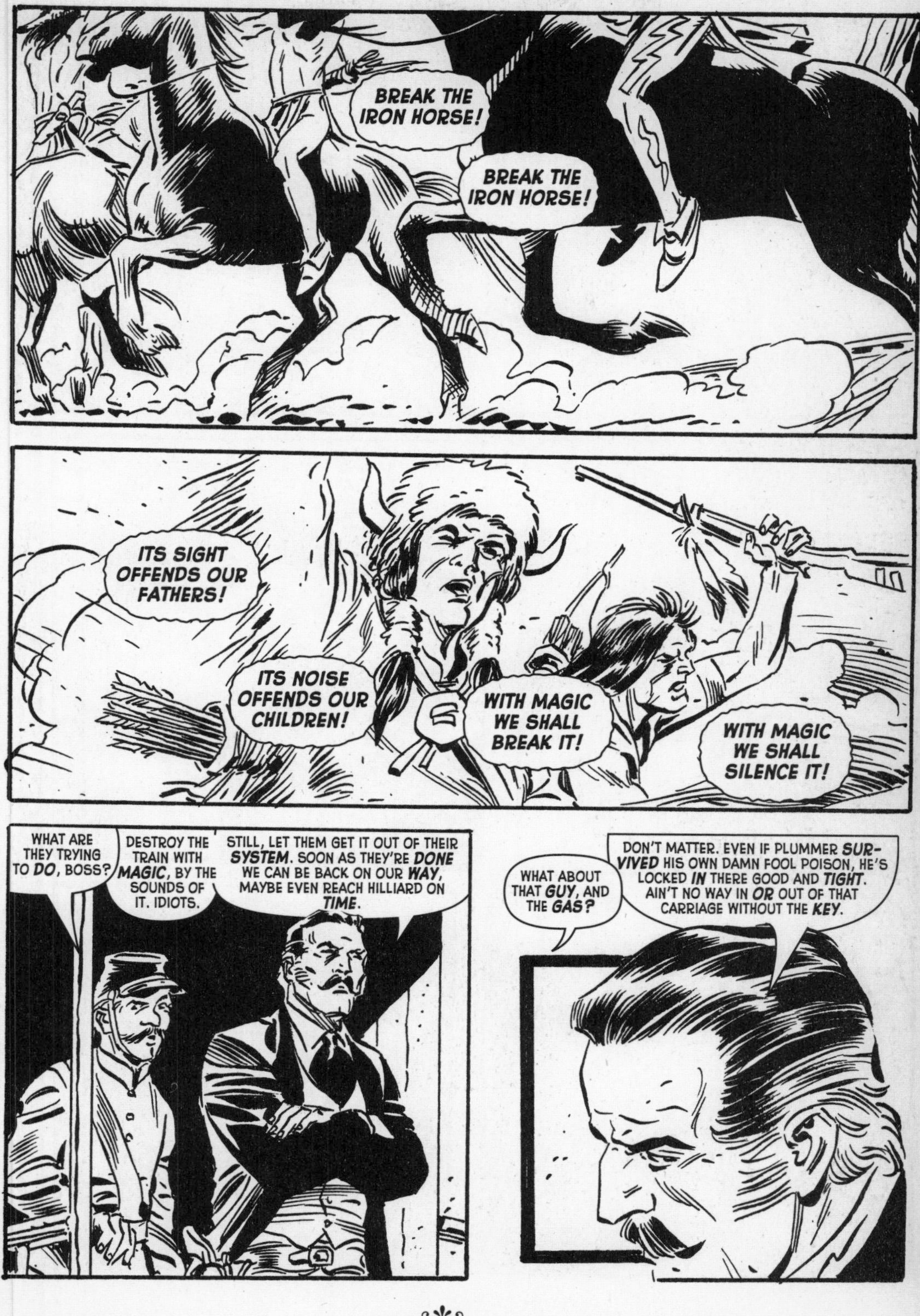
BREAK THE IRON HORSE!
BREAK THE IRON HORSE!
ITS SIGHT OFFENDS OUR FATHERS!
ITS NOISE OFFENDS OUR CHILDREN!
WITH MAGIC WE SHALL BREAK IT!
WITH MAGIC WE SHALL SILENCE IT!
WHAT ARE THEY TRYING TO DO, BOSS?
DESTROY THE TRAIN WITH MAGIC, BY THE SOUNDS OF IT. IDIOTS.
STILL, LET THEM GET IT OUT OF THEIR SYSTEM. SOON AS THEY'RE DONE WE CAN BE BACK ON OUR WAY, MAYBE EVEN REACH HILLIARD ON TIME.
WHAT ABOUT THAT GUY, AND THE GAS?
DON'T MATTER. EVEN IF PLUMMER SURVIVED HIS OWN DAMN FOOL POISON, HE'S LOCKED IN THERE GOOD AND TIGHT. AIN'T NO WAY IN OR OUT OF THAT CARRIAGE WITHOUT THE KEY.

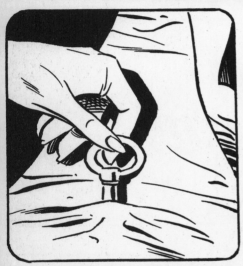

ARE YOU ALL *RIGHT*, MA'AM? LET ME HELP YOU *UP*, HERE.

WELL, *GOODNESS* ME... THANK YOU, SIR. YOU'RE VERY *KIND*.

DON'T MENTION IT, MA'AM. GOOD *NIGHT*.

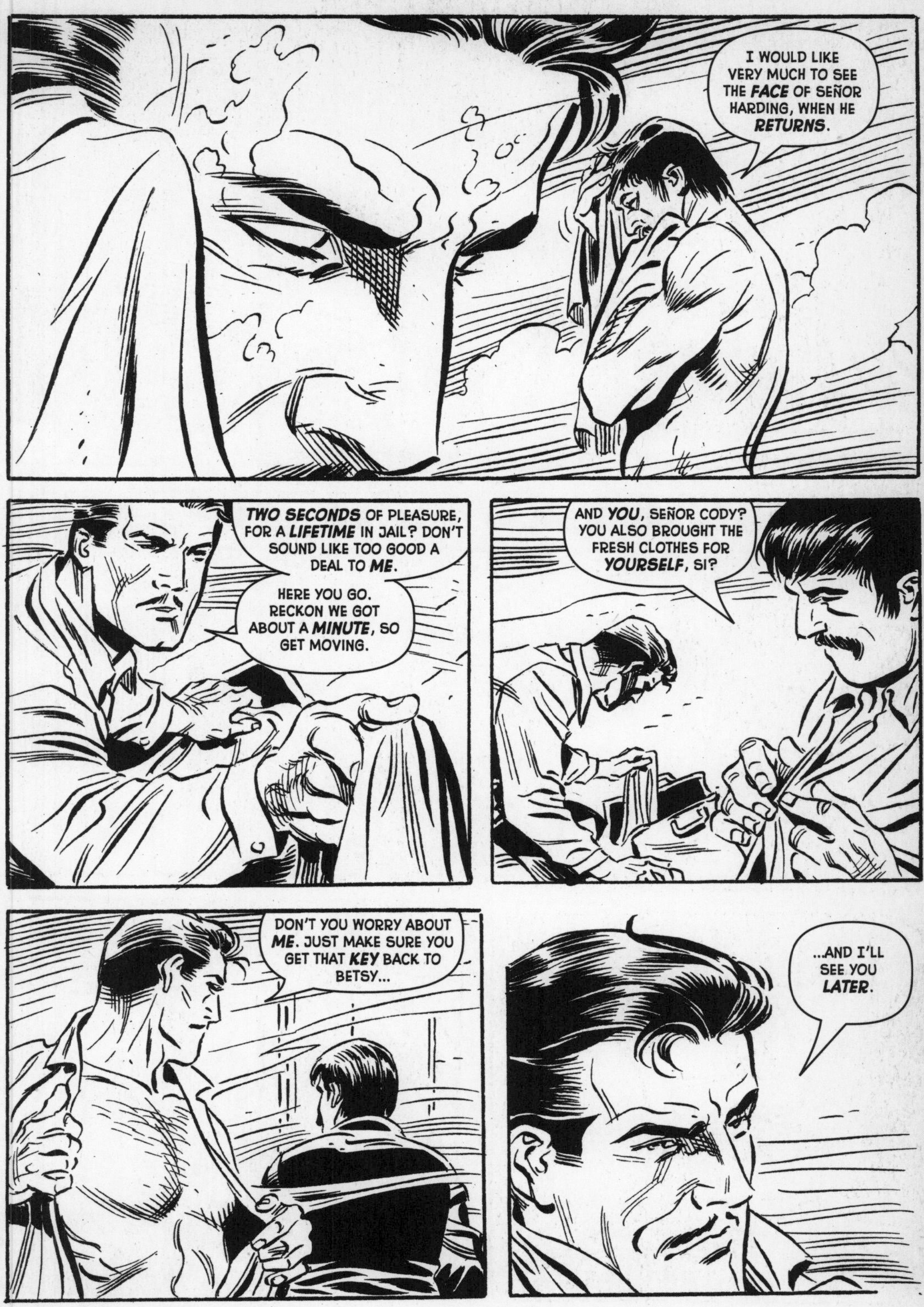
I WOULD LIKE VERY MUCH TO SEE THE FACE OF SEÑOR HARDING, WHEN HE RETURNS.
TWO SECONDS OF PLEASURE, FOR A LIFETIME IN JAIL? DON'T SOUND LIKE TOO GOOD A DEAL TO ME.
HERE YOU GO. RECKON WE GOT ABOUT A MINUTE, SO GET MOVING.
AND YOU, SEÑOR CODY? YOU ALSO BROUGHT THE FRESH CLOTHES FOR YOURSELF, SI?
DON'T YOU WORRY ABOUT ME. JUST MAKE SURE YOU GET THAT KEY BACK TO BETSY...
...AND I'LL SEE YOU LATER.

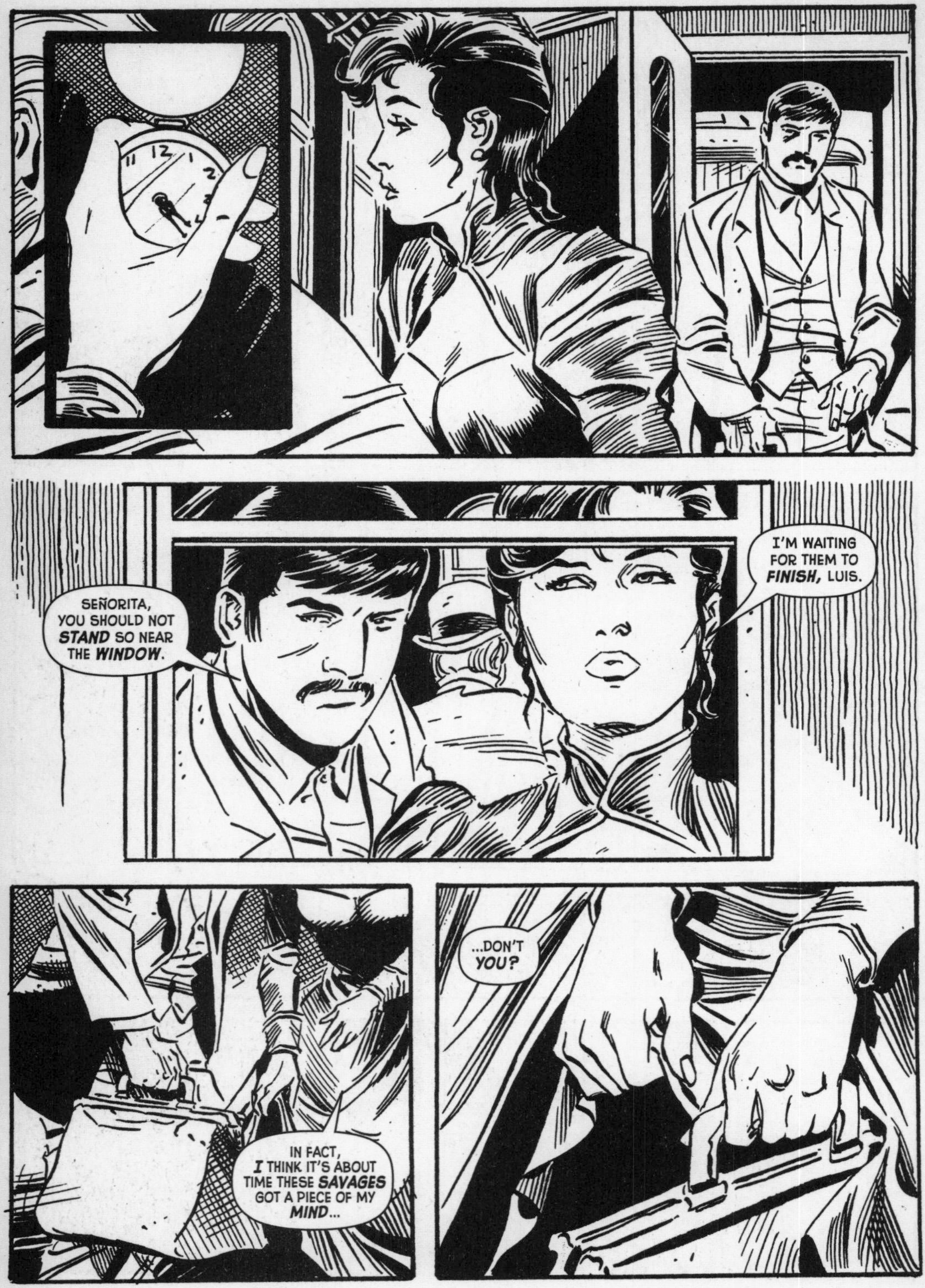
SEÑORITA, YOU SHOULD NOT STAND SO NEAR THE WINDOW.
I'M WAITING FOR THEM TO FINISH, LUIS.
IN FACT, I THINK IT'S ABOUT TIME THESE SAVAGES GOT A PIECE OF MY MIND...
...DON'T YOU?

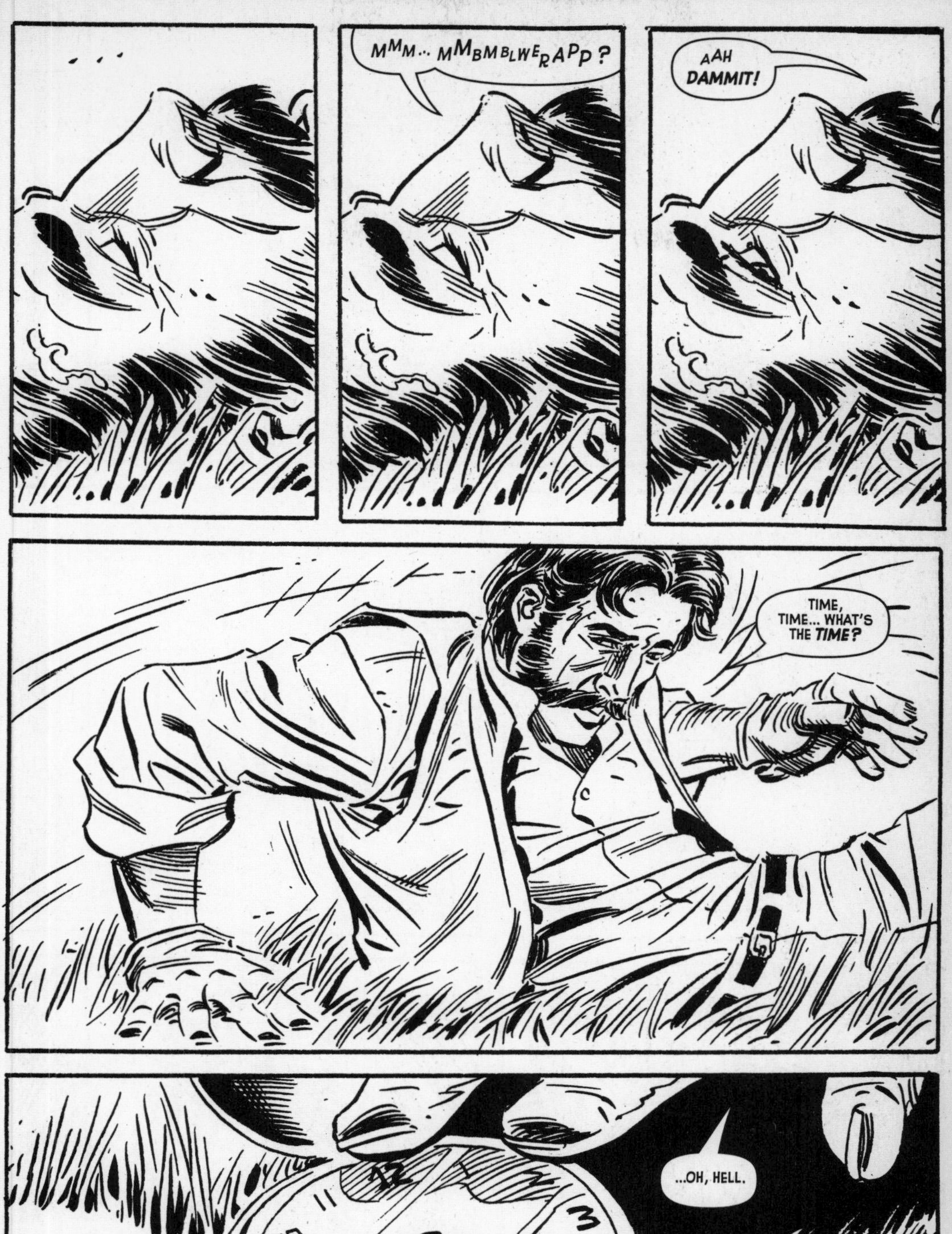
. . .
MMM... MMBMBLWERAPP?
AAH DAMMIT!
TIME, TIME... WHAT'S THE TIME?
...OH, HELL.

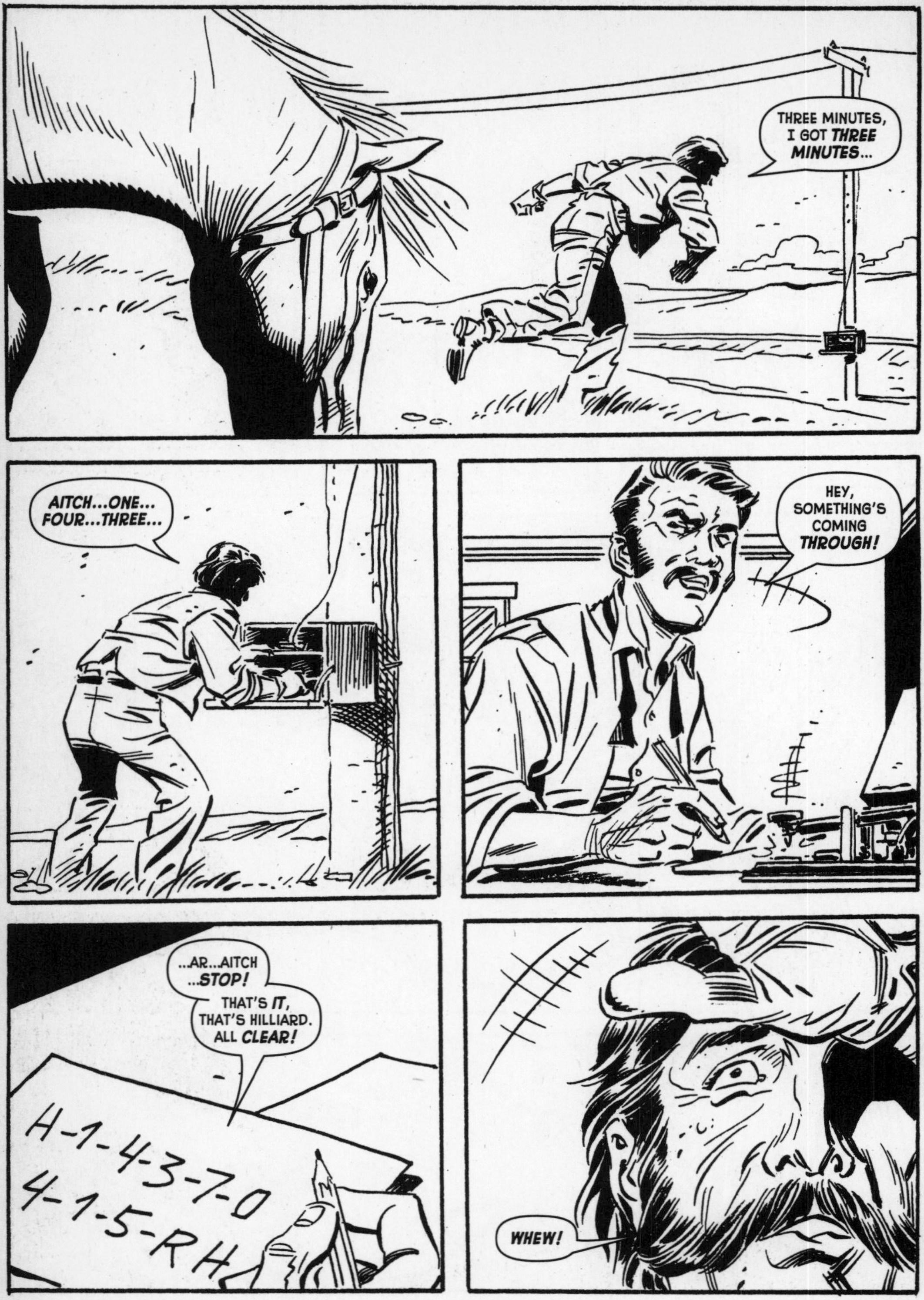

THREE MINUTES, I GOT THREE MINUTES...
AITCH...ONE... FOUR...THREE...
HEY, SOMETHING'S COMING THROUGH!
...AR...AITCH ...STOP!
THAT'S IT, THAT'S HILLIARD. ALL CLEAR!
H-1-4-3-7-0
4-1-5-RH
WHEW!

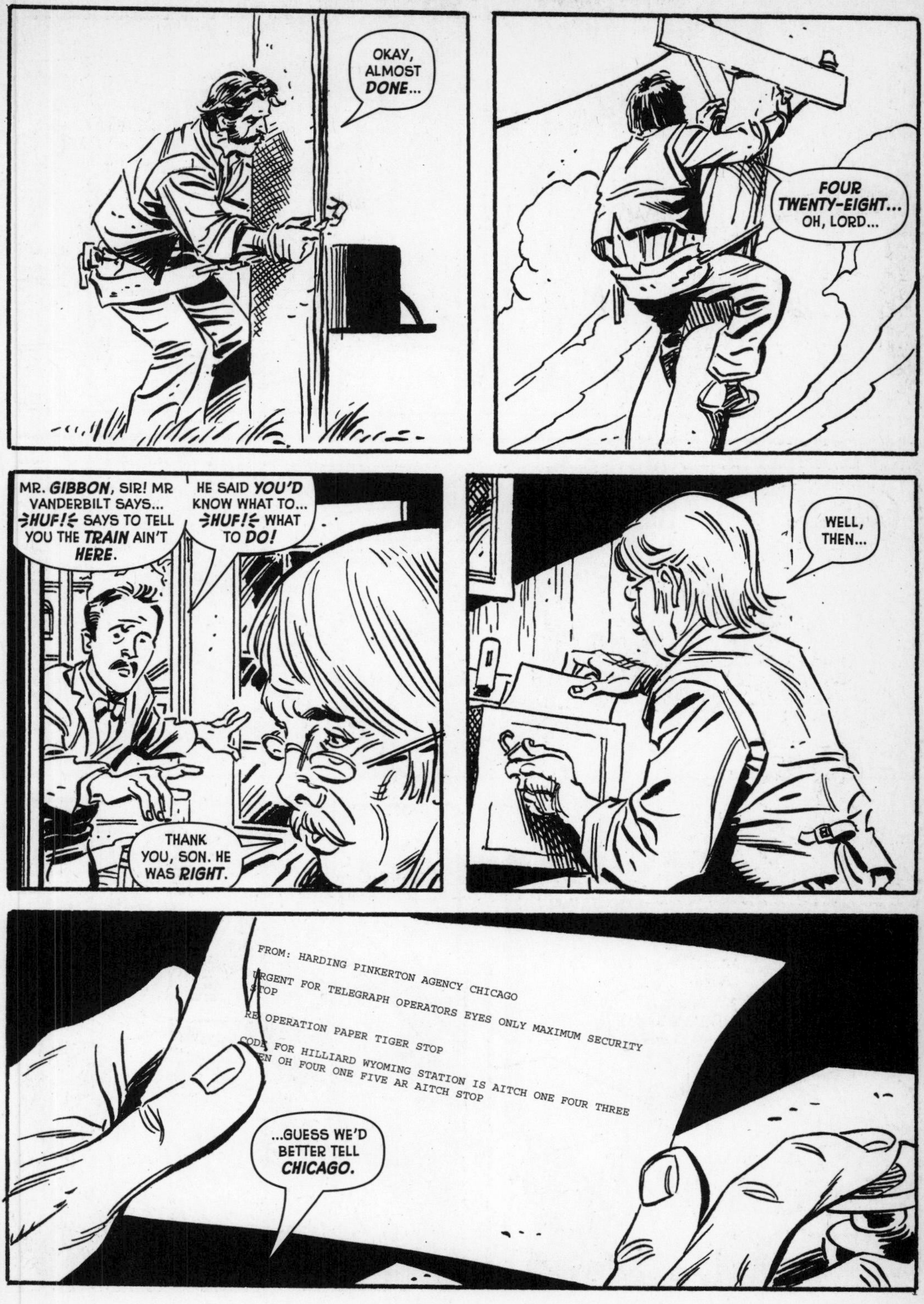

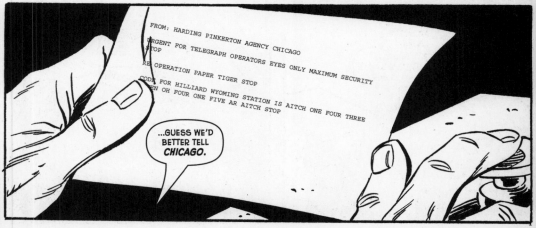

OKAY, ALMOST DONE...
FOUR TWENTY-EIGHT... OH, LORD...
MR. GIBBON, SIR! MR VANDERBILT SAYS... HUF! SAYS TO TELL YOU THE TRAIN AIN'T HERE.
HE SAID YOU'D KNOW WHAT TO... HUF! WHAT TO DO!
THANK YOU, SON. HE WAS RIGHT.
WELL, THEN...
FROM: HARDING PINKERTON AGENCY CHICAGO
URGENT FOR TELEGRAPH OPERATORS EYES ONLY MAXIMUM SECURITY STOP
RE OPERATION PAPER TIGER STOP
CODE FOR HILLIARD WYOMING STATION IS AITCH ONE FOUR THREE
EN OH FOUR ONE FIVE AR AITCH STOP
...GUESS WE'D BETTER TELL CHICAGO.

C'MON, *C'MON*...

CLAMP *OFF*, AND NOW...

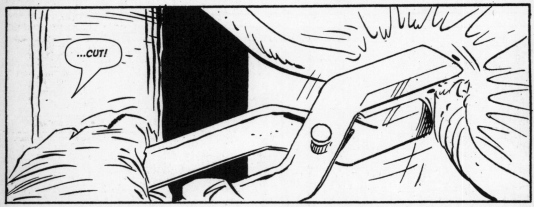

...CUT!

WELL, *THAT'S* STRANGE. THERE DOESN'T SEEM TO BE ANY *SIGNAL*...

WOOOOOOH!

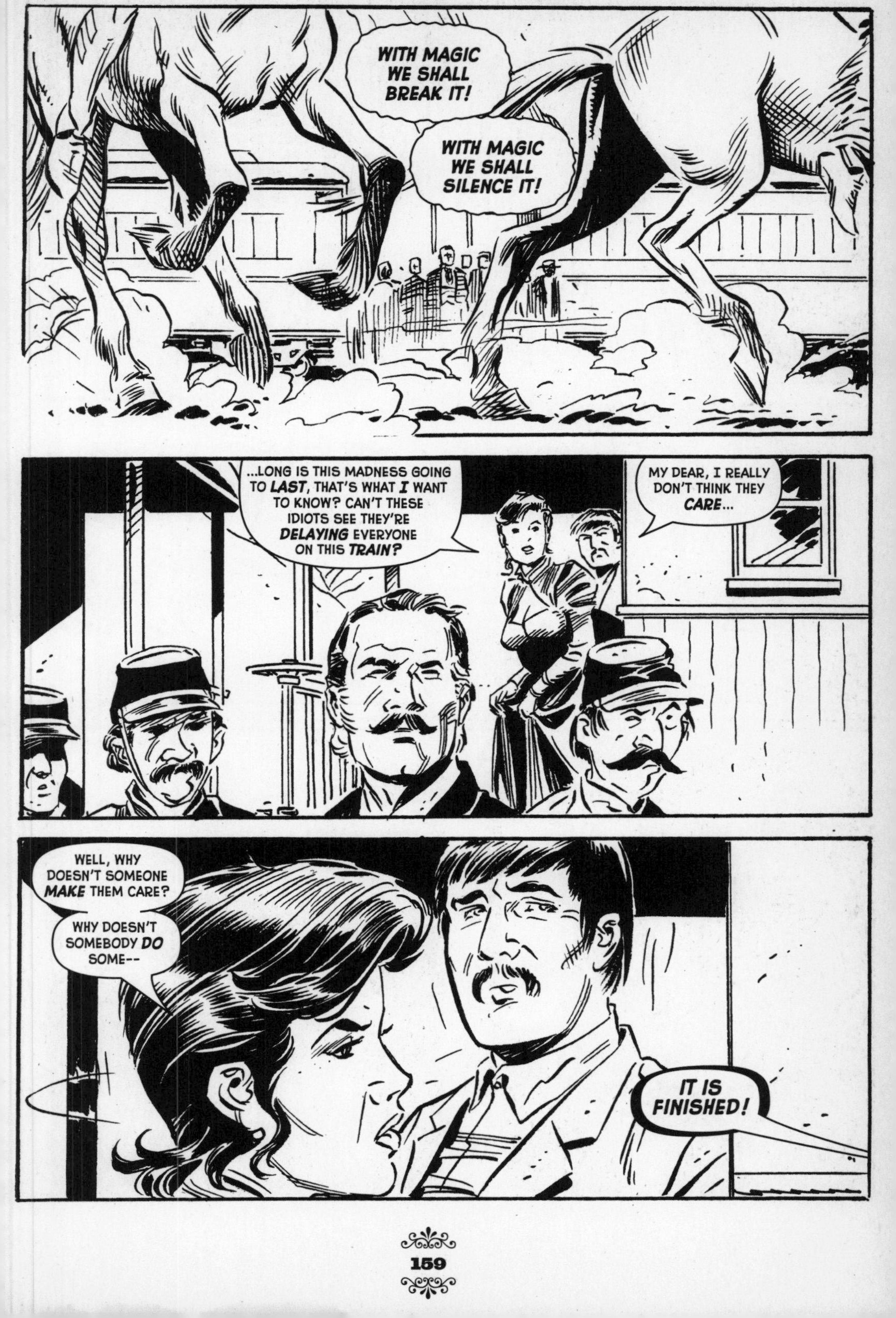
WITH MAGIC WE SHALL BREAK IT!
WITH MAGIC WE SHALL SILENCE IT!
...LONG IS THIS MADNESS GOING TO LAST, THAT'S WHAT I WANT TO KNOW? CAN'T THESE IDIOTS SEE THEY'RE DELAYING EVERYONE ON THIS TRAIN?
MY DEAR, I REALLY DON'T THINK THEY CARE...
WELL, WHY DOESN'T SOMEONE MAKE THEM CARE?
WHY DOESN'T SOMEBODY DO SOME--
IT IS FINISHED!

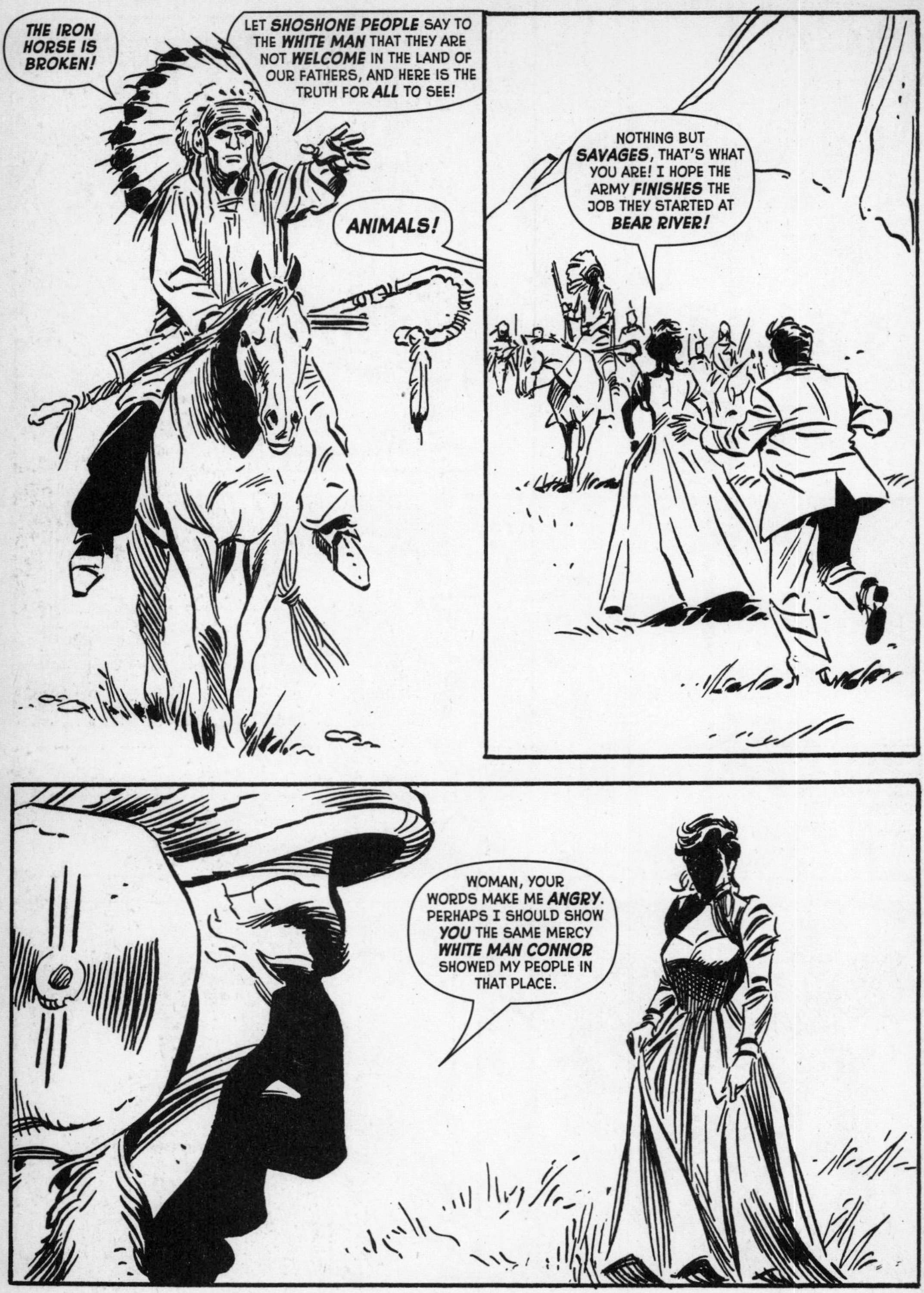
THE IRON HORSE IS BROKEN!
LET SHOSHONE PEOPLE SAY TO THE WHITE MAN THAT THEY ARE NOT WELCOME IN THE LAND OF OUR FATHERS, AND HERE IS THE TRUTH FOR ALL TO SEE!
ANIMALS!
NOTHING BUT SAVAGES, THAT'S WHAT YOU ARE! I HOPE THE ARMY FINISHES THE JOB THEY STARTED AT BEAR RIVER!
WOMAN, YOUR WORDS MAKE ME ANGRY. PERHAPS I SHOULD SHOW YOU THE SAME MERCY WHITE MAN CONNOR SHOWED MY PEOPLE IN THAT PLACE.

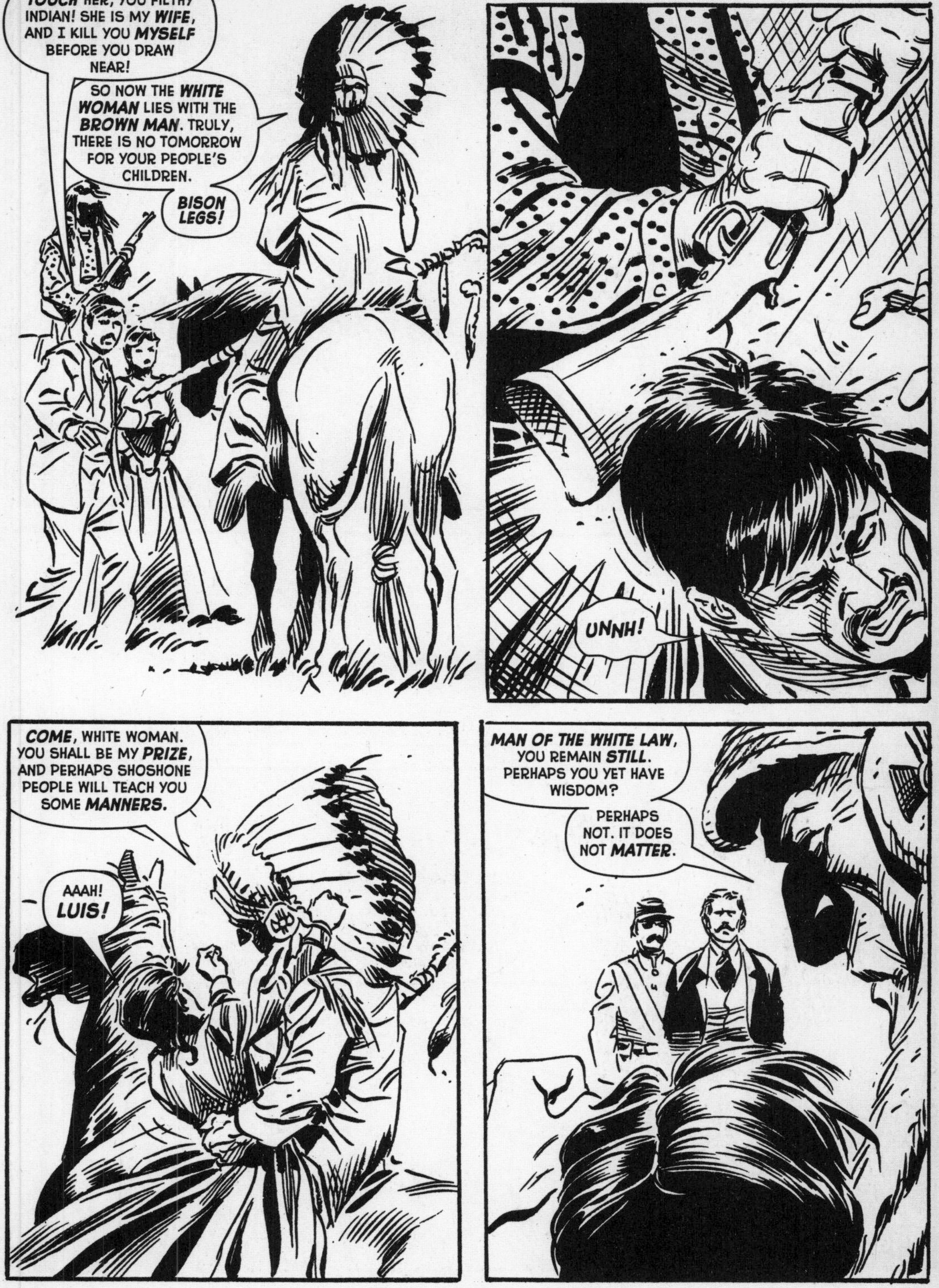
YOU WILL NOT TOUCH HER, YOU FILTHY INDIAN! SHE IS MY WIFE, AND I KILL YOU MYSELF BEFORE YOU DRAW NEAR!
SO NOW THE WHITE WOMAN LIES WITH THE BROWN MAN. TRULY, THERE IS NO TOMORROW FOR YOUR PEOPLE'S CHILDREN.
BISON LEGS!
UNNH!
COME, WHITE WOMAN. YOU SHALL BE MY PRIZE, AND PERHAPS SHOSHONE PEOPLE WILL TEACH YOU SOME MANNERS.
AAAH! LUIS!
MAN OF THE WHITE LAW, YOU REMAIN STILL. PERHAPS YOU YET HAVE WISDOM?
PERHAPS NOT. IT DOES NOT MATTER.

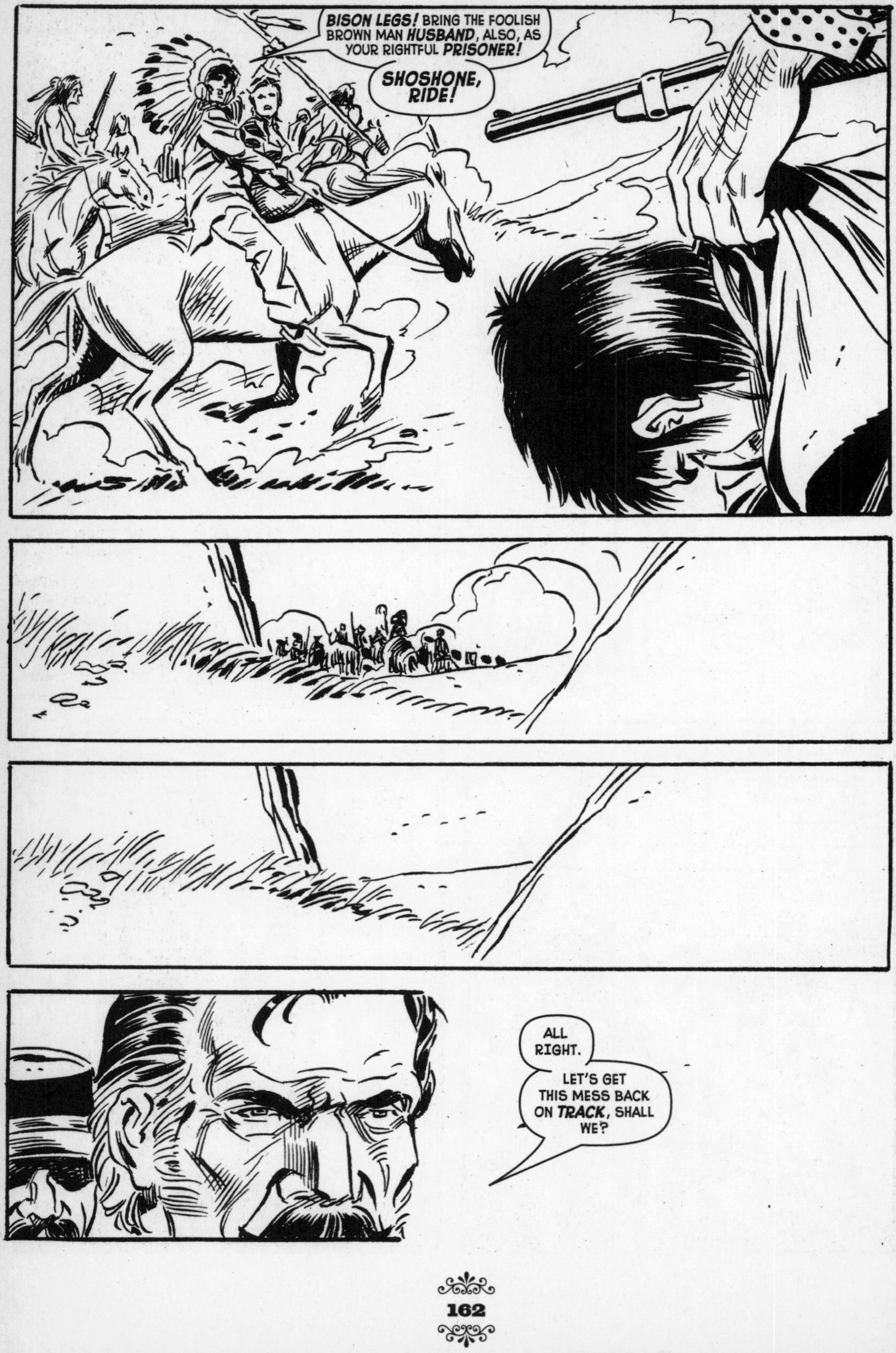
BISON LEGS! BRING THE FOOLISH BROWN MAN HUSBAND, ALSO, AS YOUR RIGHTFUL PRISONER!
SHOSHONE, RIDE!
ALL RIGHT.
LET'S GET THIS MESS BACK ON TRACK, SHALL WE?

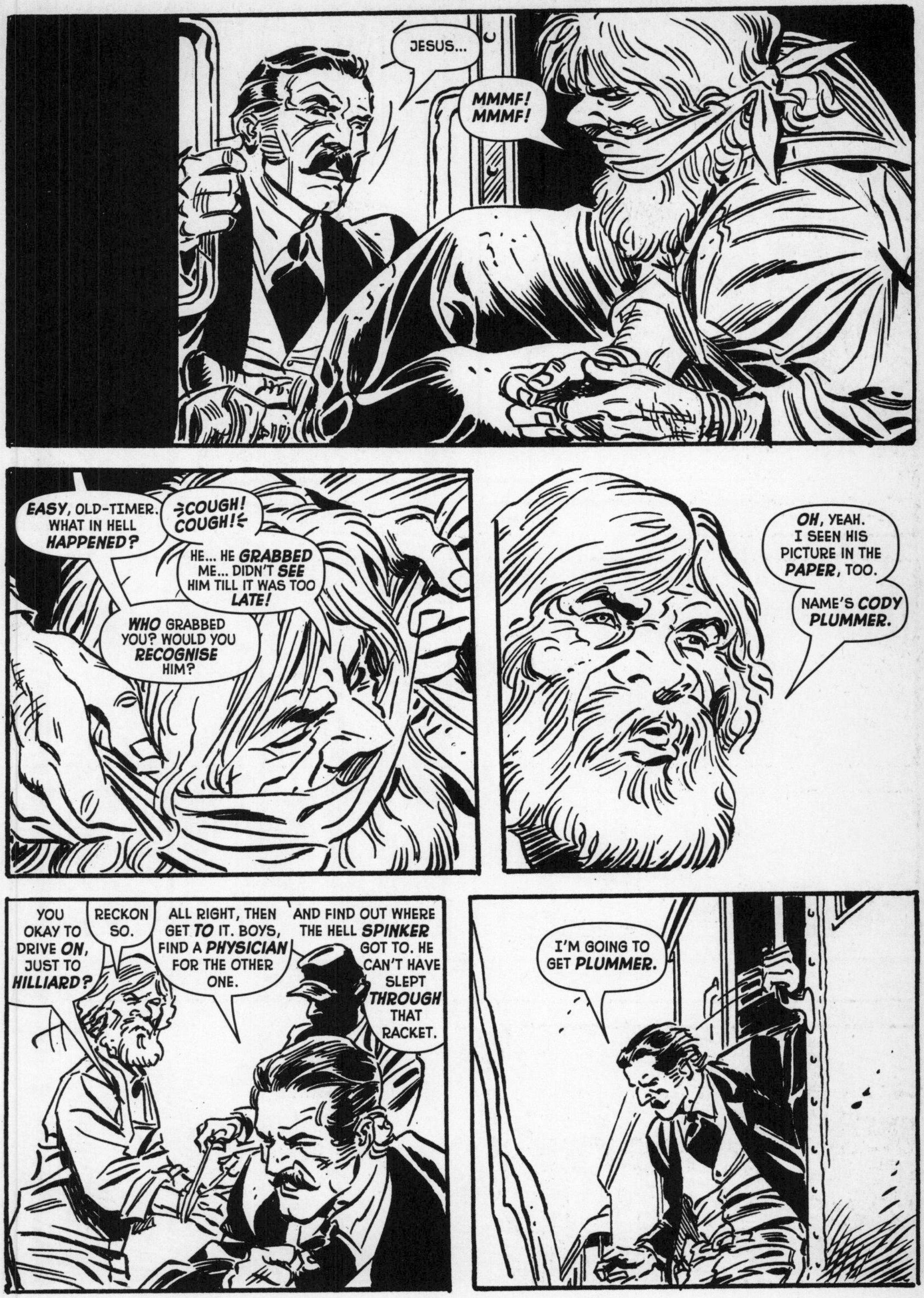
JESUS...
MMMF! MMMF!
EASY, OLD-TIMER. WHAT IN HELL HAPPENED?
COUGH! COUGH!
HE... HE GRABBED ME... DIDN'T SEE HIM TILL IT WAS TOO LATE!
WHO GRABBED YOU? WOULD YOU RECOGNISE HIM?
OH, YEAH. I SEEN HIS PICTURE IN THE PAPER, TOO.
NAME'S CODY PLUMMER.
YOU OKAY TO DRIVE ON, JUST TO HILLIARD?
RECKON SO.
ALL RIGHT, THEN GET TO IT. BOYS, FIND A PHYSICIAN FOR THE OTHER ONE.
AND FIND OUT WHERE THE HELL SPINKER GOT TO. HE CAN'T HAVE SLEPT THROUGH THAT RACKET.
I'M GOING TO GET PLUMMER.

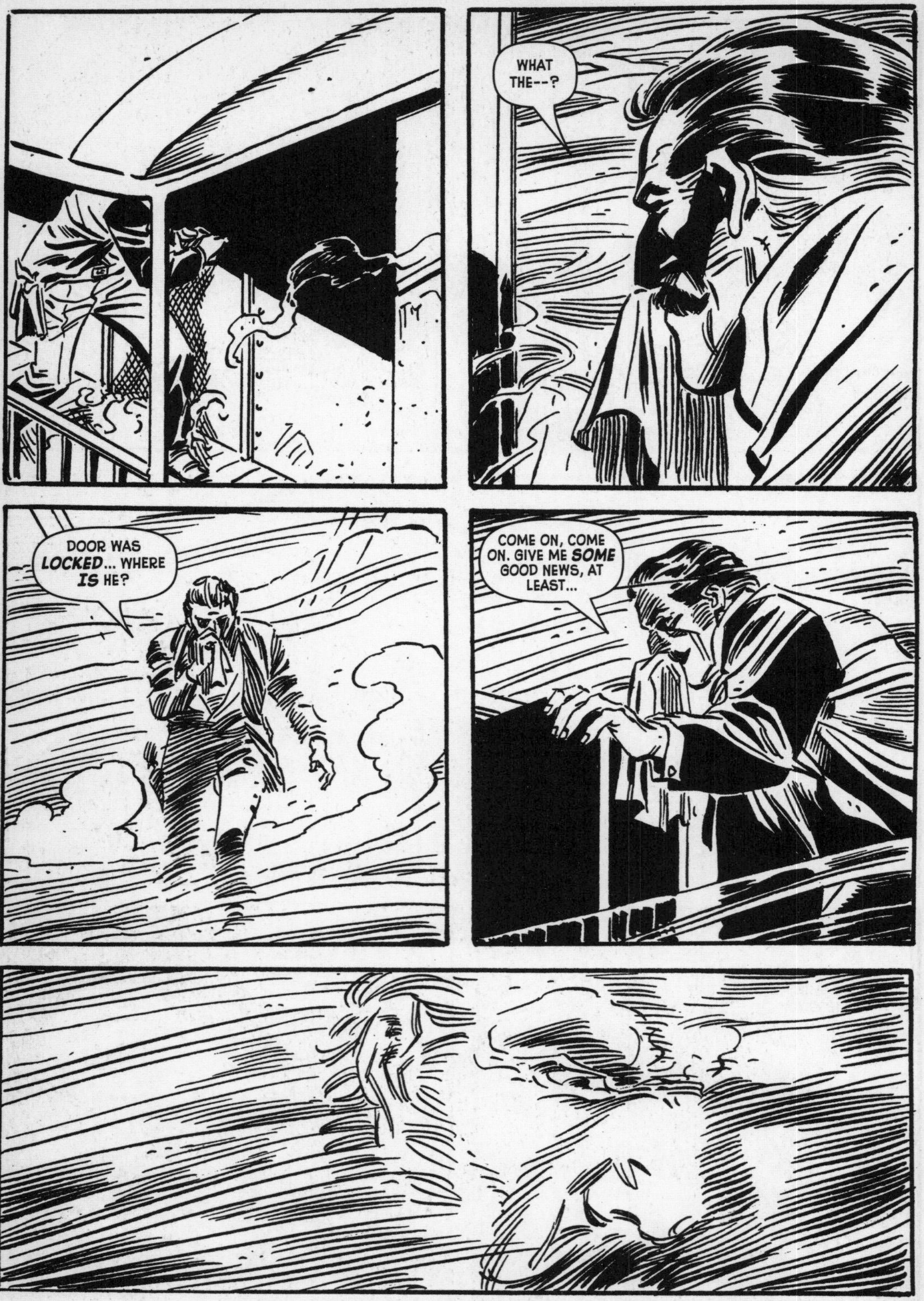
WHAT THE--?
DOOR WAS LOCKED... WHERE IS HE?
COME ON, COME ON. GIVE ME SOME GOOD NEWS, AT LEAST...

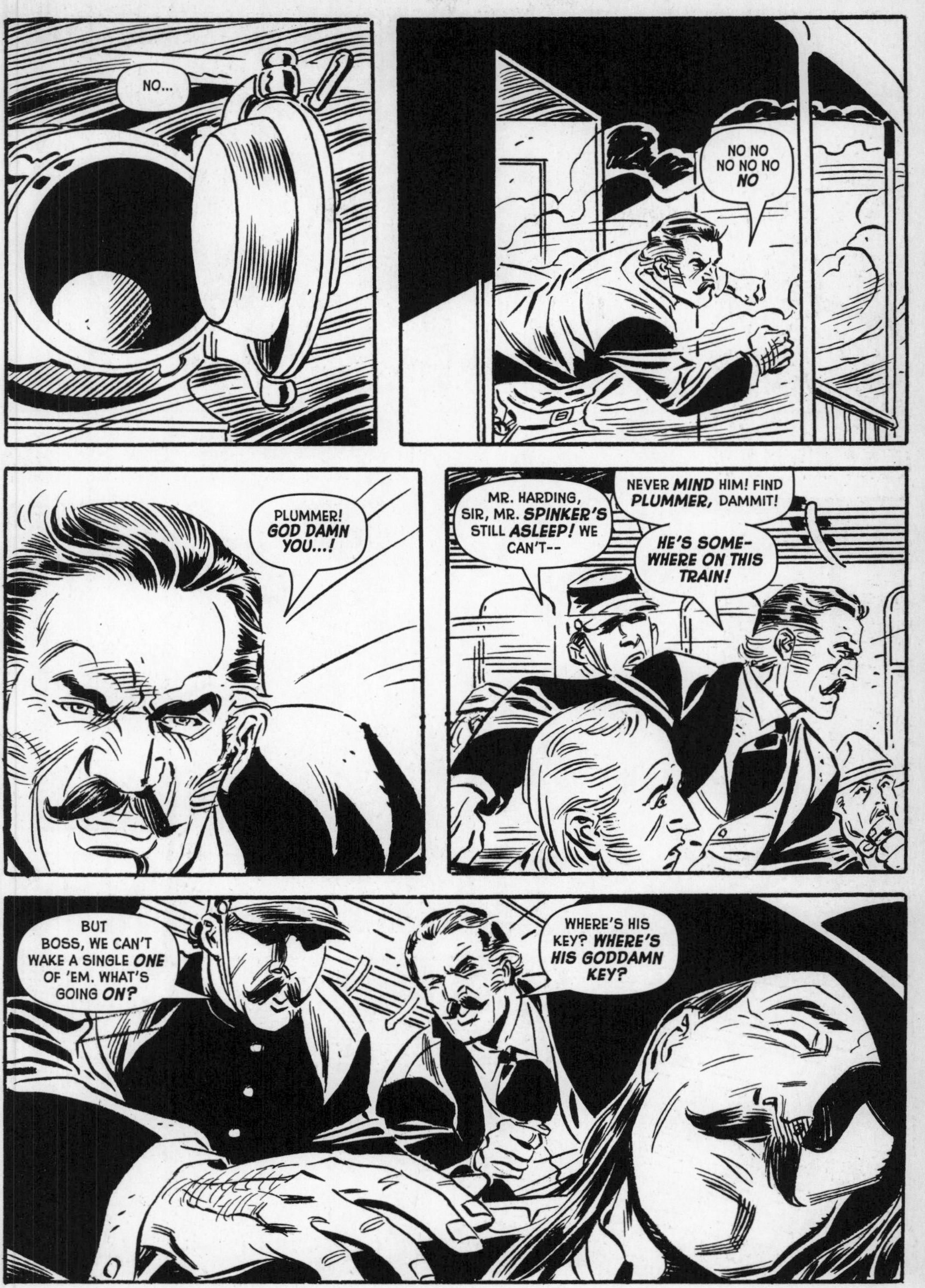
NO...
NO NO NO NO NO NO
PLUMMER! GOD DAMN YOU...!
MR. HARDING, SIR, MR. SPINKER'S STILL ASLEEP! WE CAN'T--
NEVER MIND HIM! FIND PLUMMER, DAMMIT!
HE'S SOMEWHERE ON THIS TRAIN!
BUT BOSS, WE CAN'T WAKE A SINGLE ONE OF 'EM. WHAT'S GOING ON?
WHERE'S HIS KEY? WHERE'S HIS GODDAMN KEY?

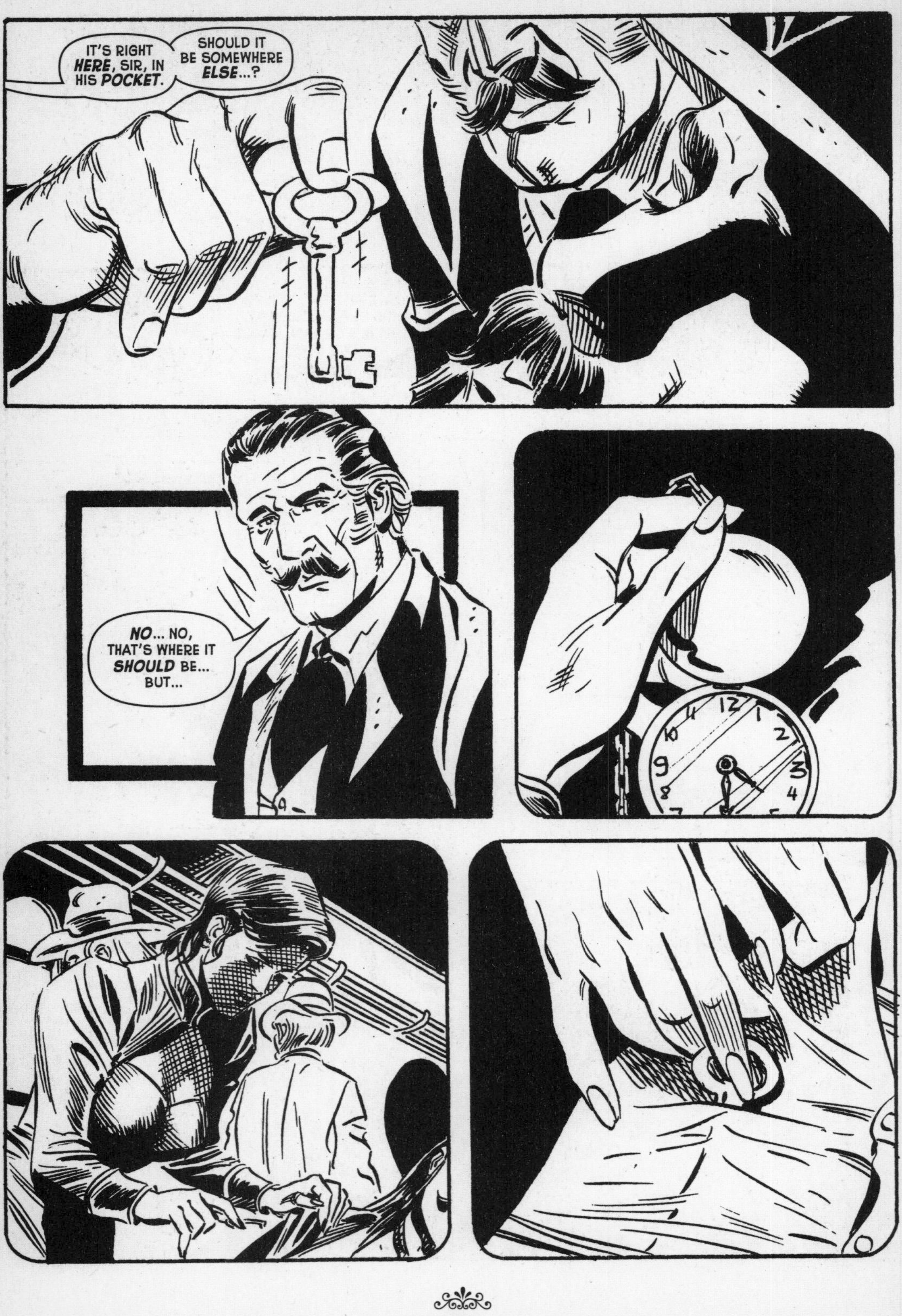
IT'S RIGHT HERE, SIR, IN HIS POCKET.
SHOULD IT BE SOMEWHERE ELSE...?
NO... NO, THAT'S WHERE IT SHOULD BE... BUT...

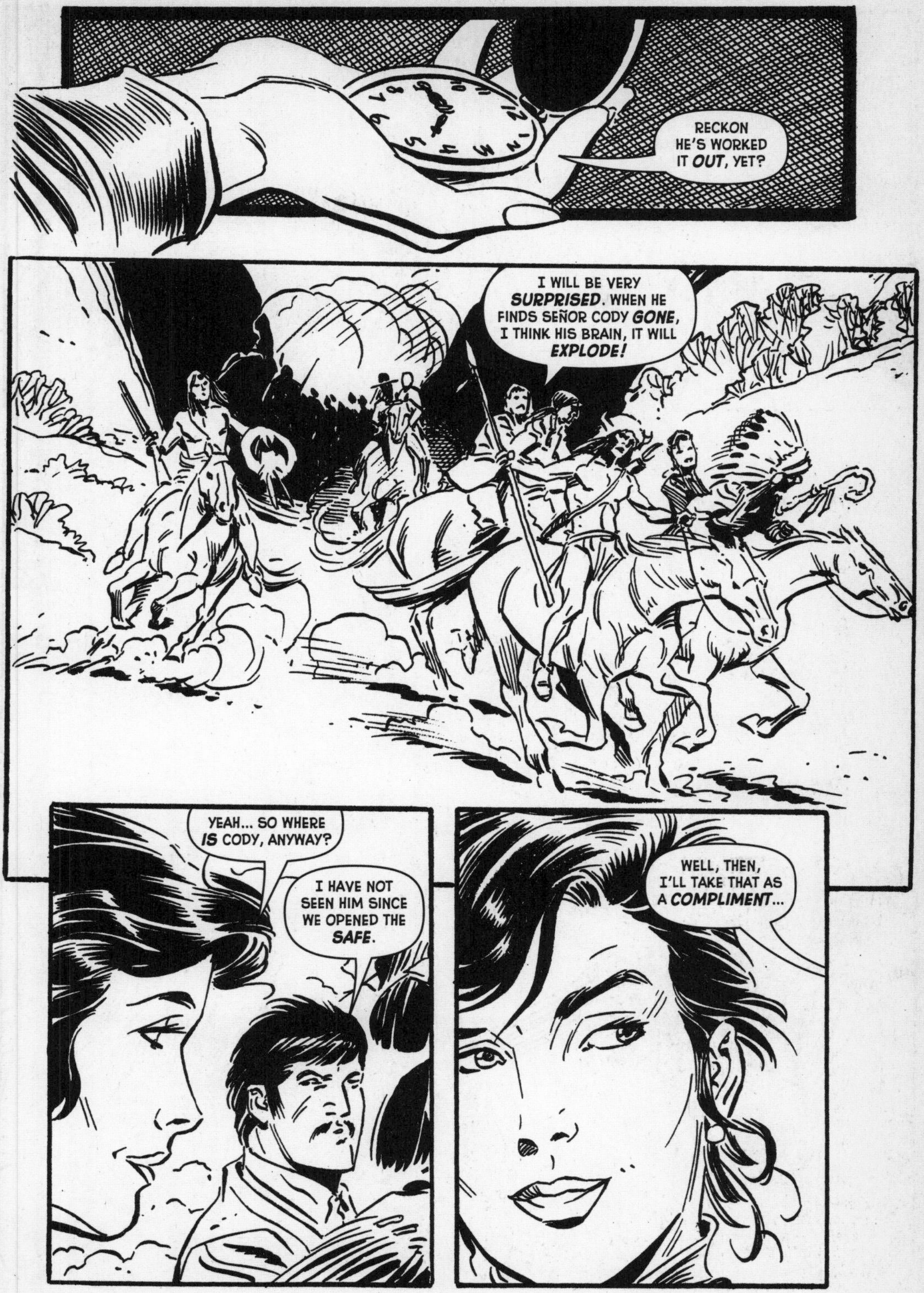
RECKON HE'S WORKED IT *OUT*, YET?
I WILL BE VERY *SURPRISED*. WHEN HE FINDS SEÑOR CODY *GONE*, I THINK HIS BRAIN, IT WILL *EXPLODE!*
YEAH... SO WHERE *IS* CODY, ANYWAY?
I HAVE NOT SEEN HIM SINCE WE OPENED THE *SAFE*.
WELL, THEN, I'LL TAKE THAT AS A *COMPLIMENT*...

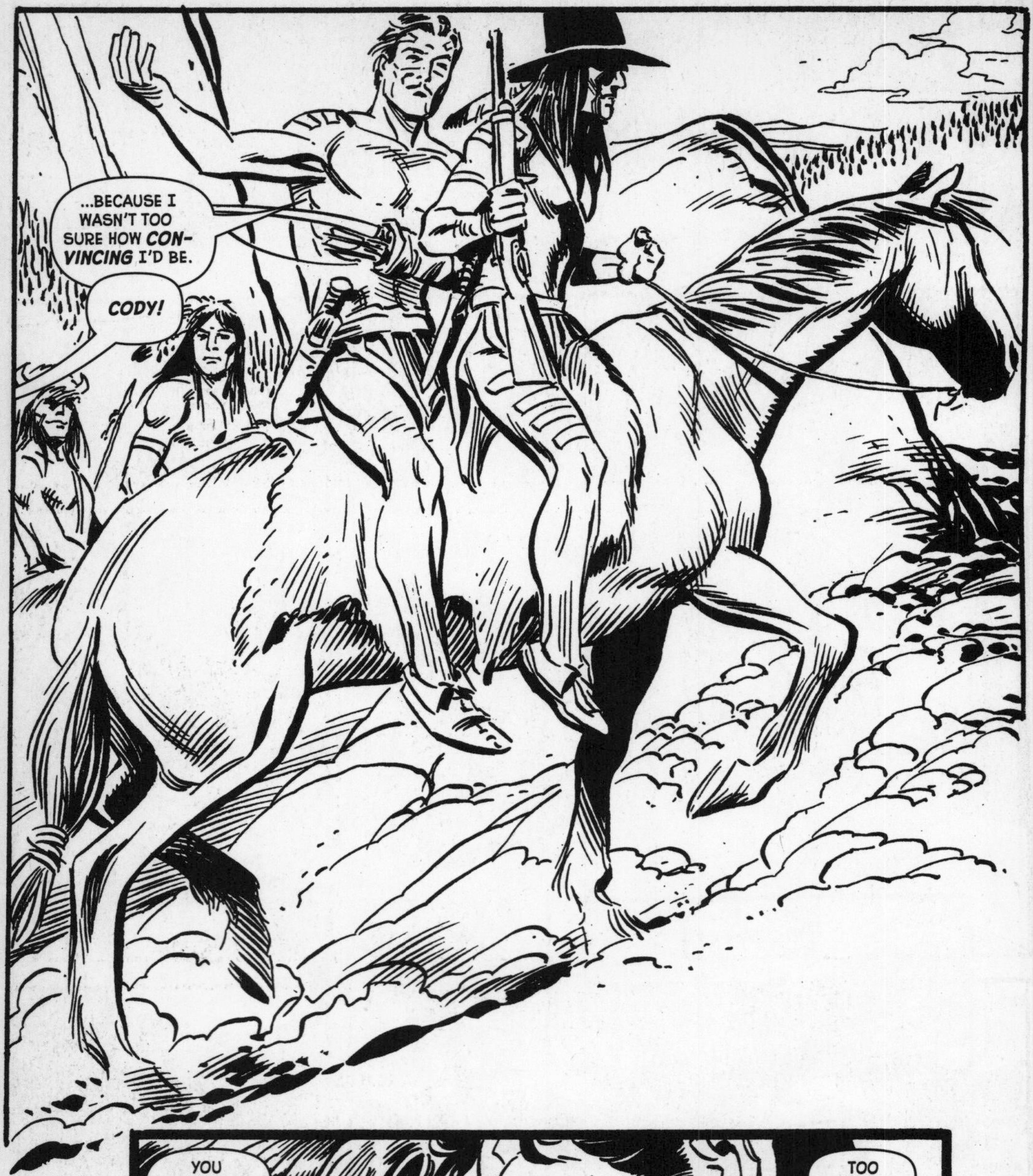
...BECAUSE I WASN'T TOO SURE HOW CON-VINCING I'D BE.
CODY!

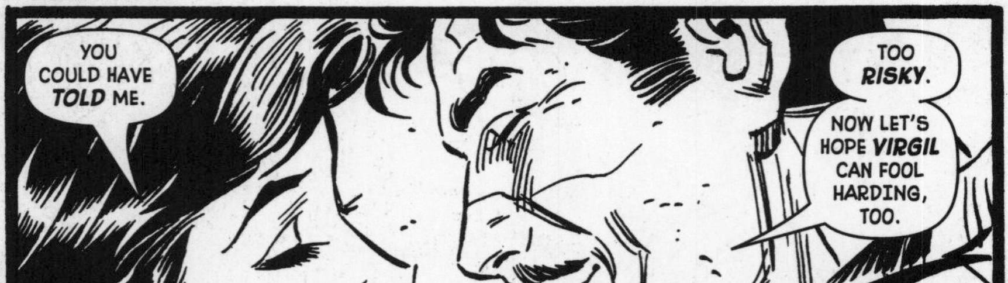
YOU COULD HAVE TOLD ME.
TOO RISKY.
NOW LET'S HOPE VIRGIL CAN FOOL HARDING, TOO.

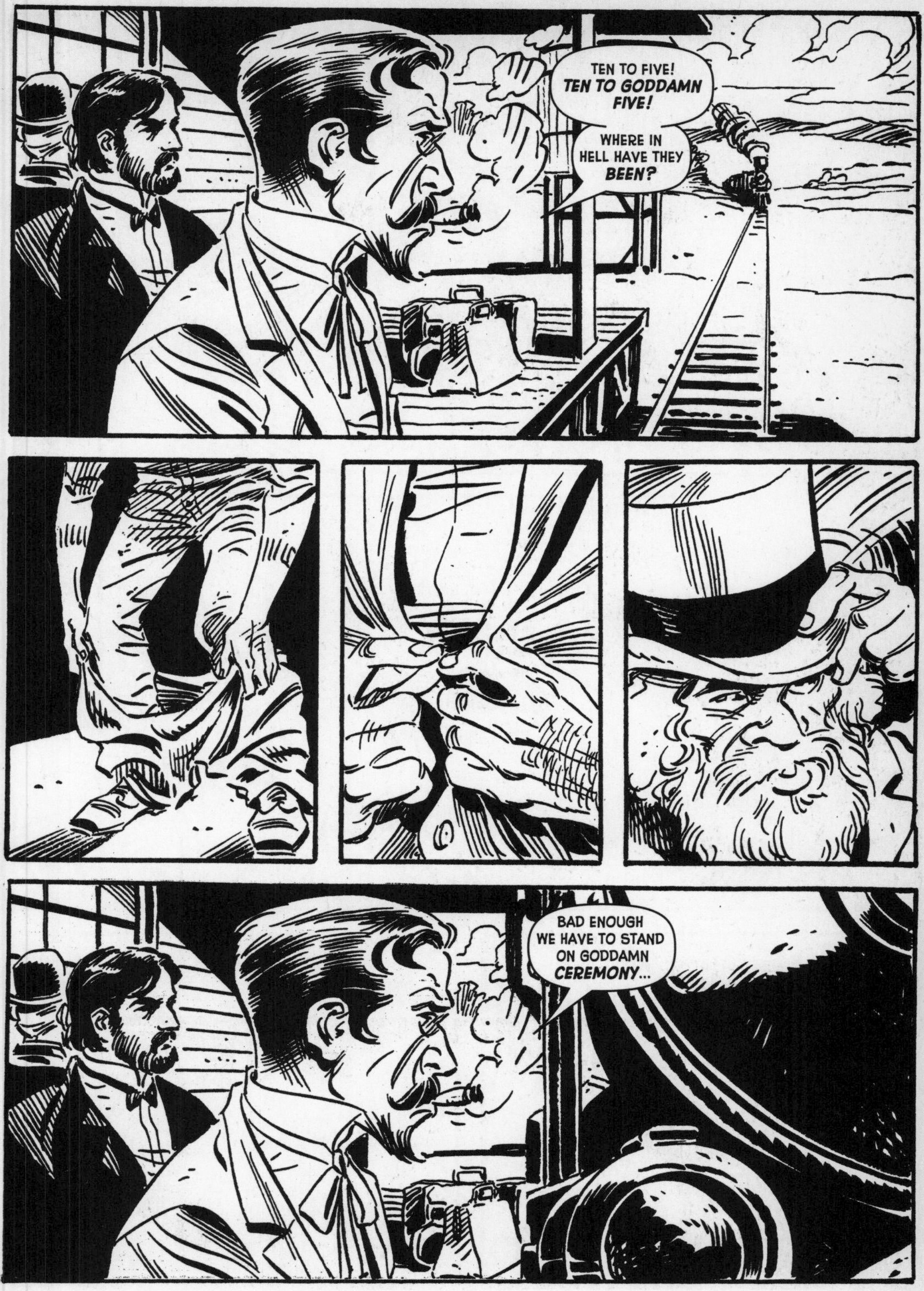
TEN TO FIVE! *TEN TO GODDAMN FIVE!*
WHERE IN HELL HAVE THEY *BEEN?*
BAD ENOUGH WE HAVE TO STAND ON GODDAMN *CEREMONY*...

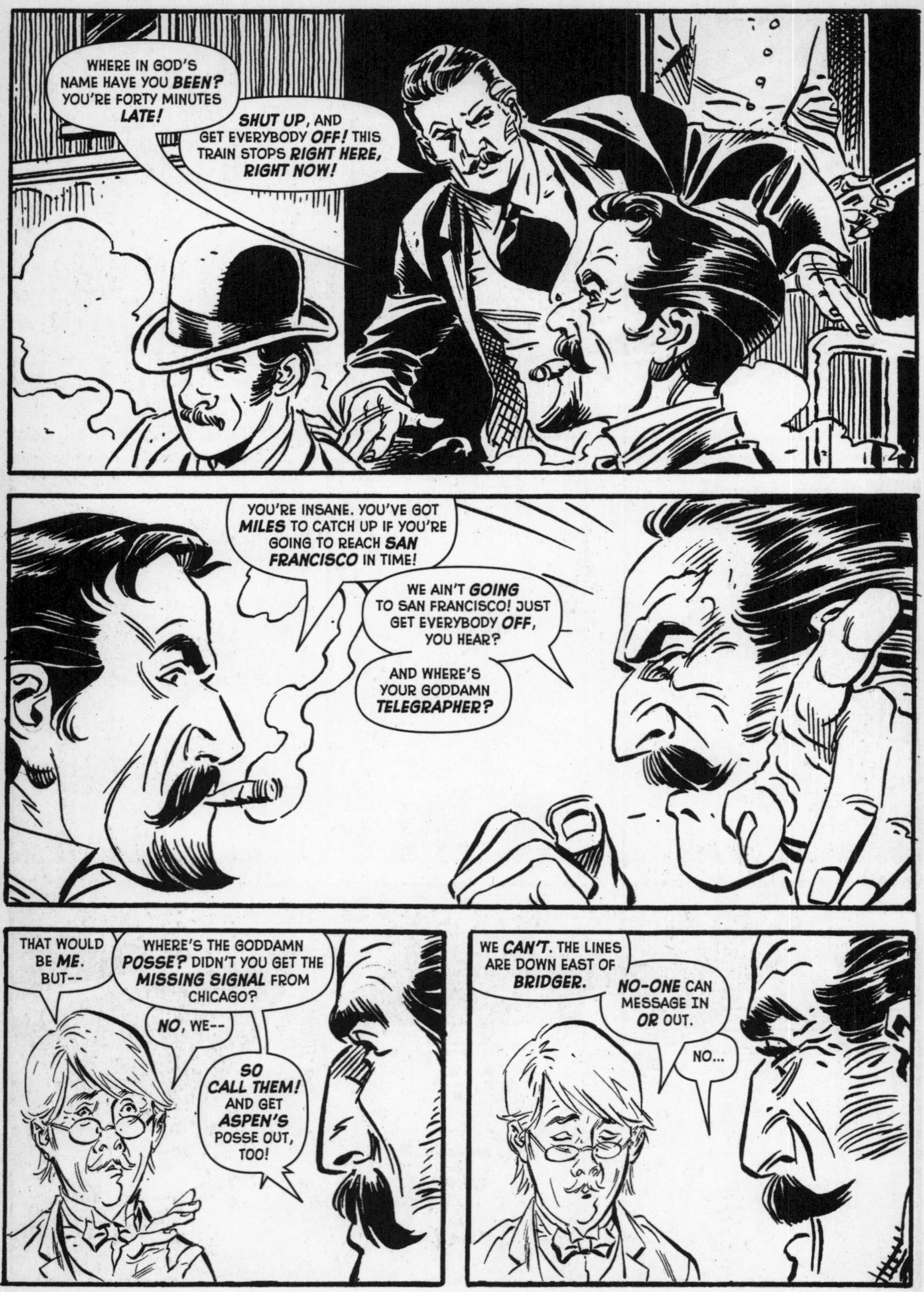
WHERE IN GOD'S NAME HAVE YOU BEEN? YOU'RE FORTY MINUTES LATE!
SHUT UP, AND GET EVERYBODY OFF! THIS TRAIN STOPS RIGHT HERE, RIGHT NOW!
YOU'RE INSANE. YOU'VE GOT MILES TO CATCH UP IF YOU'RE GOING TO REACH SAN FRANCISCO IN TIME!
WE AIN'T GOING TO SAN FRANCISCO! JUST GET EVERYBODY OFF, YOU HEAR?
AND WHERE'S YOUR GODDAMN TELEGRAPHER?
THAT WOULD BE ME. BUT--
WHERE'S THE GODDAMN POSSE? DIDN'T YOU GET THE MISSING SIGNAL FROM CHICAGO?
NO, WE--
SO CALL THEM! AND GET ASPEN'S POSSE OUT, TOO!
WE CAN'T. THE LINES ARE DOWN EAST OF BRIDGER.
NO-ONE CAN MESSAGE IN OR OUT.
NO...

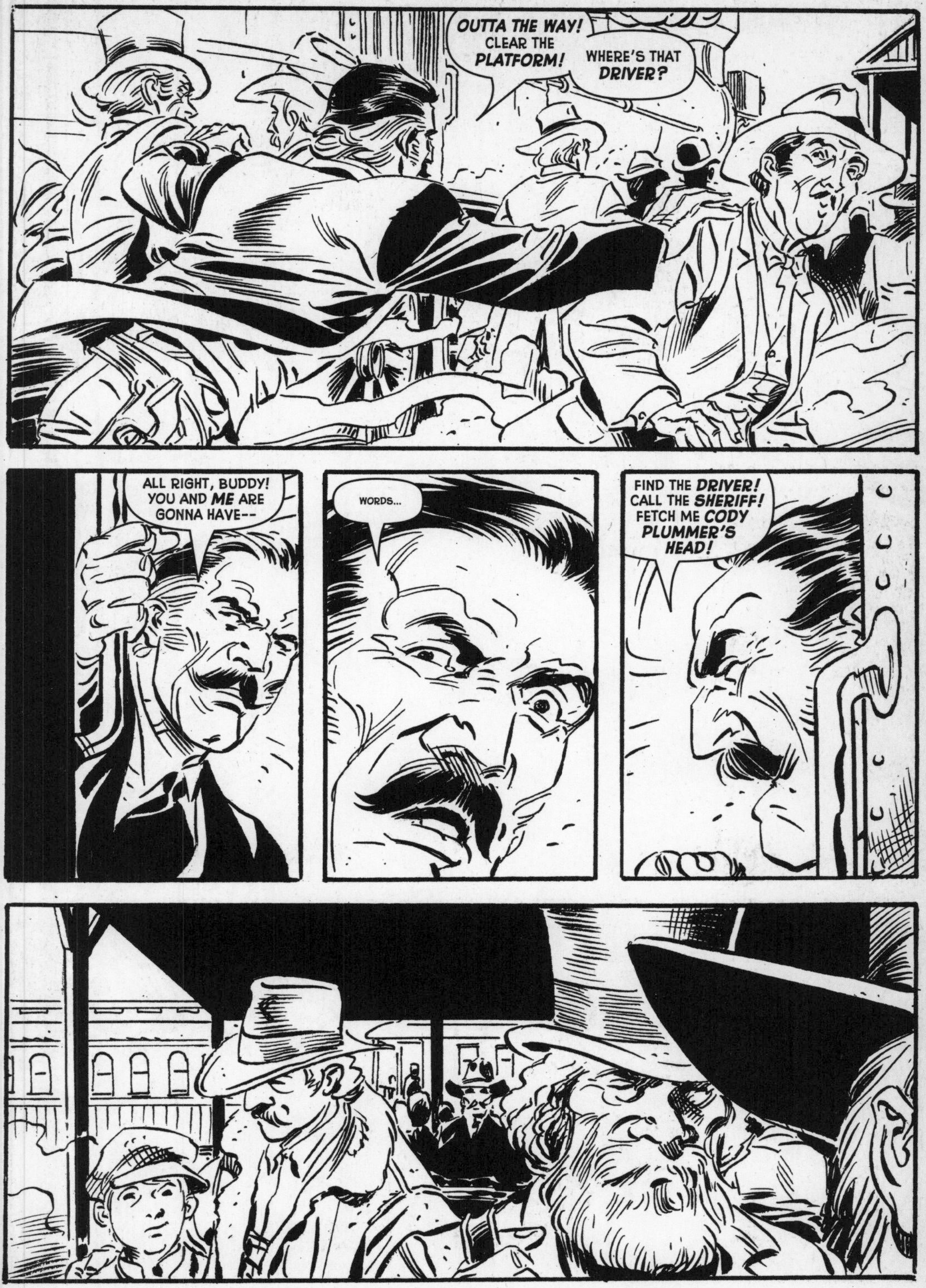
OUTTA THE WAY! CLEAR THE PLATFORM!
WHERE'S THAT DRIVER?
ALL RIGHT, BUDDY! YOU AND ME ARE GONNA HAVE--
WORDS...
FIND THE DRIVER! CALL THE SHERIFF! FETCH ME CODY PLUMMER'S HEAD!

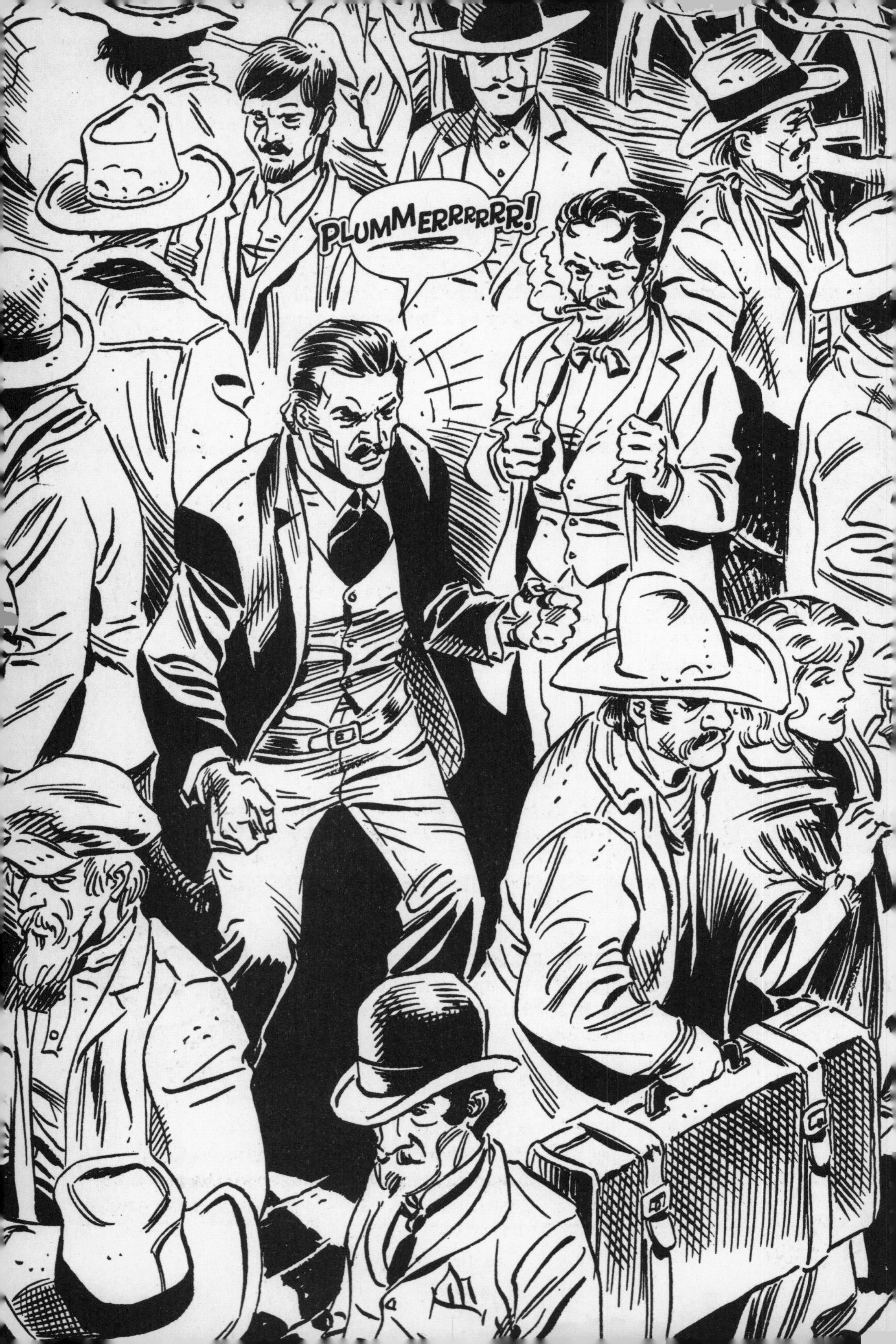
PLUMMERRRRRR!

LUIS CAVAÑOS

pursued a new career as an escapologist, touring America as "Cavaños, The Amazing Spaniard!" He eventually retired to Texas, where he married his Mexican stage assistant.

GEORGE WENDELL

bought a Mississippi steamboat and ran the most lucrative poker tournament on the river, until his retirement in 1879. He famously debarred anyone found carrying a lucky horseshoe.

VIRGIL SMITH

bought a ranch in Utah and constructed the largest clockwork model train set in the country. In 1878 he converted to Mormonism and married a local clockmaker's daughter.

DAVID HOROWITZ

invested his share in Montana livestock and reaped huge profits, but lost it all in the cattle-decimating blizzard of 1887. He returned to Chicago as a lowly financial advisor.

THE SHOSHONE PEOPLE

dwindled further at the hands of the white man, eventually being forced onto reservations. Long Foot's tribe refused to comply, instead dividing the robbery money between families and scattering across the land. Long Foot's son Broken Horse used his share to open a ski resort in the Rocky Mountains.

BENJAMIN SPINKER

resigned from the Pinkerton Agency to set up a railroad catering business with his wife Annie. In 1878 they sold the business to Union Pacific for an undisclosed sum and retired to Oregon.

ROBERT HARDING

also resigned from the Pinkerton Agency, but did not retire to San Francisco as intended. Instead, Harding spent the rest of his days travelling the length and breadth of America, hunting down Cody Plummer. He never succeeded.

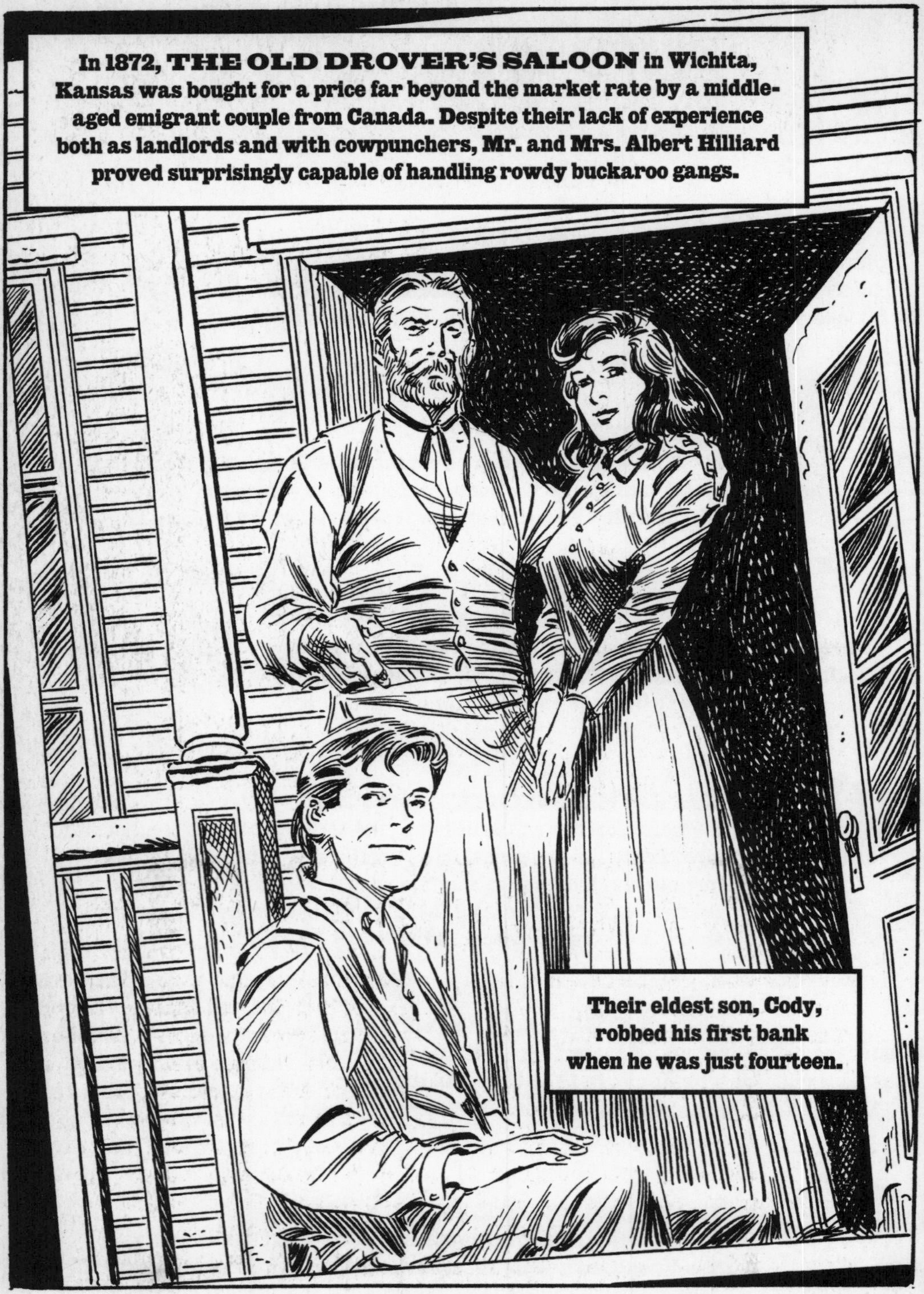
In 1872, THE OLD DROVER'S SALOON in Wichita, Kansas was bought for a price far beyond the market rate by a middle-aged emigrant couple from Canada. Despite their lack of experience both as landlords and with cowpunchers, Mr. and Mrs. Albert Hilliard proved surprisingly capable of handling rowdy buckaroo gangs.
Their eldest son, Cody, robbed his first bank when he was just fourteen.

THE END